Professional Ethics

Professional Ethics

The City Law School
CITY UNIVERSITY LONDON

Authors

Susan Blake, Barrister, Associate Dean, The City Law School
Julie Browne, Barrister, Senior Lecturer, The City Law School
Ros Carne, Barrister, Senior Lecturer, The City Law School
Nigel Duncan, Principal Lecturer, The City Law School
Oliver Hanmer, Professional Practice Manager, Bar Standards Board
Stuart Lindsay, Barrister, Lecturer, The City Law School
Keith Simpson, Barrister, Senior Lecturer, The City Law School
Jonathan Smith, Bar Standards Board
Marcus Soanes, Barrister, Principal Lecturer, The City Law School
Simone Start, Barrister, Lecturer, The City Law School

Editor

Ros Carne, Barrister, Senior Lecturer, The City Law School

Series Editor

Julie Browne, Barrister, Senior Lecturer, The City Law School

OXFORD
UNIVERSITY PRESS

OXFORD

UNIVERSITY PRESS

Great Clarendon Street, Oxford OX2 6DP

Oxford University Press is a department of the University of Oxford.
It furthers the University's objective of excellence in research, scholarship, and education by
publishing worldwide in

Oxford New York

Auckland Cape Town Dar es Salaam Hong Kong Karachi
Kuala Lumpur Madrid Melbourne Mexico City Nairobi
New Delhi Shanghai Taipei Toronto

With offices in

Argentina Austria Brazil Chile Czech Republic France Greece
Guatemala Hungary Italy Japan Poland Portugal Singapore
South Korea Switzerland Thailand Turkey Ukraine Vietnam

Oxford is a registered trademark of Oxford University Press
in the UK and in certain other countries

Published in the United States by Oxford University Press Inc., New York

British Library Cataloguing in Publication Data
Data available

Library of Congress Cataloging in Publication Data
Data available

Typeset by Laserwords Private Ltd, Chennai, India
Printed in Great Britain on acid-free paper by
Ashford Colour Press Ltd, Gosport, Hampshire

ISBN 978–0–19–959185-5

10 9 8 7 6 5 4 3

FOREWORD

I am delighted to write this foreword to the manuals. They are written by a combination of practitioners and members of staff of The City Law School, formerly the Inns of Court School of Law and are designed primarily to support training on the Bar Professional Training Course (BPTC), wherever it is taught. They embrace both compulsory and optional subjects. They provide an outstandingly useful resource for all those involved in the teaching and acquisition of the skills and knowledge that practising barristers need. Originally designed for the Bar Vocational Course, they have been comprehensively revised to meet the requirements of the new BPTC. They are updated regularly and, in addition, the publishers maintain a complementary website for the series, an Online Resource Centre, which can be used by readers to keep up-to-date throughout the academic year.

The manuals, together with the Online Resource Centre, exemplify the practical and professional approach that is central to the BPTC. I congratulate the authors on the excellent standard of the series and I am grateful to Oxford University Press for its ongoing enthusiastic support. The manuals are not only invaluable to all prospective barristers, but reflect an ongoing commitment to raise standards in the public interest.

Professor Adrian Keane
Barrister
Director of Professional Programmes
The City Law School
City University, London
2010

PREFACE

Students joining the Bar Professional Training Course in September 2010 will be the first to sit a new separate assessment in Professional Ethics and Conduct. The Bar Standards Board is concerned that these topics should play a more prominent role in the training of barristers. They are right. The new module will prepare you for your career with the rigour that is required in an age of high public scrutiny and expectation. This manual has been renamed to reflect these changes, both in training for the Bar and at the Bar itself. The barristers' Code of Conduct, while it remains the primary reference point, is no longer sufficient to indicate the far-reaching ethical considerations that should inform a barrister's working life. Ethics denotes a much wider scope for the values that underpin the profession. Thus the Code is increasingly supplemented by Guidance, case law, and Practice Directions which need to be considered and absorbed. Those of you developing an interest in the subject for its own sake may wish to read more widely and further texts are suggested in Chapter 4, 'The letter and the spirit of the Code'.

This is a time of great change for the Bar and for the way it is regulated. The barristers' complaints procedure has recently undergone a major overhaul, and for the first time this year complaints involving Inadequate Professional Service will be heard by a new Office for Legal Complaints (OLC) which is a single independent body, entirely separate from the Bar Council or the Bar Standards Board. In addition, the Legal Services Act 2007 has led to new ways of working for solicitors and barristers with the introduction of multi-disciplinary teams known as Legal Disciplinary Practices (LDPs). The Code of Conduct itself is in the process of revision and is likely to be substituted by new Conduct Rules, based around a number of core values. Students on this year's BPTC, however, should be reassured. You will be assessed on the existing Code and Guidance, set out in Appendix 1 of this manual and on the Bar Standards Board website. The new Conduct Rules are likely to be introduced at the end of 2011.

The increasing public prominence of both the Bar Council and the Bar Standards Board, through their websites and other publications, indicates a concern to demonstrate transparency and accountability in a profession that has often been criticised in the past. Many of those criticisms are unjustified. But if the Bar is to be proof against all challenges, the highest ethical standards are required. A proper approach to ethics in a specialist area can only arise through thorough knowledge and understanding of the relevant sources.

The aim of this manual is to give you the necessary grounding. By studying the manual and by putting to use what you have read in the exercises and discussions that take place throughout the course, you should be in a position to take an informed decision on any ethical problem that arises in the course of your practice. There will always be areas of uncertainty. If ethics were easy, the world would be a different place. But with thoughtful application of what you learn you will be in a position to choose the best of a number of possible options and to justify your choice.

As a barrister you will have a weighty responsibility. You have a duty to the court and a duty to the client. You have a duty to the public at large to help maintain confidence in the legal profession. Problems most commonly arise when these duties appear to conflict. Decisions on professional ethics can be difficult. They will be even more difficult when you are dealing with real clients. So make the most of this year of preparation. Professional ethics and conduct are central to everything you will do in practice.

Ros Carne
Barrister, Senior Lecturer,
The City Law School

ACKNOWLEDGMENTS

Grateful acknowledgment is made to the publishers of copyright material which appears in this book:

The Bar Standards Board <http://www.barstandardsboard.org.uk> for kind permission to reproduce Sections 1, 2 & 3 of the Code of Conduct of the Bar for England and Wales, Part I & II Pupillage Guidelines, Written Standards for the Conduct of Professional Work, Witness Preparation—*Momodou and Limani*, The Preparation of Witness Statements, Guidance on Preparation of Defence Case Statements, Non-practising Barristers Supplying Legal Services—Guidance on New Rules, Reporting Professional Misconduct of Barristers by Members of the Bar, and Sections 1 & 2 of the Equality and Diversity Code for the Bar.

GUIDE TO USING THIS BOOK

The Bar Manuals series includes a range of tools and features to aid your learning. This guide will outline the approach to using this book, and help you to make the most out of each of the features within.

Practical based approach

The authors have taken a practical based approach to Professional Ethics at the Bar. This manual uses realistic examples of ethical dilemmas that may confront a barrister, indicating the best way to resolve them.

The code and beyond

The manual looks beyond the letter of the Code to consider related issues such as effective representation in a diverse society. There is comprehensive coverage, from the Bar Standards Board, of the complaints procedure and the requirements placed on barristers under the Proceeds of Crime Act 2002.

Core texts

The barristers' Code of Conduct, selected Annexes, and essential Guidance are included in the Appendix to the manual. Recent amendments relating to Legal Disciplinary Practices are included.

Court etiquette

The manual includes answers to frequently asked questions ranging from what to wear to what to do when the judge enters the courtroom.

Examples

Examples of professional conduct and ethical dilemmas are set out throughout the manual with clear advice as to how you should respond, giving reference to relevant paragraphs of the Code or Guidance.

Pedagogical features

Lists of problems based on genuine cases are included. These allow students to apply what they have learnt in the text to real life situations.

ORC updates

The barristers' Code of Conduct and Guidance change rapidly. The Bar Standards Board has published important new Guidance for barristers on Public Access Work, Legal Disciplinary Practices, Investigating or Collecting Evidence, Conduct of Correspondence, Sharing of Premises and Attendance at Police Stations. For these Guidance documents and other materials relating to manuals in this series please visit the Online Resource Centre at www.oxfordtextbooks.co.uk/orc/barmanuals/.

OUTLINE CONTENTS

DETAILED CONTENTS

Introduction

Paragraph 301 of the Code of Conduct states that:

A barrister . . . must not:

(a) engage in conduct whether in pursuit of his profession or otherwise which is:
   (i) dishonest or otherwise discreditable to a barrister;
   (ii) prejudicial to the administration of justice; or
   (iii) likely to diminish public confidence in the legal profession or the administration of justice or otherwise bring the legal profession into disrepute.

You are hoping to join this profession at a time of change. The courts, for example, are no longer the exclusive adversarial platforms of barristers, but are now open to solicitor advocates, in-house solicitors, and the employed Bar. In the course of your career you may find yourself working closely with non-lawyers in a 'Legal Disciplinary Practice', a new form of business structure permitted by the Legal Services Act 2007. You may act as a mediator or arbitrator, in addition to your court practice. Furthermore, the nature of your work is likely to change rapidly, with an increasing emphasis on the interpretation of regulations and the defining of quality standards. In these changing times, there is nothing more important to practise at the Bar than maintaining the highest standards with respect to the way in which barristers conduct themselves, and the regard in which they are held by their peers, judges they appear before, their instructing solicitor, and members of the public with whom they come into contact during their professional lives.

1.1 The Code of Conduct

Underpinning the profession is the Code of Conduct (the Code) and no matter what challenges you will face individually or as part of a profession, your comprehension and application of the Code must be thorough. Without this solid foundation the Bar's efforts in the face of change would crumble to nothing. The way that you conduct yourselves in practice and towards those whom you meet in your professional lives is rightly under scrutiny. Barristers never work in isolation. Ignoring the application of the Code not only affects an individual's reputation and career at the Bar, it can have far-reaching implications to those affected by such oversights and thus the behaviour of the Bar as a profession is brought into question. Consequently, the Code set out in **Appendix 1** is perhaps the most important text to comprehend and then apply throughout your career at the Bar.

There are three sections to the Code of Conduct:

- Section 1 contains the Code of Conduct itself, which sets out the core rules and ethics of the profession.
- Section 2 contains Annexes A to S to the Code dealing with some more specific forms of practice and rules, for example, the International Practice Rules, Employed Barrister Rules, etc.
- Section 3 contains the 'Written Standards for the Conduct of Professional Work', which are referred to frequently in this manual, on the BVC course, and in practice.

The amount of guidance published by the Bar Standards Board is steadily increasing. For this reason not every guidance document is published in this manual. BPTC students, are well advised to check the Bar Standard Board's website where up-to-date guidance is regularly posted. Further guidance is published alphabetically on the Bar Council's website. Students should also be familiar with the Equality and Diversity Code for the Bar which is set out in full in Appendix 1.

At the time of writing the Bar Standards Board is engaged in finalising a new set of Conduct Rules. No fundamental changes from the current Code of Conduct are anticipated: the aim of the new Rules is to set out existing ethical concerns in a more helpful way, with less repetition and a clearer focus. The Rules will also incorporate more effectively the new provisions arising as a result of the Legal Services Act 2007. It is anticipated that the Rules will come into force towards the end of 2011.

1.2 The ethical challenge

It would be comforting to think that at this stage of your legal training the Code will expressly deal with all professional conduct situations. In fact it does not and during the BPTC and in early practice it becomes apparent that not only does the letter of the Code need to be understood, but also the application of its spirit to many situations is crucial. **Chapter 4**, 'The letter and spirit of the Code', prompts you to think carefully about the way in which you choose to interpret the Code and it also suggests that you recognize the 'underpinning values' of the Code. This approach is vital if as a barrister you are to operate within the spirit of the Code, where there is no letter, albeit that this is so often based on an interpretation of the combination of the fundamental tenets. Indeed, the chapter also advises that you are wise to be aware of your own personal morality and to ensure that it does not cloud your objective professional judgment in dealing with the ethical difficulties you will meet in practice.

Chairman's speech to Bar Conference, Guy Mansfield QC, 15 October 2005

Our great profession is critical to the administration of justice. We are listened to in many quarters at home and abroad when we speak. We have a vital place in society. But we must adhere to the highest standards. We must adapt and embrace new concepts. We must work for and preserve freedom under the law. We must secure a modern Bar with a strong future.

1.3 A profession under scrutiny

Popular perceptions about the Bar are often wrong. Conclusions portrayed in the media about alleged 'fat cat' lawyers overlook the serious deficiencies in Legal Aid funding. Many lawyers struggle to make ends meet. Many take on a large amount of pro bono work. The reality is that there is an unglamorous side to the profession—long, unsocial hours and, for some, serious financial difficulties.

You may be puzzled as to why it is necessary to mention such problems. The answer is simple—whatever difficulties are encountered, financial or otherwise, the application of the Code of Conduct remains paramount. Cutting corners is never an option. It is never acceptable to compromise your commitment to the highest standards on account of fees, or the lack of them, or for any other reason of personal convenience. Unfailing adherence to this self-denying ethic is one trait that marks the Bar and the barrister out as uniquely excellent in the eyes of those who actually have dealings with the profession and that puts the lie to the uninformed stereotype. Every day the way in which you choose to conduct your affairs is rightly under scrutiny by all parties you come into contact with. For example, in the context of criminal trials case law has highlighted defence counsel's professional duties with regard to procedural errors by the prosecution. The judiciary has clearly set out that such matters should be identified and dealt with at the earliest opportunity and not left until the last minute because criminal proceedings are not a game (*R v Gleeson* [2003] EWCA Crim 3357 and *Hughes v DPP* [2003] EWHC 2470).

As you become fully versed in the letter of the Code and its application, it is useful to read a list compiled by Mark Stobbs (former Head of Professional Conduct at what was then known as the General Council of the Bar) setting out the main reasons for complaints against barristers.

Principal reasons for complaints against barristers

Poor services to clients

This can cover a wide variety of circumstances but typical examples are:

- arriving late at court or for a conference without reasonable excuse;
- behaving rudely or abruptly to the client;
- failing to ensure that the client properly understands advice or the consequences of any decision or settlement;
- giving negligent advice or failing to take steps to protect the client's interest;
- double-booking and other clerks' room errors.

Misconduct

All of the above cases can amount to misconduct as well if the facts are sufficiently serious. The following types of action will also amount to misconduct:

- breach of confidence;
- expressing personal opinions in the press in matters which are continuing and in which you have been instructed;
- acting where you have an interest or where another client has an interest which is opposed to that of your client;
- bullying your client and threatening to withdraw if your client does not accept a settlement or plead guilty;
- making allegations of fraud without a proper basis for so doing no matter how hard your client may press you to do so;

- coaching or rehearsing a witness in their evidence;
- holding yourself out as a barrister when offering legal advice if you have not completed pupillage or complied with the other practising requirements;
- misleading the court or continuing in a case where your client has misled the court or failed to disclose a document that the law requires to be disclosed.

Personal problems

Generally, the Bar Standards Board does not seek to make judgments about individuals' personal lives, but there are times when conduct outside practice can call a person's suitability to remain a barrister into question. Particular examples include:

- being convicted of a criminal offence or being charged with a serious criminal offence—both must be reported to the Bar Council;
- being adjudicated bankrupt or made subject to an Individual Voluntary Arrangement or a Directors Disqualification Order, which must again be reported to the Bar Council;
- using the qualification to obtain an advantage that would not otherwise be given or to intimidate another person;
- failing to comply with the order of a court;
- other dishonest or disreputable behaviour which is likely to bring the Bar or the administration of justice into disrepute.

Breaches of the Practising Rules

- failing to pay the insurance premium to the Bar Mutual Indemnity Fund or practising certificate fee;
- not complying with the compulsory continuing education scheme.

In those situations where the complaint stems from difficulties in the relationship between barrister and lay client, the solution will often be found in putting client care at the centre of one's professional conduct and taking the time to ensure that the client understands what is happening, and why, at every stage.

1.4 Fair treatment

The Bar is committed to equal opportunities. An integral part of good professional conduct is the attitude that you adopt and display towards the variety of people with whom you come into contact in your professional life. These range from colleagues in chambers, opponents, the judiciary, professional clients, lay clients, witnesses, and court staff, to other professionals such as police officers, doctors, probation officers, and social workers. You will be dealing with people from every walk of life, every socio-economic group, with differing mental abilities, customs, religions, and expectations. It is crucial that you deal with people courteously and fairly. Your success at the Bar will depend more than anything upon the way that you treat other people. Being courteous and respectful to all people at all times, especially under pressure, is the hallmark of a successful and confident person. This is what people expect of a barrister.

It is also important that you are scrupulous to avoid discriminating directly or indirectly against any person on grounds of race, colour, ethnic or national origin, nationality, citizenship, sex, sexual orientation, marital status, disability, religion, or political persuasion (see the Code para 305.1). Such discrimination is not only a breach of the Code; it is also a breach of the Bar's Equality and Diversity Code.

Chapter 3, 'Working at the Bar today', sets out how you can develop your awareness of and approach to treating people fairly. The chapter contains information on the sources of guidance relating to fair treatment and discrimination. **Chapter 2**, which deals with 'professional relationships', is also a very useful source of guidance in ensuring that you behave towards others with the courtesy, respect, and sensitivity that the Bar requires of its members. It draws upon the experience of barristers, solicitors, judges, clerks, and organizations to which the lay client turns, such as the Bar Standards Board or the new Office for Legal Complaints (OLC). It also contains key practical texts such as the Code for Crown Prosecutors in an attempt to ensure that whatever your role is in proceedings you will know the sources of guidance that an intending barrister needs.

1.5 The consequences of misconduct

Barristers who choose the approach of keeping their head in the sand when faced with professional conduct issues in practice will inevitably meet problems. They will fall down the path of sleepless nights; their reputation will be soiled and because any failure to comply with the Code will constitute professional misconduct and may result in liability for disciplinary proceedings (see paras 901.1 to 901.8 of the Code), they may find, at worst, that they are disbarred from practice or suspended for a period of time. Consequently, because the Code of Conduct has a 'remorseless grip' and the 'disciplinary system of the Bar is very strong' (LCC 5th Annual Report 2001), barristers who choose to ignore the early warning signs in a case do so at their peril. Disciplinary proceedings are the most obvious consequence following a transgression of the Code, not to mention the possibility of a wasted costs order. If you gain a reputation as a sharp practitioner, your life in practice will become very difficult. Your fellow practitioners will treat you suspiciously, judges will give you a hard time, solicitors will no longer brief you, and you will lose the trust of your clerk. If you cannot command the respect of those you regularly come into contact with, it becomes readily apparent that you will not have a career at the Bar. Remember, the Bar is a small profession and the 'grapevine' is extremely effective. Your reputation at all times must be untarnished. **Chapter 6** is a useful guide to the Bar Standard Board's complaints procedure.

1.6 Practical advice

Chapter 7, 'The BPTC, practice, and professional conduct', is designed to help further with your analysis of professional conduct and ethical difficulties. It provides you with a central source of reference for specific problem areas which can occur frequently in practice and which you will meet during your participation in the key skill areas on the BPTC and may well be examined upon. It therefore focuses on professional conduct problems pertinent to the following skills: conference, advocacy, alternative dispute resolution, opinion writing, and drafting. The chapter refers to relevant sources of guidance to ensure that intending barristers are fully aware of why a certain approach to these issues is necessary. It includes, for example, Bar Council guidance on dealing with previous convictions. Additionally, **Chapter 5** is a useful overview of court etiquette and takes you through many of the customs you will meet in practice. **Chapter 8** provides guidance on issues raised by the Proceeds of Crime Act 2002 for the practitioner. These issues are important due to their complex interplay with obligations to the client under the Code.

It is hoped that, as you read the specific provisions of the Code and of the discussions relating to the potential areas of difficulty in practice, your skills in the following areas will develop:

- the *identification* of potential professional conduct issues;
- the *sources* of guidance on particular issues;
- the necessity of applying the *spirit* of the Code where there is no letter;
- the need to recognize obligations towards *fair treatment*; and
- how you would deal *practically* with the matter.

1.7 BPTC and professional conduct

Throughout the City Law School Bar Professional Training Course, you will be able to monitor the development of the skills set out above. The professional ethics course begins with an introductory keynote speech given by a senior member of the Bar. This is followed by two panels of practitioners of differing call who will discuss the problems set out in **Chapter 9**. During the Bar Professional Training Course, in both large and small groups, professional ethics and conduct teaching continues to pervade all aspects of the course, with a number of small group sessions on both the criminal and civil stream focusing specifically on areas of ethical concern. In preparation for these sessions you are encouraged to use the Bar Standards Board website as a source of the most current version of the Code and Guidance . You are advised to keep a separate note of all professional conduct matters arising on the course and your approach to them, together with a note of the suggested response. By keeping a note, you will also have a central reference source setting out the likely areas you will be examined upon. Very importantly, in April 2011, for the first time, BPTC students will be separately assessed on professional conduct and ethics in examination conditions by way of Multiple Choice Questions and Short Answer Questions. You will have ample opportunity to practice answering this style of question during the course.

1.8 Conclusion

In conclusion, taking the right approach to professional conduct and ethical difficulties from the outset of your professional training is crucial. One word sums up all that has been set out above. That word is '*Awareness*'. Being alert to professional conduct and ethical difficulties and knowing the Code, the Guidance and their application will hold you in good stead throughout your career at the Bar and you will, in time, inspire others through your professionalism.

2

Professional relationships

Whichever party you are instructed to represent, as counsel you must consider a number of responsibilities beyond those to your client. Of course everything possible must be done on behalf of the client, but counsel has a number of wider duties. Miscarriages of justice can and do occur when counsel forget or ignore their duties to the court, to their professional client and the Crown Prosecution Service, and to other members of the profession. There is even a duty to the Legal Services Commission. A barrister should be concerned in the administration of justice, and **not** to win at all costs.

It is common for these duties to conflict, for example, over the disclosure of an authority harmful to your case. Frequently the question is not straightforward. It is important that from the earliest days you can at the very least recognise that there is a potential problem so that you can then take steps, for example, discussion with a senior barrister or telephoning the Professional Conduct and Complaints Committee, to ensure that the right answer is reached.

In this chapter we consider a number of ways in which the duty to one's client is, and must be, fettered, so that ultimately justice is achieved. More broadly we consider the range of professional relationships that the barrister will enter into in the course of practice and the duties and obligations that are owed in conducting each relationship successfully and to the appropriate ethical standard.

2.1 Relationship with the court

2.1.1 Duties and responsibilities owed to the court

Time and again, the judiciary has stressed the paramount duty of counsel to the court. This duty is expressed in para 302 of the Code as 'overriding'. In *Rondel v Worsley* [1969] 1 AC 191, 227 Lord Reid put it in this way:

Every counsel has a duty to his client fearlessly to raise every issue, advance every argument, and ask every question, however distasteful, which he thinks will help his client's case. But, as an officer of the Court concerned in the administration of justice, he has an overriding duty to the Court, to the standards of his profession, and to the public, which may and often does lead to a conflict with his client's wishes or with what the client thinks are his personal interests.

In the same case, Lord Denning MR explained the nature of the duty to the court in these terms:

[Counsel] must accept the brief and do all he honourably can on behalf of his client. I say 'all he honourably can' because his duty is not only to his client. He has a duty to the Court which is paramount. It is a mistake to suppose that he is the mouthpiece of his client to say what he wants: or his tool to do what he directs. He is none of these things. He owes allegiance to a higher cause. It is the cause of truth and justice. He must not consciously misstate the facts. He must not knowingly conceal the truth. He must not unjustly make a charge of fraud, that is, without evidence to support it. He must produce all the relevant authorities, even those that are against him. He must see that his client discloses, if ordered, the relevant documents, even those that are fatal to his case. He must disregard the most specific instructions of his client, if they conflict with his duty to the court. The code which requires a barrister to do all this is not a code of law. It is a code of honour. If he breaks it, he is offending against the rules of the profession and is subject to its discipline. But he cannot be sued in a Court of law. Such being his duty to the Court, the barrister must be able to do it fearlessly. He has time and time again to choose between his duty to his client and his duty to the Court.

([1966] 3 WLR 950, 962.)

Please note that, with regard to immunity from suit, *Rondel v Worsley* has been overruled by the decision of the House of Lords in *Arthur J S Hall & Co (A Firm) v Simons* [2000] 3 WLR 543, [2002] 1 AC 615. Advocates no longer enjoy immunity from liability for negligent conduct of a case in court, either in civil or criminal proceedings. The sentiments expressed in the two extracts above, however, retain their full force.

2.1.1.1   Duties and responsibilities owed to the court

Your overriding duty to the court to act with independence in the interests of justice incorporates many separate responsibilities. Set out below is a non-verbatim summary of some of the relevant sections of the Code which includes a duty:

(a) To assist the court in the administration of justice, and not to deceive or knowingly or recklessly mislead the court (para 302). Note that ss 27 and 28 of the Courts and Legal Services Act 1990 are amended by s 42 of the Access to Justice Act 1999. This imports an overriding duty on advocates to the court to act with independence in the interests of justice. This would include, e.g., correcting any misleading information which is incorporated in your client's witness statement and which on your instructions is inaccurate. A further example is contained in para 708(f) of the Code—not to make a submission which the barrister does not consider to be properly arguable.

(b) To act with due courtesy to the court (Section 3, Miscellaneous Guidance, Written Standards, para 5.5).

(c) To bring to the attention of the court all relevant decisions and legislative provisions of which you are aware, whether or not their effect is favourable to your case (para 708(c)). A failure to comply with this duty, or that at (d), below, can result in costly and unnecessary appeals.

(d) To bring any procedural irregularity to the attention of the court during the trial (para 708(d)).

(e) To advise that all relevant disclosures be made and withdraw from the case if such advice is not followed (para 608(d) and (e)).

(f) To record the proceedings. You have a duty to take a note of the judge's reasons for his decision and have it typed as soon as there is any question of an appeal (see *Letts v Letts* The Times, 8 April 1987).

(g) Not to devise facts which will assist in advancing the lay client's case and not to draft any statement of case, witness statement, affidavit, notice of appeal or other document which is not supported by the lay client or by his instructions (paras 704 and 708(e)).

(h) Not to allege fraud in any statement of case or other document without clear instructions to do so and without reasonably credible material which as it stands establishes a prima facie case of fraud (para 704(c)).

(i) Not to assert a *personal* opinion of the facts or the law to the court unless invited to do so by the court (para 708(b)).

(j) Not to make statements or ask questions which are merely scandalous or intended or calculated only to vilify, insult, or annoy either a witness or some other person (para 708(g)).

(k) To take all reasonable and practicable steps to avoid unnecessary expense or waste of the court's time (Code para 701(a) and Written Standards for the Conduct of Professional Work, General Standards, para 5.11); this includes a duty not to waste an appellate court's time. In *Ainsbury v Millington* The Times, 13 March 1987, Lord Bridge stated that it was:

> the duty of counsel and solicitors in any pending appeal in publicly funded litigation whenever an event occurred which arguably disposed of the matter in contention, either to ensure that the appeal was withdrawn by consent or, in the absence of agreement, to bring the facts promptly to the attention of the appellate court and to seek directions.

2.1.1.2(A) Wasted *costs* orders: civil and criminal

A barrister can be made personally responsible for costs wasted as a result of his or her improper, unreasonable, or negligent conduct in proceedings. The legislative bases for the court's powers in this regard are as follows:

- *Court of Appeal (Civil Division), High Court, county courts*: s 51(6), (7), and (13) of the Supreme Court Act 1981 (inserted by s 4 of the Courts and Legal Services Act 1990). For civil cases, the procedural rules are to be found in CPR Part 48.7 and PD 48.

- *Court of Appeal (Criminal Division), Crown Courts, magistrates' courts (criminal proceedings)*: s 19A Prosecution of Offenders Act 1985 (inserted by Courts and Legal Services Act 1990 s 111). The Costs in Criminal Cases (General) Regulations 1986 (SI 1986 No 1335), *Practice Direction (Costs in Criminal Proceedings)* 93 Cr App R 89, and the Criminal Procedure Rules r 76.9 provide the relevant procedural background.

- *Magistrates' courts (civil proceedings)*: Magistrates' Courts Act 1980 s 145A (inserted by Courts and Legal Services Act 1990 s 112).

'Wasted costs' means any costs incurred by a party:

- as a result of any improper, unreasonable or negligent act or omission on the part of any representative or any employee of a representative; or

- which, in the light of any such act or omission occurring after they were incurred, the court considers it is unreasonable to expect that party to pay.

Note that there must be a causal connection between the conduct complained of and the waste of costs.

There have been a number of cases in which courts, including the Court of Appeal, have made wasted costs orders against barristers. In *Re A Barrister (Wasted Costs Order No 1 of 1991)* [1992] 3 WLR 662, the Court of Appeal recommended a three-stage test:

- Had there been an improper, unreasonable, or negligent act or omission?

- If so, had any costs been incurred by any party in consequence thereof?

- If so, should the court exercise its discretion to disallow, or order the representative to meet, the whole or any part of the relevant costs and, if so, what specific sum was involved?

In the Court of Appeal case of *Ridehalgh v Horsefield* [1994] 3 WLR 462 Sir Thomas Bingham MR made it clear that the judgment was applicable to criminal as well as civil courts, and made the following points.

(a) 'Improper' covered, but was not confined to, conduct which would ordinarily justify serious professional penalty. It was not limited to significant breach of the relevant code of professional conduct. It included conduct which was improper according to the consensus of professional, including judicial, opinion, whether it violated the letter of a professional code or not.

(b) 'Unreasonable' described conduct which was vexatious, i.e., designed to harass the other side rather than advance the resolution of the dispute. Conduct could not be described as unreasonable simply because it led to an unsuccessful result, or because other more cautious legal representatives would have acted differently. The acid test was whether the conduct permitted of a reasonable explanation. If it did, the course adopted might be regarded as optimistic and reflecting on a practitioner's judgement, but it was not unreasonable.

(c) 'Negligent' should be understood in an untechnical way to denote failure to act with the competence reasonably expected of ordinary members of the profession. It was not a term of art and did not necessarily involve an actionable breach of the legal representative's duty to his own client.

(d) A legal representative was not acting improperly, unreasonably or negligently simply because he acted for a party who pursued a claim or defence which was plainly doomed to fail.

(e) However, a legal representative could not lend his assistance to proceedings which were an abuse of process, and was not entitled to use litigious procedures for purposes for which they were not intended, for example, by issuing proceedings for reasons unconnected with success in the action, pursuing a case which was known to be dishonest, or knowingly conniving at incomplete disclosure of documents.

(f) Any judge considering making a wasted costs order must make full allowance for the fact that an advocate in court often had to make decisions quickly and under pressure.

(g) Legal professional privilege might be relevant. If so, the privilege was the client's, which he alone could waive. Judges should make full allowance for the inability of respondent lawyers to tell the whole story. Where there was room for doubt, the respondent lawyers were entitled to the benefit of it. It was only when, with all allowance made, a lawyer's conduct of proceedings was quite plainly unjustifiable that it could be appropriate to make the order.

(h) When a solicitor sought the advice of counsel, he did not abdicate his own professional responsibility. He had to apply his mind to the advice received. But the more specialised the advice, the more reasonable it was likely to be for him to accept it.

(i) A threat to apply for a wasted costs order should not be used as a means of intimidation. However, if one side considered that the conduct of the other was improper, unreasonable, or negligent and likely to cause a waste of costs, it was not objectionable to alert the other side to that view.

(j) In the ordinary way, such applications were best left until after the end of the trial.

(k) As to procedure, the respondent lawyer should be told very clearly what he or she was said to have done wrong. No formal process of discovery would be appropriate. Elaborate statements of case should in general be avoided. The court could not imagine circumstances in which the applicant could interrogate the respondent lawyer or vice versa. The legal representative must have opportunity to show cause why an order should not be made (Rules of the Supreme Court 1965, Ord 62, r 11(4)), but this did not mean that the burden was on the legal representative to exculpate himself. (Note that this was written before the introduction of the Civil Procedure Rules 1998.)

2.1.1.2(B) In *Medcalf v Mardell (Wasted Costs Order)* [2002] 3 WLR 172, [2002] 3 All ER 721, the House of Lords considered a wasted costs order for the first time. The case concerned an application for a wasted costs order by the claimant against leading counsel and his junior representing the defendants. The basis of the application was the claimant's allegation that both barristers had included serious allegations of fraud and other misconduct against the claimant and his solicitors in an application to amend a notice of appeal and in the skeleton arguments supporting the application. The court had refused the application. The House of Lords confirmed that applications for wasted costs orders could be made against lawyers for the opposing party, and further confirmed the approach in *Ridehalgh v Horsefield* to deciding such applications. Further, the House emphasised the problems involved where the client of a lawyer accused of wasting costs refused to waive privilege so as to allow the court to see the full facts relating to that lawyer's advice to the client (usually arising in the situation where the other party had applied against the opposing lawyers). In such a situation, the House stated that it would only be very rarely that it would be possible for the court to conclude that there was no room for doubt about the lawyer's conduct; and further, the court must not make a wasted costs order against a practitioner precluded by legal professional privilege from advancing a full answer to a complaint unless satisfied in all the circumstances that it was fair to do so—again, this would be an exceptional situation.

The House also drew attention to *Arthur J S Hall & Co (A Firm) v Simons* [2000] 3 WLR 543 (see **2.1.1** above), decided since *Ridehalgh*, regarding the removal of immunity from suit for advocates for their work in court.

Substantial guidance on the issue of wasted costs can be found on the Bar Council's website in the 'Guidance' section, 'Wasted Costs Orders'.

2.1.1.3 Problems

(1) In the course of legal argument, your opponent advances a proposition of law to the court in support of their client's case, but fails to produce a particular reported decision of which you are aware and which would plainly be of assistance. Without it you are likely to win; with it you may well fail. What do you do? Does your answer depend upon for whom you are acting and whether in civil or criminal proceedings?

(2) While sitting in court waiting for your case to be called, you listen to the previous case. Counsel for the claimant is seeking to persuade the judge that the maximum time that the judge can allow the defendant to vacate the claimant's premises is 14 days. The defendant is unrepresented. The judge is a recorder with clearly little experience of landlord and tenant law. You are aware that the judge has a discretion to allow the defendant a maximum period of six weeks. Do you do anything?

(3)   You start to cross-examine a prosecution witness about matters which you consider to be vital to your client's case. The judge, having heard argument on the matter, disallows your line of questioning. You are convinced the judge is wrong and that your client will thereby be convicted. What, if anything, can you do?

2.1.2 Specific responsibilities of prosecuting counsel

The role of prosecuting counsel carries grave responsibilities in ensuring the fairness and openness of the criminal justice system. The overriding responsibility is that the prosecutor must act fairly, impartially, and must **not** seek to obtain a conviction by all means at his or her command.

The primary source of information regarding your obligations when prosecuting is to be found in the Written Standards for the Conduct of Professional Work at Part 10. The Written Standards are in Section 3 of the Code of Conduct and can be found on the Bar Standards Board (BSB) website. Broadly, prosecuting counsel has obligations to lay all the facts before the court fairly and impartially, which includes ensuring that all evidence or matters which ought properly to be available are either adduced by the prosecution, or disclosed to the defence. There are obligations in relation to the preparation of the case in terms of advising promptly on the evidence and preparation of the matter for trial, in relation to checking that the indictment is not overloaded, and that the case is presented as simply and concisely as possible. Counsel for the prosecution is also responsible for ensuring proper service upon the defence in accordance with the Attorney General's Guidelines and the Criminal Procedure Rules. Errors of fact and/or law must be pointed out to the court at the conclusion of the summing up. In relation to sentencing, counsel for the prosecution must not attempt to influence the sentence by advocacy, but must ensure that any mitigating circumstances of which counsel is aware are communicated to the court if the defendant is unrepresented. Counsel also has obligations to assist the court as to relevant statutory provisions regarding sentencing, and any relevant Court of Appeal guidelines.

2.1.2.1 The relationship between prosecuting counsel and the judge

At **2.1.5** the question of access to the judge is considered for both prosecution and defence counsel. However, the relationship between prosecuting counsel and the judge is particularly sensitive, and is governed by the Farquharson Committee's guidance, reissued in 2002 as 'The Farquharson Guidelines: The Role and Responsibilities of the Prosecution Advocate'. These can be accessed at <http://www.cps.gov.uk/publications/prosecution/farqbooklet.html>. Part of the Guidelines are reproduced below, but it is essential that you are familiar with the entire document if you prosecute on behalf of the CPS. The Farquharson Guidelines are also subject to the Code of Conduct.

(a) It is the duty of prosecution counsel to read the instructions delivered to him expeditiously and to advise or confer with those instructing him on all aspects of the case well before its commencement.

(b) A solicitor who has briefed counsel to prosecute may withdraw his instructions before the commencement of the trial up to the point when it becomes impracticable to do so, if he disagrees with the advice given by counsel or for any other proper professional reason.

(c) While he remains instructed, it is for counsel to take all necessary decisions in the presentation and general conduct of the prosecution.

(d) Where matters of policy fall to be decided after the point indicated in (b) above (including offering no evidence on the indictment or on a particular count, or on the acceptance of pleas to lesser counts), it is the duty of counsel to consult his instructing solicitor/prosecution counsel whose views at this stage are of crucial importance.

(e) In the rare case where counsel and his instructing solicitor are unable to agree on a matter of policy, it is, subject to (g) below, for prosecution counsel to make the necessary decisions.

(f) Where counsel has taken a decision on a matter of policy with which his instructing solicitor has not agreed, then it would be appropriate for the Attorney General to require counsel to submit to him a written report of all the circumstances, including his reasons for disagreeing with those who instruct him.

(g) When counsel has had the opportunity to prepare his brief and to confer with those instructing him, but at the last moment before trial unexpectedly advises that the case should not proceed or that pleas to lesser offences should be accepted, and his instructing solicitor does not accept such advice, counsel should apply for an adjournment if instructed so to do.

(h) Subject to the above, it is for prosecution counsel to decide whether to offer no evidence on a particular count or on the indictment as a whole and whether to accept pleas to a lesser count or counts.

(i) If prosecution counsel invites the judge to approve the course he is proposing to take, then he must abide by the judge's decision.

(j) If prosecution counsel does not invite the judge's approval of his decision, it is open to the judge to express his dissent with the course proposed and invite counsel to reconsider the matter with those instructing him, but having done so, the final decision remains with counsel.

(k) In an extreme case where the judge is of the opinion that the course proposed by counsel would lead to serious injustice, he may decline to proceed with the case until counsel has consulted with either the Director or the Attorney General as may be appropriate.

2.1.3 Further duties

There are further duties of prosecuting counsel which are not expressly included in the Code.

2.1.3.1 To inform the defence of any known previous convictions of any prosecution witness

See *R v Collister and Warhurst* (1955) 39 Cr App R 100. It should be noted that previous convictions include any disciplinary offences/findings and criminal cautions against police witnesses.

2.1.3.2 To call or tender witnesses at trial

The general rule is that the prosecution must call (or tender for cross-examination) all the witnesses whose evidence was used in the committal proceedings. The exceptions are those set out in the cases of *R v Russell-Jones* [1995] 3 All ER 230 and *R v Armstrong* [1995] 3 All ER 831:

- the defence has consented to the written statement of that witness being read to the court;
- counsel for the prosecution takes the view that the evidence of that witness is no longer credible; or
- counsel for the prosecution takes the view that the witness would so fundamentally contradict the prosecution case that it would make more sense for that person to be called as a witness for the defence.

There remains a limit to the prosecution's discretion, namely that it must be exercised in the interests of justice, so as to promote a fair trial.

2.1.3.3 To adduce all the evidence upon which you intend to rely to prove the defendant's guilt before the close of your case

This is provided that such evidence is then available.

2.1.3.4 To disclose not only all of the evidence that will be called at trial, but also information of which the defence may be unaware and which will not be part of the prosecution case

This duty is dealt with mainly in the Criminal Procedure and Investigations Act 1996. The statutory scheme is covered in the *Criminal Litigation and Sentencing* manual.

In essence, there is a duty on the police officer investigating the offence to record and retain information and material gathered during the investigation. The prosecution must inform the defence of certain categories of that material that it does not intend to rely on at trial. The defence then has a duty (or for summary trial, the option) to inform the prosecution of the case that it intends to present at trial (the 'Defence Statement'). The prosecution then has a duty to present further material to the defence which might be reasonably expected to assist the accused's defence as disclosed by the defence. After this, applications can be made to the court where there is a dispute as to whether the prosecution should disclose certain material. Where public interest immunity is involved, the 1996 Act expressly preserves the existing common law.

The prosecutor remains under a continuing duty to review questions of disclosure.

The prosecution's duty of disclosure applies to summary trial where the accused pleads not guilty. The defence may make voluntary disclosure. In such a case, the prosecution will be obliged to make further statutory disclosure.

Prosecuting counsel should bear in mind at all times while he is instructed that he should use his best endeavours to ensure that all evidence or material that ought properly to be made available is either presented by the prosecution or disclosed to the defence.

2.1.3.5 To consider whether witness statements need to be edited

See *Practice Direction (Criminal Proceeding: Consolidation)* [2002] 1 WLR 2870, pt III, para 24 for the relevant considerations and practice on editing witness statements.

2.1.3.6 To be familiar with the *Practice Direction: Crown Court (Plea and Directions Hearings)* [1995] 1 WLR 1318

The purpose of a Plea and Case Management Hearing (PCMH) is to ensure that all necessary steps have been taken in preparation for trial and to provide sufficient information for a trial date to be arranged. The *Practice Direction* stresses that 'it is expected that the advocate briefed in the case will appear in the PCMH wherever practicable'. With the demands of a busy practice this will not always be possible. Pupils and junior tenants should be very conscious of the fact that it is regarded as a serious dereliction of duty for counsel to turn up at a PCMH and say 'Sorry, this isn't my brief and I can't provide the information required'. If you are going to appear at a PCMH in the place of counsel who will be appearing in the case, go armed with all the relevant information. Information required includes informing the court of the issues in the case, number of witnesses and the form that their evidence will take, exhibits and schedules to be admitted at trial, points of law and admissibility of evidence that will arise at trial, applications for evidence to be given via television links etc, witness availability, length of witness testimony, counsel availability. The Bar Council has guidance, 'Preparation for PCMH Hearings', on the website <http://www.barcouncil.org.uk> in the 'Guidance' section.

2.1.3.7   Problems

(1)   You are instructed to prosecute a case in which the allegation is that the defendant and associates burst into the victim's flat intent on causing injury. The victim, seeing the group arrive, tried to escape by jumping off a fifth-floor balcony. He fell and was seriously injured. The defendant was charged with causing grievous bodily harm with intent. After the victim has given evidence, you are shown a note by the officer in the case which the officer says was written by the victim about ten days before these events. It shows that at that time the victim was threatening suicide. You do not think that that is the reason why he jumped that day and it certainly does not accord with the evidence the victim has just given. Should you take any action in relation to the note?

(2)   In the course of a ruling given following argument by counsel for both prosecution and defence, the judge gives reasons which are based on a case cited in argument. The ruling is favourable to you, the prosecution. It is, however, clear that the judge has misunderstood the passage quoted. What do you do?

(3)   You arrive in court to prosecute a defendant. You realise that the defendant was a client of a solicitor's firm for which you worked during the holidays. You learned details about the defendant which might well help you in prosecuting the case. The defendant does not appear to recognise you. Do you do anything?

2.1.4   Specific responsibilities of defence counsel

The Written Standards for the Conduct of Professional Work also contain specific requirements for conduct of criminal proceedings by defence counsel. These are contained in Section 11. You should consult this for yourself, but broadly, the obligations are as follows: if briefed for more than one defendant in a trial, defence counsel should satisfy him or herself that a conflict between the interests of those defendants is not likely to arise. Counsel should see the defendant in conference in good time, and as often as required to prepare the case adequately; he or she should consider in advance the necessary evidence, including which witnesses are required, whether further enquiries are necessary, whether a Notice of Alibi needs to be served, whether expert evidence is required, and what prosecution witnesses will be required for cross-examination. He or she should also consider what admissions can properly be made by the defendant, consistent with proper conduct of the case, and what admissions should be sought from the prosecution—in both cases, to save court time. By 11.3, counsel must specifically advise the defendant about his or her plea—that advice can be couched in strong terms if appropriate, but always making clear that the final decision is the defendant's; and by 11.4, counsel must advise the defendant on the issue of whether to give evidence in his or her own defence. Again, it must be plain that the final decision is the client's.

Whereas the key sensitivity in representing the prosecution relates to the relationship with the judge, the most likely source of ethical difficulty in representing the defendant while fulfilling obligations to the court relates to the following areas:

- The client confesses his or her guilt to you but wishes to plead innocent.
- The client changes his or her instructions.
- The client insists upon you conducting the case in a manner detrimental to his or her interests (e.g., by calling unhelpful witnesses).
- The client wishes to plead guilty for his or her own reasons, but insists upon his or her innocence to you in conference.
- The client discloses a previous conviction to you in conference which the prosecution appear to be unaware of.

The key to all these situations lies in giving the client full advice about the risks of his or her proposed course of action, the limitations it puts upon you in presenting his or her case, and in clear advice to the client that the decision in each case is ultimately his or hers. Three situations are particularly provided for in the Written Standards or guidance issued by the Bar Council.

First, by 11.5, where the defendant tells you that he or she is innocent, but wishes to plead guilty for his or her own reasons, you must act with great care. You must first advise the defendant that if he or she is not guilty, then that is how he or she should plead, while making clear that the decision is of course his or hers alone. If the defendant insists, you should point out that you can only mitigate on the basis that he or she is guilty, and the consequences of this should be explained. The consequences include acquiring a criminal record, and the fact that it would be very unlikely that the conviction could be overturned if he or she changed his or her mind later and wished to appeal. You should also explore with the client why it is that he or she wishes to plead guilty and whether anything could be done that would help him or her to enter a not guilty plea—he or she may, for example, be under a false impression that persisting with a trial could affect an individual he or she has a relationship with adversely. If, despite thorough advice, the defendant persists in wishing to plead guilty, you will need to take steps to ensure that this decision, and your warnings, are properly recorded. Record in writing the reasons for the plea prior to the plea being entered, and ask the defendant to endorse a declaration that he or she has given you unequivocal instructions of his or her own free will, and that he or she understands your advice. If he or she does not wish to sign, then ensure you have a good contemporaneous note of the advice you gave.

Second, the defendant may confess guilt to you, but wish to run the trial on the basis of a not guilty plea. This is a tricky situation, but it pays to remember that the burden of proof is on the prosecution to prove guilt, not for the defendant to disprove it. You can therefore continue to represent the defendant but only on a heavily restricted basis, about which you should fully advise the defendant before continuing. As counsel, you cannot assert to be true that which you know to be false since this would be conniving at fraud. Therefore you can object to the prosecution's case on procedural matters, such as the form of indictment or the court's jurisdiction to hear the case. You *cannot* run the case on the basis that another person committed the crime, or call evidence which you now know to be false, such as evidence of an alibi. In other words, you cannot present an affirmative case on the defendant's behalf which is inconsistent with your knowledge of the confession. How far you can go in challenging the prosecution evidence is also tricky. The guidance in Part 12 of the Written Standards suggests that you are entitled to test the evidence of prosecution witnesses (for example, in an identification case, it would be quite proper to test the witnesses' perception along the *Turnbull* lines), and argue in closing that the case as a whole does not provide sufficient evidence to prove the defendant's guilt. But to go further would probably mislead the court. If the defendant accepts your advice about how you will be obliged to run the trial, you can and indeed should continue to represent him or her. However, if he or she insists that you must present an affirmative case inconsistent with your knowledge of his or her confession, you would be obliged to withdraw, since the defendant is effectively seeking to require you to mislead the court. The Written Standards also point out the need for great care in identifying the situation you find yourself in—is the defendant clearly asserting his or her guilt to you? Or have you simply formed that conclusion from inconsistencies in his or her account to you? Is the client of sound mind? These issues raise different considerations and you must be astute to the need to analyse the situation clearly first.

Third, the situation where the defendant discloses to you a previous conviction of which the prosecution appear to be unaware. This is dealt with in the 'Standards and

Guidance' section of the Bar Standards Board website, <http://www.barstandardsboard .org.uk>, 'Duty to Disclose Previous Convictions'. In this situation, the guidance states that counsel has no duty to disclose this information to the prosecution or the court, nor is counsel obliged to withdraw. However, you must advise the defendant in full on all the options. He or she can be told that the information about the conviction will remain confidential between you unless he or she specifically waives the privilege. Nevertheless, you must advise that you will be considerably restricted in what you can properly say in mitigation on his or her behalf, since you may not mislead the court. Therefore, you cannot implicitly or explicitly adopt the prosecution's position that this conviction does not exist, and this means that you cannot assert that the defendant is a person of good character (if there are no other previous convictions); that you cannot point to a period free of convictions or free of convictions of a specific type if the conviction in question occurred during that time or was of that type; and that you cannot point to a lack of a particular type of sentence in the antecedents if in fact this conviction resulted in such a sentence. To do otherwise would mislead the court. The defendant must also be advised about what would happen if the conviction was revealed, as against how he or she would be sentenced if not—this will include consideration of mandatory sentencing provisions. This ensures that the defendant makes his or her decision on the basis of full information. Of course, you must also address the effect if the prosecution or court subsequently discovered the conviction—the possibilities being an adjournment, relisting for alteration of the sentence, or even a reference by the Attorney General under s 36 of the Access to Justice Act 1999. Inevitably, there is the clear risk of an experienced prosecutor or judge quickly realising that you were failing to make mitigation points on your client's behalf that were apparently open to you to make. This would raise suspicion and probably lead to discovery of the conviction. You will also need to discuss with the defendant the significant credit that his or her decision to reveal the conviction would probably receive in sentencing, should he or she so decide. Ultimately, as ever, your duty is to ensure that the client has full information, while ensuring that he or she clearly understands that the final decision is his or hers.

2.1.4.1   Problems

(1)   You represent a defendant in a trial at the Crown Court having advised and appeared (without your instructing solicitor having been present) at the magistrates' court. The defendant, having been given the new caution, did not answer any question in his or her police interview. During your client's cross-examination by the prosecution, it is suggested that the account that he or she is giving has been thought up recently. You know that he or she gave that account to you on the first remand date. You were alone with him or her at the time. What should you do?

(2)   There is crucial prosecution evidence of your client's presence at the scene of the crime at a material time. Your instructions are that your client was present but merely an onlooker, not a participant in the crime. You conduct your cross-examination on that basis and do not challenge the evidence of your client's presence at the scene. When he or she gives evidence, the defendant denies his or her presence at the material time by saying that he or she had just left the scene. The judge points out the difference and demands that you clarify the situation.

(3)   Your client is pleading guilty in the magistrates' court. Your instructions are that he or she has a number of previous convictions. The police antecedents given to the court show him or her as a person of good character. How do you mitigate? Would your approach be different if the omitted previous conviction had involved the imposition of a suspended sentence of which the defendant was in breach by virtue of the instant conviction?

2.1.5   Access to the judge

2.1.5.1   Indications on sentence

In certain circumstances it is possible to seek an indication on sentence from the judge. Until very recently, the guidance on this area was to be found in the decision of the Court of Appeal in *R v Turner* [1970] 2 QB 321. However, the Court of Appeal in *R v Goodyear* [2005] EWCA Crim 888 considered that the modern practice of criminal litigation required a fresh approach to indications on sentence. While you should read the judgment in *Goodyear* for yourself, there follows a summary of the guidance issued by the Court of Appeal in that case:

- The fundamental starting point remains that the defendant is exclusively responsible for his plea. He must enter it voluntarily and without improper pressure.
- Provided that the defendant seeks the indication of sentence, there is no automatic assumption that responding to that request with an indication of sentence constitutes improper judicial pressure in respect of the defendant's decision on plea.

The role of the judge

- The judge should not give an advance indication of sentence unless one has been sought by the defendant.
- As recognised in *Turner*, the judge remains entitled to indicate that the sentence, or type of sentence, for the defendant would remain the same whether the defendant pleaded guilty, or on conviction following trial. The Court of Appeal considered that this situation would now be unusual given that a guilty plea will normally attract credit.
- The judge is entitled in an appropriate case to remind the defendant's counsel that the defendant is entitled to seek an advance indication of sentence.
- The judge has an unfettered discretion to refuse to give an indication. The Court of Appeal recognised that there may be cogent reasons why a judge would not want to give an indication for fear of creating additional pressure on the defendant. Paragraph 57 of the judgment contains a number of examples of situations where a judge may feel unable to indicate sentence. The judge would not be obliged to give his reasons for refusal.
- A judge should also be able to reserve his position on sentence until such time as he feels able to give an indication. In such circumstances the judge would normally explain why he wished to postpone the indication, together with an indication of the circumstances in which he would be prepared to give an indication in future.
- Any advance indication of sentence should normally be *confined to the maximum sentence if a plea of guilty were tendered at the stage at which the indication is sought.*
- The judge should *not* then indicate the maximum possible sentence following conviction by the jury.
- *An indication, once given, is binding upon both the judge giving the indication and any other judge who becomes responsible for the case.*
- However, if the defendant does not then plead guilty, after a reasonable time and opportunity in which to consider his plea, the indication ceases to have effect.

Obligations upon counsel for the defence

- Counsel for the defence should not seek an indication of sentence without written authority, signed by his client, that the client wishes to seek an indication.
- The advocate is personally responsible for ensuring that his client understands:

1   he should not plead guilty unless he is guilty;
2   any sentence indication given by the judge remains subject to any entitlement in the Attorney General to refer an unduly lenient sentence to the Court of Appeal;
3   if the judge does give an indication, it reflects the situation at the time it is given and will cease to have effect if a guilty plea is not tendered after a reasonable opportunity for consideration;
4   the indication relates only to the matters on which it is sought. Therefore, certain steps which follow automatically, such as confiscation proceedings, remain unaffected.

- The basis of the plea must be clear, agreed between prosecution and defence, and reduced into writing. There should be no disagreement about acceptable plea or pleas to the indictment, nor disagreement about the factual basis of the plea.
- The judge should never be asked to indicate levels of sentence depending on possible pleas—for example, asking the judge to indicate sentence depending on whether the plea was to s 18, s 20, or s 47 as alternatives. This would be to involve the judge in plea bargaining.

Role of the prosecution

- The prosecution can only react to, not initiate the process of, requesting an indication.
- Prosecution counsel is responsible for reminding the judge of this guidance where the defence seeks an indication, although the basis of the plea is not agreed.
- The prosecution is also obliged to check that the judge has had access to all prosecution evidence, including personal impact statements from any victims and the relevant previous convictions of the defendant.
- Prosecution counsel will normally draw to the judge's attention, prior to an indication being given, any minimum or mandatory sentencing requirements, together with any guideline cases or views of the Sentencing Guidelines Council if appropriate. Further, where it applies, to remind the judge that the power of the Attorney General to refer any sentencing decision as unduly lenient is unaffected by the indication process.
- Counsel should not say anything which gives the impression that the sentence indication has the support or approval of the Crown.

Procedural points

- The Attorney General's power to refer unduly lenient sentences to the Court of Appeal under s 36 of the Criminal Justice Act 1988 is unaffected by the sentence indication process, provided that prosecution counsel has followed the above guidance.

- Equally, the defendant's entitlement to apply for leave to appeal against sentence is unaffected.

- Any sentence indication should normally be sought at the plea and case management hearing, although the possibility of seeking an indication at a later stage is available.

- In a complex or difficult case, the judge is unlikely to be able to give an indication unless the basis of the plea and related issues are resolved as between prosecution and defence. Therefore, in such cases, at least seven days' notice in writing of an intention to seek an indication should be given to the prosecution and the court. A failure to do so might result in an unnecessary adjournment and reduction of the credit for a guilty plea accordingly.

- Hearings should normally take place in open court, fully recorded, in the defendant's presence.

- The fact that notice of intention to seek an indication has been given in a complex case, and the request for indication itself, would be inadmissible in any subsequent trial. Additionally, reporting restrictions would apply until the defendant pleads, or is found, guilty.

- The procedure does not apply in the magistrates' court. Schedule 3 of the Criminal Justice Act 2003 proposed changes to create a comparable system in the magistrates' court, but those sections have not been brought into force. Consequently, at this time there is no method for requesting an indication of plea in the magistrates' court.

2.1.5.2 Situations where it is permissible to see the judge

There are a variety of other situations in which it is permissible and indeed advisable for counsel to ask to see the judge. These include:

- if your client is thinking of pleading guilty but, for instance, wants to discuss the matter with your instructing solicitor who is not present at court that day, counsel may see the judge and ask for an overnight adjournment. To mention that the client is thinking of pleading guilty in these circumstances is sensitive information that ought not to be mentioned in open court;

- if the defendant has given information or assistance to the police he or she may not wish details to be given to the judge in open court. His or her safety or that of his or her family may be at risk;

- any matters that would be embarrassing to the defendant if mentioned in open court, for instance, if he or she is suffering from an illness that may make him or her appear drowsy or uninterested while in court;

- any matters that are personal to counsel and would be embarrassing to mention in open court, e.g., illness, a bereavement necessitating an adjournment, etc.

2.2 Relationship with the lay client

2.2.1 The hierarchy of duties

Your overriding duty is to the court under Code para 302, and it provides limitations as to how you represent your lay client, for example by prohibiting you from misleading the court or devising facts for which you have no evidence in order to advance your client's case.

What is the barrister's proper role in relation to a lay client? The Written Standards at 2.1 state:

The work which is within the ordinary scope of a barrister's practice consists of advocacy, drafting pleadings and other legal documents and advising on questions of law. A barrister acts only on the instructions of a professional client, and does not carry out any work by way of the management, administration or general conduct of a lay client's affairs, nor the management, administration or general conduct of litigation nor the receipt or handling of client's money.

By Code para 303(a), you have a duty to 'promote and protect fearlessly and by all proper and lawful means the lay client's best interests and do so without regard to [your] own interests or to any consequences to [yourself] or to any other person (including any professional client or other intermediary or another barrister)'. Further, para 303(b) indicates that your primary duty is to the lay client rather than your professional client.

The position of prosecuting counsel is slightly different in this context. As was seen earlier, at **2.1.2**, prosecuting counsel is obliged to act fairly and must not seek to obtain a conviction by all means at his or her command. Of course, the prosecution is instructed by the Crown Prosecution Service, who is the professional client, and the prosecutor cannot really be considered as having a lay client as such.

Note the wording of para 303 carefully—you cannot use *any* means to promote your client's interests—your methods must be 'proper and lawful'. This provides an indication as to how your duty to your client fits with your duty to the court—you may not mislead the court in the course of representing your client since this would be improper and contrary to your duty under Code para 302. The Written Standards at 5.2 supports this interpretation.

So, the lay client's interests take priority above those of the professional client. The classic example would be where you became aware that your instructing solicitor had acted negligently in the lay client's case. You are professionally obliged to consider whether the lay client's interests would be best served by instructing another professional adviser, and if so, you must advise the lay client so. You are required to take steps actively to ensure that the lay client receives that advice, if necessary by sending a copy of your advice in writing directly to the lay client—Code para 703.

Such a result will doubtless have uncomfortable consequences for your instructing solicitor, and for yourself—you may have a good professional relationship with that solicitor involving regular instructions, and having to advise a lay client in these terms will inevitably put it in jeopardy. But para 303 is clear—you act in the lay client's best interests *regardless* of the consequences to yourself and your instructing solicitor.

The primacy of your duty to the lay client does not mean that the lay client can put you under improper pressure. By Code para 307, you have a responsibility to exercise independent judgement, act with integrity, and resist external pressure to the contrary. This includes not compromising your professional standards in order to please the client (or indeed anyone else, including the court)—para 307(c). Note that you are also obliged to ensure that you never give the *impression* that your professional standards are compromised—the classic example in the Code at para 307(b) is acceptance of gifts in inappropriate circumstances. A modest gift (such as a bunch of flowers) could be accepted, but *only* once the case is over, including any possibility of appeal.

In publicly funded cases, the lay client's interests have to be considered against those of the Legal Services Commission (LSC) in particular respects. By Code para 303(c), 'A barrister, when supplying legal services funded by the Legal Services Commission as part of the Community Legal Service or the Criminal Defence Service owes his primary duty to the lay client subject only to compliance with paragraph 304'. In these situations, para 304 imposes on the barrister in connection with the supply of such services an obligation to comply with any duty imposed on him or her by the Access to Justice Act 1999, or regulations or codes in effect under that Act, and in particular the duties set out in Annexe E. Annexe E (which refers to the Code of Conduct of the Bar) is the 'Guidelines on Opinions under the Funding Code', prepared by the LSC. Barristers play an important role in advising the LSC as to the merits of cases, which the LSC uses to assist it in making decisions on whether to fund, or continue to fund, the lay client's case. *Where the barrister is acting under a funding certificate, the barrister owes direct obligations to the LSC.* For the obligations this imposes on counsel with regards to writing opinions on the merits of applications or certificates issued under the Funding Code, see **7.5** and in particular **7.5.3.3**. In short, if you are acting for a client under a funding certificate (whether advising in writing or performing some other service for the client), you are under an obligation to bring to the attention of the LSC any matter which comes to your attention that could affect the client's entitlement to funding or the terms of his or her certificate. An example might be if you became aware that the client was earning 'cash in hand' which had not been declared to the LSC. It is sufficient to draw the matter to the attention of your instructing solicitors and request that they inform the LSC, or contact the LSC directly if circumstances are such that contacting the client through your solicitors is inappropriate. You owe an obligation to the lay client to explain and advise where funding has been wrongly obtained or where their financial circumstances have changed in such a way as to affect entitlement to funding. If they then refuse to remedy the situation, you will also be obliged to withdraw from the case (Code para 608(c)).

2.2.2   Duties owed specifically to the lay client

You have the following additional specific obligations to the lay client:

- Duty to maintain the confidentiality of the client's affairs—Code para 702. This relates both to the period when the barrister is instructed, and is a continuing duty in that it survives the end of the case, or the withdrawal of the barrister's instructions. The obligation of confidentiality can only be waived by the client.

- The obligation to satisfy yourself that you have the competence, and adequate time to prepare for and represent the client in the matter in question, prior to accepting instructions—Code para 603.

- A duty to consider whether at any time the client's interests would be best served by having different representation, and if so, to advise the client—Code para 607. There are also obligations to consider whether the client is best served by instructing more than one advocate (Code para 606.2); and whether in the interests of the client or the interests of justice, it would be appropriate for the client to instruct a solicitor as well as, or instead of, you—Code para 606.3.

- A duty to consider potential conflicts of interest. This may be between the lay and professional client (in which case the conflict must be resolved in favour of the lay client)—Written Standards 3.3; or between clients—Written Standards 3.4 and 3.5. These latter provisions reflect Code para 606.4. A barrister may well be representing more than one party in a case involving several parties, and must consider, and keep under review throughout the case, whether it is appropriate for him or her to continue to represent all those clients, or whether at any point it is more appropriate for clients to be separately represented—usually because their interests are likely to conflict, or because a conflict has now arisen. Written Standards 3.4 suggests that the barrister can continue to represent all clients if they all consent in writing. By 3.5, even if there is no conflict, where the barrister has accepted a brief or instructions for any party in any proceedings, he or she should not accept a brief or instructions in respect of an appeal or further stage of proceedings without obtaining the prior consent of the original client.

- Conversely, it may be appropriate for a party represented by the barrister to be represented together with another party in the case—Code para 606.4, and the barrister should consider this possibility at all stages. This is most likely to be relevant where one or more parties have an identical interest in the proceedings.
- A duty to act with reasonable competence and maintain professional independence.
- A duty to keep the client informed of the estimate and likely impact of costs—while the professional client will have the most accurate information on current and estimated costs, you share an obligation with him or her to ensure that the client is aware of the size of the costs exposure, both in relation to his or her own costs and the situation if he or she loses and is obliged to pay the other party's costs.

2.2.3   The cab-rank rule, withdrawal from a case, and return of instructions

One of the cardinal principles of professional conduct at the Bar is the 'cab-rank rule'. This is contained in the Code paras 601 and 602. By para 601:

A barrister who supplies advocacy services must not withhold those services:

(a) on the ground that the nature of the case is objectionable to him or to any section of the public;

(b) on the ground that the conduct opinions or beliefs of the prospective client are unacceptable to him or to any section of the public;

(c) on any ground relating to the source of any financial support which may properly be given to the prospective client for the proceedings in question (for example, on the ground that such support will be available as part of the Community Legal Service or Criminal Defence Service).

It is obvious why this is a central tenet of professional conduct. There is a clear public interest in the proper administration of justice, which requires the availability of high-quality, objective, professional representation for all litigants regardless of their personal beliefs, characteristics, and means. This clearly could not be met if barristers could pick and choose their clients for any reason ranging from the size of that client's funds to personal (and even baseless) dislike or political persuasion. Para 602 of the Code is therefore quite specific as to your obligations in this situation:

A self-employed barrister must comply with the 'Cab-rank rule' and accordingly except only as otherwise provided in paragraphs 603 604 605 and 606 he must in any field in which he professes to practise in relation to work appropriate to his experience and seniority and irrespective of whether his client is paying privately or is publicly funded:

(a) accept any brief to appear before a Court in which he professes to practise;

(b) accept any instructions;

(c) act for any person on whose behalf he is instructed;

and do so irrespective of (i) the party on whose behalf he is instructed (ii) the nature of the case and (iii) any belief or opinion which he may have formed as to the character reputation cause conduct guilt or innocence of that person.

The fundamental need for such a rule is clear. However, it is equally clear that there will be situations in which it is inappropriate for a barrister to represent or, as the case may be, continue to represent certain clients, hence the concept of 'professional embarrassment'.

2.2.3.1   Professional embarrassment

This is defined in Code para 603.

A barrister must not accept any instructions if to do so would cause him to be professionally embarrassed and for this purpose a barrister will be professionally embarrassed:

(a)   if he lacks sufficient experience or competence to handle the matter;

This is quite obvious. Of course, para 602 expressly provides that you are not obliged to accept instructions outside the field in which you practise, so if you were purely a criminal specialist, you should not accept instructions in a commercial matter. But your obligations go further—even within your field of practice, you need to consider whether the instructions before you require greater experience and competence than you currently possess. Evidently, you should consider instructions as soon as they come in, and form an early view as to your ability to fulfil them, in order to give the client and the instructing solicitor as much notice as possible if you are unable to do so.

(b)   if having regard to his other professional commitments he will be unable to do or will not have adequate time and opportunity to prepare that which he is required to do;

Again, a similar exercise to (a)—you need to consider instructions that come in early on, check your diary with the clerks, and be sure that you have the time to carry out the task in question. An awkward situation can arise when a case 'goes part-heard'. This is a situation where a matter in which you are acting exceeds the time limit before the court. This will result in it either continuing into the following day (or days), or possibly being relisted at a time in the near future. While the court will try to take counsel's other obligations into account when setting another date, this is not always possible. If you have been booked to represent another client the next day, or at the relisted date, the instructions will have to be returned, and it is important that you let your clerk know as soon as possible if there is a possibility of the matter you are acting in going part-heard, so that he or she can try to plan ahead to cover the other brief, or return it with as much notice to the other solicitor as possible. What you must *never* do is abandon the part-heard case in which you are already acting. It would be nigh on impossible for another barrister to 'pick up where you left off', and would most definitely prejudice the client. This can, on occasions, result in you missing out on a pre-booked holiday. This is an unfortunate but inevitable consequence of practice at the Bar. This obligation is reflected in Code para 610(c).

There is another avoidable, and unacceptable practice that can occur. It is very tempting both for the barrister and the clerk to 'double-book' days in the diary, in other words, to book the barrister for two or more matters which will conflict if both are effective (i.e., go ahead). The reason the temptation exists is that a case will often settle prior to the booked date, in which case it is scrubbed out of the diary and the barrister may find him or herself without work to replace it on that day. This also disadvantages the clerk, who will lose his or her percentage of the fee for that work. If another matter is also in the diary and does not settle, then the day is not lost. However, this practice is clearly wrong with regards to (b) above, since quite clearly at the time of accepting the instructions, the barrister cannot guarantee to be able to do the case. Quite apart from the ethical wrongdoing, this is a very effective way to destroy a good working relationship with your instructing solicitors. Of course, it is possible for two matters to be in the diary on one day and for there to be no conflict—they could be at different times of day, with time estimates that do not overlap. Clerks are very skilled at managing the time of their barristers, and ensuring that they have 'cover' from another member of chambers if two apparently clashing dates are effective. However, the solicitor should be informed by the clerk of the possibility of a clash and the need to transfer to another member of chambers if it occurs.

(c)   if the instructions seek to limit the ordinary authority or discretion of a barrister in the conduct of proceedings in Court or to require a barrister to act otherwise than in conformity with law or with the provisions of this Code;

This is clearly a situation in which you should not be bound by the cab-rank rule. What the client, or solicitor is effectively asking you to do is to act contrary to your other obligations under the Code. For example, there could be an effort to require you to mislead the court by demanding that you present the case in a manner contrary to the true facts, or there may be a refusal to disclose a document which the client is obliged to disclose by law or rules of court.

(d)   if the matter is one in which he has reason to believe that he is likely to be a witness or in which whether by reason of any connection with the client or with the Court or a member of it or otherwise it will be difficult for him to maintain professional independence or the administration of justice might be or appear to be prejudiced;

This very much goes back to the fundamental principles in para 307 of the Code—that you must not permit your independence, integrity, and freedom from external pressures to be compromised, nor do anything leading to the inference that this might be so. Therefore, if you know one of the magistrates, or the client, socially or you might be called to give evidence in the matter, you should not accept the instructions, because otherwise, whether it be true or not, the impression will be that you were not able to act objectively and independently, in particular in relation to your obligations to the administration of justice.

(e)   if there is or appears to be a conflict or risk of conflict either between the interests of the barrister and some other person or between the interests of any one or more clients (unless all relevant persons consent to the barrister accepting the instructions);

Clearly, if you have some kind of personal interest in the outcome of the case, you should not be acting in it, because your independence has been compromised. For example, you may be a significant investor in the private company that you represent. Equally, as discussed earlier, you must be astute to the possibility of conflicts between clients—with every client, you are in a position of acute trust, charged with preserving the confidentiality of their affairs, and in possession of legally privileged information about their case which would not ordinarily be known to other parties. Therefore, if you are in a situation where you represent two people and their interests no longer coincide, it can be very difficult for you to continue to act. You are in a position as regards each of them that counsel for opposing parties never usually is.

(f)   if there is a significant risk that information confidential to another client or former client might be communicated to or used for the benefit of anyone other than that client or former client without their consent;

This is a similar situation to that discussed under (e) above. The danger to your independence and to your clients' interests is clear, and unless they consent, you cannot continue to act.

Paragraph 603(g) and (h) is fairly self-explanatory and should be read for yourself. Note also para 604, regarding specific situations in relation to which you have a choice as to whether to accept instructions or not.

2.2.3.2   Withdrawal and return of instructions

This is an area of significant ethical difficulty. Getting the decision wrong as to whether you are obliged, or entitled, to withdraw has profound consequences for the client who may be left without representation, and could amount to serious professional misconduct. The decision of the Court of Appeal in *R v Ulcay and Toygun* [2007] EWCA Crim 2379 makes it clear that the Court cannot oblige counsel to continue to act when he had made a professional judgement that he was obliged, for compelling reasons, to withdraw. The decision as to whether and if so for how long a trial should be adjourned to accommodate new counsel lay solely with the judge. Counsel is required to comply with the 'cab-rank rule' whenever and however late he was instructed, so even if counsel has insufficient time to prepare, he must 'soldier on' and do the best he could, as that in itself is not a sufficient ground to withdraw.

The circumstances in which you *must* withdraw are stated in Code para 608, and the circumstances in which you *may* withdraw are to be found in para 609. In all cases, you must comply with para 610 in relation to the manner in which you withdraw.

You should read para 608 with care. It is largely self-explanatory, but do note in particular that by 608(a) and 608(f) your obligation to withdraw is qualified with reference to whether withdrawal would jeopardise the client's interests if your withdrawal is due to a risk of being a material witness *of fact* (608(a)) or where you have accidentally read a privileged document belonging to another party.

As to para 609, you have a choice in these situations. You can continue to act, but para 609 basically enables you to withdraw where the relationship with the client has become untenable. Be quite clear—this has nothing to do with basic dislike or the fact that your client may be difficult or demanding—the cab-rank rule binds you in such situations. Therefore, ensure that you are quite clear in your own mind why you are in a position to withdraw. By para 609, you *may* withdraw where:

(a) Your instructions have been withdrawn. Evidently, you have to act on instructions and if the client is not prepared to instruct you, you are going to be in substantial difficulties representing him or her, and will probably be unable to do so effectively. Of course, make sure that your instructions really have been withdrawn and the client no longer wishes you to act for him or her.

(b) Your professional conduct is being impugned. The client may accuse you of trying to deceive him or her, or being somehow in league with the other party, or may make it quite clear that for some reason he or she does not trust you. This can make it very difficult to represent him or her effectively. There may be a situation in which he or she is making dishonest allegations about advice you previously gave, and so forth. If you do decide to withdraw for this reason, be quite clear about the basis on which you are doing so—it is too easy to blame 'a lack of trust' when simply trying to get out of representing a difficult client. Another situation to be very careful of is this—many clients want to know that you are 'on their side', and you 'believe them'. They do this because they are seeking reassurance, not because they do not trust you. You must explain carefully that your beliefs are irrelevant, and focus on discussing how to persuade the court of their case. You must not start reassuring them that you believe them, and so forth—this could compromise your independence—you are there to represent them not judge them. However, this situation calls for enormously tactful handling.

(c) Advice which you gave under Code paras 607 or 703 has not been heeded. Para 607 relates to a situation where you feel that the client's interests would be best served by having different representation, and para 703 to the situation where you have advised the client that there is a conflict between his or her interests and that of (usually) the solicitor. Again, the basic situation here is that you are involved in a conflict of interest which you feel is not in the client's interests, and feel that you cannot continue to represent the client fairly.

(d) 'Any other substantial reason.' This is something of a 'catch-all' phrase. Again, be most careful in relying on this to be clear in your mind of the exact reasons justifying withdrawal, because your conduct may well be scrutinised later by a court or by professional disciplinary bodies.

Whatever the reason for your withdrawal, whether it is a situation in which you must withdraw, or in which you may withdraw, bear in mind that you must withdraw in accordance with para 610. You must *always* explain the reasons for withdrawal to the lay client, and (apart from para 608 situations) you must not withdraw in such a way that the client cannot find other representation in time to avoid being prejudiced. In a para 608 situation, that may be unavoidable and you cannot avoid withdrawing for that reason.

Lastly, if you are in any doubt about whether you must or may withdraw, you should discuss the issue with a senior member of chambers if you are in a position to do so. If not, for example, because you are out at court, phone the Bar Council's ethics hotline for advice.

2.2.4 Problems

(1)   You are acting for the mother of a 12-month-old boy. His father is seeking contact to him, and also wishes to obtain a parental responsibility order. You meet the mother and your instructing solicitor on the morning of the hearing for a short conference. The mother is a difficult, unpleasant, and rather vindictive character as far as you can tell. Part-way through the conference, the mother states, 'I don't know why he wants contact—he's not even the father'. There is no reference to this anywhere in the papers, so you ask her why she is raising it for the first time today. She replies, 'It's not the first time. I told my solicitor about it and told her to demand a paternity test'. You look at your solicitor, who looks surprised and says that this is the first she's heard of it. What action should you take? Must you, or may you, withdraw? In considering your approach, think forward to what will happen in court. What are your client's instructions likely to be, and the other party's cross-examination of her?

(2)   You are acting in a public law Children Act case. The local authority is seeking a care order in respect of a two-year-old boy. You represent the parents, as well as the maternal grandmother. Until the local authority took action to remove the child seven days ago, the parents cared for him with frequent baby-sitting help from the maternal grandmother. The paternal grandparents are also represented, and are broadly supportive of the parents' desire to retain care of the child. In particular, they are a fairly wealthy middle-class couple who are happy to help the parents by providing a home and supervision for both the parents and the child while social services make ongoing assessments of the ability of the parents to parent the child safely. The major allegations against the parents are that the child has suffered injuries which would appear to be non-accidental, and therefore the parents have physically abused him. The medical evidence is unclear as to exactly when the injuries occurred, although it is clear that they have occurred in the last two months. The parents deny the abuse, but cannot provide an alternative explanation as to how it could have occurred accidentally. There is no direct evidence of who has harmed the child. During the first day of the hearing,

the mother asks to see you on her own. She tells you that the father and his parents now suspect the maternal grandmother of causing the injuries. She herself does not know what to think and is greatly distressed. You are aware that she and her mother are from a much more disadvantaged background than the father and his parents, and you wonder how well she is able to articulate her views to them. You personally suspect the father, who has already demonstrated displays of anger when things get stressful at court. What do you do?

(3)   You have been instructed to prepare an advice on the merits of a nuisance case, which your instructing solicitor will need to show to the Legal Services Commission in order to obtain an extension of funding in the case. Your advice is that the merits do not justify any continuation of funding. Three days after sending the advice to the solicitor, she telephones you in chambers. She makes aggressive demands that you change your advice to favour continuation of funding. What are your obligations in this matter under the Code?

(4)   You act for the claimant in a personal injury matter. Three months ago, you were instructed to prepare draft particulars of claim, which your instructing solicitor stated were going to be filed and served with the claim form in the matter. You prepared the draft within two days, since you realised that expiry of the limitation period was imminent. You have now received instructions to advise in writing on the matter. As soon as you open the papers, you realise that your instructing solicitors have failed to issue the claim before the limitation period expired. What are your obligations in this situation?

(5)   You are representing the defendant in a complicated contractual dispute. The matter was originally listed for three days, but it is now lunchtime on the third day and the judge has just called counsel into chambers to fix a date to which the matter can go part-heard. The court listings are under considerable pressure and the judge has been quite clear that counsel's other obligations cannot be accommodated in relisting the matter. Therefore, the matter has been listed for Wednesday of next week for a further day's hearing. On that day, your diary shows that you were due to start a two-day hearing in a landlord and tenant matter in which you would be representing the claimant. You have seen the claimant in conference twice so far. He is a very vulnerable person, with mental health problems, and for whom English is not his first language. He has found it very hard to trust his advisers, and you have succeeded in gaining his trust where three other counsel have failed. What action should you take?

2.3   Relationship with the professional client and other intermediaries

2.3.1   Duties and responsibilities owed to the professional client and other intermediaries

You may now accept instructions from professional clients (see para 401) and from members of approved professional bodies, for example, accountants and surveyors. You must comply with the Licensed Access Rules and Recognition Regulations and the Public Access Rules reproduced in Annexes F1 and F2 of the Code of Conduct (see para 401).

With regard to your relationship with those who instruct you, problems can arise in circumstances where they seek to limit the way in which you present the case; where they take a different view of the lay client's prospects of success; where you consider they have been remiss/negligent in their handling of the client's affairs, or where they consider you have 'let them down' by not being available to do a case or have been guilty of delay. Sometimes these problems are due to poor communication, lack of control of your clerk, or an unjustifiable attitude that you are somehow superior to them.

It is important that you foster good relations with those who instruct you, discuss any differences of opinion, and ensure that he or she is kept fully informed of any potential difficulties or conflicting dates in your diary. Your clerk should always inform any person who seeks to instruct you on a case if there is likely to be a conflicting engagement. Watch the chambers diary yourself to ensure this is being enforced. Do not delay your paperwork. If some delay cannot be avoided due to other pressing work, telephone them and explain the position so that he or she is free to instruct other counsel.

Do not criticise your solicitor or those who instruct you in front of the lay client without first discussing your view with the solicitor or the person who instructs you. Do not criticise your solicitor or those who instruct you in court unless they agree that some fault lies with them and they accept that the court must be told to prevent the lay client suffering the consequences.

A further area in which the relationship with a solicitor, in particular, may become problematical, arises out of the growth of the number of solicitors with rights of audience in the higher courts. This can lead to a variety of difficulties—not least if you are co-defending with a solicitor whose firm is acting for your defendant too, who may be more likely to go to him or her than you. Be tactful.

The Legal Services Committee of the Bar Council has in the past provided guidance on the area of solicitors acting as juniors to silks, which it quaintly describes as 'mixed doubles'. The committee stressed the importance of ensuring that the right amount of advocacy expertise is properly used, and in particular:

- if a case requires both a leader and junior, it is inappropriate for a solicitor advocate to try to perform both roles;

- the junior in any case (whether he or she be a barrister or solicitor advocate) must have appropriate skills and experience for the roles he or she is to perform and must be competent and available to perform the junior work required by the leader including examination of witnesses, the preparation of skeleton arguments and chronologies, the drafting of statements of case, etc., as the case may require;

- if a case is suitable for a silk to conduct alone, there should be no junior. But, if a junior is genuinely necessary, it would be manifestly inappropriate for a solicitor without rights of audience to seek to dispense with a junior on the basis that he or she will carry out the junior work, excluding advocacy, while also acting as a solicitor.

Guidance upon your main duties to the professional client and other intermediaries can be found in paras 603, 610, 701(e), 703, 706, and 707 of the Code. Remember that your primary duty is to the lay client (para 303(b)). Note also Annexe G, which covers the Terms of Work on which Barristers Offer their Services to Solicitors and the Withdrawal of Credit Scheme 1988.

2.3.1.1 Problems

(1)   You are asked to advise on quantum in a personal injuries case where the defendants have offered to negotiate a settlement. It is clear that the claimant's general damages will be substantial but their assessment is not straightforward. In conference you state that in your opinion the case is worth £30,000 to £35,000 on full liability. Your solicitors (who value the case more highly) ask you for an opinion in writing that the bracket is

£40,000 to £45,000 in order to support their negotiations and to achieve a settlement at £35,000. What should you do?

(2)   You act for the claimant in civil proceedings. Unlike your client, the defendant has the benefit of a full legal aid certificate. You arrive at court on the day fixed for the hearing to find that the defendant's solicitor has forgotten to warn any of his or her witnesses. The judge accedes to the defendant's request for an adjournment. The defendant's solicitor is in fact well known to you and briefs you on a regular basis. What application, if any, do you make for costs?

2.3.2 Relationship between prosecuting counsel and the Crown Prosecution Service

If acting on behalf of the CPS, you will need to be fully familiar with the following sources of guidance:

- The Farquharson Guidelines: The Role and Responsibilities of the Prosecuting Advocate. The weblink is at **2.1.2.1**.

- The Code for Crown Prosecutors, available from the CPS website at <http://www.cps.gov.uk>.

- CPS Instructions for Prosecuting Advocates, which is automatically incorporated into every prosecution brief. This again is available from the CPS website at the above link.

The above documents provide very detailed guidance on a whole raft of issues which are particular to prosecution, many of them sensitive, such as the prosecutor's role in sentencing, approach to young offenders, or restarting a prosecution. It is important that you follow this guidance—quite apart from anything else, the CPS is a public body and it is important that its approach, through you, is consistent and implements the policy and procedures that have been decided upon as appropriate in the public interest.

2.3.3 Problem

A jury fails to agree in a case in which you have prosecuted. Given the nature of the case and the evidence available to you, its inability to reach a verdict is wholly understandable. You take the view that on the customary retrial the prosecution is almost certain to fail. You also consider that a rehearing would cause considerable distress to the principal witness. You decide to offer no further evidence when the case is relisted. Your instructing solicitors do not agree. How do you deal with the situation?

2.4 Relationship with other members of the profession

2.4.1 Duties and responsibilities to the profession as a whole

The main obligations that you are bound to observe are set out in the Code of Conduct and include a duty:

(a) To uphold at all times the standards set out in the Code of Conduct and to comply with its provisions.

(b) Not to engage directly or indirectly in any other occupation if your association with that occupation may affect adversely the reputation of the Bar or prejudice your ability to attend properly to your practice (para 301(b)).

(c) To ensure that you are insured with Bar Mutual Indemnity Fund Limited against claims for professional negligence (paras 204, 402).

(d) To have a current practising certificate and comply with any training and Continuing Professional Development requirements (para 202).

(e) To ensure that your practice is efficiently and properly administered (para 403.1–403.5).

(f) To exercise your own personal judgement in all your professional activities (para 306).

(g) Not to permit your absolute independence, integrity, and freedom from external pressures to be compromised or to compromise your professional standards in order to please your client, the court, or a third party (para 307).

(h) Not to engage in any advertising or promotion in connection with your practice other than as may be permitted by the provisions of the British Codes of Advertising and Sales Promotion, and otherwise permitted under para 710.2 (paras 710.1, 710.2).

The rules relating to self-employed practice have recently changed and should be checked in paras 403.1–403.5 of the code.

2.4.2 Duties and responsibilities owed to other members of the profession

The most important aspect of your relationship with other members of the Bar is to ensure that you never knowingly mislead or deceive them. It is equally important to treat them with courtesy (para 701). Your other responsibilities include a duty:

(a) To inform counsel previously instructed in the same matter that you have received a brief or set of instructions in place of that other barrister (this appears to be a custom rather than a duty under the Code).

(b) To return, unread, a document belonging to another party which has come into your possession other than by the normal and proper channels (para 608(f); para 7.2 of the General Standards in Written Standards for the Conduct of Professional Work, section 3 of the Code of Conduct).

(c) To pay, upon receipt of any fees in respect of work done by another barrister, the whole of that fee forthwith to the other barrister (para 406.1).

(d) To pay any pupil except where they are in receipt of an award or remuneration which is paid on terms that it is in lieu of payment for any individual item of work, for any work done for you which, because of its value to you, warrants payment (para 805).

In the course of negotiating with a view to a compromise, your relationship with your opponent is of particular importance. The ethics of negotiation are discussed further in **Chapter 7.**

2.4.3 Relationship with the clerks

In the early days of practice, it is quite common for members of the Bar to shy away from challenging the authority of the clerks in chambers. While it is important to recognise the position of the clerks and build up a good rapport, trust, and working relationship with them, it is vital that you remember you are responsible for ensuring that your practice is properly and efficiently administered. If your clerk makes an error, you must take the blame. Remember that you employ the clerks, they do not employ you. On occasions, it may be necessary to 'have words with' the clerks. Do so in a polite manner and on a one-to-one basis. Do not embarrass the clerks in front of each other or other members of chambers. If you do not succeed in obtaining the clerks' cooperation, consider speaking to your head of chambers.

2.4.3.1 Problems

(1) A colleague in chambers comes to your room to discuss with you a quantum in a case in which he or she is giving some preliminary advice. He or she gives you the outline of the medical report and after you have exchanged valuations of the level of general damages, leaves you with the words, 'We have terrible problems on liability'. Some months later, you receive instructions to settle a defence and, having read the papers, you realise that it is the same case which you discussed with your colleague. Do you continue to deal with the papers?

(2) You have a row with your clerks. During the following week, one of the pupils in chambers asks your advice upon a brief which he or she has been given for the next day. You realise it is a case you advised upon last year, yet the clerks have informed you that you have no work for the following day. What do you do?

3

Working at the Bar today

3.1 Introduction

Britain in the twenty-first century is a richly diverse and multicultural society. Statistics from the 2001 census show that 4.6 million people, 7.9 per cent of the population, are from a non-white ethnic group. In certain urban areas, such as London, West Midlands, Greater Manchester, and West Yorkshire, the percentage figure is much higher. Surveys by local education authorities show that over 100 different home languages are spoken. This diversity is further reflected by the number of religious beliefs, changes in the nature of the family, positive changes with regard to gender roles, and the rights of the disabled, children, and the gay and lesbian community. However, despite many positive changes in attitude, it is a society in which discrimination still exists and in which access to justice for all remains a burning issue. Yet, it is also a society whose diversity adds to the dynamism, excitement, and challenges that you face as lawyers, irrespective of the area of practice you choose to enter.

The First Report on Legal Education and Training published in April 1996, the Lord Chancellor's Advisory Committee on Legal Education and Conduct (ACLEC) stated:

From the earliest stages of legal education and training, intending lawyers should be imbued not only with the standards and codes of professional conduct, but also more generally with the obligations of lawyers to help protect individuals and groups from the abuse of public and private power.

In the spirit of this statement, the aims of this chapter are to consider how the Code of Conduct operates in the areas of discrimination, diversity, and equality of opportunity and how it impacts on your responsibilities to all those you work with, whether as colleagues or clients. Simply to understand the Code is not enough, if barristers working at the Bar today are to rise to the obligation 'to help protect individuals and groups from the abuse of public and private power'. To represent effectively individuals you need to have an understanding of the different views, beliefs, and customs of all those that make up Britain's diverse and multicultural society. The second part of this chapter gives some general guidance and sources of information which will help you to meet this challenge. The barrister that has this understanding will not only have risen to this challenge, but will have completed a vital step in having a vibrant and successful practice.

3.2 The Code of Conduct and discrimination

An act of direct discrimination by a barrister amounts to a breach of the Code of Conduct. Paragraph 305.1 of the Code states:

A barrister must not in relation to any other person (including a client or another barrister or a pupil or a student member of an Inn of Court) discriminate directly or indirectly or victimize because of race, colour, ethnic or national origin, nationality, citizenship, sex, sexual orientation, marital status, disability, religion or political persuasion.

The breadth of this provision means that it covers a barrister's relationship with all of those people with whom he or she comes into contact in the course of carrying out a professional practice.

3.2.1   Fair representation: the 'cab-rank' rule

Fair treatment under para 305 would include fair representation, though this concept is specifically enshrined in para 602 of the Code and is known as the 'cab-rank rule'.

A self-employed barrister must comply with the 'cab-rank rule' and accordingly except only as otherwise provided in paragraphs 603, 604, 605, and 606, he must in any field in which he professes to practise in relation to work appropriate to his experience and seniority and irrespective of whether his client is paying privately or is publicly funded:

  (a) accept any brief to appear before a court in which he professes to practise;
  (b) accept any instructions;
  (c) act for any person on whose behalf he is instructed;

and to do so irrespective of

  (i)   the party on whose behalf he is instructed
  (ii)   the nature of the case and
  (iii) any belief or opinion which he may have formed as to the character reputation cause conduct guilt or innocence of that person.

(See also paras 104, 303 of the Code and para 2.2 of the Written Standards for the Conduct of Professional Work in Section 3, Miscellaneous Guidance.)

The only permissible exceptions to the 'cab-rank rule' are set out in paras 603–610 of the Code. The rule otherwise means that a barrister must accept a brief or instructions to represent a client, no matter how repugnant the client is to the barrister on political, religious, or moral grounds. Consequently, if the system is correctly and properly adhered to at all times, whatever a barrister's individual views are, effective representation of an individual is rightly ensured.

3.2.2   The Equality and Diversity Code for the Bar

The Equality and Diversity Code for the Bar was adopted by the Bar Council in 2004. The Code is designed to assist barristers to apply good equal opportunities practices in the development and running of chambers. The Code states that 'Equality of opportunity is *fair, commercially advantageous, necessary for compliance with non-discrimination law and constitutionally important*'. The Code is set out in **Appendix 1** on page 243 of this Manual. For the Annexes to the Code, you will need to refer to the Bar Council's website at <http://www.barcouncil.org.uk>.

3.3   Effective representation in a diverse society

The Bar is gradually becoming more representative of the society it serves. In December 2008 of the 12,136 self-employed barristers recorded by the Bar Council, 3,772 (31 per cent) were women and 10 per cent were from black and minority ethnic backgrounds.

As the Equality Code points out, 'Direct discrimination may frequently be subconscious, based on stereotypical assumptions about particular minority ethnic groups or about the difference in capabilities, characteristics, personalities and motivation between women and men'. From whatever background a barrister comes, at some time all will need help and advice on the customs and beliefs of the individuals that they represent. The Judicial Studies Board (JSB), the body responsible for training all those who sit in a judicial capacity, has issued specific guidance on these matters in the Equal Treatment Bench Book (ETBB). While this book is aimed at those sitting in a judicial capacity, you are advised that it holds equally invaluable information for those who are representing others. The full text of the ETBB is available on the JSB website at <http://www.jsboard.co.uk>. In addition, an easy-to-use companion booklet has been produced dealing with fairness before the courts, 'Fairness in Courts and Tribunals'. This deals with racial issues, and other issues of general equality before the courts. You are strongly advised to read this—it offers a general introduction to some of the matters dealt with in more detail in the ETBB. It is reproduced at the end of this chapter with the kind permission of the JSB.

3.4 Sources of useful information

3.4.1 The Bar Council and Bar Standards Board

The Bar Council Equality and Diversity Adviser is Pamela Bhalla (PBhalla@BarCouncil. org.uk) and she is based at the Bar Council, 289–293 High Holborn, London, WC1V 7HZ (tel: 020 7242 0082). If you wish to speak to her in confidence, there is a confidential line (tel: 020 7611 1310). Her role is to provide advice on any equality or discrimination matter to chambers wishing to improve their equality and diversity practice, to barristers with equality and diversity problems or queries, practice managers, clerks, pupils, BPTC/ law students. Angela Campbell (ACampbell@BarCouncil.org.uk) has information about the Bar Council panel of Disabilities Advisers who can offer practical advice to students with a disability on developing a career in self-employed practice.

Marc Adams (MAdams@BarStandardsBoard.org.uk) and Sarah Loutfi (Sloutfi@ BarStandardsBoard.org.uk) are the Bar Standards Board's Equality and Diversity Advisers.

3.4.2 Other useful contacts

The Equality and Human Rights Commission
3 More London,
Riverside Tooley Street
London SE1 2RG
Tel: 020 3117 0235
Fax: 020 7407 7557
Email: info@equalityhumanrights.com

Society of Asian Lawyers (SAL)
Society of Asian Lawyers
Chair: Sundeep Bhatia
Beaumonde Law Practice

Evans House
107 Marsh Road
Pinner
HA5 5PA
Tel: 0208 429 6731/33

Association of Women Barristers (AWB)
c/o Angela Campbell
The General Council of the Bar
289–293 High Holborn
London WC1V 7HZ
Website: <http://www.womenbarristers.co.uk>

Association of Muslim Lawyers (AML)
Student Officer
The Association of Muslim Lawyers
PO Box 148
High Wycombe
Bucks HP13 5WJ
Tel: 01494 526 955
Email: aml@aml.org.uk

Bar Lesbian and Gay Group (BLAGG)
<http://www.blagg.org>
contactus@blagg.org

Commonwealth in England Barristers' Association (CEBA)
Michel Aslangul (Hon. Secretary)
Email: M.Aslangul@hotmail.co.uk

The Society of Black Lawyers
c/o Peter Herbert
Tooks Court Chambers
Chambers of Michael Mansfield QC
8 Warner Yard
Warner Street
London EC1R 5EY
DX 68 Chancery Lane
Tel: 020 7841 6100
Fax: 020 7841 6199

Association of Asian Women Lawyers'
Hanisha Patel
email: hpatel@7BR.co.uk

Turkish Lawyers' Group
Emma Edhem email: emma_edhem@yahoo.co.uk

Bar Council Disability Group
c/o Angela Campbell
The General Council of the Bar
289–293 High Holborn
London WC1V 7HZ

3.5 Judicial studies board—fairness in courts and tribunals

Foreword

This booklet updates the previous *Fairness in courts and tribunals*, in light of some of the revisions to the *Equal Treatment Bench Book* since its relaunch in May 2004. It continues to provide a summary of the key points contained in the Bench Book in a format that has been well received in the past, particularly by magistrates and members of tribunals. As with its previous incarnations, this booklet is not intended to replace the *Equal Treatment Bench Book* but rather to complement it by being a quick practical point of reference. Cross-references to further information in the *Equal Treatment Bench Book* (ETBB) are included throughout the text.

Although, as before, many of the general principles in this booklet may be familiar to you, I do hope that you continue to find it useful, particularly as the judiciary continues to be under ever-increasing public scrutiny.

Mrs Justice Cox
JSB's Equal Treatment Advisory Committee
April 2007

Equality and Justice
(see Part 1, ETBB)

What can be done to tackle the existence, appearance or risk of discrimination in the courtroom? How can court and tribunal proceedings be fair and be seen to be fair? Those who administer justice must be aware of, and responsive to, the differences among people who come to court in any capacity, while remaining fair, independent and impartial. How can the judiciary meet this challenge?

This short guide, which complements the Judicial Studies Board's *Equal Treatment Bench Book* (ETBB), offers some pointers. This guide contains numerous cross-references to the Bench Book and is intended to be used as a quick, practical point of reference rather than as an alternative to it.

Equality before courts and tribunals
(see Chapter 1.1, ETBB)

- Most people find an appearance before a court or tribunal to be a daunting experience and it is vital that justice is seen to be done.

- Ensuring fairness and equality of opportunity may mean providing special or different treatment.

- People who are socially and economically disadvantaged in society may assume that they will be at a disadvantage when they appear before a court or tribunal.

- Those at particular disadvantage may include people from minority ethnic communities, from minority faith communities, individuals with disabilities (physical or mental), women, children, those whose sexual orientation is not heterosexual, and those who through poverty or for any other reason are socially or economically excluded.

- Just because someone remains silent does not mean that they necessarily understand, or that they feel that they have been adequately understood. They may simply feel too intimidated, too inadequate or too inarticulate to speak up.

- People who have difficulty coping with the language, procedures or facilities of courts or tribunals are equally entitled to fairness and justice.

The Equal Treatment Bench Book is not about political correctness nor preaching nor moralising. It is there to inform and assist judges.

Lord Irvine of Lairg, Lord Chancellor, September 1999.

Discrimination
(see Chapter 1.1, ETBB)

Discrimination can be:

- **Direct.** Where a person is treated less favourably on the grounds of race, colour, religion, gender, sexual orientation, ethnic or national origin, or disability, than others would be in similar circumstances.

- **Indirect.** Where a requirement is applied equally to all groups, but has a disproportionate effect on the members of one group because a considerably smaller number of members of that group can comply with it. This applies whether intentional or not.

Discrimination must not be permitted, whether direct or indirect. Recognizing and curbing our prejudices is essential to prevent erroneous assumptions being made about the credibility of those with backgrounds different from our own.

Most people understand behaviour in terms of their own familiar cultural conventions and by so doing may misinterpret or fail to understand those who are different.

Communicating fairness
(see Chapter 1.2, ETBB)

- The judicial process must be seen to be fair and must inspire the confidence of all who enter into it.

- Fairness is demonstrated by effective communication.

- All of us view the world from our own perspective, which is culturally conditioned.

- People with personal impairments or who are otherwise disadvantaged in society are entitled to a fair hearing.

- Our outlook is based on our own knowledge and understanding: there is a fine line between relying on this and resorting to stereotypes which can lead to injustice.

- Effective communication is the bedrock of the legal process—everyone involved in proceedings must understand and be understood or the process of law will be seriously impeded. We must reduce the impact of misunderstandings in communication.

Unless all parties to proceedings accurately understand the material put before them, and the meaning of the questions asked and answers given during the course of the proceedings, the process of law is at best seriously impeded. At worst, justice may be denied.

The responsibility for ensuring equality and fairness of treatment rests on everyone involved in the administration of justice. A litigant, claimant, defendant or representative may not encounter a member of the judiciary until the final stages of his or her case, but may only think in terms of a single system—finer points about who does what are meaningless. If anyone feels hard done by at any stage, it reflects on everyone who represents that system.

DO . . .

- Get names and modes of address correct by asking parties how they wish to be addressed.

- Make a point of obtaining, well in advance if possible, precise details of any disability or medical condition that a person appearing before you may have.

- Allow more time for special arrangements, breaks, etc. to accommodate special needs at trial.

- Give particular thought to the difficulties facing disabled people who attend court—prior planning will enable their various needs to be accommodated as far as possible.

- Try to put yourself in the position of the individual—the stress of attending court should not be made worse unnecessarily through a failure to anticipate foreseeable problems.

- Bear in mind the problems facing unrepresented parties.

- Admit a child's evidence, unless the child is incapable of giving intelligible testimony.

- Ensure that appropriate measures are taken to protect vulnerable witnesses, for instance children, those with mental or physical disabilities, or those who are afraid or distressed.

- Be polite, courteous and patient at all times.

- Make provision for oath-taking in accordance with different belief systems.

- Take the initiative to find out about different local cultures and faith communities.

- Display an understanding of difference and difficulties with a well-timed and sensitive intervention where appropriate.

And in conjunction with administrators . . .

- Encourage the availability of court documents and advance information in different local languages and alternative formats, e.g. Braille, large print, audiotape, etc.

- Encourage the provision of access to interpreters and signers.

- Encourage the provision of appropriate facilities for all court users.

- Help to promote a high standard of service to all court users.

- Support the provision of posters and leaflets in English and local minority languages and in alternative formats, e.g. large print.

DON'T . . .

- Underestimate the stress and worry faced by those appearing in court, particularly when the ordeal is compounded by an additional problem such as a disability or having to appear without professional representation.

- Overlook the use—unconscious or otherwise—of gender-based, racist or 'homophobic' stereotyping as an evidential shortcut.

- Allow advocates to attempt over-rigorous cross-examination of children or other vulnerable witnesses.

- Use words that imply an evaluation of the sexes, however subtle—for instance, 'man and wife', girl (unless speaking of a child), 'businessmen'.

- Use terms such as 'mental handicap', 'the disabled'—use instead 'learning disability', 'people with disabilities'.

- Allow anyone to be put in a position where they face hostility or ridicule.

- Make assumptions based on stereotypes or misinformation.

- Use offensive words or terminology.

Language
(see Chapter 1.2, ETBB)

- Careful use of language and current terms increases confidence in the judicial process.
- Those who are disadvantaged may be more sensitive to the insensitive use of terms.
- Owing to increasing sensitivity in our diverse society we cannot underestimate the importance of using correct terms.
- It is often helpful to ask the person themselves how they describe their status, as that is the description which will be most accurate and least likely to offend them.

Just as the legal process uses a technical language, users of the court system are entitled to benefit from the enlightened use of terms that generate confidence in the judicial process. Our choice of language is an indication of our attitude—the importance of correct etiquette has never diminished, but an appropriate sensitivity to the outward form always commands respect, particularly from those who may hitherto have been excluded or neglected.

People from minority ethnic communities or with disabilities should always be described as people: Black, disabled, etc. are adjectives and should always be used as such, as in 'Black person', 'disabled person', etc.

However committed a judge may be to fairness and equality, they may still give the opposite impression by using inappropriate, dated or offensive language. There are no right answers. Language and ideas are living and developing all the time. Some words that were once acceptable no longer are. The following can be advanced with confidence.

British. Care should be taken to use the term 'British' in an inclusive sense, to include all citizens. Exclusionary use of the term as a synonym for White, English or Christian is unacceptable.

Minority ethnic/minority cultural/minority faith/multi-faith. These terms for communities are now widely used and considered acceptable as the broadest terms to encompass all those groups who see themselves as distinct from the majority in terms of ethnicity, culture or faith. The term 'minority ethnic' has the advantage of making it clear that ethnicity is a component of all people's identity whether from the minority or majority. Reference to minority communities as 'ethnics' is a patronising expression which should certainly be avoided. It is for this reason, and for the sake of clarity, that the plural terms 'minorities ethnic' or 'minority ethnics' should also be avoided.

Visible minorities. The expression 'visible minorities' has gained ground in the last few years as an acceptable term whose scope is wider than 'Black', but is itself problematic, as it seems to imply invisible minorities.

People of colour. This expression is more popular in the USA, although it is occasionally used in the UK. It also implies a status based on racial (and therefore inferior) categories and so should be avoided.

Race. Is often used in the specific context of delineating personal characteristics, such as physical appearance, which are permanent and non-changeable.

Ethnicity. Used to define those factors determined by nationality, culture and religion and therefore, to a limited extent, subject to the possibility of change.

Culture. Characterized by behaviour and attitudes, which although determined by upbringing and nationality are perceived as changeable.

Mixed-parentage/dual-heritage/mixed-race/half-caste. The term 'half-caste' is generally found offensive and should be avoided. The term 'mixed-parentage' is an acceptable term for those born to parents who are from a mixture of cultural and ethnic backgrounds, while the [term?] 'dual heritage' may sometimes be used to describe children born of parents with two distinct backgrounds. The term 'mixed-race' may be considered slightly pejorative to the extent that it focuses upon the racial identity of the parents as opposed to other factors such as culture or ethnicity.

Coloured. An offensive term that should never be used.

Black. The term 'Black' has a positive meaning and is not used in the sense of the colour but as a term of reference. As a descriptive term, Black can refer to all people of Caribbean or African descent.

West Indian/African Caribbean/African. The term 'West Indian' may not necessarily give offence, but in most contexts it is inappropriate. Where it is desirable to specify geographical origin, use of the term 'African Caribbean' (as opposed to Afro-Caribbean) is both appropriate and acceptable. The term does not, however, refer to all people of Caribbean origin, some of whom are White or of Asian origin. Young people born in Britain will probably not use any of these designations, simply referring to themselves as Black where racial identity is relevant. However, increased interest among young Black people in their African cultural origins is resulting in a greater assertion of the African aspect of their identity, and the term 'African Caribbean' or 'Black Caribbean' is now more widely used in some circles. Likewise, the term 'African' is acceptable and may be used in self-identification, although many of those of African origin will refer to themselves in national terms as 'Nigerian', 'Ghanaian', etc.

Asian/Oriental/British Asian. People from the Indian sub-continent do not consider themselves to be 'Asians', this term being only applied to them for the sake of convenience in Britain. People from the Indian sub-continent identify themselves rather in the following sets of terms: their national origin ('Bangladeshi', 'Indian', 'Pakistani'); their region of origin ('Bengali', 'Gujarati', 'Punjabi'); or their religion ('Hindu', 'Muslim', 'Sikh'). The term most appropriate to the context should be used: national, regional or religious.

The term 'Asian' may be acceptable in cases where the exact ethnic origin of the person is unknown. Strictly speaking, however, it would be more accurate to make a collective reference to people from the Indian sub-continent as being of South Asian origin, so as to distinguish them from those of South Eastern Asia (e.g. Malaysians and Vietnamese) and from the Far East (e.g. Hong Kong Chinese). The term 'Oriental' should be avoided as it is imprecise and may be considered racist or offensive.

Young people of South Asian origin born in the UK may accept the same identities as their parents. However, this is by no means always the case, and some may choose to assert themselves as 'Black' or 'British Asians', although the use of either of these phrases requires great sensitivity.

Immigrants. The description of all people of minority ethnic origin as 'immigrants' is highly inaccurate given the period of time the majority have been settled in the UK. The term is exclusionary and liable to give offence. Except in reference to 'immigrants' in the strict, technical sense, all such terms should be avoided. Likewise any expression referring to 'second/third generation' immigrants is likely to cause offence.

Refugee/asylum-seekers. The term 'refugee' refers to those people who have had to escape from persecution in their home country. These are 'asylum-seekers' but the term is now associated with people without a genuine claim to be refugees, and is almost pejorative. Care must be taken when using these terms to ensure accuracy in factual or technical terms.

Unrepresented parties

(see Chapter 1.3, ETBB)

There are various reasons why people choose to represent themselves, rather than instructing a lawyer. For many, it is because they do not qualify for Legal Services Commission funding. Whatever their reason for not employing a lawyer, unrepresented parties are likely to be particularly anxious. There may be much at stake, and yet they may be unaware of basic legal principles and court procedures. It is to be expected that they will be experiencing feelings of fear, ignorance, frustration, bewilderment and disadvantage, especially if appearing against a represented party. Judges and tribunal chairs must try to maintain a balance between assisting the unrepresented party and protecting their represented opponent from problems arising from the unrepresented party's lack of legal knowledge.

Problems that may face those without legal representation

Those who appear without legal representation may:

- Lack understanding of legal terminology and specialist vocabulary.
- Be ignorant of law and procedure and in some cases may have difficulty with reading and writing.
- Have no experience of advocacy.
- Lack objectivity.
- Lack the ability to cross-examine or test evidence.
- Not grasp the true issues of a case.
- Have difficulty in marshalling facts.
- Fail to understand court orders or directions, or their obligations to comply with pre-hearing directions.
- Not appreciate the importance of documentary or photographic evidence, or the duty to disclose documents.
- Misunderstand the purpose of a hearing.
- Need court papers to be translated if English is not their first language.
- Not have ready access to legal textbooks or libraries.

At the hearing, the judge should explain to an unrepresented party:

- Who they are and how they should be addressed.
- Who everybody else is, and their respective functions.
- That the unrepresented party should tell the judge immediately if they do not understand something.
- The purpose of the hearing and the issue which is to be decided.
- The rule that only one person at a time may speak and that each side will have a full opportunity to present its case.
- That a party may take notes (but not tape recordings).
- That if the unrepresented party would like a short break in the proceedings, they have only to ask.
- That the issue is decided on the evidence, documented and oral, before the court and nothing else.
- That mobile phones must be switched off, or at least in silent mode.

Cross-examination by the defendant

Throughout a trial, a judge must be ready to assist a claimant or defendant in the conduct of their case, particularly when they are examining or cross-examining witnesses and giving evidence. The judge should always ask whether they wish to call any witnesses, and should be ready to restrain any unnecessary, intimidating or humiliating cross-examination by an unrepresented defendant.

In criminal cases, for certain offences of assault, child cruelty or of a sexual nature, the Youth Justice and Criminal Evidence Act 1999 prohibits unrepresented defendants from cross-examining adult witnesses and child witnesses. The Act also gives courts the discretion to forbid such cross-examination in other types of case.

After the hearing, unrepresented parties often do not understand the outcome of the case or the reasons for it, especially if they have lost. A judge should always set out clearly the reasons for the decision. The judge should also explain the requirement to seek permission to appeal, if appropriate, and should tell the unrepresented party to consider their rights of appeal, but explain that the court cannot give any advice as to the exercise of those rights.

Social exclusion

(see Chapter 1.4)

The term 'social exclusion' refers to a situation of economic or social disadvantage. It incorporates, but is broader than, concepts like poverty or deprivation, and includes disadvantage which arises from discrimination, ill health or lack of education, as well as that which arises from a lack of material resources.

A disproportionate number of those appearing before courts and tribunals are from socially excluded backgrounds. This may affect the way individuals present and understand evidence, and how they respond to cross-examination.

Race and justice

(see Part 2, ETBB)

The experience of racism in one sector of society may influence an individual's perceptions about another sector, such as the administration of justice. If an individual or someone known to an individual has suffered racism at school, from the police, from the health or social services or at work, then what happens in the courtroom will most probably be viewed with mistrust.

For most people, the administration of justice is about going to court, lawyers and judges. Whether it is a criminal or civil court or a tribunal will matter little from the point of view of racism or expectations of unfair treatment.

From the point of view of experiencing racism, it does not matter if you are the defendant, plaintiff, witness, respondent, juror, lawyer or judicial office-holder.

Institutional racism. Defined by the Stephen Lawrence Inquiry Report as '. . . the collective failure of an organization to provide an appropriate and professional service to people because of their colour, culture or ethnic origin. It can be seen or detected in processes, attitudes and behaviour which amount to discrimination through unwitting prejudice, ignorance, thoughtlessness and racist stereotyping which disadvantages minority ethnic people.' Institutional racism does not mean that all individuals in an organization are racist, but that their structures and working methods may have an unfair outcome.

It is fundamental to the stability of society that everyone should have confidence and trust in the institutions and agencies of justice. The judicial oath itself embodies the concept of fair treatment 'without fear or favour, affection or ill will'. However, there continues to be evidence of a lack of confidence in the justice system, particularly among minority ethnic communities. The task of ensuring that in terms of rights, remedies and treatment, courts and tribunals are perceived as fair, continues to present the judiciary and those who work in the administration of justice with a major challenge.

Background statistics

Some statistics are given below to place into context comments about minority ethnic communities in the UK. (Further details can be found at <www.statistics.gov.uk>.)

UK population, 58.7 million, of which:

- White, 54.2 million (92%)
- South Asian or Asian British, 2.3 million (4%)
- Black or Black British, 1.1 million (2%)
- Mixed, 0.7 million (1.2%)
- Chinese, 0.2 million (0.4%)
- Other ethnic groups, 0.2 million (0.4%)

Roma Gypsies and Irish Travellers are currently recognised as racial groups under the Race Relations (Amendment) Act; unfortunately while there are no official statistics various research studies indicate that this population is estimated to be around 300,000 (see section 1.5.8, ETBB).

Among those who migrate to the UK there are a growing number of refugees and asylum-seekers who may come into contact with the administration of justice in various ways: as part of the adjudication process of their case, as claimants in civil or family cases, as alleged criminals, and increasingly as victims of racist attacks.

In 2002, applications for asylum increased by 18% to 84,130. About 42% resulted in grants of asylum, exceptional leave to remain or allowed appeals.

Research also shows that:

- Pakistanis, Bangladeshis and Black Caribbeans experience significantly higher unemployment and lower earnings than White people.
- All minority ethnic groups, even those doing relatively well, are not doing as well as they should be given their education and other characteristics.
- 70% of all minority ethnic communities live in the 88 most deprived local authority areas.

Minority ethnic communities before courts and tribunals

Since 1999 (the year in which the Stephen Lawrence Inquiry Report was published), a great deal has been achieved to ensure that the administration of justice in England and Wales is free of racism and discrimination. It is important, however, to guard against complacency.

Analysis of *British Crime Survey 2000* shows that people from minority ethnic communities are less confident that the criminal justice system respects the rights of, or treats fairly, people accused of committing a crime—although the concern appears to be directed more at the police than the courts. Only 52% of Black people felt that these rights were respected compared with 70% of White and 66% of Asian people. However, according to the same survey, Black and Asian people are more confident than White people that the system is effective in bringing people to justice and meeting the needs of victims of crime.

The Home Office's 2001 *Citizenship Survey* showed that people from minority ethnic groups were more likely than White respondents to say that they would be treated worse than people of other races when engaged with public authorities, the police, the CPS and the courts.

Racism is an attack on the very notion of universal human rights. It systematically denies certain people their full human rights just because of their colour, race, ethnicity, descent (including caste) or national origin. It is an assault on a fundamental principle underlying the Universal Declaration of Human Rights—that human rights are everyone's birthright and apply to all without distinction.

Racism and the administration of justice,
Amnesty International 2001.

As victims
(see Chapter 2.2, ETBB)
Successive British Crime Surveys, most recently in 2000, have shown that minority ethnic groups are more likely to be victims of crime for both household and personal offences.

- Judges need to be aware that minority communities are more at risk of crime in general as victims and that research has shown that the impact of racist crimes affects all victims more severely.
- It is valuable to make inquiries about measures that local victim support groups can take, and the national and local patterns of racist crime.
- Racially aggravated offences ought to be utilised as fully as possible to promote confidence and encourage the reporting of racist crime.

As suspects and offenders
(see Chapter 2.2, ETBB)
Section 95 of the Criminal Justice Act 1991 in conjunction with the Race Relations (Amendment) Act 2000 introduced the wider collection of data detailing ethnicity. These statistics have shown consistent patterns of outcomes, as summed up in the Home Office publication *Race and the Criminal Justice System 2002.*

- People from minority ethnic groups are more likely to be stopped and searched by the police.
- In 2001–02, Black people were eight times more likely to be stopped and searched than White people, an increase over the previous year.
- Minority ethnic people were more likely to be arrested, and Black people were five times more likely to be arrested than any other group.
- Black people are less likely to be cautioned than either Asian or White people.
- People from minority ethnic communities were more likely to be remanded in custody.
- Those from minority ethnic communities are more likely to plead not guilty and more likely to be acquitted.
- Black people were less likely to be fined or discharged and more likely to receive a community sentence.
- Black defendants, dealt with by the Youth Justice Board, were more likely to be remanded in custody than White or Asian young people; in most areas they were more likely to be given Detention and Training Orders than White young people and less likely to be discharged or fined.

A report by Roger Hood, *Ethnic minorities and the criminal courts 2003*, showed:

- 33% of Black defendants, 27% of Asian defendants and 29% of White defendants at Crown Court said their treatment had been unfair, as did 25% at magistrates' courts.

- Most complaints were about severity of sentence rather than the conduct or attitude of judges or magistrates.

- There were no complaints about racist remarks from the Bench.

- 38% of Black defendants at Crown Court, 34% of Asian defendants and 40% of White defendants said they would not expect to be treated fairly next time they came to court.

- However, at magistrates' courts, 39% of Black defendants and 35% of Asian defendants said this, compared with 15% of White defendants—though only 9% said this was because of their racial origin.

It must be clear when sentence is passed that the hearing and decision are free from racial stereotyping and bias.

In civil courts and tribunals
(see Chapter 2.3, ETBB)
Statistical material and research concentrates overwhelmingly on race within the criminal justice system. Little is so far known about the effect on minority ethnic communities of other types of proceedings. Some factors that may be relevant here are:

- In family proceedings, a need for an understanding of different family patterns and structures.

- Problems arising from subjective assessments of what constitutes a 'good parent'.

- Increase in the numbers of litigants in person, who may not understand vital procedures, e.g. the pre-action protocols under the Civil Procedure Rules and some of who may not have English as a first language.

More systematic monitoring of the work of courts and tribunals would ensure there is no improper discrimination and help courts and tribunals deal fairly and sensitively with all those appearing before them.

This research suggests a substantial change for the better in perceptions of ethnic minorities of racial impartiality in the criminal courts. Several judges mentioned that attitudes have altered markedly in recent years and magistrates reported a substantial decline in the frequency of racially inappropriate remarks. Many lawyers also reported that racial bias or inappropriate language was becoming a thing of the past.

Ethnic minorities and the criminal courts,
Roger Hood, 2003.

As practitioners
(see Chapter 2.4, ETBB)
Steps that can promote greater openness and equality in the justice system:

- Making ourselves aware of the impact of the system on different communities and what it means for those coming to court, whether as claimants, victims, witnesses, representatives or suspects.

- Recognizing the different impact of the system of justice on different groups.

- Effectively managing court and tribunal hearings to ensure that they are free from any form of discrimination.

- In the light of the Crime and Disorder Act 1988, being alert to possible racist motivations for crimes that may have been missed by the police or CPS.
- Helping to support appropriate community-based groups to become involved in providing support.

What therefore can judges do to demonstrate fairness and build confidence? The basic principles can be expressed in a short list of dos and don'ts.

DO . . .

- Treat everyone who comes to court with dignity and respect.
- Remember that everyone has prejudices. Recognize and guard against your own.
- Be well informed—being independent and impartial does not mean being isolated from issues which affect people from minority communities.
- Remember that fair treatment involves taking account of difference.
- Ask if in any doubt. A polite and well-intentioned inquiry about how to pronounce a name or about a particular religious belief or a language requirement will not be offensive when prompted *by a genuine desire to get it right.*

DON'T . . .

- Assume that treating everyone in the same way is the same thing as treating everyone fairly. It would not be fair to treat a wheelchair user in the same way as someone who is able to walk, for example, by expecting him or her to climb stairs to reach a courtroom.
- Make assumptions—all White people are not the same, nor are all Black, South Asian, Chinese or Middle Eastern people.
- Project cultural stereotypes, for example, that all young Black people avoid eye contact. Most young Black and Asian people are second and third generation British-born citizens and may be no different from any other teenager when faced with authority figures.
- Perceive people from minorities as 'the problem'—the problem may lie in the working methods and traditions of some institutions, which may put some groups, such as women, people with disabilities or those from minority ethnic communities, at a disadvantage.

Religious diversity
(see Part 3, ETBB)

- Awareness of a person's religious belief or non-belief is an integral element of being aware of equal treatment issues.
- Taking notice of religious matters helps create an atmosphere of trust and reduces alienation.

The 2001 Census shows that 71.6% of respondents (37 million) stated their religion as Christian, while 15.5% (9.1 million) stated they had no religion and a further 7.3% (4.2 million) did not respond to the question.

Some 3.1% of England's population and 0.7% of the Welsh population give their religion as Muslim, making this the most common religion after Christianity. Some 8.5% of London's population gave their religion as Muslim, 4.1% are Hindus and 2.1% Jewish.

When compared with the provision on race, the law does not provide comprehensive protection from religious discrimination or incitement to religious hatred.

The interrelationship between ethnicity and religion is complex. Ethnic groups are often multi-religious. Indians, for example, may be Hindus, Muslims, Sikhs, Christians or members of other belief systems. Religious practice can also cut across ethnic groups. Ethnic and religious identities can also coincide: both Jews and Sikhs are recognised as ethnic groups under the Race Relations (Amendment) Act.

To add to the complexity, each religion has a considerable internal diversity of traditions, movements, cultures and languages. There are many variations within minority religions, just as within Christianity, where Black-led churches have joined traditional Christian groups.

Oath taking
(see Chapter 3.2, ETBB)
The Oaths Act 1978 makes provisions for the forms in which oaths may be administered and states that a solemn affirmation shall be of the same force and effect as an oath. In to-day's multicultural society all citizens, whether or not they are members of faith traditions, should be treated sensitively when making affirmations, declarations or swearing oaths.

As a matter of good practice:

- The sensitive question of whether to affirm or swear an oath should be presented to all concerned as a solemn choice between two procedures, which are equally valid in legal terms.

- The primary consideration should be what binds the conscience of the individual, since detailed questions of theology cannot be resolved in the courtroom.

- One should not assume that an individual belonging to a minority community will automatically prefer to swear an oath rather than affirm.

- All faith traditions have differing practices with regard to court proceedings and these should be treated with respect.

- In many faith traditions the holy scripture is believed to contain the actual presence of divinity and is accordingly revered.

- Requests to perform ritual ablutions before taking the oath should be treated sympathetically.

- Jewish, Hindu, Muslim and Sikh women may prefer to affirm if having to give evidence during menstruation or shortly after childbirth.

- Some witnesses may want to remove shoes or cover their heads or bow with folded arms while taking an oath in order to manifest respect to the presence of the divine in their holy scripture. All holy books should be covered in cloth bags at all times. If in the process of oath-taking the book needs to be uncovered, this should be done by the witness rather than a member of court staff since questions of ritual impurity may arise.

Detailed guidance on the major religions likely to be encountered in England and Wales can be found in Appendix V of the ETBB.

Names and naming systems
Naming systems vary between minority groups and some are complex. More detailed information can be found in Appendix II of the ETBB. A few basic principles may, however, be stated:

- It is more important to ask people how they would like to be addressed, how to pronounce their name and how to spell it, rather than trying to learn all the different naming systems.

- Ask for the full name: first, middle and last names. Do not ask for 'Christian' names or 'surname'.

- Do not address or record people by their religious or honorific titles only; see Appendix II of the ETBB for further details.

Veils in court
(see Chapter 3.3, ETBB)

At the heart of the guidance on the wearing of the full veil, or *niqab*, in court, is the principle that each situation should be considered individually in order to find the best solution in each case, with the interests of justice remaining paramount.

If a person's face is almost fully covered a judge may have to consider if any steps are required to ensure effective participation and a fair hearing—both for the woman wearing a *niqab* and for other parties in the proceedings.

- **Jurors.** If a challenge is presented to a woman wearing a full veil serving on a jury, a judge may wish to consider excusing her, on the proviso that she may serve on another jury where no challenge is made. Much will depend on the views of the parties, but the judge must be satisfied there is a genuine basis for such a challenge.

- **Victims and complainants.** It is clearly important that people are not deterred from seeking justice or not getting a fair hearing by a sense that they are excluded from court. It may be possible for evidence to be given wearing a veil, or for the woman to agree to remove it while giving evidence. Other measures are available to the court, such as screens, video links, clearing the public gallery. A short adjournment may be provided to enable the woman to seek guidance. What is clear is that a decision on these matters should ideally be reached after discussion at a preliminary hearing.

- **Witnesses and defendants.** Similarly a sensitive request to remove a veil may be appropriate, but should follow careful thought as attending court itself is a daunting prospect for witnesses and may affect the quality of evidence given. While it may be more difficult in some cases to assess the evidence of a woman wearing a *niqab*, the experiences of judges in other cases have shown that it is possible to do so. Where identification is an issue, it must be dealt with appropriately and may require the witness to make a choice between showing her face or not giving evidence.

- **Advocates.** The starting point should be that an advocate wearing a full veil should be entitled to appear when wearing it. The interests of justice will be paramount and the judge may need to consider—in the particular circumstances that arise—if the interests of justice are being impeded or not by the fact the advocate's face cannot be seen, or they cannot be heard clearly.

Children in court
(see Part 4, ETBB)

Court proceedings are traumatic experiences for children and we should be aware of their particular anxieties.

- Sensitive preparation of the child before court can minimise distress.

- Thorough case management can also alleviate anxiety for children.

- Some children, such as those from some cultural groups or those with disabilities, may be more vulnerable.

The appearance in court of a child or young person—as victim, witness or defendant—requires particular procedures to be followed. A significant number of vulnerable witnesses are children, and there are various initiatives to protect them. It is important for the judicial office-holder to be conversant with these facilities.

The testimony of the child must be adduced as effectively and fairly as possible. The judge must be satisfied as to the child's competence; this issue should be dealt with as early as possible in proceedings. Under the Youth Justice and Criminal Evidence Act 1999, a lack of competence in a witness is described as an inability to understand questions or to give answers which can be understood. Any hearing to determine competence shall be in the presence of the jury and may include expert evidence.

Children may be prone to particular anxieties in court which may include fear of the unknown, fear of retaliation or publicity, pressure to withdraw a complaint, fear of having to relate personal details before strangers, fear of having to see the defendant or of being sent to prison, or feelings of guilt connected with family breakdown. Adolescent witnesses are more likely to exhibit adverse psychological reactions to the stress of appearing in court than younger ones. It is very important for the judicial office-holder at a hearing to give the child directions on:

- The need to tell the truth.
- The importance of leaving nothing out when answering questions.
- The need to say so if the child does not understand a question.
- The importance of not guessing the answers to questions.
- The need to tell the judge if the child has any problem of any sort at any time during the hearing.

Judges should ensure that advocates do not attempt over-vigorous cross-examination, and that they use language which is free of jargon and which is appropriate to the age of the child. Judicial vigilance is always necessary.

Special measures and children's evidence
(see Chapter 4.4, ETBB)
The Criminal Justice Acts of 1988 and 1991 allowed children's evidence to be given via live television link and later by previously recorded video. Provision for children's evidence to be given in special ways extends back to the Children and Young Persons Act 1933.

The Youth Justice and Criminal Evidence Act 1999 has introduced further measures, which extend to children and young persons, as well as witnesses with mental or physical impairments or whose evidence is likely to be impaired by reason of fear or distress.

- Screens may shield witnesses.
- The court can be cleared so that evidence may be given in private.
- Evidence-in-chief, cross-examination and re-examination may all be carried out by video recordings.
- Evidence may be given through an intermediary, who may also explain questions and answers to and from the witness, to enable them to be understood.
- The court can make available any device to aid communication with a witness with any disability.

A judge conducting a trial involving a video recording of an earlier interview should be thoroughly conversant with the Home Office 'Memorandum of Good Practice on Video Recorded Interviews with Child Witnesses for Criminal Proceedings', which provides guidance on how to conduct such interviews with children, including how to confine their answers to comply with the law of evidence. The memorandum is of principal relevance to criminal proceedings, although its guidance is also of use in civil and family proceedings.

The judge has absolute discretion as to whether or how to admit the evidence of children. The first question must be the potential relevance of what the child might have to say. Much will also depend on the age of the child and the nature of the case.

Disability

(see Part 5, ETBB)

Disability has two elements. The first is the limitation imposed upon the individual by reason of their physical, mental or sensory impairment. The second is the disadvantage which this imposes on the individual in their environment. Any disadvantage that a person with a disability is subject to should not be reinforced by the legal system. Everyone is entitled to justice, regardless of whether or not they are able to cope with the facilities and procedures of the courts.

It is not simply a question of judges being polite and understanding when faced with people whose disabilities are clearly apparent. All members of the judiciary should be able to recognize disabilities as they exist, identify the implications, know what powers they have to compensate for the resulting disadvantage and understand how to use these powers without causing prejudice to other parties.

If any of the parties, witnesses or advocates involved in court proceedings has a disability which might impair their ability to participate, it is important that this is identified as early as possible. Steps can then be taken to ensure that any hearings take place in accessible rooms and suitable facilities are available.

A litigant in civil or family proceedings is treated in a different manner under the court rules only in the case of incapacity. The procedures then ensure that a representative is appointed, compromises and settlements are approved by the court, and there is supervision of money recovered (see Chapter 5.4, ETBB).

It is estimated that there are at least 8.5 million people who currently meet the definition of disabled person under the Disability Discrimination Act 1995. This provides that a 'disability' is any 'physical or mental impairment which has a substantial and long-term adverse effect on . . . normal day-to-day activities'. 'Disability' may for example relate to mobility, manual dexterity, physical co-ordination, incontinence, speech, hearing or sight, memory, and ability to concentrate, learn or understand.

The Disability Discrimination Act 1995, Youth Justice and Criminal Evidence Act 1999 and Human Rights Act 1998 all impose on courts a duty to take account of disabilities. Courts must be able to accommodate the special needs of litigants, defendants and witnesses arising from disability.

Under the Disability Discrimination Act 1995 it is unlawful to discriminate against disabled persons in the provision of facilities and services. There is a duty on all service providers—including courts—to take reasonable steps to change any practice that makes it impossible or unreasonably difficult for people with disabilities to make use of a service which they provide to other members of the public.

The Human Rights Act 1998 also provides support for litigants who are disabled, particularly in respect of the right to a fair trial. Awareness of the issues which a disability might raise in the management of a trial are important in this respect and special arrangements may have to be made with regard to:

- Memory and comprehension—form of questioning, courtroom procedures.

- Mobility—access requirements; individuals may be unable to attend court.

- Communication—visual aids, speech interpreters.
- Some forms of disability mean concentration is impaired, or the person needs to eat or drink more frequently, or take medication, or go to the lavatory at frequent intervals. The presence of carers or helpers may be necessary, perhaps even in the dock or witness box.
- The order in which evidence is heard—attending court can be even more stressful for people with disabilities than for others, so it might be helpful to arrange the hearing of evidence so that they are not kept waiting.

Some types of disability

- **Alzheimer's disease.** A progressive disease predominantly affecting the elderly. It can take the form of lapses of memory and unsettling behaviour patterns. The stress of appearing in court can have a detrimental effect.
- **Autism.** A lifelong development disability which impedes the ability to communicate and to relate socially.
- **Cerebral palsy.** Includes disorders of movement as well as posture and communication problems.
- **Cerebral vascular accidents ('stroke').** Symptoms can include weakness or paralysis, speech difficulties, loss of balance and incontinence.
- **Deafness.** This covers a range of hearing impairments. All courtrooms should be fitted with an induction loop. The use of sign language interpreters may be necessary.
- **Diabetes.** This can be controlled by medication, but symptoms can range from irritability to slurred speech and loss of consciousness.
- **Down's syndrome.** This is associated with a low IQ and varying communication difficulties.
- **Dyslexia.** May cause difficulty with information processing linked with short-term memory and visual co-ordination.
- **Epilepsy.** May cause seizures or fits, which may be brought on by the stress of a court appearance.
- **Incontinence.** This may arise in conjunction with other disabilities or in isolation, and may worsen with stress. Additional breaks in proceedings may have to be arranged.
- **Inflammatory bowel disease.** A pre-arranged signal for an urgent trip to the lavatory may be necessary.
- **Mental health problems.** These vary greatly and the judge will have to make a careful assessment of affected individuals and how to deal with them in the witness box.
- **Motor neurone disease.** A progressive degenerative disease with symptoms extending to loss of limb function and wasting of muscles.
- **Multiple sclerosis.** Symptoms can include visual damage and restricted movement and individuals are likely to fatigue rapidly.
- **Spina bifida and hydrocephalus.** The range of mobility is wide, and individuals may have impaired brain function.
- **Thalidomide.** Individuals are usually limb-disabled; some have hearing impairment.
- **Visual impairment.** One of the commonest disabilities. The best method of communicating in court should be established at the outset.

The Juries Act 1974 provides that it is for the judge to determine whether or not a person should act as a juror. In the event of a person with disabilities being called for jury service, the presumption is that the person should so act unless the judge is of the opinion that the person will not, on account of their disability, be capable of acting effectively as a juror. The full-time attendance of a carer for a jury member would, however, pose difficulties because it would be an incurable irregularity for the carer to retire with the jury to the jury room.

Mental disability
(see Chapter 5.3, ETBB)
A mental disability may arise due to mental ill health, learning disability or brain damage.

Adjustments to court procedures may be required to accommodate the needs of persons with mental disabilities whether as witnesses, litigants in civil or family proceedings or defendants in criminal proceedings.

Only mental incapacity (as distinct from the mere existence or a history of a mental disability) will generally have legal significance in civil and family matters.

Lack of mental capacity may also be significant in criminal prosecutions (i.e. is the accused fit to plead?) and sentencing options may be affected by the mental state of the defendant.

The judge is responsible for the conduct of the hearing and should ensure that people with mental disabilities can participate to the fullest extent possible while avoiding prejudice to other parties.

Mental capacity
(see Chapter 5.4, ETBB)
An adult who lacks mental capacity will not be able to make decisions that others should act upon. Such decisions may relate to financial affairs (e.g. contracts, the conduct of litigation) or personal welfare (including health care).

The Mental Capacity Act 2005 will be fully implemented in England and Wales on 1 October 2007. It improves and clarifies the decision-making process for people unable to make decisions for themselves. It establishes the jurisdiction of a new Court of Protection, but also has an impact on the day-to-day work of all judges, who may need to make assessments of the capacity of adults appearing before them. It redefines mental incapacity, focusing on the time when a decision is made and the matter to which the decision relates, and includes an obligation to take 'all practicable steps' to support individuals in making their own decisions.

Courts should always investigate the question of mental capacity whenever there is any reason to suspect that it may be absent. The question then to ask is 'Is he (or she) incapable of this particular act or decision?' It may be necessary to determine the issue of capacity at a separate hearing.

Mental capacity is a question of fact to be determined by the court on all the available evidence, of which the views of a doctor only comprise a part. The Act defines capacity and provides a two-stage test for determining whether a person is incapable of making a particular decision. Mental capacity depends upon the individual's understanding rather than status or the outcome of any decisions made. The general law also provides specific tests for particular purposes (e.g. signing a will, getting married, conducting litigation).

Under the Act, a person is unable to make a decision if unable to:

- Understand the information relevant to the decision.

- Retain that information.

- Use or weigh that information as part of the process of making the decision, or

- Communicate his decision (whether by talking, using sign language or any other means).

Any decision made on behalf of a person who lacks capacity must be made in that person's best interests—a different concept from what the decision-maker thinks is best. The Act sets out a checklist of factors to be considered in deciding what is in a person's best interests, aimed at identifying those issues most relevant to that person.

The Official Solicitor may be referred to where capacity issues arise and assistance is not available from any other source (see: <www.officialsolicitor. gov.uk>).

Gender
(see Part 6, ETBB)

- Though women and girls comprise more than half the population, they remain disadvantaged in many areas of life.
- Stereotypes and assumptions about women's lives can unfairly impede them and might frequently undermine equality.
- Care must be taken to ensure that our own experiences and aspirations, as women or of women we know, are not taken as representative of the experiences of all women.
- Factors such as ethnicity, social class, disability, status and age affect women's experience and the types of disadvantage to which they might be subject.
- Women may have particular difficulties participating in the justice system; for example, because of maternity or child-care issues.
- Women's experiences as victims, witnesses and offenders are in many respects different from those of men.
- Women are underrepresented in many areas of public life and among law-makers, including the judiciary.
- As judges, we can go some way to ensuring that women have confidence in the justice process and that their interests are properly and appropriately protected.

There have been many positive changes in society regarding gender roles. Law-makers and law-enforcers have in the past, however, mostly been men and a male outlook can still prevail. The disadvantages that women can suffer range from inadequate recognition of their contribution to the home or society to an underestimation of the problems women face as a result of gender bias.

- 67% of women are employed, as opposed to 78% of men.
- Women's employment is more likely to be casual or part-time.
- 60% of all primary carers for another adult are women.

Despite the increasing number of women in the workforce, they remain primarily responsible for unpaid domestic duties. The economic contribution of such labour can be undervalued, resulting in disadvantageous assessments of damages and liability in civil actions, including the settlement of property claims.

In court, women witnesses may feel patronized and disbelieved. A recent Home Office survey revealed that significant (most often disadvantageous) stereotyping exists in the manner in which women are sentenced. Sexual complainants, and those complaining of sexual harassment in discrimination cases, can suffer when there is over-rigorous cross-examination regarding their previous sexual history or where the assailant is known to them.

Domestic violence
(see Chapter 6.1, ETBB)

Research commissioned by the Northern Ireland Office shows two out of every five serious assaults on women involve a current or former partner. Violent behaviour is often a means of coercion, control and reinforcement of power over the other partner in a relationship. The difficulty always stems from the fact that, until allegations are proven, they remain as such.

- Two women are killed every week by their current or former partners.
- Domestic violence accounts for 25% of all violent crime.
- One in four women experience domestic violence, which can escalate during pregnancy or when a woman attempts to leave her violent partner.

Recent guidance encourages the Crown Prosecution Service and courts to take into account the paramount need to ensure the safety of the woman and any children of the household, in particular by ensuring that their whereabouts are not revealed. When granting bail or an injunction, other factors to take into account are: any history of violence in the relationship, the seriousness of the allegations, the victim's injuries, the use of any weapon and whether the attack was planned, whether any subsequent threats have been made, and the effect on any children.

When appearing in court, there are analogies to be drawn with vulnerable witnesses, such as the possibility of intimidation, the need for escort to and from court, and the presence of supporters in court. Other specific measures should be considered, such as providing screens in court, allowing the giving of evidence by television link and the video recording of testimony. The consequences of leaving the perpetrator of the violence alone with the woman in any part of the building should be considered most sensitively. Domestic violence, particularly that occurring over a long period of time, can affect the ability to give coherent testimony. Much depends upon the quality of legal advice received, and whether there are innovative procedures in place, such as the use of Polaroid cameras in police stations.

An apparent inability to change or leave a violent situation should not be interpreted as an acceptance of the violence, so as to render the woman responsible for the violence, or to serve to undermine a women's credibility.

Between a third and a half of all perpetrators of domestic violence also physically abuse children in their care. The effect of domestic violence upon children might include post-traumatic anxieties such as depression, anxiety, behavioural problems, and other psychosomatic symptoms. Readers are referred to Section 5 of the Report to the Lord Chancellor on the question of parental contact in cases where there is domestic violence, which contains guidelines for good practice in such cases, and can be found at <www.dca.gov.uk/family/abfl mr.htm>. [Detailed Guidance in such cases can now be found at www.justice.gov.uk]

Gender Recognition Act 2004
(see Chapter 6.2, ETBB)

The Gender Recognition Act 2004 creates a framework for the legal recognition of transsexual people in their reassigned sex, and permits a person of either gender to make an application for a 'Gender Recognition Certificate' on the basis of living in the other gender or having changed gender under the law of a country or territory outside the UK. The Act makes provision for a 'Gender Recognition Panel' to determine such an application. The granting of a Gender Recognition Certificate does not depend upon a transsexual person first having surgery.

However, not all transsexual people will apply for a Gender Recognition Certificate. The fact that a person does not have a Gender Recognition Certificate should not be assumed to mean that they are not properly transsexual and entitled to respect and legal protection as appropriate in their reassigned sex. A reassigned person who has been issued with a full Certificate by the Panel is entitled to marry in his or her acquired gender.

Sexual orientation
(see Chapter 7.1, ETBB)

- Lesbians or gay men still often experience unequal treatment in their daily lives.
- When dealing with apparent lack of candour, courts and tribunals should remember that being a lesbian or gay man is an individual experience that may have led to fear and concealment.
- Sexual orientation is just one of the many facets of a person's identity. Being a lesbian or gay man is sometimes described as being as much an emotional orientation as a sexual one.
- Nearly all lesbians and gay men were brought up in a heterosexual home.
- Objective mainstream research shows that children brought up by lesbian or gay parents do equally well as those brought up by heterosexual parents.
- Most lesbians and gay men feel that their sexual orientation was there from birth and is unalterable—just as most heterosexuals do.
- Some scientific research claims a genetic determinant for sexual orientation, suggesting that sexuality is not chosen.
- Parliament has now recognised that a same-sex couple can, as a matter of law, constitute an enduring family relationship.
- Gay couples are not the same as straight couples. Courts and tribunals should be careful not to judge same-sex relationships according to the principles of heterosexual married life. Families that do not conform to the traditional model are an increasingly common social reality.

There is a historical background of widespread discrimination against homosexuals. Verbal abuse and physical violence are not infrequently directed against homosexuals, and discrimination in the workplace is not uncommon. Perceptions of prejudice by the gay and lesbian community extend to their experiences in court. There is no evidence that homosexuality implies a propensity to commit crime, nor is there an established link with paedophile orientation.

The Human Rights Act 1998 raises a number of issues relating to the equal treatment of lesbians and gay men, most particularly whether the respect for family life under Article 8 includes lesbian and gay couples. It will certainly be argued that the employees of public authorities cannot be dismissed on the grounds of sexuality, and this is likely to have implications both for the private sector and for the Employment Tribunal.

Concerns about undermining the institution of marriage assume that to promote the rights of one category of citizen necessarily undermines those of another. Further, the Civil Partnership Act 2004 now creates a structure for the establishment and formal recognition of 'civil partnerships'—the relationship between two people of the same sex which is formed when they register as civil partners of each other. The Act also repeals provisions found in other statutes which define families and couples, for the purpose of imposing burdens or granting benefits, based on a heterosexual relationship or marriage. The effect of the Civil Partnership Act 2004 is that for most purposes same-sex couples are treated as equivalent to opposite-sex couples and civil partners are treated as equivalent to married partners.

The Civil Partnership Act also provides for the breakdown of a civil partnership in much the same way as marriage, and amends laws relating to children, the succession of tenancies, wills and inheritance, social security, child support, taxation and domestic violence to provide same-sex partners with much the same rights as heterosexual partners.

Families that do not strictly conform to the traditional model are an increasingly common social reality. There is no evidence that children are excessively teased because their parents are unmarried, or even because their parents are lesbian or gay. Indeed, such children do equally well as those brought up by heterosexual parents in terms of emotional well-being, sexual responsibility, academic achievement and avoidance of crime.

There are also increasing non-discrimination rights afforded to gay and lesbian people. In the context of employment, the Employment Equality (Sexual Orientation) Regulations outlaw discrimination connected to sexual orientation.

Further, the Equality Act 2006 gives the Secretary of State power to make regulations outlawing discrimination and harassment connected to sexual orientation more widely and, in particular, in the provision of goods, facilities and services, in housing, in education and in the exercising of public authority functions.

It is misguided to:

- Attribute masculine characteristics to lesbians, or feminine characteristics to gay men.

- Make any assumptions as to the sexual orientation of transvestites or transsexuals Where there is a question relating to a person's gender, the person should be asked what gender they consider themselves to be, and what gender they would prefer to be treated as.

- Assume that AIDS and HIV-positive status are necessarily indicative of homosexual activity.

HIV treatment can prevent a person from developing the symptoms of AIDS indefinitely, but the fear and stigmatization resulting from an out-of-date understanding of the issues can be very damaging.

AIDS is becoming an outmoded concept in countries able to afford effective HIV treatments.

For further information
Please contact:

Judicial Studies Board, 9th Floor, Millbank Tower, Millbank, London SW1P 4QU
Tel: 020 7217 4708
Fax: 020 7217 4779
E-mail: publications@jsb.gsi.gov.uk

The Equal Treatment Bench Book can be found on the JSB's website at <www.jsboard. co.uk>.

4

The letter and spirit of the Code

4.1 The lawyer joke

A layperson, an accountant and a lawyer were all asked: 'What do two and two make?'
The layperson replied: 'Four, of course.'
The accountant replied: 'Four—or five.'
The lawyer replied: 'What do you want it to make?'

Lawyers are the butt of many jokes, many of which flow from a perception that lawyers are capable of acting quite unethically in pursuit of their client's interests. While this perception has, fortunately, never developed in the UK to the extent that it has in the USA, the characteristics of practice in common law jurisdictions expose lawyers to many ethical dilemmas, and responses to these vary. This chapter (and indeed this manual) will provide you with some answers, but in other areas it will simply provide you with a framework within which you will still have to make your own decisions. In these cases it should provide you with tools and ideas which may help you to arrive at conclusions which satisfy the ethical demands of practice.

The issues have been neatly presented by Ross Cranston:

An important policy issue is the extent to which the Code of Conduct ought to be infused by wider ethical notions. There are two aspects to this. One is encapsulated in the question: 'Can a good lawyer be a bad person?'. In other words, are the standards in the Code of Conduct untenable when laid alongside ethical thought or common morality? The second aspect is that if there is a discrepancy between the Code of Conduct and secular ethical thought, what is special about barristers that exempts them from the precepts of the latter? To put it another way, how is it that barristers can decide ethically on a course of action for a client which is different from that which they would adopt for themselves?

(Cranston, R (ed.), *Legal Ethics and Professional Responsibility*
(Oxford: Clarendon, 1996)

The Bar Standards Board recognises this dilemma. Amongst the things it requires you to achieve on the BPTC are 'knowledge and understanding of the philosophical issues and purposes underpinning ethical behaviour'.[1] More specifically, you are expected to 'understand and appreciate the core professional values which underpin practice at the Bar or England and Wales, particularly the additional moral responsibilities held by the profession (over and above the population in general) due to decision-making roles, functions and authority which are key to practice at the Bar'.

---

1 These and other quotations are from the BPTC Handbook, section 2.2.4, accessible at <http://www.barstandardsboard.org.uk/assets/documents/BPTC%20-%20handbook%20version%2001-08-08.pdf>.

4.2 The Code of Conduct

The Bar Code of Conduct provides you with the rules and standards that should inform all aspects of your practice at the Bar. It looks, at first sight, very much like a statute and this recognition should lead you to approach it with respect, but also to consider carefully how you should use it. It is not a statute, but a Code of Conduct. Bear in mind that it is supported by Guidance, available through the Bar Council and Bar Standards Board websites.

There is a risk that, if the Code is perceived as essentially like any other piece of legislation, you will approach it in the same way. Why should this be a problem? It stems from the underlying principle within UK substantive law that all actions are permitted unless they are forbidden. Thus Acts that regulate behaviour are to be construed in a restrictive manner and loopholes may properly be exploited.

For example, the Theft Act 1968 s 9 provides:

(1) A person is guilty of burglary if:
    (a) he enters any building or part of a building as a trespasser and with intent to steal anything in the building or part of a building in question, to inflict on any person in it any grievous bodily harm or to rape any woman in it, or to do unlawful damage to the building or anything in it; or
    (b) having entered any building or part of a building as a trespasser, he steals or attempts to steal anything in the building or that part of it or inflicts or attempts to inflict on any person in it any grievous bodily harm.

Your client has entered a building as a trespasser but with no particular intention, and, once inside decides to do unlawful damage to property within the building. Your advice to him should be to plead not guilty to a charge of burglary. This is because his actions fall within neither paragraph of the subsection even though his actions have produced the same result as behaviour which would lead to guilt (had he formed the intention to cause the damage before, rather than after entering the building). This conclusion may be hard for a layperson to understand but would be natural to any lawyer versed in statutory interpretation.

To adopt the same approach to following the Code may enable you to avoid successful disciplinary proceedings by the Bar Standards Board. In other words, in so far as it acts in an analogous manner to a criminal statute, the Code may be treated in the same way. However, to approach the Code in this way could carry dangers for the reputation of the profession. Your interpretation of the Code should be informed by ethical values and where the Code permits a variety of responses your choice between them should be similarly informed. This is why the Bar Standards Board requires that you understand these underpinning values.

An example of how the Code regulates your professional response arises from para 704:

704 A barrister must not devise facts which will assist in advancing the lay client's case and must not draft any statement of case, witness statement, affidavit, notice of appeal or other document containing:

[. . .]

(c) any allegation of fraud unless he has clear instructions to make such allegation and has before him reasonably credible material which as it stands establishes a prima facie case of fraud;

The concept of 'reasonably credible material' inherently carries a degree of subjectivity. Suppose that you have been instructed by your lay client that the opponent has been perpetrating a fraud. It is not uncommon for hostility between the parties to lead to all sorts of allegations which are discovered later to be impossible of formal proof. That being the case, it would be unwise to incorporate such an allegation into any draft on the client's assertion alone. What, however, if the client (who has behaved in a temperate manner throughout) tells you that the opposing party has admitted to committing fraud, but no other independent evidence is available? What if, in addition, the client is prepared to make a statement of truth in respect of this allegation? Would such a statement be 'reasonably credible material' given that it is in essence no more than the original assertion presented formally in a way which is admissible in court? Should you still insist on some independent evidence?

In practical terms you would doubtless advise your professional client to seek independent evidence to corroborate your lay client's oral evidence before settling a statement of case which contained an allegation of fraud. If it is not forthcoming, should you pursue the allegation? The only guidance the Code offers is that the material must be credible and establish a prima facie case. The assertion of an intemperate client would clearly be inadequate (it is the mischief the rule is designed to avoid). To rely on a statement of truth may be sufficient to avoid a finding of misconduct (although if there were no other evidence the client should be advised of the dangers of pressing the matter in court: a wasted costs order may loom). However, to refuse to incorporate such an allegation in those circumstances will upset your client, and is likely to upset them more if the allegations are in fact well founded. You must not let your independence be compromised (para 307(a) and (c)), yet you should act on your client's behalf (para 303(a)).

Note that the House of Lords' decision in *Medcalf v Mardell and others* [2003] 1 AC 120 (for details see **7.5.4.2**), while addressing this area, does not resolve this issue. If you check the specific guidance on this matter on the Bar Council website you will find:

The Professional Standards Committee (PSC) takes the view that there is no litmus test for determining whether it is proper to allege fraud. As Lord Bingham made clear at para 22: 'Counsel is bound to exercise an objective professional judgment whether it is in all circumstances proper to lend his name to the allegation'. That decision will depend on the individual facts of each case.

It should be noted that although paragraph 704 refers specifically to fraud, the same principle would apply to any other allegation of serious misconduct.

No doubt you should err on the side of caution and advise that further evidence should be obtained if possible, but it may not be available. Moreover, if, after settling the statement of case, it becomes clear that there is no credible evidence of fraud (for example, the opposing party may have made the admission to provoke a reaction or as an act of bravado) or if other facts come to light showing that the allegation of fraud has no prospect of success, you will no doubt recognise that the fraud allegation should no longer be pursued. It is submitted that the proper approach is not to seek a 'way around' the provisions of the Code, but to consider underlying values, so that your response is likely to assist to maintain the Bar's reputation as a thoroughly ethical profession. Fortunately, problems as awkward as this should not be a daily occurrence, and you should remember that advice will be available from your Head of Chambers or from the Bar Council.

An understanding of the underpinning values will give you a basis for deciding ethical questions beyond what the Code provides. Remember that behaviour prohibited by the Code is not made acceptable by a contrary underpinning value, but an underpinning value might validate conduct upon which the Code is silent or in circumstances which generate conflict between its provisions. Ultimately, where, having thought through matters in this degree of depth, you remain uncertain as to the proper way of proceeding, you should contact the Bar Council Ethical Queries Helpline available for advice in emergencies.

4.3 Underpinning values

Here are a number of values which may be said to underpin the Code of Practice. It is not intended to be exhaustive.

- Justice.
- Respect for the law.
- Client autonomy.
- Confidentiality.
- Honesty.

How these values apply to the demands of practice at the Bar may best be understood by reading them in the context of the core principles identified by the Bar Standards Board as underpinning the Code and Bar Council guidance. These are:

- the principle of professional independence;
- the principle of integrity;
- the principle of duty to the court;
- the principle of loyalty to the lay client;
- an understanding of the problems and perception of conflict of interest;
- the principle of non-discrimination on grounds of gender, race, ethnicity, or sexual orientation; and
- commitment to maintaining the highest professional standards of work, to the proper and efficient administration of justice, and to the Rule of Law.[2]

4.3.1 Conflict in underpinning values

Conflict between values is inherent in legal practice. Lord Reid makes this clear in his opinion in *Rondel v Worsley* [1969] 1 AC 191, 227:

Every counsel has a duty to his client fearlessly to raise every issue, advance every argument and ask every question, however distasteful, which he thinks will help his client's case. But, as an officer of the court concerned with the administration of justice, he has an overriding duty to the court, to the standards of his profession, and to the public, which may and often does lead to a conflict with his client's wishes or what the client thinks are his personal wishes.

Consider a concrete situation. If your client in a criminal matter has provided you with information which is relevant (but adverse) to your case you will be faced with a conflict between maintaining confidentiality and not misleading the court. A perusal of the Code will throw up relevant provisions.

104 The general purpose of this Code is to provide the requirements for practice as a barrister and the rules and standards of conduct applicable to barristers which are appropriate in the interests of justice and in particular:

(a) in relation to self-employed barristers to provide common and enforceable rules and standards which require them:
  (i) to be completely independent in conduct and in professional standing as sole practitioners;
  (ii) to act only as consultants instructed by solicitors and other approved persons;
  (iii) to acknowledge a public obligation based on the paramount need for access to justice to act for any client in cases within their field of practice;

[. . .]

---

2 Ibid.

301 A barrister must have regard to paragraph 104 and must not:

(a) engage in conduct whether in pursuit of his profession or otherwise which is:
   (i) dishonest or otherwise discreditable to a barrister;
   (ii) prejudicial to the administration of justice; or
   (iii) likely to diminish public confidence in the legal profession or the administration of justice or otherwise bring the legal profession into disrepute;. . .

302 A barrister has an overriding duty to the Court to act with independence in the interests of justice: he must assist the Court in the administration of justice and must not deceive or knowingly or recklessly mislead the Court.

[. . .]

702 Whether or not the relation of counsel and client continues a barrister must preserve the confidentiality of the lay client's affairs and must not without the prior consent of the lay client or as permitted by law lend or reveal the contents of the papers in any instructions to or communicate to any third person (other than another barrister, a pupil . . . or any other person who needs to know it for the performance of their duties) information which has been entrusted to him in confidence or use such information to the lay client's detriment or to his own or another client's advantage.

[. . .]

708 A barrister when conducting proceedings in Court: . . .

(e) must not adduce evidence obtained otherwise than from or through the client or devise facts which will assist in advancing the lay client's case;

These rules are helpful in identifying what is expected in relation to each of the underlying values. However, they provide little guidance as to how conflicts should be resolved. In fact, the conflict identified occurs so regularly in practice that a proper way of responding is well established. You will not necessarily be required to withdraw unless your client wishes you to present information you now know to be incorrect. Your precise duties will depend on the nature of the information being withheld. This may range from a full confession to dishonesty in obtaining public funding or an indication of past offences of which the prosecution appears to be unaware. You will find detailed guidance as to how to respond ethically to these different situations at **7.2** below.

Note that further guidance on the preparation of witness statements is available on the Bar Standards Board website. This is expressly described as applying to civil matters only, as barristers do not draft witness statements in criminal cases. Thus you should note that striking a balance between different values might produce different results in the criminal and the civil context.

This itself throws up an important value, associated with client autonomy and justice. Our adversarial system of justice requires as close as possible an approach to equality of arms. The assumption is that representation by competent and qualified lawyers achieves that equality. In a civil matter the parties are to some extent equal (although one may be able to spend more money than the other in preparing the case). In a criminal matter, however, it is normal to find individuals (often impecunious and possibly facing loss of liberty) with all the forces and resources of a powerful state arranged against them. This goes some way to explaining:

- the cab-rank rule, which requires barristers to accept any case which is within their competence and ability to undertake (there are exceptions—see Part VI of the Code); and
- the lesser expectations to disclose adverse factual information in criminal, as opposed to civil matters (given that the task is for the prosecution to prove the case, not for the defendant to prove his innocence).

So your response to a clash of underlying values may need to differ depending on the context.

You may find yourself in a situation where you face such a clash of values or where you are challenged by a client holding different values to your own. Consider the following situations.

EXAMPLE

What if my client is impecunious and facing a wealthy opponent?

For example, you are acting pro bono for an unemployed client who claims to have been unfairly dismissed for fighting at work. Your professional client instructs you to contact the respondent's lawyers in order to seek a settlement. The evidence from a number of witnesses and from personnel records suggests that your client had, indeed, been fighting, had done so on many occasions, and was only dismissed after proper warnings had been given. In conference, however, your client continues to deny the allegation while offering no explanation for the evidence against him. You are confident that should the matter proceed to trial your client will lose. You are, however, aware that many cases can result in a technical finding of unfair dismissal for procedural failings, even if the compensation in such cases is likely to be minimal. Your lay client has indicated that he is willing to accept £2,000 in settlement. You recognise, moreover, that for the employer to defend the claim, should you make many demands on them for disclosure or further questions, will cost them over £2,000.

Should you contact the employer, pointing out that the hearing will be a long one and that you will be requiring considerable disclosure of documents and answers to detailed questions about personnel practices in the firm, suggesting that your client will withdraw the case if they pay £2,000 in settlement? To do so would promote the value of client autonomy and (by subverting the normal consequences of inequalities in wealth) promote a particular view of social justice.

Should you, instead, avoid putting that pressure on the employer when negotiating, recognising that this might make it less likely that the employer will settle for £2,000? To do so would promote the values of respect for the law and a particular (but different) perception of justice.

The Code does not prevent either course, provided you are acting on your client's instructions after giving proper advice. This is thus one example where your own values may have an impact on your choice of whether to use the 'we'll make this expensive for you' tactic.

What if my client is seeking to achieve, by instructing me, a goal which I regard as immoral?

For example, your clients, who are a couple seeking to have an exceptionally bright child, wish to carry out genetic checks to screen out any foetuses which appear not to be intelligent. You feel strongly that this is an abuse of the genetic research which has been done. Although the motive appears to be one which is forbidden under the relevant legislation you understand that similar checks (which are permitted) can indirectly provide information which would enable them to screen for intelligence.

Should you simply advise them that their proposed course of action would contravene the law and that they should not therefore attempt to pursue it? To do so may promote the value of (your particular view of) morality. This itself will be based on a value such as the integrity of the individual (in this case the unconceived child).

Should you, instead, indicate how they might achieve their goal without technically breaking the law? To do so would promote the value of client autonomy.

When considering the propriety of your response you must remember that your duty is to act for your client and you should not make moral judgments about your client's actions. You should also consider what your client needs to know in order to make a properly informed decision. These principles are addressed in the Code and clearly prioritise the value of client autonomy.

What if my client is seeking to achieve, by instructing me, a goal which involves a breach of the law?

For example, you are instructed by solicitors to advise a corporate client which wishes to reduce some of its production costs. The proposed savings will increase the risk of a release of toxic chemicals into a river. Such a release will constitute a breach of regulations designed to protect the environment and expose the client company to the risk of fines. However, you are aware that the local authority with responsibility for enforcing those regulations is extremely short of finance and is unable to make regular checks. A minor release is therefore unlikely to be noticed.

Should your advice be to explain the legal situation and simply point out that the proposed cost reductions place the company at risk of committing an illegal action for which they might suffer a penalty? To do so may promote the value of respect for the law.

Should your advice extend to your assessment of the very small risk of discovery? To do so may promote the value of client autonomy.

Does the principle indicated in the previous example (that you should not make moral judgments about your client's actions) apply equally here, when the proposed action involves your client committing a criminal offence? The Code indicates that you must do nothing dishonest or bring the profession into disrepute. Incitement to break the law clearly falls within that concept. You can therefore protect yourself from breach of the Code by giving clear advice not to break the law. However, you may be doing that in the realistic knowledge that your client may well ignore you and break the law. Note that if this has occurred to you it is probably your own sensitivity to ethical issues that alerts you to the risk that this may have the effect of indirectly inciting a breach of the law.

You will see that none of these three examples produces a single, clearly correct answer. Regrettably, this may well arise in practice. I have my personal preferences as to the most appropriate response, but you may well take a different view. Any such difference will flow in part from the personal values that you or I espouse. For this reason we need to be aware of those values and how they impact on our responses when faced with ethical dilemmas (as we undoubtedly will be). At the same time it is important that we remember that we must not apply our personal values unrestrained. As barristers, we are bound by the Code and that recognition may assist when you are faced with a conflict of potentially applicable values. You cannot justify a departure from the clear requirements of the Code by pleading an inconsistent personal value, no matter how strongly you espouse it.

4.4 Role morality

One concept which may assist in resolving conflicts of this sort is that of role morality. A lawyer may be required to do something for a client which she could not morally justify doing for herself. That proposition may initially appear to be wrong, or at least counter-intuitive. However, it is explained to a degree by the recognition that the basis of litigation in the UK is adversarialism. The lawyer is the skilled partisan advocate of the client and is (in theory) opposed by a similarly skilled partisan advocate for the opponent. The neutral decision-maker is neither lawyer but the tribunal.

This concept only works if the lawyer is genuinely partisan and the parties are equitably resourced. A client whose lawyer adopts a neutral role will be severely disadvantaged if opposed by a client whose lawyer adopts a partisan approach. In order to shoulder this burden properly, lawyers may well have to seek to achieve conclusions of which they disapprove, or carry out actions which they would not carry out on their own behalf. To justify this, many have introduced the idea of 'role morality'. This concept prioritises the value of client autonomy and is the source of the cab-rank rule (see Code para 601). Many lawyers regard it as enabling them to do for their clients what they would not do for themselves.

It may have surprising consequences. As Boon and Levin point out:

Paradoxically, whilst lawyers are expected to act cooperatively, altruistically and ethically when dealing *with* their clients, they are expected to be uncooperative, selfish and possibly unethical in pursuing the objectives *of* their clients. This creates considerable moral strain, . . .

(Boon, A and Levin, J, *The Ethics and Conduct of Lawyers in England and Wales*
(Oxford: Hart, 2nd ed, 2008) at 192)

That moral strain will alert you to the fact that while the concept of role morality may justify your doing for your client what you would not do for yourself, it does not give you guidance as to how far you can go. Take an example.

EXAMPLE

It may well be that if you clearly owed a debt you would not take advantage of the limitation provisions to evade it. However, would you apply the same moral judgment if it were your client who owed the debt? Suppose, for example, your client is very short of money and had forgotten the debt, which is owed to a large corporation? Suppose, instead, your client is the large corporation and the person owed the debt is impecunious?

Your view may be identical in those two situations or you may regard their relative wealth as a key issue. That is a matter for you. However, identifying the issue should make it clear that role morality, while potentially justifying actions which you would feel uncomfortable about on your own behalf, does not resolve questions about whether a particular course of action is ethically acceptable. For that, once again, you need to follow the Code and, where necessary, consider your underlying values.

The underpinning principle here is client autonomy. The Code permits you to do whatever your client wants provided that it is not illegal, you are not dishonest, and you give the court the full benefit of your knowledge of the law, whether helpful to your case or not. Equally, you must provide your client with advice that helps him or her to take an informed decision as to whether to pursue a case or not. It would be improper (as with the second example at **4.3.1**) to prioritise your views over those of your client. There is nothing to stop you identifying ethical considerations to your client, but the decision must remain with the client.

The adversarial nature of the UK legal system may be some justification for a barrister behaving differently in professional and personal contexts, but it also carries its own limits to professional behaviour. Because (unlike in an inquisitorial system) the court does not have the resources to explore the truth for itself, it relies on the honesty of advocates and their ability to research the law fully. This is the source of the requirements not to mislead the court and to cite authorities that go against your client's interests. This should identify two insights:

(a) A claim to role morality does not justify all behaviour. A balance between conflicting values must still be maintained. This is clear from the Marre Report (para 6.1):

The client is frequently acting under physical, emotional or financial difficulties and may well wish to take every step he can, whether legal or extra-legal, to gain advantage over the other party. In this situation the lawyer has a special duty and responsibility to advise his client as to the legal and ethical standards which should be observed and not to participate in any deception or sharp practice.

(Lady Marre, CBE, *A Time for Change: Report of the Committee on the Future of the Legal Profession* (General Council of the Bar and Council of the Law Society, London: 1998))

This is helpful guidance, but leaves much to the individual lawyer.

(b) No advocate will be able to meet the standards expected unless the requisite knowledge, understanding, and skills have been mastered. The knowledge, understanding, and skills that you have acquired in your undergraduate study and which you are now developing on your Bar Professional Training Course are central to your effectively meeting the demands of an adversarial system. Competence itself is an ethical issue.

For further discussions of role morality, see Boon, A and Levin, J, *The Ethics and Conduct of Lawyers in England and Wales* (Oxford: Hart, 2nd ed. 2008) at 15–17 and 191–194, and Nicolson, D and Webb, J, *Professional Ethics: Critical Interrogations* (Oxford: OUP, 1999) at 169–171.

4.5 Ethical behaviour and self-interest

It is often said that ethical behaviour is in the individual lawyer's best interest because 'the Bar is a small profession and your reputation will quickly get around'. Barely hidden behind this assertion is the suggestion that if you acquire a reputation for poor ethical standards opponents will not trust you and you will find it increasingly difficult to meet your clients' needs. This may be true. However, it is important to recognise that ethics and self-interest should not be equated.

Some help may be available from the recognition that taking a long-term view of self-interest is highly likely to be an ethically safer approach than taking a short-term view. Thus, an approach which ensures that you have a reputation for honesty is likely to enable you to represent many future clients in negotiation. It is also therefore likely to enhance your long-term income. Willingness to deceive an opponent may achieve something your current client values but will inhibit your ability to come to desirable solutions for future clients. Not only would this inhibit long-term income, it would involve a breach of the Code (para 301(a)).

One other aspect of self-interest is worth addressing here. You have an interest in your profession continuing to be perceived as in good ethical standing. If you comply with the provisions of the Code, this will preserve you from the risk of disciplinary proceedings. However, where the Code provides a framework within which different courses of action are permitted you should be alert to maintain the highest possible ethical standards.

This insight helps us to identify those aspects of self-interest which will assist us to maintain high ethical standards, but relying on self-interest is altogether insufficient. It ignores most of the underpinning values which we have identified earlier and leaves the individual lawyer without ethical guidance. Thus it remains necessary to comply with the requirements of the Code and to consider its underpinning values in those situations where conflicts nevertheless arise.

4.6 The lawyer joke again

So which of the three was acting most ethically? I have no problem with the layperson's response and am sufficiently ignorant to accept that there may be justification for the accountant's response. However, to judge the lawyer I need to go back to my core values again. If I prioritise client autonomy, this lawyer may be responding perfectly correctly. There are few situations in reality where one simple answer is the only one available. The lawyer here is seeking the client's instructions as to what the desired outcome is. It may be that that outcome is not legally available, in which case the lawyer should advise the client to that effect. It may be readily available, in which case the lawyer is in the fortunate position of giving the client good news. It is just as likely, however, that the answer is somewhere between the two. How far should you go to achieve the client's desired result? That is a matter of your professional responsibility. The Code of Conduct is your guide ('a barrister must not . . . compromise his professional standards in order to please his client, the Court, or a third party'—Code para 307(c)), which makes it clear that you should never allow your personal values to override the requirements of the Code. However, within the boundaries provided by the Code, the Guidance available on the Bar Council and Bar Standards Board websites, and always remembering the availability of the Ethical Queries Helpline, the final decision is your responsibility.

Suggested further reading:

Andrew Boon and Jennifer Levin: *The Ethics and Conduct of Lawyers in England and Wales* (2nd ed. Oxford, Hart, 2008). This is the most up-to-date of the books suggested and explores the principles underlying the ethics of solicitors and barristers. It looks critically at the conflicts which may arise and the ways in which the ethical principles apply in different areas of lawyers' work.

Richard O'Dair: *Legal Ethics: Text and Materials* (Cambridge, Cambridge University Press, 2001). This book covers the underlying principles of ethics as well as applying them to a variety of the situations in which lawyers find themselves. Many of the materials it provides are still valid, although some are out of date. It is particularly useful in that it contains problem questions and case studies.

Donald Nicolson and Julian Webb: *Professional Legal Ethics: Critical Interrogations* (Oxford, OUP, 2000). This is a more theoretical book which provides a wide-ranging and critical analysis of the ethical principles of the English legal professions.

5

Court etiquette

5.1 Introduction

Each time you appear in court you are on a public stage, in full view of the judge, the client and, usually, the public at large. How you appear and conduct yourself in front of that audience is of great importance if you are to do the job of a barrister properly. If you are discourteous, inappropriately dressed, or do not behave in the way that you ought to, you risk alienating the tribunal you are seeking to persuade. Remember that as a barrister you are always appearing on behalf of someone other than yourself: unfavourable views formed about you by the tribunal because of an unprofessional manner may rebound onto your client. Some of the requirements of the etiquette that you must observe are to be found in written sources, such as the Code of Conduct, or the occasional Practice Direction (for example, *Practice Direction (Court Dress) (No. 4)* [2007] All ER (D) 390 and *Practice Direction (Court Dress) (No. 5)* (2008) The Times, 19 August), but others have been established through custom, tradition, and common sense.

5.2 Courtesy

It should go without saying that in every sphere of practice you ought to be courteous, and this is reinforced by the Code of Conduct, which states '[a] barrister must at all times be courteous to the Court and to all those with whom he has professional dealings' (para 5.5 of the Written Standards for the Conduct of Professional Work). You are, of course, required by the Code of Conduct to 'promote and protect fearlessly and by all proper and lawful means the client's best interests and do so without regard to [your] own interests or to any consequences to [yourself] or to any other person . . .' (para 303(a)), but this does not give you *carte blanche* to be as rude as you like to judges, witnesses, or your opposing counsel. Ultimately, discourtesy by counsel in court could amount to a contempt.

5.3 Dress in court

The Code of Conduct requires that 'a barrister's personal appearance should be decorous, and his dress, when robes are worn, should be compatible with them' (para 5.12 of the Written Standards for the Conduct of Professional Work in Section 3, Miscellaneous Guidance). In practice, this means that you should dress conservatively. A courtroom is not the place to make an individual fashion statement: you may like wearing Paisley waistcoats and bright orange socks, but save that for your own time.

As a barrister, you are a professional: dress like one. Dressing conservatively means, amongst other things:

(a) Men should wear a suit (the traditional black jacket and grey striped trousers is an alternative, although less common now among younger members of the Bar). Do not wear blazers or linen jackets in court, even in hot weather. Either single or double-breasted suits are acceptable, but a waistcoat should be worn if the former is chosen. Suits and dresses should be dark in colour, i.e., black, dark navy, or grey, and of a traditional cut. In May 1995 the then Lord Chief Justice, Lord Taylor of Gosforth, decided that it was perfectly acceptable for women to wear trousers when appearing in court. These should be worn as part of a trouser suit.

(b) Dresses or blouses should be long sleeved and high to the neck, even in warmer weather.

(c) Shirts or blouses should be predominantly white; collars should be white. For men (when robes are worn) a separate wing collar is the norm: avoid, as has been seen in court, a dress evening shirt.

(d) Shoes should be black; avoid wearing boots in court.

(e) Jewellery should be discreet: avoid studs and rings through places other than ears. Men should avoid wearing an earring in court.

(f) When a wig is worn, wear it so that it covers your hair as far as possible; avoid fringes showing at the front, and keep long hair neatly tied back.

The Professional Conduct Committee of the Bar Council has been asked about the propriety of a barrister who customarily wears a turban to do so in place of a wig. The Committee was of the view that such matters were properly determined by the court concerned rather than the Committee itself. However, it expressed the view that it is entirely reasonable for a barrister who customarily wears a turban to do so in court in place of a wig.

5.4 Robes

For counsel, being robed means wearing wig, gown, and bands.

However, what barristers wear in court may be affected by proposed reforms to what the judiciary wear. On 27 July 2007 the Lord Chief Justice, Lord Worth, announced that the dress of judges will be simplified; the changes include a simpler gown and not wearing a wig. These changes took effect from 1 October 2008 (see *Practice Direction (Court Dress) (No. 5)* (2008) The Times 19 August).

The Bar Council has issued a Guidance Note on Court Dress dated 31 July 2008. It provides that:

(a) In the Court of Appeal, in the House of Lords, and in the Privy Council, counsel will wear court dress (meaning wigs, gowns, wing collars, and bands or collarettes).

(b) In the Commercial Court, Admiralty Court, and Technology Court, business suits will be worn on all occasions.

(c) In the Chancery Division court dress should be worn for all trials (which includes a final hearing of a Part 7 claim, a Part 8 Claim, and a Petition) and appeals and business suits on all other occasions.

(d) In the Family Division, counsel should wear business suits except for contested divorce/nullity petitions, when court dress will be worn.

(e) In the Administrative Court, court dress should be worn on all occasions.

(f) In the Queen's Bench Division, on occasions not covered by the above, court dress should be worn for trials (which includes a final hearing of a Part 7 claim, a Part 8 Claim, or a Petition), and business suits should be worn on all other occasions.

(g) In the county court, business suits should be worn for applications (including all interim and final hearings in children and ancillary financial relief cases) and court dress for trials (including contested divorce/nullity petitions). Also, in the county court, counsel should wear court dress for appeals from trials and appeals under ss 204 and 204A Housing Act 1996, and business suits for appeals from applications.

(h) Before masters, registrars, and district judges, counsel should wear business suits (except for hearings in the Chancery Division which take place before masters, registrars, and district judges *in court* rather than in the judge's room, when court dress should be worn).

(i) In the magistrates' court, counsel should wear business suits.

(j) In the Crown Court, court dress should be worn (except for bail applications in chambers).

(k) Despite what is set out above, in *any* case where the liberty of the subject is in issue (except for magistrates' court and Crown Court bail applications which are held in chambers), counsel should wear court dress.

It is always advisable, though rather inconvenient, to take your robes to court in case the judge before whom you are appearing chooses to take the matter robed and in open court.

Always turn up to your chambers prepared to appear in court in robes, even if you were planning a day on papers, i.e., wear a suit, have your robes with you, and a collarless shirt to hand. It is not at all unusual for you to arrive at chambers to be told by your clerk that you are to attend court, when you thought you were going to have a paperwork day!

5.5 Customs

Much of court etiquette is derived from custom. Some of the more common customs are:

(a) Do not move or speak while a witness is being sworn; you should stay completely still and silent while this is being done, even if you are not involved in the case.

(b) Do not enter or leave court while a verdict is being taken, or when a defendant is being sentenced.

(c) When the judge enters the courtroom you must stand; he or she will normally bow to counsel before being seated—you should return the bow. You should also bow to the judge when leaving court, and, if you have just come in to a court when the judge is already sitting, as you sit down.

(d) Do not stare (indeed, try not to look) at members of a jury when they come into court to deliver their verdict. At this stage, they have made their decision: you can no longer influence them one way or the other, and there is no reason why you should make them feel uncomfortable by trying to guess their verdict.

(e) You should not show your emotions at a verdict, or a judge's ruling.

(f) By convention, briefcases are not usually carried by counsel when robed. Do not take a bag into court (other than a handbag). If you have to, for whatever reason, ensure it is concealed as far as possible. Similarly, newspapers and other miscellaneous items should be kept from the view of the tribunal you are before.

(g) There is a courtesy known as 'dressing the judge' which should be observed. A judge in robes should never be left without a member of the Bar being in court, unless the judge has indicated that he or she can leave. If your case is over, and you are the only barrister in court, do not leave unless the judge has given such an indication. In virtually every case the judge will so indicate.

(h) If your opponent rises to object, sit down. Two barristers should never be on their feet at the same time unless being addressed directly by the judge.

(i) Sometimes you will go into court where leading counsel will be appearing; by convention, junior barristers sit in the row behind leading counsel, rather than the same one. Constraints of space sometimes mean that this is not always observed.

In addition to the above customs there are also a number of less common situations where there is still an element of custom and etiquette, for example, on the death of a judge, it will usually fall to the most senior member of the Bar present in the robing room that day to perform some form of valediction before the business of the court is resumed.

5.6 Modes of address

Reference should be made to the *Advocacy* manual which contains a guide to the appropriate modes of addressing the court and the use of the correct form of address.

5.7 Problems

(1) You are instructed to represent the defendant in a high court case at 10.30 a.m., at the Royal Courts of Justice. You sleep through your alarm clock and, to your horror, wake up at 10 a.m. The court is an hour's journey from your home. What do you do?

(2) You are the junior pupil in chambers. At 4.30 p.m. on Thursday your clerk tells you that you have two cases listed at Exeter Crown Court for the following day: one at 10 a.m. in court one, and one at 10.30 a.m. in court two, and that no one else in chambers is available to do either of them. At 10.35 a.m. you are still conducting the case in court one, when you are passed a note by the usher from court two that that court has convened and that the judge is waiting for you and furious to know that you are in a different court. What do you do?

6

Professional misconduct: the complaints procedure

6.1 General

The Bar Standards Board (BSB) came into existence on 1 January 2006 following a decision to separate the regulation of the Bar from the representative functions of the Bar Council. This decision was taken in light of the report on the Regulatory Framework for Legal Services by Sir David Clementi, and anticipated the legislative reforms now enshrined in the Legal Services Act 2007.

The Board has been established to regulate barristers called to the Bar of England and Wales in the public interest. It is responsible for:

- setting the education and training requirements for becoming a barrister;
- setting continuing training requirements to ensure that barristers' skills are maintained throughout their careers;
- setting standards of conduct for barristers;
- monitoring the service provided by barristers to assure quality;
- promoting equality and diversity within the Bar, including guidance on good practice relating to access to pupillages and tenancies, the conduct of work in chambers, and issuing guidance on both complaints handling and the avoidance of disability and age discrimination, amongst other things.
- handling complaints against barristers and taking disciplinary or other action where appropriate.

These activities are carried out by the Board through five regulatory committees: Complaints; Education and Training; Qualifications; Quality Assurance; and Standards. Both the Board and Committees have both barrister and lay members; the Board is chaired by a lay person.

As part of its regulatory role, the BSB investigates complaints against barristers and, where appropriate, takes disciplinary action. The procedures that it follows in doing so are laid down, or repeated, in the Code of Conduct:

(a) Complaints Rules—Annexe J.

(b) Disciplinary Tribunal Regulations—Annexe K.

(c) Hearings before the Visitors Rules—Annexe M.

(d) Adjudication Panel and Appeals Rules—Annexe P.

(e) Chambers Complaints Handling—Annexe S.

There are two important figures in the complaints procedure: the independent Complaints Commissioner (the Commissioner) and the Complaints Committee (CC), which was formerly known as the Professional Conduct and Complaints Committee. Their roles are explained in detail at **6.3** and **6.4** below.

6.2 Administration of disciplinary hearings

On 24 January 2005, the Visitors of the Inns of Court handed down their decision in the case of *P v the General Council of the Bar*. They decided that the lay member of the Visitors panel was, by virtue of her membership of the Bar Council's Professional Conduct and Complaints Committee (the PCCC), precluded from hearing the appeal for the following reasons:

- the lay member was automatically disqualified because she shared an interest with the PCCC, the prosecuting body, in securing a conviction;

- the lay member's participation meant that the Visitors panel was not 'independent and impartial' within the meaning of Article 6(1) ECHR; and

- the lay member's participation gave rise to an appearance of bias.

Following this decision, the Bar Council:

- amended the composition of disciplinary panels where necessary to remove any connection of members with the CC, or the Bar Council or any of its committees;

- made clear that the President of the Council of the Inns of Court (COIC), rather than the Bar Council, is responsible for choosing the disciplinary panels;

- moved the administration of the disciplinary panels to COIC and away from the Bar Council.

6.3 The Complaints Commissioner

The Complaints Commissioner is not a lawyer and oversees how the BSB handles complaints when they first arrive. The Commissioner can dismiss a complaint that is made outside the time limit, or if the evidence does not show a case of professional misconduct or inadequate professional service. The Commissioner can also decide to refer a complaint to a barrister's chambers or employer, or refer it to another regulatory body (for example, the Office of the Immigration Services Commissioner). If a complaint does warrant investigation, the Commissioner will direct the Complaints Team to make enquiries of the barrister subject to the complaint, and any other relevant witnesses. At the end of this process, the Commissioner reviews the information obtained through the investigation to determine whether the complaint should be referred up to the Complaints Committee for consideration of disciplinary action

Additional powers of the Complaints Commissioner include the referral of a barrister to a Medical Panel, under the Fitness to Practise Rules (Annexe O to the Code), or refer a barrister to a Suspension Panel, under the Interim Suspension Rules (Annexe N to the Code), if he or she has been convicted or charged with an indictable offence which could form the subject of disciplinary charges at a Disciplinary Tribunal.

6.4 Complaints Committee

The Complaints Committee's role is to decide whether disciplinary action should be taken against a barrister, based on the evidence available. The CC is made up of practising barristers from a variety of specialisms and independent lay members (non-lawyers). All its members are appointed through open competition and on merit by an independent Appointments Board. In 2010, the CC consists of about 45 members of the Bar and 18 lay members. Apart from dealing with complaints, the CC also deals with applications from members of the Bar for waivers from requirements of certain provisions of the Code of Conduct and the referral of barristers to Suspension Panels under the Interim Suspension rules.

6.5 The nature of complaints

In 2009, about 560 external complaints were received from a wide variety of complainants including members of the lay public, prisoners, judges, solicitors, and other members of the Bar. In addition, the Bar Standards Board raised about 180 complaints itself against its members for offences such as failure to comply with the practising requirements, failure to complete Continuing Professional Development, failure to have a practising certificate, or failure to have professional indemnity insurance. Of the external complaints, about 55 per cent are dismissed prior to referral to the CC; 50 per cent dismissed by the Commissioner and the remaining 5 per cent dismissed following a reference to chambers' internal complaints procedure. The remainder are considered by the CC.

The nature of complaints can vary widely but the most common are as follows:

(a) Dissatisfied lay clients alleging:

(i)   incompetence and/or negligence;

(ii) undue pressure to accept a settlement or to plead guilty;

(iii) poor advocacy, style, or tactics.

(b) Misbehaviour in/out of court, especially rudeness to other counsel, the complainant, or to the judge and failure to accept the latter's rulings.

(c) Misleading the court.

(d) Breach of the practising requirements, including:

(i)   failure to comply with Continuing Professional Development requirements;

(ii) failure to renew practising certificate.

(e) Criminal convictions (including driving and public order offences).

6.6 Types of breach of the Code

There are two types of breach of the Code that a barrister can be charged with:

• professional misconduct; and

• inadequate professional service (IPS).

The definition of each can be found in Part 10 of Section 1 of the Code of Conduct. From 1 October 2005, professional misconduct is defined in paras 901 and 902 of the reissued

8th Edition of the Code. IPS is defined in Part 10 of the Code as being *conduct towards a lay client or performance of professional services for that client which falls significantly short of that which is to be reasonably expected of a barrister in all the circumstances.*

6.7 Complaints process

When a complaint is received (other than one made by the Bar Standards Board of its own motion) it is referred to the Complaints Commissioner, who will make an initial decision as to whether the complaint should be referred to the barrister's chambers or employer, whether it should be investigated by the BSB, or whether it should be dismissed. If there are ongoing legal proceedings related to the complaint (such as a pending appeal), the Commissioner may decide to adjourn consideration of the complaint until the related legal proceedings have concluded.

If the Commissioner decides to refer the complaint to the barrister's chambers, a copy of the complaint will be sent to the barrister and the Head of Chambers for the complaint to be considered under the chambers' complaints handling procedure. The Head of Chambers is required to report the outcome of the investigation of the complaint to the BSB.

If the Commissioner decides to investigate a complaint, the BSB will send the full details of the complaint, including all the material provided by the complainant, to the barrister for his or her comments. Relevant witnesses will also be contacted. After all the comments are received, they will be sent to the complainant to read and respond to. When the investigation is complete, the Commissioner will again consider the complaint and all the evidence and comments. The Commissioner can:

(a) Dismiss the complaint because there is not sufficient evidence of IPS or professional misconduct.

(b) Decide that the complaint should be referred to the CC, where there is some evidence of IPS or professional misconduct which is apt for further consideration.

(c) Decide that the barrister may have provided an inadequate professional service and refer the complaint to an Adjudication Panel.

(d) Decide that there is prima facie evidence of a professional misconduct (without or without IPS) and refer the complaint to be dealt with under the Determination by Consent (DBC) process.

The primary purpose of consideration by the CC is to determine whether disciplinary action should be taken against a barrister. The Committee considers only documentary evidence and none of the parties attend. Having considered the evidence, the CC may:

(a) dismiss the complaint (if the majority of the lay members present agree);

(b) dismiss the complaint but decide that the barrister should be given advice regarding his or her behaviour;

(c) decide that no further action should be taken;

(d) decide that the barrister may have provided an inadequate professional service and refer the complaint to an Adjudication Panel;

(e) decide that there is evidence of professional misconduct (with or without IPS) and refer the complaint to the Determination by Consent (DBC) process;

(f) decide that there is evidence of professional misconduct (with or without IPS) and refer the complaint to a Disciplinary Tribunal.

The complainant and the barrister are informed of the Committee's decision.

6.8 Adjudication Panels

If the Commissioner or the Committee decides that the barrister may have provided inadequate professional service to his or her client, they may refer the complaint to an Adjudication Panel to make the final decision. Their procedures are governed by the Adjudication Panel and Appeals Rules (Annexe P to the Code). The Panel will consider all the evidence and decide whether the barrister has provided inadequate professional service to his or her client, and if so, what should be done to remedy it. Remedies include ordering the barrister to:

- apologise;
- refund fees;
- pay compensation to the lay client of up to £15,000.

6.9 Disciplinary Tribunals

If the Complaints Committee decides that there is evidence of professional misconduct, it can refer the complaint to a Disciplinary Tribunal. A Disciplinary Tribunal is able to consider IPS, but only if the complaint also involves professional misconduct. Tribunal panels have either three or five members.

Three-person Tribunals normally include:

- a Queen's Counsel;
- a barrister member;
- a lay member.

Five-person Tribunals normally include:

- a judge;
- two barrister members;
- two lay members.

Disciplinary Tribunals are usually held in public. It is a formal process; parties may be legally represented and witnesses may be called to give evidence. Charges are put to the barrister in the form of a statement of offence, similar to those found on an indictment and the hearing follows a similar process to criminal trials.

The Tribunal will consider all the evidence and decide whether the barrister is guilty of professional misconduct, IPS, or both. If the charges of professional misconduct are proved, the Tribunal can impose sanctions, which could include any of the following:

- ordering the barrister to apologise;
- ordering the barrister to pay a fine of up to £15,000 to the BSB;
- suspending the barrister from practice;
- disbarring (striking off) the barrister.

There are other sanctions, and combinations of sanctions, that the Tribunal can impose. The Council of the Inns of Court has published comprehensive Sentencing Guidance, which can be found on the BSB's website.

6.10 Determination by consent

This is a new process (from 31 March 2009) that allows the Complaints Committee to make a final determination on complaints of professional misconduct and/or inadequate professional service with the barrister's consent. The Complaints Committee's sentencing powers are limited and it cannot suspend or disbar a barrister. This process is intended to conclude complaints more quickly and is primarily used for complaints raised by the BSB.

6.11 Written warnings/fines

From 1 October 2005, the definition of professional misconduct within the Code of Conduct changed. The basic premise that all infringements of the Code constitute professional misconduct remains but specific Code provisions, set out at para 901.1 of the Code, are now no longer treated as misconduct unless the breach is serious. A failure to comply with the relevant provisions of the Code may be classed as a serious due to the nature or extent of the failure, if there are multiple breaches of the Code, or if the barrister has previously failed to comply with the same or any other provision of the Code.

If the breach of the relevant Code provisions is not considered to be serious, a written warning or fine may be imposed for the breach. A written warning or fine does not amount to a finding of professional misconduct.

If a barrister is given two or more written warnings/fines in a three-year period, a further failure will automatically constitute professional misconduct even if the failure would not in itself amount to professional misconduct.

Administrative fines are most commonly applied for breaches of the practising requirements; however, they may be imposed in relation to external complaints.

6.12 Appeals

Findings of professional misconduct and subsequent sentences imposed by Disciplinary Tribunals are open to appeal under the Hearings Before the Visitors Rules 2005 (found at Annexe M to the Code). The Bar Standards Board may appeal against a finding or sentence of a Disciplinary Tribunal. Findings of inadequate professional service only may be appealed to an Appeal Panel under the Adjudication Panel and Appeal Rules (found at Annexe P to the Code).

6.13 Publication of findings and sentence

All findings of professional misconduct (whether made by a Disciplinary Tribunal or by the Complaints Committee with the barrister's consent) are published on the BSB's website and by the Inns of Court. Findings of professional misconduct are also included in the barrister's formal disciplinary record and will be disclosed if any organisation or a member of the public requests details of disciplinary action against the barrister. Adjudication Panel decisions are not published.

6.14 Legal Services Ombudsman

The Legal Services Ombudsman, who is neither a barrister nor a solicitor, is appointed under the Courts and Legal Services Act 1990 to oversee the handling of complaints against members of the legal professions. If complainants are dissatisfied with the way their complaints have been dealt with, they have the right to request the Ombudsman to examine the BSB's handling of the complaint and decide whether it was investigated fully and fairly. The Ombudsman then asks to see the BSB's file. If, after considering the matter, the Ombudsman thinks the complaint was not dealt with properly, the Ombudsman can recommend further action including reconsideration of the matter by the Commissioner or the CC, or the payment of compensation to the complainant by the Bar Standards Board.

Complaints have to be referred to the Legal Services Ombudsman within three months of the letter notifying the complainant of the Commissioner's, CC's, or Disciplinary Tribunal's decision. The Ombudsman has no power to investigate the substance of a complaint that has been decided by a court or by a Disciplinary Tribunal or where an appeal is being, or could still be, made against the CC's decision though the Ombudsman may look at the Bar Standards Board's handling of the matter.

6.15 Advice to counsel who are the subject of a complaint

The number of complaints received by the Bar Standards Board from lay clients and others has generally been going up over the last ten years and it is becoming more likely that, at one stage or another, a barrister, particularly if he or she specialises in criminal or family work, will be required to respond to a complaint. Counsel will normally be informed of this in a letter from the Bar Standards Board enclosing a copy of the material sent by the complainant to the Bar Standards Board. That letter will indicate that counsel's comments are required within three weeks of its date.

It is worth making clear that, at this stage, neither the Bar Standards Board nor the Commissioner has taken any view on the merits of the complaint but considers there may be some evidence of a breach of the Code; for this reason, counsel's comments (and also those of any relevant witnesses, if any) are sought so that a decision can be made as to whether there is prima facie evidence of a breach of the Code that warrants referral for further action. The majority of complaints are dismissed, however, the Legal Services Ombudsman oversees the working of the system and has power to refer matters back to the Commissioner or CC for reconsideration. Counsel should feel free to contact the Complaints Team to discuss the handling of the complaint, the procedure generally, or to seek advice. Clearly, the Complaints Team cannot advise on whether there is or is not a prima facie case of misconduct and cannot give a barrister advice on how to present his or her case. That said, the following questions arise frequently.

6.15.1 I am in a long case and cannot prepare my response adequately in time

The Complaints Team is usually able to agree reasonable extensions for good reasons over the telephone. It is essential that a barrister responds within the time stipulated on the correspondence from the Bar Standards Board; failure to do so constitutes a breach of the Code. Barristers should make every effort to produce their response as soon as is reasonably possible. The CC can and does take action against barristers who are unreasonably dilatory in preparing their replies.

6.15.2   This matter took place many months ago and I have little recollection of the case

There is no reason why counsel cannot approach his or her instructing solicitors for a copy of the original instructions in the case and such other details as he or she may need in order to refresh his or her memory. It is certainly open to him or her to seek an extension of time in order to obtain such documentation.

6.15.3   May I approach solicitors and other witnesses for their views?

There is no reason why counsel should not approach instructing solicitors, judges, etc., to provide statements or other information in support of counsel.

6.15.4   The client has issued/is likely to issue proceedings against me in negligence

Counsel should seek the advice of the Bar Mutual Indemnity Fund on how to deal with the complaint. If proceedings have been issued, normally consideration of such a complaint is adjourned until the matter has been considered by the civil courts. In any case if, on the advice of your insurers or for reasons of professional privilege, it is inappropriate for certain matters to be sent to the complainant which, nevertheless, it would be helpful for the Commissioner or the Committee to see, such material should be provided. If this is the case, counsel should make it clear which parts of the response should not be sent to the complainant. The Commissioner or the Committee will consider how to deal with such evidence.

6.15.5   What should I say in my response?

The content of the response to the complaint is very much a matter for the individual barrister to consider. There is nothing to stop him/her seeking advice from other colleagues, his/her head of chambers or a member of the Barristers' Complaints Advisory Service as to his/her reply. A good rule is to address specific allegations, providing relevant comment and material in support of the same.

6.15.6   How will it affect my application for silk/judicial appointment?

A complaint which has been dismissed is not at present required to be mentioned to the Judicial Appointments Commission (JAC) or QC Appointments in connection with any application for silk/judicial appointment and the Bar Standards Board will not disclose such a complaint, though the barrister may have to do so. The Bar Standards Board will, however, disclose any finding of professional misconduct or any unresolved complaint. The exact effect of such disclosure is for the JAC/QC Appointments to consider and will clearly depend on the circumstances of each case.

6.15.7   Should I be represented at Tribunals or panel hearings?

Most barristers choose to be represented before Disciplinary Tribunals and may approach other counsel direct in order to be so represented. There is a long tradition at the Bar of silks agreeing to act for no fee in such cases. It is, however, in each case, a matter for the individual concerned as to whom he or she seeks to approach and whether he or she needs to instruct solicitors to assist. The individual should bear in mind that he or she will not always get his or her costs back even after a successful defence at a Tribunal, although the Bar Mutual Indemnity Fund (BMIF) now provides indemnity cover for costs and expenses incurred in the defence of disciplinary proceedings. This cover is available for certain types of complaints with the prior consent of BMIF. However, some types of complaints are specifically excluded; these are usually complaints relating to a barrister's failure to comply with the relevant practising requirements or for complaints relating to a criminal charge/conviction.

6.15.8 Is there any organisation that can help me?

The Bar Council established the Barristers' Complaints Advisory Service (BCAS) which consists of about 40 barristers of all levels of seniority and types of practice who are prepared to advise barristers on how to deal with complaints. A list of members and details of the scheme are included in the material sent to barristers when they are asked for comments on complaints. The London Common Law and Commercial Bar Association operate a similar scheme. Additionally, the Bar Mutual Indemnity Fund has recently extended its cover to provide support to barristers responding to some types of complaint.

6.16 Interim suspension and fitness to practise

Additionally, the Bar Standards Board has rules to deal with cases where a barrister has been charged or convicted of a serious criminal offence (the Interim Suspension Rules) or is medically unfit to practise (the Fitness to Practise Rules). The Interim Suspension and Fitness to Practise rules essentially allow the Bar Standards Board to suspend a barrister from practice pending a final decision from a relevant panel/court, where applicable.

The Code provisions relevant to interim suspension are found at para 905(b) which requires a barrister to report to the Bar Standards Board if he or she is charged with an indictable offence or convicted of a relevant criminal offence (which covers everything apart from fixed penalty or parking offences). Depending on the type of offence, barristers who report themselves under these provisions may be considered under the Interim Suspension Rules found at Annexe N to the Code of Conduct. Where a barrister has been convicted of a criminal offence, these rules give the Bar Standards Board the power to suspend the barrister until a Disciplinary Tribunal deals with the complaint arising from the conviction. Where a barrister has been charged with a serious indictable offence, the rules give the Bar Standards Board the power to impose certain conditions on the barrister's practice until the offences for which he or she has been charged are considered by the court. The rules empower the Bar Standards Board to set early dates for hearings and to enable the barrister concerned to make appropriate representations.

The Fitness to Practice Rules are used where it comes to the attention of the Bar Standards Board that a barrister may be unfit for medical reasons to practise. The rules allow a Medical Panel to require a barrister to attend on an appointed medical adviser for an examination. On receipt of a report from the medical adviser, the panel can consider whether a barrister is unfit to practise by reason of incapacity (including addiction) and that a suspension is necessary for the protection of the public. The rules can be found at Annexe O to the Code of Conduct.

6.17 Future regulation of the Bar

The Legal Services Act 2007 reforms the way in which the Bar is regulated. In relation to complaints the most relevant provisions are the creation of a new independent Legal Ombudsman (under the supervision of the Office of Legal Complaints (OLC)) which has been given statutory responsibility for dealing with all consumer complaints about all legal professionals including barristers. The new service is due to come into operation in Autumn 2010 and at that stage the BSB will no longer be able to deal with consumer complaints (inadequate professional service). However, the BSB will continue to have full responsibility for considering complaints about misconduct and taking disciplinary action. As a result of the creation of the Legal Ombudsman, the 'Legal Services Ombudsman' will cease to exist at the end of March 2011.

The new Legal Ombudsman has wide statutory powers to compel barristers to co-operate with its investigations but only after the complaint has first been considered in accordance with chambers' complaints procedures. The intention is to try to settle most complaints by informal agreement but the Legal Ombudsman has the power to make binding determinations which can be enforced through the courts if necessary. The Legal Ombudsman will be able to order that a barrister pays up to £30,000 in total redress (covering compensation, return of fees, and other sums to redress the effects of the complaint). Failure to comply with Legal Ombudsman investigations and/or orders will constitute a breach of the BSB Code and leave barristers open to disciplinary action.

The changes under the Legal Services Act 2007 are substantial and all barristers should familiarise themselves with the new remit of the Legal Ombudsman and its statutory powers. Further information can be found on the BSB or Legal Ombudsman websites.

The BPTC, practice, and professional conduct

7.1 General introduction

This chapter will focus on professional conduct problems pertinent to the key skills you will undertake during the BPTC. It therefore concentrates on the following assessment areas: conference, advocacy, negotiation, opinion writing, and drafting.

Undoubtedly, the issues discussed will arise in practice. A sound understanding of these areas will ensure that when you are conducting a case you can identify these professional conduct points and, as a result, because you will be familiar with the fundamental tenets of the Code and of relevant statutory law (the Proceeds of Crime Act 2002), the matters can be properly dealt with at the earliest opportunity, no matter in what context the problem arises.

All the contributors to this chapter are experienced lecturers, academic authors, and subject coordinators at The City Law School and, as such, are not only drawing on their own experiences of practice in these areas, but upon the types of professional conduct points which you will inevitably be examined upon as you complete your skills assessments. Consequently, it is particularly useful not only to use this chapter as a central source of reference for professional conduct difficulties, but also as you go through the BPTC to take a note of your approach to the areas which have arisen in your small group discussions. You will then be in a position, as the course progresses, to check upon your development in handling these areas and how it compares to the advice set out below.

7.2 Conference skills

Conferences come in a variety of forms, most often involving the lay client, with or without the professional client in attendance. In some cases, for example when you are prosecuting on behalf of a body such as the CPS, Serious Fraud Office, or HM Revenue and Customs your conference may involve a number of other people. It would not be unusual, for example, to have a conference involving Crown prosecutors, police officers, and forensic scientists in a serious criminal case. At the other end of the range, you may be sent to the magistrates' court with little information and have to deal with finding your lay client and maybe even taking instructions through a wicket in a cell door or while standing in a corridor.

As stated in the *Conference Skills* manual, these problems often arise without warning and in situations where you cannot readily seek advice. This means that you have to have a sound understanding of the principles that guide a barrister in practice, as well as the spirit of the Code. There are common duties, which apply in all of these situations and they are discussed below.

7.2.1 Instructions from your lay client

With limited exceptions, the instructions that you receive from your lay client are to be treated in the strictest confidence. The Code states:

702 Whether or not the relation of counsel and client continues, a barrister must preserve the confidentiality of the lay client's affairs and must not without the prior consent of the lay client or as permitted by law lend or reveal the contents of the papers in any instructions to or communicate to any third person (other than another barrister, a pupil . . . or any other person who needs to know it for the performance of their duties) information which has been entrusted to him in confidence or use such information to the lay client's detriment or to his own or another client's advantage.

Clearly, you will expect to be able to use your client's instructions to cross-examine, draft statements of case, or even draft witness statements. This will necessarily involve disclosing those instructions and the client will have given you permission to do so. A problem may, however, arise when the client makes a disclosure to you in conference, which they do not want to have revealed. A number of common disclosures are considered below.

7.2.2 Whether to disclose?

7.2.2.1 Disclosure to the National Criminal Intelligence Service (NCIS) under the Proceeds of Crime Act 2002 (POCA)

In practice you must be aware of how the POCA 2002 impacts on your disclosure obligations to NCIS, when as counsel you are concerned in an arrangement which you know or suspect relates to the proceeds of crime. Further, since 1 March 2004, barristers have been included in the 'regulated sector' by virtue of the Money Laundering Regulations 2003. **Chapter 8** and the ***Conference Skills*** manual consider these issues, with which you must be fully familiar.

7.2.2.2 Confessions

Every barrister has been asked by someone, 'how can you represent someone when you know that they are guilty?' The answer that you may have given is that you are not the judge or a juror and if your client says that they are not guilty then those are the instructions you follow in presenting their case. So far, so good. But what happens if the client actually tells you that they did commit the offence?

Using a criminal case as an example and assuming that the client's instructions to date have been that they want to plead not guilty, what do you do when they appear to admit to you in conference that they did commit the offence? In the first place, do not panic. Recognise that there is a potential problem and continue your questioning to explore exactly what the client is saying—the client is not a lawyer and may not appreciate what defences are available. If your questioning reveals that, without doubt, the client has told you that they do not have a defence, then you will need to advise on this clearly and advise that the best course of action would be to plead guilty and make the most of the mitigation.

If the client tells you that, nonetheless, they wish to continue to plead not guilty, you will need to consider your duty to the court. The Code expresses it as follows:

302   A barrister has an overriding duty to the Court to act with independence in the interests of justice: he must assist the Court in the administration of justice and must not deceive or knowingly or recklessly mislead the Court.

You may not make representations to the court that you know to be untrue—this would involve you in misleading the court. You will need to explain this to the client. The client may well be concerned that this 'overriding' duty means that you will have to reveal their guilt to the court. You may well be concerned that your duty to the court appears to clash with your duty of confidentiality to your client.

The correct approach is that, first of all, you cannot reveal the client's instructions without the client's permission. However, you equally cannot put forward any positive case that they are not guilty as this would be knowingly misleading the court. You may, however, still test the prosecution evidence in cross-examination. This means that you can explore with a witness how reliable their evidence is, but you cannot put any positive case to the witness on behalf of your client. For example, if the issue were identification you might well question a witness about the conditions in which the identification was made, but, if your instructions are that the identification was correct, then you cannot put to the witness that they are mistaken in that identification. Practically, it can make it extremely difficult to run a successful case or to make any clear closing speech. You will have to explain all of this to the client and also remind them of the potential advantages of pleading guilty in terms of sentencing, reiterating your advice to plead guilty. If the client chooses to ignore that advice, as they are entitled to do, you may be wise to have the client endorse your brief to say that you have advised them of the consequences of their choice.

7.2.2.3   Information damaging to your client's case

Your lay client may reveal information in conference, which would be damaging to their case. For example, the client discloses that they have previous convictions which the CPS does not seem to know about, and the client wants to keep those secret at trial. In such a situation, you should advise the client that you have a duty of confidentiality and that, without their express permission, you cannot disclose the previous convictions to the court. However, you should also remind yourself that you have a duty not to mislead the court. While you do not have to volunteer information which is potentially damaging to your client's case, if the judge were to ask you, for instance, whether your client wanted a good character direction in the summing up, then you must not mislead the court when answering the question.

In your conference, you would have to advise your client that you may be asked a direct question by the judge and would need to ask whether they would allow you to disclose the previous convictions in such a situation. If the client says no, then when you are in court you would have to use a form of words such as "Your Honour, I cannot assist the court". The judge and prosecutor will easily work out why that is and the prosecutor will probably take the opportunity to have the client's record rechecked by police. You will certainly not get a good character direction. The effect, therefore, is the same as if you had revealed the previous convictions—but without the credit to your client of 'coming clean'. You should advise of this in your conference and may suggest that they would gain credit for being so honest.

The Bar Standards Board has offered guidance to barristers on what they can and cannot say in such situations. The full text is available on the Bar Standards Board's website (<http://www.barstandardsboard.org.uk>) (Standards and Guidance/BSB Guidance/Duty to disclose previous convictions), but some key points are extracted below:

In circumstances where counsel is aware of previous convictions, regardless of the nature of the case or potential sentence, counsel should give the defendant clear advice as to all the options. He should:

- Inform the defendant that the information as to the previous conviction will remain confidential unless the client specifically waives privilege;
- Inform the defendant that whilst the information remains confidential, he will be restricted in what he can say in mitigation;
- Advise the defendant that nothing can be said as to the defendant's record which expressly or impliedly adopts the position as outlined by the prosecution and in particular, that nothing can be said as to:

  (a) the absence of convictions of the type or gravity of the undisclosed conviction;

  (b) a period of time as being free from convictions if the undisclosed conviction occurred during that period;

  (c) the absence of a particular sentence or disposal in the defendant's antecedents if such sentence or disposal was in fact imposed in respect of the undisclosed conviction; or

  (d) an apparently good character of the defendant.

- Specifically advise the defendant as to the nature of the sentencing exercise if the court became aware of the undisclosed conviction, whether by virtue of the defendant's voluntary disclosure or by some other means.
- Advise the defendant as to the possibility of the prosecution subsequently discovering the undisclosed conviction.
- Advise of the real possibility that failure of counsel to refer to the defendant's antecedents would not go unnoticed by experienced prosecution counsel or judge. This could lead to an adjournment, to the matter being relisted for alteration of the sentence, or to a reference by the Attorney General under section 36 of the Criminal Justice Act 1988.

The defendant should be told that the choice as to what course to adopt is his, but that if he decides to reveal the qualifying conviction, he would be entitled to expect significant credit from the court.

The Bar Council's guidance notes also make clear that this would not be an appropriate situation for counsel to withdraw.

7.2.2.4 Prosecutors

The Criminal Procedure and Investigations Act 1996 creates a positive duty on prosecutors to disclose information which undermines the Crown's case or which is helpful to the defendant's. Section 9 of the 1996 Act makes this a continuing duty to review information. The Code for Crown Prosecutors makes this clear:

2.2 It is the duty of prosecutors to review, to advise on and to prosecute cases or to offer an appropriate out-of-court disposal to the offender. Prosecutors must ensure that the law is properly applied; that all relevant evidence is put before the court; and that obligations of disclosure are complied with, in accordance with the principles set out in this Code.

This duty to disclose damaging information illustrates the different approaches that defending and prosecuting counsel are obliged to take. The Code for Crown Prosecutors states clearly that, the Prosecutor should not be primarily motivated by winning the case.

2.4 Prosecutors must always act in the interests of justice and not solely for the purpose of obtaining a conviction.

As prosecutor, if some piece of information (a disciplinary finding against a police officer, for example) were to come to light during a conference, your advice would have to be that it must be disclosed—even though it might expose your witness to cross-examination.

7.2.2.5   Civil cases

In civil matters, counsel is bound by the same duty of confidentiality to the lay client and the duty not to mislead the court. See further the *Civil Litigation* manual. However, in fast-track and multi-track cases, a party is required to disclose any documents upon which they rely and documents which adversely affect their own or another party's case or which support another party's case. This means that if counsel were told in conference about a relevant document, which had not been disclosed, he or she would have to advise the client to disclose it to the other party. If the client refused, then counsel would have to advise that he or she could not continue to act for the client unless that disclosure were made. The Code of Conduct deals with this situation as follows:

608   A barrister must cease to act and if he is a self-employed barrister must return any instructions: . . .

> (e) if having become aware during the course of a case of the existence of a document which should have been but has not been disclosed on discovery the client fails forthwith to disclose it.

Before withdrawing from the case, counsel is obliged to consider whether he or she is prejudicing the client by the timing of that withdrawal. He or she is also obliged to explain why it is necessary to withdraw from the case. The Code says:

610   A barrister must not:

> (a) cease to act or return instructions without having first explained to the client his reasons for doing so;
>
> [. . .]
>
> (d) except as provided in paragraph 608 return any instructions or withdraw from a case in such a way or in such circumstances that the client may be unable to find other legal assistance in time to prevent prejudice being suffered by the client.

However, the wording of para 610 clearly suggests that the client's failure to make proper disclosure will be an overriding consideration—even if the revelation occurs during a trial. For guidance on disclosure of illegally obtained evidence, refer to the Bar Council's website, 'Guidance on Illegally Obtained Evidence in Civil and Family Proceedings'.

7.2.2.6   Public funding

It may well be that your lay client has the benefit of public funding through the Legal Services Commission (LSC). This adds another dimension to your duties in conference, as the Code says that a barrister has a duty to the LSC in the following terms:

303   A barrister:

> [. . .]
>
> (c) when supplying legal services funded by the Legal Services Commission as part of the Community Legal Service or the Criminal Defence Service owes his primary duty to the lay client subject only to compliance with paragraph 304.

304   A barrister who supplies legal services funded by the Legal Services Commission as part of the Community Legal Service or the Criminal Defence Service must in connection with the supply of such services comply with any duty imposed on him by or under the Access to Justice Act

1999 or any regulations or code in effect under that Act and in particular with the duties set out in Annexe E.

Annexe E deals with counsel's obligations when drafting opinions on the suitability of cases for public funding by the LSC. At para 20, this states that:

...counsel acting under a funding certificate is under a duty to bring to the attention of the Commission any matter which might affect the client's entitlement to funding, or the terms of his or her certificate, at whatever stage of the proceedings that might occur.

In criminal matters, there is a similar duty to report abuse of the system. The relevant regulations under the Access to Justice Act 1999 are contained within the Criminal Defence Service (General) (No. 2) Regulations 2001 (SI 2001 No. 1437). This provides:

24 Notwithstanding the relationship between or rights of a representative and client or any privilege arising out of such relationship, where the representative for an applicant or assisted person knows or suspects that that person:

(a) has intentionally failed to comply with any provision of regulations made under the Act concerning the information to be furnished by him; or

(b) in furnishing such information has knowingly made a false statement or false representation the representative shall immediately report the circumstances to the Commission.

If your publicly funded lay client revealed facts in conference, which would affect this entitlement, you would have to advise them to pass the correct information to the LSC immediately. If the client refused to do this, then you would have to explain that you could not continue to act:

608 A barrister must cease to act and if he is a self-employed barrister must return any instructions: . . .

(c) if in any case funded by the Legal Services Commission as part of the Community Legal Service or Criminal Defence Service it has become apparent to him that such funding has been wrongly obtained by false or inaccurate information and action to remedy the situation is not immediately taken by the client;

(d) if the client refuses to authorise him to make some disclosure to the Court which his duty to the Court requires him to make . . .

If you are forced to withdraw, para 610(a) of the Code obliges you to explain to your lay client why you are doing so, and, as far as possible, not to leave your client in a position where he or she will suffer prejudice (para 610(d)). However, as noted above, the wording of the Code makes clear that counsel cannot in any circumstances continue to act when he or she believes that one of the conditions within para 608 of the Code applies.

7.2.2.7 Sensitive information

The client may reveal information in conference that they wish to be kept confidential, but which you believe would assist either at trial or in mitigation. For example, they may be able to assist the police by revealing the names of others involved in the same offence. This would assist the mitigation considerably. The duty of confidentiality to the client means that without his or her express permission you cannot reveal that information—even if you believe that it is in the client's interests to do so. You should advise clearly on how you believe that revealing the relevant information would assist them. However, if your client is clear that they will not reveal it, remember that it is your client's case and not yours. Only your client can say what is in their 'best interests', after having been presented with the full picture by you.

In these circumstances, you may wish to invite the client to endorse your brief to say that you have advised him or her about the consequences of not revealing the relevant information and that he or she has nonetheless decided not to do so. This should protect you from any complaint that he or she might make about your advice if, for example, your client receives a more serious sentence than he or she was expecting. However, if the brief is endorsed great care should be taken so that the wording does not overtly refer to sensitive matters, which the client has chosen not to reveal. Any documentation revealing a client's decision to assist the police should be treated with the highest degree of confidentiality.

7.2.3   The professional client

As a general rule, you would expect your solicitor (or the firm's representative) to attend a conference between you and a lay client. They will take notes, record action points and, depending on how involved they are with the case, participate in talking to the lay client and clarifying points. The solicitor also acts as a witness to what is discussed. There may be times when you do not have this luxury—for example, in your early cases where you may meet the client for the first time at court and conduct your conference then and there. Solicitors, mindful of costs, may also not attend some court hearings simply to keep costs down for their clients or funding may not have been granted for a solicitor to attend. This raises a number of professional conduct issues:

706   A self-employed barrister who is instructed by a professional client should not conduct a case in Court in the absence of his professional client or a representative of his professional client unless the Court rules that it is appropriate or he is satisfied that the interests of the lay client and the interests of justice will not be prejudiced.

The Code does not make it mandatory that the professional client attends with you at court—indeed he or she will rarely attend at the magistrates' court. You will have to decide whether your lay client risks being prejudiced by this absence. Take a careful note of your instructions from your client and be prepared to explain to the client, and, if necessary, the judge, why the solicitor is not there. The client may be unhappy that the solicitor (perhaps someone who deals with them regularly, or the only lawyer they believe is dealing with the case) is not there at court. If the professional client is absent it will help to build your lay client's confidence if you can demonstrate your knowledge of the case and your skill in conference and as an advocate.

7.2.4   Witnesses

It is not prohibited for a barrister to meet and speak to witnesses. Extreme caution is, however, needed to avoid any suggestion of coaching witnesses. The Code says:

705   A barrister must not:

   (a) rehearse, practise or coach a witness in relation to his evidence;

You must, of course, exercise care not to coach your lay client or suggest how the evidence should be given at any time. This caution extends to all witnesses of fact in a case. Remember also that interviewing witnesses includes not only sitting down in an interview room, but also chatting in the corridor or over a cup of coffee about the case. You need to be conscious of what you say about the case at all times. Clear guidance is given regarding counsel's obligations in respect of contact with witnesses in Pt 6 of the Written Standards for the Conduct of Professional Work. This is reproduced in **Appendix 1**, Section 3, in this manual, and it is important that you are fully familiar with that guidance. See also the 'Guidance on Witness Preparation' available from the Bar Standards Board's website.

You may have a conference, which involves an expert witness or someone giving character evidence on your client's behalf. The same rules apply—that you are not to seek to influence the way that the witness gives their evidence (save by your expertise in questioning in court). This does not prevent you from asking experts questions about matters within their expertise, or their view on the evidence given by other experts, only your suggesting the answers that they should give.

If a witness of fact attends court in a criminal matter and wants to give evidence on behalf of the defendant, then you will want to know what he or she will say. If you have no proof from the witness, and if you have a professional client in attendance, then you will be able to leave it to him or her to take a proof from the witness. If you are alone, then this leaves you in a more difficult position.

Note that the previous prohibition on barristers attending at police stations to advise a suspect or interviewee has now been lifted. See Code, para 401(b)(iv). The Code says that this may be permissible if necessary:

707   A self-employed barrister who attends Court in order to conduct a case in circumstances where no professional client or representative of a professional client is present may if necessary interview witnesses and take proofs of evidence.

This situation is most likely to arise in the magistrates' court, where you may well be representing your client without your professional client in attendance. As the professional client will more often be in attendance at the Crown Court, it will less frequently be necessary to take a proof or interview witnesses in such matters.

You will have to take care not to lead the witness or coach them in any way. If the witness asks you what they should say, then your advice must be for them to tell the truth. You would be unwise to offer any more information than that. If you take a note of what the witness says to you, you may wish to have the witness sign it as an accurate record of what he or she told you.

At court, you will never speak to or contact a witness while he or she is giving evidence, save by asking questions in examination-in-chief or cross-examination. The Code expressly prohibits such contact:

705   A barrister must not: . . .

  (a) except with the consent of the representative for the opposing side or of the Court, communicate directly or indirectly about a case with any witness, whether or not the witness is his lay client, once that witness has begun to give evidence until the evidence of that witness has been concluded.

Clearly this prohibition extends even to your client—for example, if the case is adjourned overnight while your client is still giving evidence, you will not speak to him or her until the next day, after he or she has finished his or her evidence. If this situation is likely to arise, then you will need to explain this to your client before he or she goes into the witness box. If you are seen to be speaking to him or her (even if you are not discussing the evidence), it may appear that you are coaching your client and you can expect opposing counsel to protest to the judge in the strongest terms.

7.2.5   Fair treatment

It should come as no surprise that the Code of Conduct forbids you to discriminate in the following terms:

305.1   A barrister must not in relation to any other person (including a client or another barrister or a pupil or an employee or a student member of an Inn of Court) discriminate directly or indirectly because of race, colour, ethnic or national origin, nationality, citizenship, sex, sexual orientation, marital status, disability, age, religion or belief.

What this means in terms of conference skills is that you must be sensitive to the differing needs of your lay client. The range of issues this may cover is necessarily wide. For example, you may be unfamiliar with the naming system of your client's culture, or you may find that your client has never learned to read—you may find his or her lifestyle or personal views unattractive. Of course, whether or not you like your client or the way that your client lives their life—or any other of your personal views—must not affect your dedication to conducting their case as effectively as possible. Equally, if you are unsure how to pronounce your client's name or how to address him or her, use your common sense and show your client the courtesy of asking.

Fair treatment goes beyond these obvious points. If your client could not read, for example, it would be up to you to do all you could to enable him or her to take a full part in proceedings. In consultation with your client, you would seek to find ways of overcoming that problem. Ignoring the problem would amount to discrimination.

Most importantly, your duty not to discriminate requires you to be aware of what discrimination is and the wide variety of circumstances where you might be found to be discriminating inappropriately. The examples above are merely the tip of the iceberg. It is recognising that there is or may be an issue, which is vital to dealing with a situation correctly. Once you know that there is an issue, you will then have to use your common sense and your sense of what is right, within the spirit of the Code, to deal with it depending on the individual circumstances. Remember, if you are in doubt, you can always consult another member of chambers or, in emergencies, the Bar Council's adviser on professional conduct problems.

7.2.6   What the lay client is entitled to expect from you

Finally, remember that your duty to the lay client includes giving full and accurate advice to them on all matters. This involves you in applying the spirit of the Code, as well as good business sense. Your function is to give information to your client on options and consequences, as well as your opinion on which line of action they should pursue and why. This enables your client to exercise informed choice. It is never your function to make choices for your client or to force them to do what you want.

Thinking back, for example, to the client who has information on others involved in his or her offending. Your duty to your client is to advise them on what might be done with that information, the consequences of what they decide to do and also your opinion on the best course of action to pursue. You will give your client the information that they need to make a fully informed decision. Your opinion on the best course of action may be to reveal this information to the judge so that your client can receive maximum credit when being sentenced. You will explain to your client why you think that this best serves their interests, but make clear that the final decision is theirs to make. If you have done your job in fully informing your client about the potential choices, then they are ideally placed to make a decision. If the client decides not to follow your advice and you feel that this is a mistake, you may wish to have your client endorse your brief stating that he or she understands the consequences of the choice and that he or she still wishes to proceed in this way (taking care if sensitive information is involved). As long as your client's choice does not involve your having to act unethically, then you will have to run the case as they instruct. It is, after all, your client's case.

Many trainee barristers seem to believe that the lay client's function is simply to listen respectfully to counsel's wise pronouncements, rather than play an active part in the conference. This is not correct. You are providing a service for which you are being paid and the lay client is entitled to expect professionalism and courtesy at all times rather than irritation or condescension. Remember that the most important person in any conference is the lay client.

7.3 Advocacy skills

The role of an advocate in court is very demanding and you will soon find yourself in challenging and highly stressful situations. Throughout, however, your conduct must meet the rightly demanding standards of the profession. If you do so, you will avoid adverse criticism and know that you have acted to the best of your abilities in the interest of your client. For a recent example of unprofessional behaviour, see *Boodram v State of Trinidad and Tobago* [2002] 1 Cr App R 12. In that case defence counsel conducting a trial for murder had failed to realise that it was in fact a retrial. This was described as 'the worst case of the failure of counsel to carry out his duties in a criminal case that their lordships have come across' (para 40).

This section will help you to identify the main duties of the advocate; it is not exhaustive and should be read in the context of the general guidance offered in the rest of this manual. Many of the rules of professional conduct that are relevant to courtroom advocacy are longstanding; however, the precise wording of the rules and duties do change from time to time to adapt to the changing circumstances of modern life. It is therefore vital that you are up to date with any amendments to the rules. A full and up-to-date version of the Code is available on the Bar Standards Board's website <http://www .barstandardsboard.org.uk>.

In the context of advocacy, the main areas of the Code for BPTC students to concentrate on are:

(a) Part III which contains the Fundamental Principles, including the duty not to act dishonestly or bring the profession into disrepute and the particular duties to the court and to act in the best interests of the client. It also includes the duties to the Legal Services Commission and not to discriminate on grounds of race, sex, and so forth, and the duties which safeguard a barrister's independence.

(b) Part VII which sets out the duties of barristers when conducting work including the general duties to act courteously and promptly, the duty of confidentiality, duties where there is a conflict between clients, duties when drafting documents and appearing in court, the rules concerning contact with witnesses, media comment, and advertising.

One of the main concerns for practising barristers is striking the balance between the overriding duty to the court and promoting the client's case:

(a) A barrister has an overriding duty to the court to act with independence in the interests of justice: he must assist the court in the administration of justice and must not deceive or knowingly or recklessly mislead the court (Code para 302).

(b) A barrister must promote and protect fearlessly and by all proper and lawful means the lay client's best interests and do so without regard to his own interests or to any consequences to himself or to any other person (including any professional client or other intermediary or another barrister) (Code para 303(a)).

See *R v McFadden* (1976) 62 Cr App R 187, where James LJ at page 190 offered the following stark observation on the competing considerations of duty to the court and the status of the Bar Council's guidance.

The Bar Council issues statements from time to time to give guidance to the profession in matters of etiquette and procedure. A barrister who conforms to the Council's rulings knows that he cannot be committing an offence against professional discipline. But such statements, although they have strong persuasive force, do not bind courts. If therefore a judge requires a barrister to do, or refrain from doing, something in the course of a case, the barrister may protest and may cite any relevant ruling of the Bar Council, but since the judge is the final authority in his own court, if counsel's protest is unavailing, he must either withdraw or comply with the ruling or look for redress in a higher court.

In this section we will discuss some of the duties that should help to inform your decision about how to act in the face of such significant competing interests. Before doing so you will be advised to know where else you can find guidance on your duties and conduct in court.

7.3.1 Guidance on duties and conduct in court

7.3.1.1 The Crown Prosecutors' Code

The Crown Prosecution Service (CPS) is a public service for England and Wales headed by the Director of Public Prosecutions (DPP) and is answerable to Parliament through the Attorney General. While the police are responsible for investigating crime, the CPS is the public prosecutor; however, it cooperates closely with the police while remaining independent of them.

The DPP is empowered under s 10 of the Prosecution of Offences Act 1985, to give guidance on the general principles to be applied when making decisions about prosecutions and this is the main function of the Code for Crown Prosecutors. For the purposes of this Code, the term 'prosecutors' is used to describe members of the prosecution service who are designated as Crown Prosecutors; prosecutors who are members of the RCPO; Associate Prosecutors who are designated under s 7A of the Prosecution of Offences Act 1985 and who exercise their powers in accordance with the instructions issued by the DPP; and other members of the RCPO who are designated by the DPP in his capacity as the Director of the Revenue and Customs Prosecutions under s 39 of the Commissioners for Revenue and Customs Act 2005.

The Code sets out the basic principles that Crown prosecutors should follow when they make case decisions. The Code helps the Crown Prosecution Service to play its part in making sure that justice is done. It contains information that is important to police officers and others who work in the criminal justice system and to the general public. The Code is also designed to make sure that everyone knows the principles that the Crown Prosecution Service applies when carrying out its work. By applying the same principles, everyone involved in the system is helping to treat victims fairly and to prosecute fairly but effectively.

The Code is a public document. It is available on the CPS website: <http://www.cps .gov.uk>. Translations into other languages are available, as are audio and Braille copies.

7.3.1.2   Guidance for prosecuting counsel

In the mid-nineteenth century, Crompton J said that prosecuting counsel 'are to regard themselves as ministers of justice, and not to struggle for a conviction' (*R v Puddick* (1865) 4 F & F 497). Nearly a century and a half later the Court of Appeal repeated the concept of ministers of justice in *R v Gonez* [1999] All ER (D) 674. The role of the prosecuting counsel was also the focus of the Farquharson Committee in 1986. It concluded that such counsel have wide duties to the court and the public at large. Prosecuting counsel, it said, are under a duty to present cases for the prosecution fairly to the jury and that they have a greater independence of those instructing them than that enjoyed by other counsel. Prosecuting counsel should not strive unfairly to obtain convictions; they must not press a case beyond the limits that the evidence permits. The Written Standards for the Conduct of Professional Work, appended to the Bar's Code of Conduct at para 10.6 remind prosecuting counsel at all times to have regard to the Farquharson Committee report. Further and more detailed discussion of the conclusions of the committee can be found in *Blackstone's Criminal Practice*, 2010, para D15.4ff. Additionally, the Farquharson guidelines have recently been produced and although the principles established by the Farquharson Committee will continue to apply, this new guidance can be found on the CPS website.

Paragraph 10 of the Written Standards of the Bar's Code of Conduct sets out the responsibilities of prosecuting counsel in detail. These standards and principles apply as appropriate to all practising barristers, whether in independent practice or employed and whether appearing as counsel in any given case or exercising any other professional capacity in connection with it (para 10A). Paragraph 10.1 encapsulates the spirit of Mr Justice Crompton's statement:

Prosecuting counsel should not attempt to obtain a conviction by all means at his command. He should not regard himself as appearing for any party. He should lay before the Court fairly and impartially the whole of the facts which comprise the case for the prosecution and should assist the Court on all matters of law applicable to the case.

For example, a prosecutor should take special care not to prejudice the defendant's trial by engendering inappropriate amounts of sympathy for the alleged victim of an assault.

7.3.1.3   Equal Treatment Bench Book

When working as an advocate in court you will have your ability to deal with people regularly tested. One of the keys to being effective in court is to know and understand the people you deal with and address. The trial process rests on the presumption that everyone in court has an ability to follow and understand oral communication and nowhere is this presumption more significant than in the oral testimony of the witnesses. The advocates and the judge will all have highly developed skills in questioning witnesses, analysing their evidence, and communicating their arguments to the jury. If at any point the witnesses or jury fail to comprehend the questions, answers, or arguments (i.e., the oral communications) the trial system begins to fail justice. The Judicial Studies Board's Equal Treatment Bench Book (ETBB) has identified what it labels 'cross-cultural misunderstanding' as one way in which oral communication can fail the justice system. Guidance is offered on all aspects of interpersonal communication in a multicultural and multi-faith society. Not only is helpful guidance offered on technical matters such as oaths and affirmations but also on interpreting how people answer questions and display respect in court. In addition there are sections on disability, gender, and sexuality. The full text of the ETBB is available on the website: <http://www.jsboard.co.uk>.

7.3.2   Advocacy and professional conduct

7.3.2.1   General

In the context of civil practice it has been said that a barrister has complete authority over the conduct of litigation and all that is incidental to it, but not over matters which are collateral to the case: *Swinfen v Lord Chelmsford* (1860) 5 Hurl & N 890. Lord Esher MR stated (at 143) in *Matthews v Munster* (1888) LR 20 QBD 141:

> When the client has requested counsel to act as his advocate . . . he thereby represents to the other side that counsel is to act for him in the usual course, and he must be bound by that representation so long as it continues . . . The request does not mean that counsel is to act in any other character than that of advocate or to do any other act than such as an advocate usually does. The duty of counsel is to advise his client out of court and to act for him in court, and until his authority is withdrawn he has, with regard to all matters that properly relate to the conduct of the case, unlimited power to do that which is best for his client.

Under the Civil Procedure Rules 1998, r 1.3, the parties are required to help the court to further the overriding objective, that is, to enable the court to deal with cases justly. The Access to Justice Act 1999, s 42, has inserted a new provision into the Courts and Legal Services Act 1990, s 27 (rights of audience), that any person exercising a right of audience before any court has a duty to the court to act with independence in the interests of justice and that duty shall override any other obligation with which it is inconsistent (other than an obligation under the criminal law). Should you receive instructions that are in conflict with these requirements you may find yourself to be professionally embarrassed and need to withdraw from the case.

As a barrister, you have a duty to the court to ensure that it is informed of all relevant decisions and legislative provisions of which you are aware whether they are favourable or unfavourable to the contention which you are arguing (Code para 708(c)). Similarly, any procedural irregularity must be brought to the court's attention during the hearing—you must resist the temptation to reserve the matter for an appeal (Code para 708(d)). These provisions are reiterated in the Written Standards at para 5.10(c).

7.3.3   Submissions

It is well known that counsel should not give evidence personally in court. However, inadvertent attempts to do so do occur. You should avoid statements that personalise your submissions, so avoid 'I think', 'I feel', and 'I believe'. If you remember that your role in court is to speak on behalf of your client and the judge will only accept your submissions you should be able to avoid this pitfall.

Similarly, when appearing in a case you should maintain a professional detachment. Do not attempt to impose your own personality onto the application. So, avoid expressions of personal opinion, do not thank judges for administering justice in your client's favour and likewise, resist the temptation to express disappointment when they do not! (In any event the hearing may not be the end of the matter—are there meritorious grounds of appeal?) You should also avoid visible or audible reactions to your opponent's case as it is presented in court—wait until you have an opportunity to reply. And if the judge's questions are inconvenient or unhelpful to your case maintain a poker face and attempt to turn your answer to your client's advantage.

The following provisions of the Code are of direct relevance to submissions and applications, but most of them equally apply to trial advocacy. Remember that these duties apply to both oral advocacy and written advocacy (for example skeleton arguments).

(a) Preservation of *confidentiality* of lay client's affairs (para 702). Clients sometimes give their lawyers information on the understanding that it will not be communicated to others—including the court. Occasionally this information would be of assistance to their case. In such circumstances you must get the lay client's express permission to disclose the fact. It is often wise to have the client endorse your brief to confirm his or her permission—this is particularly advisable if the professional client is not present. If the court or an opponent attempts to draw you on a point that your client has identified as confidential, you must still respect your client's wishes. Neither the court nor an opponent is in a position to require you to make a disclosure, though of course both are at liberty to draw their own conclusions. In civil proceedings the court can use its wide powers to stay proceedings until the information is disclosed. This may be a wholly consistent manoeuvre by the judge in order to meet the overriding objective of the rules of enabling the court to deal with cases justly; see CPR, r 1.1.

(b) Counsel must not deceive or knowingly or recklessly *mislead* the court (para 302). Fortunately, few barristers would countenance the former, but the latter can occur often through poor preparation and sheer carelessness. Note that recklessness will leave you on the wrong side of the line—hence the importance of finding adequate time for thorough preparation, marking your brief in such a way that you can find relevant facts readily and giving yourself adequate time to answer questions. If your brief or the pre-hearing client conference is unable to supply the answer do not speculate as to what it might be. The court will be sympathetic that you are not in possession of all the facts in a case (so long as you are not personally at fault) especially at the interim stage.

(c) A barrister must not adduce *evidence* obtained otherwise than from or through the client or devise facts which will assist the lay client's case (para 708(e)).

(d) A barrister must not devise facts which will assist in advancing his lay client's case (Written Standards para 5.8).

This follows on from what has just been said about avoiding speculation and filling in gaps. It also reminds us that a barrister cannot (in the ordinary run of events) give evidence in open court. (For the extraordinary circumstances when it is appropriate for counsel to give evidence, see the Court of Appeal's guidance to the Bar Council and Law Society in *R v Jaquith* [1989] Crim LR 563.) While you should do everything in your legitimate powers to promote the cause of your client, there are limits—and this is one of the most significant.

7.3.3.1 Full and frank disclosure

In civil applications that are without notice there is a duty to give full and frank disclosure. This means that adverse facts and potential arguments that the other side either does intend to raise or may raise should be brought to the attention of the judge. The Civil Procedure Rules require parties to address in their evidence 'all material facts of which the court should be made aware' (PD 25, para 3.3). However, it is not sufficient to assume that the judge is aware of an adverse fact simply because it is in the witness statement or your skeleton argument. You have a duty to draw the court's attention to such facts orally. This is a continuing duty, so if something material subsequently comes to light before the return date, the court must be informed of it. Failure to disclose will usually result in an order being set aside as of right and would additionally be a breach of the Code of Conduct, in particular the duty not to mislead the court (para 302).

7.3.4   Trial advocacy

Before conducting—indeed before planning—a trial you need to be aware of the limits placed on contact with witnesses within the Code. Basically witness coaching is not permitted in England and Wales (see para 705(a) and the 'Guidance on Witness Preparation'). In most cases the solicitor is the main conduit for instructions and can relay important messages to the lay client. These and other points that are relevant to client conferences are dealt with in **7.2** above and discussed at length in the *Conference Skills* manual (**Chapter 9**).

The special guidance for prosecuting counsel has been discussed, that for defence counsel is given in the Written Standards at para 11. The essence of this guidance is found at para 11.1:

When defending a client on a criminal charge, a barrister must endeavour to protect his client from conviction except by a competent tribunal and upon legally admissible evidence sufficient to support a conviction for the offence charged.

The rest of para 11 and the following paragraph on confessions of guilt should be read carefully before preparing the case, making any contact with the prosecutor, offering advice to clients in conference and attending court to represent them.

Attendance of counsel at court is considered in para 15 of the Written Standards. These should be read with care, as some of the guidance is complex. However, one point is clear:

Defence counsel should ensure that the defendant is never left unrepresented at any stage of his trial.

(Written Standards para 15.2.1)

7.3.4.1   Formulating a theory of the case and witness handling

One of the most important aspects of trial preparation is the theory of the case—a reasoned explanation of your side's case that will form the basis of your closing speech. Your sources are the uncontested evidence in the case and your client's version of the matters that are in issue. Naturally, there are professional conduct considerations attached to the formulation of case theories. First and foremost of these is the duty to limit your theory to the facts in the case (according to your client's instructions and those facts that are not in issue) and any reasonable inferences that can be drawn from those facts. There are special limits for prosecutors, as has been set out previously under para 10.1 of the Written Standards.

On the other hand a defence barrister:

Must not suggest that a victim, witness or other person is guilty of crime, fraud or misconduct or make any defamatory aspersion on the conduct of any other person or attribute to another person the crime or conduct of which his lay client is accused unless such allegations go to a matter in issue (including the credibility of the witness) which is material to his lay client's case and which appear to him to be supported by reasonable grounds.

(Code of Conduct para 708(j) and Written Standards para 5.10(h))

When appearing for either the defence or prosecution you:

Must not make statements or ask questions which are merely scandalous or intended or calculated only to vilify insult or annoy either a witness or some other person;

(Code of Conduct para 708(g) and Written Standards para 5.10(e))

Must if possible avoid the naming in open Court of third parties whose character would thereby be impugned;

(Code of Conduct para 708(h) and Written Standards para 5.10(f))

With these very significant caveats, your theory of the case will lead you to formulate a short explanation of why the events took place and why your client's version of the events is the preferable one. Not only will this form the basis of your closing speech but it will also suggest themes that will run through your examination of your own witnesses and cross-examination of those of your opponent. Thus checking that your theory does not offend any of the rules of professional conduct is an essential stage in its formulation.

You will have to exercise personal judgement upon the substance and purpose of questions asked and statements made, since you are personally responsible for the conduct and presentation of your case. See Code of Conduct para 708(a) and Written Standards para 5.10(a). This is in keeping with para 306 of the Code of Conduct:

A barrister is individually and personally responsible for his own conduct and for his professional work: he must exercise his own personal judgement in all his professional activities.

7.3.4.2 Cross-examination

After the other side has brought out evidence from its witness in chief examination, or in civil trials has tendered the witness statement as evidence, you are given the opportunity to question that witness to advance your client's case. You can achieve this in ways that are positive or negative:

Positively:

- seek or emphasise agreement between your client's case and what this witness has just said or can say;
- elicit additional information from the witness that did not come out in examination-in-chief.

Negatively:

- undermine the evidence of this witness;
- undermine this witness.

The rule against unnecessary unpleasant statements and insults that applied to formulating a theory of the case and examination-in-chief is perhaps even more pertinent to cross-examination, so it is worth repeating it. Code of Conduct para 708(g) and Written Standards para 5.10(e) states:

A barrister when conducting proceedings at Court: . . .
must not make statements or ask questions which are merely scandalous or intended or calculated only to vilify insult or annoy either a witness or some other person.

Tempting as it may be to get carried away during a particularly successful cross-examination, it will in all likelihood damage rather than advance your client's case. Judicial reprimands in open court not only embarrass counsel, they can also potentially jeopardise the lay client's case.

7.3.4.3 Putting your case

A crucial feature of cross-examination is the obligation to put your case. You must put your client's version of a particular event to a witness who is in a position to dispute that version. You may not want to do so, because the witness will disagree with your version of events, but you must. Indeed, if the denial or disagreement is unconvincing this will have an impact on the jury: it may not believe the witness. Even if you strongly suspect that the witness will deny your case convincingly, you must still put the relevant questions to that witness. You cannot merely leave the point and deal with it in your closing speech—the Code prevents you from following this route. Code of Conduct para 708(i) and Written Standards para 5.10(g) states:

A barrister when conducting proceedings at Court: . . .

must not by assertion in a speech impugn a witness whom he has had an opportunity to cross-examine unless in cross-examination he has given the witness an opportunity to answer the allegation.

So, if you fail to put your case to the witness:

(a) You are acting incompetently at best, unethically at worst.

(b) You run a danger that you will not be allowed to deal with that point in your closing speech.

(c) When your client goes into the box and gives his or her evidence, and adduces evidence that the jury has not heard put to the other side's witnesses, it may conclude that the defendant has recently invented it.

If, through your own fault, you have failed to put the client's case, you will have to explain to the judge that it is your fault and not your client's. Witnesses may need to be recalled, the trial delayed and all parties inconvenienced. The consequences therefore are likely to be embarrassing in the extreme.

7.3.4.4   Conclusion of the trial and sentencing

At the conclusion of the judge's summing up the prosecuting counsel is under a duty to draw to the judge's attention any apparent omissions or errors of fact or law (Written Standards para 10.7). If you are acting as defence counsel, you would not appear to be under such a duty (except in the case of provocation in a murder trial: *R v Cox* [1995] 2 Cr App R 513). However, if you were not to assist the court at this stage you could jeopardise any subsequent appeal raised by your client.

In relation to sentence, prosecuting counsel should not attempt by advocacy to influence the court with regard to sentence. However, the prosecutor should draw the court's attention to any aggravating or mitigating factors disclosed by their case, any victim personal statement, any evidence of the impact of offending on the community, and any relevant statutory provisions relating to ancillary orders such as anti-social behaviour orders (see Code for Crown Prosecutors, para 11.1). Indeed, if a defendant is unrepresented, it is proper for prosecuting counsel to inform the court of any mitigating circumstances about which he or she is instructed (Written Standards para 10.8(a)). The prosecutor also should assist the court with sentencing guidelines and statutory provisions and other technical matters relevant to compensation, forfeiture, and restitution (Written Standards para 10.8(b)–(d)). Further, the prosecutor should draw the attention of the defence to any assertion of material fact made in mitigation which the prosecutor believes to be untrue. If the defence persists with the assertion, prosecuting counsel should invite the court to have the matter determined in a Newton hearing (Written Standards para 10.8(e)).

There are also duties for defence counsel in the sentencing process. If a barrister acting for the defence is instructed to submit in mitigation anything which casts aspersions on the conduct or character of a victim or witness in the case, you must notify the prosecution in advance so as to give prosecuting counsel sufficient opportunity to consider the requirement for a Newton hearing (Written Standards para 11.2(k)). See also the Bar Standards Board's guidance, 'Duty to Disclose Previous Convictions'.

It is sometimes appropriate for counsel—both for the prosecution and the defence—to see the judge prior to sentencing. Specific guidance is offered on this in the cases of

R v Turner [1970] 2 QB 321 and *R v Goodyear* [2005] 3 All ER 117; guidance on the application of *Goodyear* has been given in *R v Kulah* [2008] 1 All ER 16 and see also Amendment No 22 to the *Consolidated Criminal Practice Direction (Criminal Proceedings: Victim Personal Statements; Pleas of Guilty in the Crown Court; Forms)* [2009] 1 WLR 1396. See further **2.1.5**. It is essential that you understand the limits on such contact and what you can expect judges to indicate about the sentence and perhaps more importantly what they will not indicate. The issue of access to the judge for both prosecution and defence counsel is considered at **2.1.5**.

7.3.4.5   Appeals

When deciding whether to appeal the outcome of a case and especially when settling grounds of appeal you must remember the guidance offered in the Code of Conduct. This includes the dogmatic statement that counsel should not settle grounds of appeal unless they consider that such grounds are properly arguable (para 704(b) and Written Standards para 16.3). Further, if at any stage you are of the view that the appeal should be abandoned, you should at once set out your reasons in writing and send them to your professional client (Written Standards para 16.6). Naturally, you should not devise facts which will assist in advancing the lay client's case and a barrister must not draft grounds of appeal or any other document containing:

(a) any statement of fact or contention which is not supported by the lay client or by their instructions;

(b) any contention which he does not consider to be properly arguable;

(c) any allegation of fraud unless he has clear instructions to make such allegation and has before him reasonably credible material which as it stands establishes a prima facie case of fraud; . . .

provided that nothing in this paragraph shall prevent a barrister drafting a document containing specific factual statements or contentions included by the barrister subject to confirmation of their accuracy by the lay client or witness.

(Code of Conduct para 704)

7.4   Resolution of disputes out of court

Professional conduct is as important in alternative forms of dispute resolution as in any other aspect of a barrister's work. The Code of Conduct applies equally to your conduct in settling a dispute as it does to your conduct as an advocate. Indeed professional conduct and ethics can be more important in a relatively informal process such as mediation, not least because there may be more grey areas where it is important to take ethical decisions, and issues requiring an ethical approach may arise suddenly.

Resolution of a dispute out of court is often referred to as alternative dispute resolution or ADR, and this term will be used in this section. There are many forms of ADR, and they cannot all be covered in detail. The three types of ADR that a barrister is most likely to be engaged in are as follows, and ethical considerations for other forms of ADR can be illustrated by these models:

- Arbitration. This is an adjudicative form of ADR where an independent third party makes a decision on a case presented in an adversarial way. There may be a hearing broadly similar to a trial or the case may be decided on paper.

- Mediation. This is non-adjudicative—an independent third party seeks to assist the parties to reach an agreement, usually meeting the parties jointly and separately. Procedure is by agreement and lawyers may or may not attend.

- Negotiation. This is non-adjudicative—the lawyers for each party seek to reach an agreement within the instructions of their clients.

- In all cases the duty to the court will not figure in the same way as it does in litigation as ADR does not involve a court hearing. Nonetheless the barrister should still act with a duty to the court in mind, not least because a case that goes through an ADR process may still go to court, for example because a mediation or negotiation process fails.

The duty to the client is of particular importance when trying to settle a case in any ADR process. It is as important to get the best possible outcome for the client in settling as it is in advocating a case in court. It is also vital to act within the instructions of the client, especially in a process like negotiation where the barrister has substantial control of the process. An important potential benefit of ADR is the saving of costs, and a client should be advised about ADR options even if this might result in lower fee payments to the lawyer in relation to the case.

This section highlights the more common professional conduct issues that arise where a barrister is instructed to try to reach a settlement on behalf of his or her client. It focuses on the general duties when seeking a settlement in a civil case, as negotiating in a criminal case (or plea bargaining) has very specific rules which are beyond the scope of this manual. When instructed to use an ADR process, a barrister needs to be aware of his or her duties to a variety of people: the professional client, the lay client, the opposing lawyer (whether barrister or solicitor), any independent third party (in a process such as mediation), and the court (when negotiating a settlement within the litigation process).

7.4.1 General duties

Of particular relevance to ADR are those paragraphs of the Code which are applicable to all practising barristers (paras 301–307) and those under Part VII relating to the conduct of work by practising barristers. Note in particular the duty in para 701(a) to be courteous, in para 702 the duty of confidentiality, in para 703 the duties in respect of conflicts between lay client and intermediaries, and para 704 the duty not to mislead, which although headed 'drafting documents' is of more general application. You should also have regard to the Written Standards for the Conduct of Professional Work of the Code of Conduct, under the Conduct of Work at paras 5.5 and 5.11.

As with other aspects of your work as a barrister, the Code can only give general guidance on ethical rules when taking part in an ADR process, it cannot deal specifically with every situation that may arise. Although ADR is conducted privately with only those involved knowing what happened, it is as important to act as ethically as when you are acting in the public eye (for example, as an advocate in court). Your reputation is based on how you conduct yourself in practice, whether in public or private. The Bar is a small profession!

7.4.2 Confidentiality/privilege

Confidentiality is an important benefit of all ADR processes, and may indeed be a reason for choosing ADR rather than a court hearing. The first aspect of this is that an ADR process and information that arises in it cannot normally be referred to in court, even if the ADR process fails. The second aspect is that information provided by a client should not be discussed without instructions.

7.4.2.1 'Without prejudice'

Negotiation or mediation with a view to settlement should be conducted 'without prejudice' whether by letter, fax, phone, or face-to-face meeting. This basically means that the contents cannot be revealed to the court to assist it to determine the case. While any negotiation with a view to compromise is impliedly without prejudice, the position is also frequently expressly stated, for example in a mediation agreement, or by putting the words 'without prejudice' on a letter. Negotiations between counsel with a view to a compromise are impliedly made 'without prejudice'. Such discussions are in effect privileged and must not be repeated in court or in open correspondence. In the event of a failure to reach a satisfactory compromise, warn your client not to repeat in court what has been said during a negotiation or mediation. More detailed guidance on the evidential position of 'without prejudice' communications is contained in the *Evidence* manual.

There are two exceptions to the rule that what is discussed with a view to settlement is privileged and cannot be repeated. The first is where an admission of fact, which should properly have been openly disclosed, is made in the course of negotiations. For example, 'My client now admits he gave your client a gift of £500 although the balance of his claim for £2,000 was a loan'. The umbrella of 'without prejudice' does not protect such an admission. You may therefore use the admission if it is in your lay client's best interests to do so, though you should inform your opponent of your intention to do this. On the other hand, 'My client is prepared to waive £500 of his claim provided your client pays him the balance of £1,500 within 28 days' is not an admission. It is a concession made 'without prejudice' in the context of an offer of compromise.

The second is where agreement is reached. The phrase 'without prejudice' was discussed in *Guinness Peat Properties v Fitzroy Robinson Partnership* [1987] 2 All ER 716, where it was held to mean 'without prejudice to the position of the writer if the terms he proposes are not accepted'. If a 'without prejudice' offer is accepted, it is a formal agreement to settle the claim, is immediately binding, and can be revealed to a court, if for example the terms are disputed. If the offer is not accepted, it is ignored, and nothing said in a letter making the offer can be used as evidence (*Rush and Tompkins Ltd v GLC* [1988] 3 WLR 939).

7.4.2.2 Discussions between lawyers

Discussions between counsel about a possible settlement or how to assist the case to run smoothly frequently take place without either client being present. Both counsel may therefore be more informal than if the clients are present, using language and saying things which might not be said if the clients are present. However, you must always remember that your first duty is to your client; that you are negotiating on his or her behalf. Your duty of confidentiality means that you should not reveal anything to the other side which might be damaging to your client or your client's case. As a general rule, you should not disclose anything that your client would not wish the other side to know. If something is revealed to you by your opponent, which it is in your client's interest to know or which may affect the way in which you conduct the case, you must disclose this to the client. You should also tell your opponent that you will inform your client.

Do not be persuaded to reveal matters which you feel you should not, or not inform your client of things you feel you should, by your opponent saying or implying that 'counsel-to-counsel' discussions exempt you from your duty to your client. There is no such thing within the Code of Conduct or professional ethics as 'counsel-to-counsel confidentiality'.

Most mediation agreements or decisions given in an arbitration will be subject to a confidentiality clause by agreement.

7.4.3   The professional client

Both the solicitor and counsel may become involved in the use of an ADR process in a case. The division of roles should be kept clear. You might be asked to advise the solicitor on possible terms of settlement, in which case the solicitor might file a Part 36 offer or proceed with any negotiation. Alternatively, you might be instructed to try to negotiate a case, in which case you must keep the solicitor informed of progress. If there is a mediation, the barrister and solicitor should agree with the client who should attend. As general principles:

(a) Keep your professional client informed of developments.

(b) If a professional client is present, listen to his or her views on the merit of any proposal that has been made.

(c) Be courteous and even-tempered in your dealings with your professional client. Do not argue in front of the lay client. If there is a difference of opinion between you, discuss it out of the lay client's hearing.

(d) Do not, however, keep your professional client happy at the expense of your lay client's interests. For example, do not advise your client to reject a fair offer of compromise merely because your solicitor insists that his firm, rather than the one proposed, handles the conduct of the sale of the property in dispute. The Code states:

> **303(b)**   A barrister owes his primary duty as between the lay client and any professional client or other intermediary to the lay client and must not permit the intermediary to limit his discretion as to how the interests of the lay client can best be served . . .

> **703**   If a self-employed barrister forms the view that there is a conflict of interest between his lay client and a professional client or other intermediary (for example because he considers that the intermediary may have been negligent) he must consider whether it would be in the lay client's interest to instruct another professional adviser or representative and, if he considers that it would be, the barrister must so advise and take such steps as he considers necessary to ensure that his advice is communicated to the lay client (if necessary by sending a copy of his advice in writing directly to the lay client as well as to the intermediary).

7.4.4   The lay client

The lawyer is the expert, the professional adviser, and the representative acting on behalf of the client. However, it is the client's case. The client should decide which ADR option to follow on the basis of advice, and the client's objectives and interests should remain central, even in a process like negotiation where the individual lawyer has substantial control. The professional conduct issues which arise as a result are as follows.

7.4.4.1   Act only on instructions and within your client's instructions

As a lawyer, you act as your client's agent, and this is particularly important in a negotiation, with general agency rules applying. You have actual authority to act only within the client's instructions and should never settle outside this actual authority. However, from the other party's point of view, you are acting for the client and have the apparent or ostensible authority to settle a case after proceedings have been issued. The extent of this apparent authority can of course be cut down by giving the other side notice of any limit on it. If you act outside your actual authority but bind the client because the agreement comes within your apparent authority, you will be in breach of duty to your client and liable to him or her.

You must therefore only negotiate when your client instructs you to do so, and you can only negotiate within the authority given to you by your client. You must ensure that you really do understand the client's objectives, interests, and needs and pursue these in the negotiation and that you have your client's clear authority to either propose or accept an offer of compromise.

Your brief will normally contain a lot of information which makes it clear what the client will or will not accept, i.e., sets the parameters of your actual authority in negotiating a settlement. However, there may well be matters of detail on which it is not clear exactly what the client wants. Making it apparent to the other side that any negotiation is subject to the authorisation or approval of the client, leaves you open to agree detail on condition that the client does approve (i.e., giving notice of the limited authority). By setting this parameter, it leaves you free to try to tie up the detail in the best way possible without binding the client.

In a mediation the client will normally play a larger role in presenting his or her own case, though if a lawyer attends the lawyer is likely to take a significant role. Similar rules as to following instructions apply, though this may be more straightforward when the client is also present.

7.4.4.2   Ensure that the client's claim is legitimate

Although it is the lay client's case, you have a duty not to knowingly allow yourself to be used as a tool to obtain settlement in respect of a groundless or fraudulent claim. If your client's case is without any foundation, you should not act for him or her. The Code sets out:

704   A barrister must not devise facts which will assist in advancing the lay client's case and must not draft any statement of case, witness statement, affidavit, notice of appeal or other document containing:

(a) any statement of fact or contention which is not supported by the lay client or by his instructions;

(b) any contention which he does not consider to be properly arguable;

(c) any allegation of fraud unless he has clear instructions to make such allegation and has before him reasonably credible material which as it stands establishes a prima facie case of fraud;

(d) in the case of a witness statement or affidavit any statement of fact other than the evidence which in substance according to his instructions the barrister reasonably believes the witness would give if the evidence contained in the witness statement or affidavit were being given in oral examination;

provided that nothing in this paragraph shall prevent a barrister drafting a document containing specific factual statements or contentions included by the barrister subject to confirmation of their accuracy by the lay client or witness.

7.4.4.3   Ensure your client's interests are protected

The use of ADR may involve some element of compromise, but the outcome should still be the best that is reasonably available to the client. A settlement should rarely be reached on a basis that is significantly less favourable than might be achieved by going to court. As counsel, it is also your duty to ensure your client's interests are adequately protected by the machinery and terms of the compromise. For example, a judgment debt is likely to affect your client's prospects of obtaining future credit, whereas an agreement to pay the debt contained in a Tomlin order will not.

7.4.4.4   Advise the client clearly and fully on their case

You have a duty, as counsel, to ensure that when the client decides whether or not to accept an offer or agree to settle, the decision is a fully informed one. You must advise the client both of your view of the case and of what, in your judgment, is the best course of action. Ensure that the client understands how the strengths and weaknesses of the case or any procedural or evidential matters affect the chances of achieving the objectives that he or she is seeking. Ensure that he or she is aware of the risks involved in making, accepting, or rejecting an offer of compromise, for example, the incidence of costs, and that he or she understands the nature and effect of any agreement and/or any undertaking he or she is proposing to give to the court. The terms of the settlement must be fully explained as must the effect, in particular that settlement will mean the end of the matter and there will normally be no possibility of reopening it or seeking more. Such advice may need to be given at the end of a negotiation, or during a mediation process.

Failing to advise the client properly or just accepting a decision where the client clearly does not understand his or her legal position or consequences of the decision, is a breach of duty to the client.

7.4.4.5   It is the client's decision, not yours

Decisions about substantive matters, for example, whether or not to negotiate or enter mediation, what issues are open to settlement, and whether or not an offer should be accepted, must be made by the client. It is the client's case and you must ensure that any decision about whether to settle or not is that of the client and not yours. Whether the settlement is acceptable must be measured against the client's objectives, needs, and interests. Having advised fully (see above), you must then accept the client's decision and abide by it. If the client is not prepared to accept a settlement, that is his or her prerogative. The only exception to this may arise if the client is funded by the Community Legal Service. The solicitor will be under a duty to report to the Regional Director of the Community Legal Service that the client has declined to accept an offer to settle (Funding Code Procedures, Section 12 Reporting Obligations, C43.2.vi.a Duties of the Solicitor). In such a case, advice may have been required from a barrister on the merits of the case prior to funding being granted. You may have given that advice which included an assessment of quantum. If the settlement offer is within that which you advised, then you too may fall under the duty of any Legal Representative in the Funding Code Procedures (C44 i) to ensure that the Regional Director is informed, if it appears to you that the client has required the case to be conducted unreasonably, or so as to incur an unjustifiable expense to the Fund or has unreasonably required that the case be continued.

7.4.4.6   Conditional fee agreements

Barristers are increasingly entering conditional fee agreements whereby no fee is charged if the client loses the case but the barrister receives a 'success' fee if the client wins. These agreements raise novel practical problems and have significant potential pitfalls for the Bar. In particular, it is recognised that a conditional fee agreement could impact on the barrister–client relationship in respect of settling a case.

Guidance is given by the General Council of the Bar in its 'Conditional Fee Guidance' set out under Rules and Guidance on the Bar Council's website (<http://www.barcouncil .org.uk>). Part I deals specifically with Ethical Guidance. The paragraphs of particular relevance to negotiation are as set out below.

Conditional Fee Guidance

6.   Form of agreement

In particular, the barrister should ensure that no term increases or tends to increase pressure on the lay client to reach an inappropriate settlement . . .

9.   Impartiality/conflict of interest

Having accepted instructions to act under a CFA, a barrister shall thereafter give impartial advice to the lay client at all times and take all reasonable steps to identify and declare to the lay client and to the instructing solicitor any actual or apparent conflict of interest between the barrister and the lay client.

10.   Advice and interests of lay client

During the currency of a CFA, the barrister should use his/her best endeavours to ensure that:

(a) any advice given by the barrister in relation to the case is communicated and fully explained to the lay client;

(b) any offer of settlement is communicated to the lay client forthwith;

(c) the consequences of particular clauses in the solicitor–lay client agreement and the solicitor–barrister agreement are explained to the client as and when they become relevant, particularly after an offer of settlement has been made.

This last obligation applies in particular to the financial consequences which may arise from the making of an offer to settle the case including consideration of: (1) any increase in the offer of settlement; (2) 'conventional' costs consequences; and (3) the success fees which are or may become payable.

11.   Advising on settlement

When advising on a settlement of the action the barrister should at all times have in mind his/her obligation under paragraph 303(a) of the Code to 'promote and protect fearlessly and by all proper and lawful means the lay client's best interests and do so without regard to his own interests or to any consequences to himself or to any other person (including any professional client or other intermediary or another barrister)'. The barrister's duty must be, when advising the client on a settlement or on a payment in or Part 36 offer, to advise as to the best course of action from the lay client's point of view only.

12.   Disagreement over settlement

Difficulties may arise when the lawyers disagree about the wisdom of continuing the case or accepting an offer, whether that disagreement is:

(a) between them on the one part and the lay client on the other; or

(b) between solicitor and counsel; or

(c) between leading and junior counsel.

In such event careful consideration must be given to the lay client's interests. Every effort should be made to avoid unfairly putting the lay client in the position where having begun proceedings s/he is left without representation. However, where, for example, counsel has been misled about the true nature of the evidence or the lay client is refusing to accept firm advice as to the future conduct of the case, the terms of the CFA may permit counsel to withdraw. Before taking this serious step the barrister will have to check carefully whether s/he is entitled to withdraw.

13.   Withdrawal from the case

The barrister may withdraw from the case in any of the circumstances set out in the CFA agreement, but only if satisfied that s/he is permitted to withdraw pursuant to Part VI of the Code. In the event that the CFA agreement does not contain a term that the barrister may withdraw from the case in particular circumstances, but the Code requires the barrister to withdraw in those circumstances, the Code takes priority over the agreement.

If you are acting under a CFA agreement, you will need to ensure that your advice to your client satisfies these requirements, in particular that you advise the client on the best course of action for him or her regardless of your own position on any success fee.

In addition, you must ensure that your advice on the offer of settlement and the consequences of the CFA agreement is clear to the client, in particular advising on the usual costs consequences of settlement and any success fee payable. You should also make clear the consequences of not accepting the settlement and ensure that the client is clear on the net gain of such action (the likely better sum/outcome, the prospects of getting it and the further costs consequences of continuing including any likely success fee).

Your duty not to divulge information entrusted to you in confidence by your client without his or her consent continues after the case, even if it has been dealt with by way of a negotiated compromise. If you are acting under a CFA, the guidance of the Bar Council in para 14 states, 'The fact that the action is funded by means of a CFA, and the terms of a CFA, should not be disclosed to the other parties to the action without the express written permission of the lay client, or save in so far as such disclosure is required by the court, the CPR, statute, rule, order, or Practice Direction'.

7.4.5 The opponent

In an adjudicative process such as arbitration the relationship with the opponent is likely to be broadly similar to that in a litigation process. In a process such as mediation the approach to the case is intended to be more collaborative, and some lawyers can find the adjustment a little difficult until they become familiar with mediation. This is however a matter of approach rather than professional conduct issues.

Negotiating with the other side raises the most difficult issues of professional conduct as regards tactics and general behaviour. Depending on the format followed, mediation may involve some similar issues. There are relatively clear principles, but without detailed guidance there are some grey areas, for example as regards what will amount to misleading an opponent.

As counsel, you have a duty to conduct negotiations in a fair, honest, courteous, and trustworthy manner. You should never compromise your professional integrity. The importance of fair play should not detract from your duty to promote the interests of the lay client fearlessly. Frustration may tempt you on occasions to forget this: *don't let it*. A reputation for underhandedness or sharp practice will be retained long after the event, especially in a relatively small profession like the Bar. You need to be conscious that, even if the behaviour comes within the ethical boundaries, the tactics you use will invariably affect the reputation that you build, if for example you regularly take an aggressive stance.

7.4.5.1 Misleading your opponent

Some tactics are clearly dishonest and unethical, for example, deliberately misleading your opponent by pretending to have evidence you do not have. They are against the Bar's Code of Conduct and, even if they do not amount to an offence, for example, fraud, using them can result in being debarred. You must never deliberately deceive or mislead your opponent in order to achieve a more favourable offer of compromise (see para 301 of the Code of Conduct).

It is, however, acceptable to use 'bluff', allowing an opponent to form an impression without positively misleading him. Nonetheless managing or manipulating information may become sufficiently 'tricky' or misleading to amount to professional misconduct. You can quite properly pitch the case at its highest when trying to reach a settlement, even though you may not necessarily succeed in proving the whole case in court. There is not always a clear line between doing the best for your client and misleading or unfair tactics. But you must not pretend that you do know a fact or have particular instructions if this is simply not true. You must also not knowingly conceal something which ought properly to have been disclosed, for example a document, in the hope of securing a more favourable settlement.

7.4.5.2 Use of threats

'Threat' is defined as 'a conditional commitment by a negotiator to act in a way that appears detrimental to the other party unless the other party complies with a request', in Donald G. Gifford's book *Legal Negotiation: Theory and Applications* ((1989) (St Paul, Minn: West Publishing Co), p 143). Many negotiation tactics, although not phrased as threats, implicitly involve them; for example, 'the final offer' is basically a threat to end the negotiation if the offer is not accepted. Not all threats are unethical—arguments are often geared to put some pressure on an opponent. For example a 'threat' to make an interim application may be quite acceptable if a party has a right to make such an application and will seriously consider doing so if a concession is not made.

A threat becomes potentially unethical if unjustified pressure, misleading pressure, or pressure from something outside the issues in the case is used to try to force a concession. Clearly, it would be dishonest and unprofessional to suggest that your client intended to do something he or she did not intend. In addition, your client may be considering action which is not legitimate because it is illegal or impractical, in which case you should be advising your client in strong terms not to take it. It would also be improper to threaten to report the client for the other side to an authority in relation to a potential criminal offence or investigation for tax evasion on the basis of confidential information revealed as part of an attempt to settle. It is unprofessional and unethical to make threats that are tantamount to blackmail.

Even where the client has threatened to take particular legitimate action if their demands are not met, for example, that they will 'go to the press unless the opponent does X', whatever the facts, counsel must tread a fine line between following the client's instructions and avoiding the aggressive use of threats to secure a favourable outcome. The dividing line between a legitimate statement and an unethical threat is not clear. This is a difficult area and there is no clear guidance in the Code of Conduct. It is not always easy to distinguish an improper threat from an objective statement of potential consequences. It frequently comes down to a question of the manner in which the information is imparted to one's opponent and the exact words used.

When in doubt, err on the side of caution, i.e., do *not* threaten: 'My client will go to the press unless your client does XYZ', as this is really simply a threat. However, you may inform the opponent in appropriate language that your client is indicating an intention to go to the newspapers, for example, 'I think it is only fair to tell you that my client is so upset by this/feels so strongly about this that she's talking of going to the newspapers'. Although the difference between these two approaches is subtle, it is nevertheless there. The second example is merely a statement of the client's possible intention and *not* linked to any demand in respect of her case.

7.4.5.3 Going back on your word

Do not go back on your word, or subsequently pretend you did not say something, in order to cover your own mistake or indiscretion. Such behaviour is unacceptable. If you have made an error, admit it. Take great care with the words used when you make a concession or a potential concession to avoid any misunderstanding.

7.4.5.4 Acting without authority

Do not make an offer or commit your client to an agreement without instructions or authority to do so. Make it clear to your opponent when your proposal is subject to your lay client's agreement. For example, 'If my client were prepared to do XYZ, would your client do ABC?' You can put yourself into an impossible position if you make an agreement outside your instructions (so that your client refuses to be bound by it) but where your opponent and his client insist that you are bound and cease to enforce the agreement.

7.4.5.6   Failing to act courteously

While it is acceptable and indeed important to be appropriately assertive in your manner, aggressive behaviour may become sufficiently insulting or rude to amount to a breach of your professional duty to act courteously. Avoid bickering with your opponent; it does not do your client any good. Nor is it wise to lose your objectivity by taking on the persona of your client in the course of negotiations. For example, 'Your client is totally dishonest, he has already stolen £2,000 from us'. This merely serves to antagonise.

7.4.5.7   Litigants in person

The above considerations apply whether or not your opponent is a lawyer or a litigant in person, and apply in a mediation as in a negotiation. However, where there is a litigant in person in the case, you have the additional consideration of ensuring that you do not abuse your professional status and knowledge. This can produce other difficult issues, such as how much and the way in which you explain the law as you understand it; for example, to what extent you include in your explanation any points of law which go against you. In a mediation the mediator can assist in dealing with a litigant in person on the other side.

7.4.6   An independent third party

In all ADR processes other than negotiation an independent third party is likely to be involved. This may be on an informal basis, for example in a mediation, or on a more formal basis, where for example an adjudicator is appointed to reach a decision.

Professional guidance has not yet evolved to provide clear guidelines on the relationship to an independent third party. The process will normally be covered by an adjudication or mediation agreement, and the lawyer should normally follow that agreed process. Professional duties to the client will remain fully in force.

7.4.7   The court

Seeking to reach a settlement does not mean that the role of the court can be ignored. Any ADR process may be subject to the views of a court, for example as regards enforcement of any agreement reached, and in conducting an ADR process the lawyer will normally compare a potential outcome with what might happen if the case were litigated.

If an ADR process takes place without the issue of proceedings the court will have no direct oversight, but increasingly ADR and litigation overlap, for example because a case is stayed for mediation to take place. It is impossible to cover this interface in detail, but key professional conduct points may include:

- The need to inform the court if agreement is reached between the parties away from the court. If, for example, agreement is reached in correspondence, or as a result of mediation, remind your professional client to inform the court as soon as possible.
- Awareness of the oversight of the court and the need for approval if a consent order is agreed. The judge may suggest some amendments to your draft order.
- If negotiations are taking place at court, keep the court informed of the possibility of a compromise. It may be sufficient to relay this information to the court via the

court clerk or usher. At times, it may be necessary to explain this to the judge or tribunal.

- Provide the court with a realistic estimate of the further time you need to discuss any proposals. Inform the court immediately upon reaching agreement. The Code states:

701 A barrister:

(a) must in all his professional activities be courteous and act promptly conscientiously diligently and with reasonable competence and take all reasonable and practicable steps to avoid unnecessary expense or waste of the Court's time and to ensure that professional engagements are fulfilled;

Paragraph 5.11 of the Written Standards states:

A barrister must take all reasonable and practicable steps to avoid unnecessary expense or waste of the Court's time. He should, when asked, inform the Court of the probable length of his case; and he should also inform the court of any developments which affect information already provided.

If you have time, draw up draft minutes of the agreed terms or order.

When you go into court, either hand up the draft, or, in the absence of a written draft, inform the court of the terms which have been agreed between the parties 'subject to Your Honour/Your Lordship's approval'. It may be necessary even where you have a draft order, to take the judge through its terms. Invite the judge to make the order in the terms proposed.

7.5 Opinion writing and drafting

In written work, you must display the same high standards of integrity and honesty that apply in all other aspects of your practice. The Code of Conduct has a lot to say about the conduct of written work. This section is designed to give you some guidance on matters which arise frequently in opinion writing and drafting in civil and criminal cases.

7.5.1 General provisions relevant to written work

When undertaking any written work on behalf of a client you should have a comprehensive knowledge of:

- the Code of Conduct ('the Code');
- the Written Standards for the Conduct of Professional Work ('the Written Standards');
- Guidance on Preparation of Defence Case Statements;
- Guidance on Preparation of Witness Statements;
- the Funding Code.

The Written Standards in particular provide a guide to the way in which you should carry out your work. They must be read in conjunction with the Code and are to be taken into account in determining whether a disciplinary offence has been committed.

In undertaking any written work, advisory or drafting, or indeed any oral advisory work, you must always bear in mind the fundamental principles of the Code. In particular you:

(a) must not engage in conduct whether in pursuit of your profession or otherwise which is:

(i) dishonest or otherwise discreditable;

(ii) prejudicial to the administration of justice; or

(iii) likely to diminish public confidence in the legal profession or the administration of justice or otherwise bring the legal profession into disrepute (Code para 301);

(b) have an overriding duty to the court to act with independence in the interests of justice; you must assist the court in the administration of justice and not deceive or knowingly or recklessly mislead the court (Code para 302);

(c) must promote and fearlessly protect the lay client's best interests by all lawful and proper means and without regard to any consequences to yourself or your professional client, other intermediary or another barrister (Code para 303);

(d) are individually and personally responsible for your conduct and for your professional work; you must exercise personal judgement in all your professional activities (Code para 306);

(e) must not allow your independence, integrity, or freedom from external pressures to be compromised, or do anything which would lead to an inference that they have been compromised or compromise your professional standards in order to please your client, the court, or any third party, including any mediator. (para 307).

Although these fundamental principles lie at the heart of all written work which you may be asked to undertake on behalf of a lay client, the Code and Written Standards and the Guidance issued by the Bar Council under the Code offer specific guidance in relation to certain types of work which you may be instructed to carry out.

7.5.2 Your duty on receipt of papers

When you obtain instructions to advise or draft a document, you must read them expeditiously to ensure that you are competent to deal with the matter and have adequate time to carry out the task given the pressures of your other work (see para 701(b) and (c) of the Code and para 3.1 of the Written Standards). You must not delay in carrying out this task. You should aim to do this within a few days, or immediately if the instructions are urgent, because if the case is beyond your competence, or you cannot fulfil the task within the required time or a reasonable time, then the professional client must be informed and the instructions passed on to another barrister. Of course, you cannot return instructions without first explaining to your client the reason for doing so, and you obviously cannot pass the papers on to another barrister without the consent of your client (Code para 610(b)).

If you do accept the instructions, then you must ensure that you do the work within the time requested or agreed, or within a reasonable time. If there is a time limit laid down by the Civil Procedure Rules within which the work should be done (for example, filing a Defence, serving Witness Statements, filing a Notice of Appeal), then you must ensure the work is done and returned to your instructing solicitor in good time to enable him or her to comply with the time limit. A failure to comply with time limits laid down by the Civil Procedure Rules may result in your lay client's case being struck out, so drafting work must usually be given priority over advisory work.

Solicitors are frequently heard to complain that a failure to carry out written work within the requested or agreed time, or within a reasonable time, is a very common failing of the Bar. In practice, it sometimes happens that cases run on longer than intended, or urgent and serious matters arise, so that agreed time limits cannot be met or the work requested cannot be undertaken within a reasonable time. If this does happen, it is important to telephone your instructing solicitor immediately. The lay client may be able and prepared to wait, but if he or she is not, then you must return the instructions to the professional client or to another barrister acceptable to your professional and lay client (para 701(e) of the Code and para 5.6 of the Written Standards).

It follows that you must manage actively your practice and keep a close eye on the volume of work that you have. Be realistic and honest about: (a) the length of time it will take you to complete each item of work; and (b) the work that you are competent to do, having regard to your knowledge and expertise. Do not feel obliged to accept instructions in a complex case involving copyright and passing off if your primary area of expertise is family work and you do not know the first thing about copyright or passing off. Indeed, if you know, or ought to know, that you are not competent to handle the instructions, it would be a clear breach of the Code to accept them.

7.5.3 Opinion writing

7.5.3.1 General principles

Any advice that you give should be 'practical, appropriate to the needs and circumstances of the particular client, and clearly and comprehensively expressed' (para 5.7 of the Written Standards). This is obvious. However, in the remainder of this section, some guidance will be given about your professional obligations when specific types of advice are sought.

7.5.3.2 Advice for the benefit of the Legal Aid Board/Legal Services Commission

If you undertake publicly funded work, you have additional professional responsibilities that you must always follow when it comes to providing written advice about the case. In publicly funded cases, you will almost always be asked to provide a written opinion before proceedings are issued, and also quite often after service of witness statements, to determine whether it is appropriate for the matter to go to trial. In relation to opinions provided under Legal Aid Certificates granted before April 2000, the Opinion must comply with the *Legal Aid Guidelines* (to be found in the Legal Aid Handbook or on the Bar Council's website). In respect of Legal Services Certificates provided under the Funding Code, the advice must comply with Annexe E of the Code of Conduct 'Guidelines on Opinions under the Funding Code'. Both sets of guidelines are in fairly similar terms and give guidance to barristers on what an Advice or Opinion must contain as to the merits of funding or continuing to fund a case.

Generally, Opinions must be prepared in accordance with the Funding Code (see <http://www.legalservices.gov.uk>). When you are instructed to advise in writing, you must decide whether a conference is necessary, for example to assess the credibility or reliability of a lay client's evidence.

When you write the Opinion, you must ensure that it states: (a) the level of service under which the Opinion is given (or applied for); and (b) the case category into which the proceedings fall. In addition, every Opinion on the merits should comply with the following matters in so far as they are relevant to the issues raised in the particular case:

(a) Where factual issues are involved, set out the factual disputes in sufficient detail to enable the Commission to assess their relative strengths and express a clear opinion on whether the applicant's evidence would be accepted by the court, and give reasons for that opinion.

(b) Where there are issues or disputes of law, these must also be summarised in sufficient detail to enable the Commission to come to a view without having to have recourse to materials outside the Opinion. Express a clear view on whether the applicant's case on the law would be accepted by the court, and give reasons for that opinion.

(c) Draw attention to any lack of evidence, which might have a bearing on the applicant's case or any other factor which might affect the outcome of the case.

(d) State the prospects of success, and in particular specify whether they are:

    (i)   very good (greater than 80 per cent);

    (ii) good (60 per cent to 80 per cent);

    (iii) moderate (50 per cent to 60 per cent);

    (iv) borderline (which means that the prospects of success are not poor, but because there are difficult disputes of fact, law, or expert evidence, it is not possible to say that the prospects of success are better than 50 per cent). In this case, the fact, law, or expert evidence which leads you to put the case in this category must be identified;

    (v) poor (less than 50 per cent, so the claim is likely to fail);

    (vi) unclear (the case cannot be put into any of the above categories because further investigation is needed; in which case, you must also indicate what further investigation is needed).

(e) Cost benefit: the Opinion must set out the benefit to the client, and put a figure on the likely level of damages the client would receive if successful at trial, allowing for any reduction for contributory negligence or otherwise. Likely damages should also be discounted if there is any doubt as to whether the opponent will be able to pay the money award.

(f) Where the application is for investigative help to be granted or continued, the Opinion should indicate what investigations need to be conducted. It should also show that there are reasonable grounds for believing that when the investigative work has been carried out, the claim will be strong enough, in terms of prospects of success and cost benefit, to justify a grant of full representation.

(g) If the case has a wider public benefit, you should set out the nature of the benefit and the parties affected by it.

(h) Finally, you should suggest or formulate any appropriate limitation or condition on the certificate, if it is appropriate to do so, in order to safeguard the Fund.

7.5.3.3   What advice do you give if you become aware that your lay client has improperly obtained public funding?

Sometimes your lay client may provide you with information which suggests that public funding has been wrongly obtained by false or misleading information. If this is the case, you cannot simply turn a blind eye to the matter. You should explore the matter, tactfully, with your lay client and/or instructing solicitor. If it becomes apparent that funding has been improperly obtained, your duty, as counsel, is clearly spelled out by paras 303 and 304 and Annexe E paras 20 and 22 of the Code of Conduct. In addition to these provisions, Rule C44 of the *Funding Code Procedures* also provides that counsel must inform the Regional Director if, among other things, it appears that the lay client may have given inaccurate, misleading, or incomplete information, or new information or a change of circumstances has come to light which may affect the terms or continuation of the Certificate.

Your obligations under the Code of Conduct are therefore clear. You must inform the Commission of any matter which may affect your lay client's entitlement to funding or the terms or continuation of a Certificate. You should discuss the matter with your lay client, explain the nature of the duty imposed on you, and urge him or her personally to make the disclosure required (although personal disclosure by the lay client does not appear to negate the duty imposed on counsel). Note that para 22 of Annexe E provides that where you are under a duty to draw matters to the attention of the Commission, you can do so by drawing the matter to the attention of your instructing solicitor, and asking him or her to pass it on to the Commission, or you can contact the Commission directly if that is appropriate in the circumstances of the case. In addition to the reporting obligations set out above, you must cease to act if the lay client refuses to take action to remedy the situation. In these circumstances, you are effectively put in the position of having to make the disclosure to the Commission against your lay client's wishes, and this would obviously make any continuing professional relationship with him or her extremely difficult.

7.5.3.4   Advice on disclosure

In civil cases, it is your duty to advise your client that all relevant documents must be disclosed, even if they are fatal to his or her case (see para 608(e) of the Code and **7.2.2.5** above). If the lay client fails to follow your advice, you must withdraw from the case.

Applications made 'without notice' impose an even stricter obligation of disclosure on the lay client. In applications of this type, which will usually involve obtaining an urgent injunction or a freezing or search order, you must ensure that full and frank disclosure is made to the court. The duty of disclosure is really that of your lay client, but it is policed by the lawyers. If you fail to ensure that your lay client complies with it, or fail to draw the attention of the court to matters which should be disclosed, then you may be misleading the court, or engaging in conduct which is prejudicial to the administration of justice. You would therefore be in breach of your duties under paras 301 and 302 of the Code. Any failure to make full and frank disclosure may also result in the order being discharged. An order for costs may also be made against your lay client (or perhaps a wasted costs order may be made against you or your instructing solicitors).

Therefore, in advising a client who wishes to obtain urgent 'without notice' interim relief, such an as injunction, a freezing order, or a search order, it is imperative that your lay client understands the nature of the duty of full and frank disclosure. If necessary, you must ask questions of the client to ensure that this duty is complied with. If you are asked to draft any document, such as a witness statement, you must also ensure that all relevant matters are fully and properly disclosed in it.

7.5.3.5   Advice following receipt of further information

It is not uncommon for counsel to be asked to advise at an early stage of an action. Subsequently, you may be sent instructions to settle statements of case, or witness statements or advise on a different aspect of the matter. Sometimes the fresh instructions will contain material that will alter the advice that you gave previously.

If you find yourself in this position, you should reassess any previous advice following receipt of further information if you are instructed to do so. Even if you are not instructed to reconsider your previous advice, you should at least warn your instructing solicitor that your previous views have to be reconsidered as a result of the change of circumstances. A failure to do so may lead to a wasted costs order against you: *C v C (Wasted Costs Order)* [1994] 2 FLR 34.

7.5.3.6   Opinions under conditional fee agreements

If you are instructed to act under a conditional fee agreement (CFA) then you may face a number of ethical problems, not least when you are instructed to carry out written work. The Bar Council CFA Panel has drawn up a lengthy document to offer guidance to those undertaking CFA work. The *Conditional Fee Guidance* does not form part of the Code of Conduct, but you are strongly advised to follow the guidance to ensure compliance with the Code.

If you are acting under a CFA, then during the currency of the CFA agreement, you should use your best endeavours to ensure that:

(a) Any advice you give is communicated and fully explained to the lay client.

(b) Any offer of settlement is communicated to the lay client immediately.

(c) The consequences of particular clauses in the solicitor–lay client agreement and the solicitor–barrister agreement are explained to the lay client as and when they become relevant, particularly after an offer of settlement has been made. This last obligation in particular would require you to give advice on the usual costs consequences of settlement and the success fee that may become payable.

(d) In advising on settlement or on a payment-in or Part 36 offer you must bear in mind only the interests of the lay client (and not your own interests, such as the 'success fee' that may become payable on settlement under the CFA). You should at all times have in mind your obligations under para 303(a) of the Code. A model CFA together with Standard Terms and Conditions can be downloaded from the Bar Council's website.

7.5.3.7 Advice in criminal cases

The Code of Conduct and the Written Standards apply equally to criminal cases. However, there are a number of other specific duties which you must also bear in mind by virtue of the Written Standards.

In particular, para 10.4 of the Written Standards provides that prosecuting counsel should:

(i) decide whether any additional evidence is required, and if it is, advise in writing, setting out precisely what additional evidence is required with a view to serving it on the defence as soon as possible;

(ii) consider whether all the witness statements in the possession of the prosecution have been properly served on the defendant;

(iii) eliminate all unnecessary material so as to ensure an efficient and fair trial, and also consider the need for particular witnesses and exhibits;

(iv) draft appropriate admissions and serve them on the defence;

(v) in all Class 1 and Class 2 cases and in other cases of complexity, draft a case summary for transmission to the court.

Defence counsel must consider whether:

(i) any enquiries or further enquiries are necessary, and, if so, should advise in writing as soon as possible;

(ii) details of an alibi are required, and, if so, draft an appropriate notice;

(iii) it is appropriate to call expert evidence for the defence, and advise solicitors to comply with the rules of the Crown Court in relation to notifying the prosecution of the contents of the evidence to be given;

(iv) any admissions can be made with a view to saving time and expense at trial, with the aim of admitting as much evidence as can be admitted in accordance with his or her duty to client;

(v) he or she wishes to examine any exhibits, and if so, should ensure that appropriate arrangements are made to examine them as promptly as possible.

7.5.3.8 Advice on appeal

Frequently, barristers are asked to advise on appeal. In criminal cases, defence counsel must always consider whether there are any grounds of appeal against conviction or sentence.

Paragraph 16 of the Written Standards draws counsel's attention to the Guide to Proceedings in the Court of Appeal Criminal Division (although note that the current version in force is dated October 2008). In addition para 16.2 of the Written Standards provides that:

(i) If his client pleads guilty or is convicted, a defence barrister should see his client after sentence in the presence of his professional client or representative. If he is satisfied that there are no reasonable grounds of appeal, he should advise orally and confirm this in writing. No further advice is necessary unless a full written advice is required by the professional client, or it is necessary on the particular facts of the case.

(ii) If he is satisfied that there are reasonable grounds for appeal or he needs more time to consider the position, then he should give oral advice in these terms, and certify this in writing. Counsel would then provide written advice to the professional client as soon as possible and in any event within 14 days.

Quite often clients may want you to settle appeal documents even if you advise that the appeal is completely hopeless. In these circumstances, you must take care not to settle any grounds of appeal that you do not consider to be properly arguable (para 704 of the Code of Conduct and para 5.11 of the Written Standards). In criminal cases, para 16.3 of the Written Standards states:

Counsel should not settle grounds of appeal unless he considers that such grounds are properly arguable, and in that event, he should provide a reasoned written opinion in support of such grounds (although this is now a combined document).

7.5.3.9 Solicitor asks you to give advice which does not reflect your true opinion

You must not permit your absolute independence, integrity, and freedom from external pressures to be compromised or compromise your professional standards in order to please your client, the court, or a third party (Code para 307). You therefore must not alter your opinion to suit the needs of any professional client or lay client, and nor should you provide advice, for any purpose, which does not reflect your true opinion.

7.5.3.10 What advice do you give if you consider your solicitor to be negligent?

In practice, you may sometimes consider that your lay client may have a claim against your instructing solicitors. For example, the client's case may have been struck out because your instructing solicitors failed to serve witness statements on time. In a property dispute, you may conclude that your client has no legal title to a particular piece of land due to the negligence of your instructing solicitors who acted for the lay client during the purchase of the land. Your instructing solicitor may send you a lot of work, and you know that he or she will not want the lay client to become aware that the firm may have caused the lay client's predicament. What do you do in these circumstances?

Guidance can be obtained from paras 303 and 703 of the Code of Conduct and para 3.3 of the Written Standards. Your duty under these provisions can be broken down into the following parts:

(a) You must promote and protect fearlessly and by all proper and lawful means the lay client's best interests.

(b) You must do so without regard to your own interests or to any consequences to yourself or to any other person, including your instructing solicitors. The fact that you may receive no further instructions from the solicitors must not be allowed to influence your advice. Nor should you permit your instructing solicitor, in any way, to limit your discretion or influence your opinion on how the interests of the lay client would best be served.

(c) As between your lay client and your instructing solicitor, your primary duty is owed to the lay client.

(d) You should always be alert to the possibility of a conflict of interest between the lay client and the professional client, and any such conflict must be resolved in favour of the lay client.

(e) If you form the view that there is a conflict of interest between your lay client and your instructing solicitor (for example, because it appears that the latter may have been negligent), then you must consider whether it would be in the lay client's best interests to instruct another professional adviser or representative. If you consider that it would, you must advise in those terms. You must also take such steps as you consider necessary to ensure that your advice is communicated to the lay client, if necessary by sending a copy of your advice in writing directly to him or her, as well as to the professional client (see para 703 of the Code).

(f) In advising, bear in mind that it may not always be sensible for a lay client to instruct another firm of solicitors to act on his or her behalf immediately, even if it does appear that your instructing solicitors have been negligent. An example of when it might be proper for your instructing solicitors to continue to act for the time being, is where an appeal is pending against an order striking out the claim for failure to follow a procedural step in the action. However, even in these circumstances, it may be appropriate to ask the solicitors or their insurers to fund the appeal. It is equally clear that a firm of solicitors should not continue to act if there is any doubt over whether the litigation should be continued, or if the lay client would clearly be best advised to pursue a remedy against his or her solicitors rather than a third party. The facts of each case must be carefully considered.

(g) Finally, as a matter of common courtesy, always telephone your instructing solicitor and give him or her advance warning of the nature of the advice that it is your professional duty to give to the lay client. This may do much to preserve the relationship between you and your instructing solicitor for the future.

7.5.4 Drafting

7.5.4.1 General principles

Paragraph 704 of the Code offers general advice on drafting any statement of case, witness statement, affidavit, notice of appeal, or other document.

704   A barrister must not devise facts which will assist in advancing the lay client's case and must not draft any statement of case, witness statement, affidavit, notice of appeal or other document containing

(a) any statement or fact or contention which is not supported by the lay client or by his instructions;

(b) any contention which he does not consider to be properly arguable.

You must not settle any statement of case or any document which contains abusive or scandalous allegations or any allegation which is intended to insult, vilify, or annoy the other party or any other person (para 708(g)).

These general rules must be borne in mind every time you are asked to draft any document. In relation to para 704(b) of the Code, it is impossible to lay down any detailed rules about whether or not something is 'properly arguable'. However, it is clear that a contention will not be 'properly arguable' if it gives rise to no claim or defence at law, or, if properly analysed, there is absolutely no evidence to support it. You must therefore have a firm grasp of the relevant substantive law when drafting any legal document. Furthermore, you must ensure that any contention you put in a document can be properly argued on the facts of the particular case.

7.5.4.2 Pleading fraud

Sometimes a lay client will make allegations of fraudulent or dishonest conduct against the opposing party. Both the lay client and the professional client may ask you to include these allegations in any statement of case that you are instructed to draft. However, you are under a very strict duty not to draft any statement of case, witness statement, affidavit, notice of appeal, or other document containing any allegation of fraud unless you have 'clear instructions' to make such an allegation and you have before you 'reasonably credible material which as it stands establishes a prima facie case of fraud' (Code para 704(c)). Although this paragraph only refers to fraud, any other dishonourable or dishonest conduct should not be alleged without similar material.

The House of Lords (agreeing with the dissenting judgment of Wilson J in the Court of Appeal) has considered this provision in *Medcalf v Mardell and others* [2003] 1 AC 120. In this case, a wasted costs order was sought by the opposing party from leading and junior counsel (the barristers) acting for the other party. They had settled a notice of appeal and a skeleton argument containing allegations of fraud, which the court found were not justified by the evidence. The barristers defended the application on the ground that they had not been able to persuade their lay clients to waive privilege, and that being so, it was impossible for the court to know on what material they had acted, and so the application ought to be dismissed.

In the Court of Appeal, Peter Gibson and Schiemann LJJ (Wilson J dissenting), took the view that para 704(c) required a barrister to have reasonably credible material establishing a prima facie case of fraud before they could draft an allegation of fraud. That material had to be evidence that could be put before the court to make good the allegation. If there is material before counsel which could not be used in court, the existence of the material could not justify pleading fraud.

Wilson J carefully considered the meaning of the phrase 'reasonably credible material which as it stands establishes a prima facie case of fraud'. In his view, the word 'material' in what is now para 704(c) of the Code was wider than evidence in its proper form, and the phrase 'as it stands' means 'at face value'. He took the view (para 80) that, 'To construe the word "establishes" as something that can be achieved only by evidence admissible in court is, in this context, arguably to read too much into it'. In the absence of any evidence as to what the barristers did have before them when pleading the allegations of fraud in the notice of appeal and skeleton argument, he did not feel that he could come to a positive conclusion that the Code of Conduct had been breached.

In the House of Lords, Lord Bingham, agreeing with Wilson J, had this to say:

Paragraph 606(c) [now 704(c)] lays down an important and salutary principle. The parties to contested actions are often at daggers drawn, and the litigious process serves to exacerbate the hostility between them. Such clients are only too ready to make allegations of the most damaging kind against each other. While counsel should never lend his name to such allegations unless instructed to do so, the receipt of instructions is not of itself enough. Counsel is bound to exercise an objective professional judgement whether it is in all the circumstances proper to lend his name to the allegation. As the rule recognises, counsel could not properly judge it proper to make such an allegation unless he had material before him which he judged to be reasonably credible and which appeared to justify the allegation. At the hearing stage, counsel cannot properly make or persist in an allegation which is unsupported by inadmissible evidence, since if there is not admissible evidence to support the allegation the court cannot be invited to find that it has been proved, and if the court cannot be invited to find that the allegation has been proved the allegation should not be made or should be withdrawn. I would however agree with Wilson J that at the preparatory stage the requirement is not that counsel should necessarily have evidence before him in admissible form but that he should have material of such a character that would lead responsible counsel to conclude that serious allegations could properly be based upon it. I could not think, for example, that it would be professionally improper for counsel to plead allegations, however serious, based on the documented conclusions of a DTI inspector or a public inquiry, even though counsel had no access to the documents referred to and the findings in question were inadmissible hearsay. On this point I would accept the judgment of Wilson J.

It is clear from this that:

(a) Allegations of fraud cannot and should not be made simply because the lay client instructs you to make them.

(b) Allegations of fraud should never be made in the absence of 'clear instructions'. You should insist on written instructions from the lay client before you draft any allegation of fraud.

(c) You must scrutinise the papers carefully and decide whether there is enough material to justify pleading an allegation of fraud. The material must be credible and, as it stands, establish a prima facie case of fraud.

(d) If the material relied upon includes or consists of the evidence of a witness, it would be prudent to ensure that a signed statement is obtained from the witness before such an allegation is made.

(e) If an allegation of fraud is drafted but it later becomes clear, at any stage of the proceedings, that it cannot be substantiated (for example, because a witness has retracted his or her statement), then you should inform the opposing side immediately that the allegation of fraud is not being pursued.

7.5.4.3 Drafting orders for interim relief

Quite often counsel is instructed to make an application and draft an order for interim relief such as an injunction, search order, or freezing order. If you are instructed to make such an application, you should ensure that you personally undertake the task of drafting the order, and do so as quickly as possible. A copy of the order must be lodged with the court before the oral hearing starts, except in exceptional circumstances.

Mummery LJ had this to say in *Memory Corporation plc v Sidhu (No. 2)* [2000] 1 WLR 1443 at 1459(H)–1460(E) about counsel's duty in relation to such hearings:

It is the particular duty of the advocate to see that the correct legal procedures and forms are used; that a written skeleton argument and a properly drafted order are prepared by him personally and lodged with the court before the oral hearing; and that at the hearing, the court's attention is drawn by him to unusual features of the evidence adduced, to the applicable law and to the formalities and procedure to be observed.

It is unsatisfactory for an advocate to hand to the court for the first time during the course of an urgent hearing a long and complex draft order that requires close reading and careful scrutiny by the court. If the advocate is unable to produce a draft order for the judge to read before the oral hearing starts then the application should not be made, save in the most exceptional circumstances, until the order has been drafted and lodged.

I emphasize the special responsibility of the advocate for the preparation of draft orders for the use of the court. There may be a convenient precedent to hand on the word processor of the instructing solicitor or in their files or in counsel's chambers, but it is the duty of the advocate actually presenting the case on the oral hearing of the application to settle the draft order personally so as to ensure that he is thoroughly familiar with the detail of it and so in the best possible position to respond to the court's concerns and to assist the court on the final form of the order.

If the order differs in any respect from the standard form of order used in such applications, it is also important to draw this to the attention of the court. Failure to do so may render you in breach of your duty not to mislead the court.

7.5.4.4 Witness statements

In relation to witnesses, you may be asked to see a lay client or a witness in conference with a view to discussing their evidence. You may be asked to do this to assess the credibility of the witness or advise on the strength of the case generally, or to take a proof of evidence which can then be used as the basis of a witness statement. You may also be asked to draft a witness statement on behalf of the lay client or some other witness of fact. In civil cases, counsel is increasingly asked to draft and prepare witness statements because the witness statement will usually stand as that witness's evidence-in-chief at the trial of the action. In this section, guidance will be given in relation to:

- the contact which you may have with a witness in both civil and criminal cases;
- the rules you must adhere to when drafting witness statements.

Contact with witnesses

There is no longer any rule which prevents a barrister from having contact with any witness other than the lay client. Under the Code of Conduct (para 705), it is clear what you must not do. You must not:

- rehearse, practise, or coach a witness in relation to his evidence;
- encourage a witness to give evidence which is untruthful or which is not the whole truth.

See **7.2** above for further discussion on this point.

In relation to witnesses other than the lay client, you should exercise your discretion and consider very carefully whether and to what extent contact is appropriate for the purpose of interviewing witnesses or discussing with them the substance of their evidence bearing in mind that:

(a) it is not your function, but rather that of your instructing solicitor, to investigate the case and collect the evidence;

(b) even if you do not intend or wish to do so, as a figure in authority, you may subconsciously influence lay witnesses, and discussion of the evidence may unwittingly contaminate the witness's evidence;

(c) you should be alert to the risks that any discussion of the substance of the case with a witness may lead to suspicions of coaching, and thus tend to diminish the value of the witness's evidence in the eyes of the court. It may also place you in a position of professional embarrassment if you yourself became a witness in the case (see para 6.2 of the Written Standards).

In the case of a completely independent witness, you may think it prudent not to discuss the evidence with the witness at all, bearing in mind the matters set out above. If, however, after careful consideration of all matters, you decide to proceed, you should take the following steps to minimise the risk of suspicions of coaching. You should ensure that:

- before any discussion about the evidence takes place, you have been provided with a proof of the witness's evidence;
- any such discussion takes place in the presence of your instructing solicitor or a representative;
- the discussion of one witness's evidence does not take place in the presence of another witness of fact;
- care is taken not to disclose the factual evidence of another witness if it would be inappropriate to do so.

A failure to follow these steps will tend to encourage the rehearsal or coaching of a witness and increase the risk of fabrication or contamination of evidence.

You should also be alert to the distinction between settling a witness statement and the taking of a witness statement. Where you are asked to take a witness statement, as opposed to settling a witness statement from a proof of evidence of the witness which has been taken by your professional client, then it is not appropriate, except in exceptional circumstances, for you to act as counsel in the case because it risks undermining your independence as an advocate (see para 6.2.6 of the Written Standards). It should also be noted that the cab-rank rule does not require a barrister to undertake the task of taking a witness statement, as opposed to settling a witness statement. Exceptional circumstances when it may be appropriate for you to take a proof of evidence and continue to act as counsel in the case would be:

- the witness is a minor;
- you have no choice, other than to take a proof, for example in circumstances where a witness turns up at trial and there is no professional client in attendance;
- you are a junior member in a team and will not be examining the witness.

The 'Guidance on Preparation of Witness Statements' para 9(v) makes it clear that the following distinction should be borne in mind:

(a) Questioning a witness closely in order to:
  (i)   enable him or her to present his or her evidence fully and accurately (this must be permissible to ensure that any witness statement that you settle is complete in content); or
  (ii) test the reliability of his or her evidence (which may be necessary to form an informed view of the merits of the case and/or the credibility of the witness).
  and

(b) Questioning a witness closely with a view to encouraging him or her to alter, massage, or obscure his or her real recollection (which is clearly not permissible).

There is no objection to testing a witness's recollection robustly to ascertain the quality of the evidence or discussing the issues that may arise in cross-examination. What is objectionable is conducting a mock cross-examination of the witness or lay client or rehearsing with the witness particular lines of questioning that you propose to follow or which your opponent is likely to follow.

The rules relating to the settling or taking of witness statements in criminal cases are much more strict than in civil cases. Paragraph 6.3.1 of the Written Standards states that:

As a general principle, with the exception of the lay client, character, and expert witnesses, it is wholly inappropriate for a barrister in such a case to interview any potential witness. Interviewing involves discussing with any such witness the substance of his evidence or the evidence of other such witnesses.

Drafting witness statements in a civil case

When asked to draft witness statements in a civil case, you must bear in mind the fact that the statement is likely to stand as the witness's evidence-in-chief. One of the first questions that will be asked of the witness at trial is whether he or she confirms the truth and accuracy of the statement. It is therefore critical that the statement you draft reflects that witness's evidence.

There is often some misunderstanding of the role that counsel can play in drafting a witness statement. Counsel's duty in drafting a witness statement is to:

* understand the evidence that a witness can give;
* help the witness present his or her story *in his or her own words* in a well-structured, organised, coherent, and persuasive way;
* ensure the witness tells his or her whole story (in other words that the statement is complete in content);
* above all, ensure that the statement reflects the witness's evidence. Paragraph 6(iv) of the Guidance on Preparation of Witness Statements states that:

Save for formal matters and uncontroversial facts, [the witness statement] should be expressed, if practicable in the witness's own words. This is especially important when the statement is dealing with the critical factual issues in the case—e.g., the accident or the disputed conversation. Thus the statement should reflect the witness's own description of events. It should not be drafted or edited so as to massage or obscure the witness's real evidence.

It is *not* counsel's function to:

* put a gloss on the evidence;
* draft a statement that contains words that the witness would not use, particularly in relation to the central factual issues;
* vet the accuracy of the witness's evidence (see para 5 of Guidance on Preparation of Witness Statements);
* exclude material from the statement where the omission renders untrue or misleading anything that remains in the statement.

Paragraphs 704(a) and (b) of the Code of Conduct apply equally to witness statements as they do to any other document that you may be asked to draft. Therefore, the witness statement must not contain any statement of fact which is not supported by instructions. You should not draft any statement or fact other than the evidence which in substance, according to your instructions, you reasonably believe the witness would give if the evidence contained in the witness statement or affidavit were being given in oral examination (para 704(d) of the Code). However, you can draft a document containing facts or matters which are subject to confirmation of accuracy by the lay client or witness.

Settling defence case statements in criminal cases

It is becoming increasingly common for counsel to be asked to settle defence case statements. The Bar Standards Board has now prepared a document entitled 'Guidance on Preparation of Defence Case Statements' to assist counsel undertaking this task. You should not settle the defence case statement until you have seen all relevant documents, particularly all prosecution documents and statements, and obtained full instructions from the lay client from a properly signed proof and also preferably during a conference. In particular, you must ensure that the lay client understands the importance of the defence case statement and the potential adverse effects of an inaccurate or inadequate statement.

Once the statement is drafted, you should ensure that you get proper informed approval for the draft from the lay client. This is particularly important in case the lay client challenges or disowns the statement during the trial. You ought therefore to insist on getting *written* acknowledgment from the lay client that:

- he or she understands the importance and accuracy of the defence case statement; and

- he or she has had the opportunity of considering the contents of the statement carefully and approves it.

If you entrust your solicitor with the task of obtaining this acknowledgment, then you should also prepare a short written advice to enclose with the defence case statement on the importance of obtaining the acknowledgment before the defence case statement is served. The defendant should be asked to sign the statement before it is served.

Due to the absolute necessity for the statement to be accurate, para 6 of the 'Guidance on Preparation of Defence Case Statements' states that counsel ought not to accept any instructions to draft or settle a defence case statement unless he or she has been given adequate time and opportunity to gain proper familiarity with the case and comply with the requirements set out above.

7.5.4.5   Drafting indictments in criminal cases

Prosecution counsel is frequently asked to draft the indictment. If you do obtain instructions to undertake drafting of this type, you must do so promptly and within due time. You should also bear in mind 'the desirability of not overloading an indictment with either too many defendants or too many counts, in order to present the prosecution case as simply and as concisely as possible' (para 10.4 of the Written Standards). See also the Code for Crown Prosecutors, paras 7.1–7.3. Furthermore, even if you are not instructed to settle the indictment, you should ask to see a copy of it and should check it.

7.5.5   Can you refuse to advise and/or draft a document?

You are bound by the cab-rank rule (Code para 602). You must therefore accept any instructions at a proper professional fee in the fields in which you profess to practise, irrespective of the party on whose behalf you are instructed, the nature of the case or any belief or opinion that you may have formed as to the character, reputation, cause, conduct, guilt, or innocence of that party. This applies whether the case is privately or publicly funded.

There are a number of circumstances in which you can refuse to act when instructed. These are set out in paras 603, 604, and 701 of the Code of Conduct. You may refuse to act if:

(a) you are required to do anything other than during the course of your ordinary working year;

(b) you do not have adequate time to deal with the papers (Code paras 603 and 701);

(c) there is a conflict of interest which would prevent you acting (such as having acted for the other side);

(d) the fee is not a proper professional fee having regard to the complexity and length and difficulty of the case, your expertise and seniority, and the expenses you will incur. Note that a publicly funded matter is deemed to be at a proper professional fee;

(e) the work is to be done under a conditional fee agreement;

(f) instructions are received from a solicitor or firm who has had credit facilities withdrawn by the Bar Council on the basis that the firm has been persistently late or has failed to pay counsel's fees. You must then refuse to do any work for the solicitor or firm unless payment of an agreed fee is enclosed with the papers, or you agree in advance to accept no payment for the work (Annexe G1, The Terms of Work on which Barristers Offer Their Services to Solicitors and the Withdrawal of Credit Scheme 1988).

Otherwise, you must accept and carry out your instructions to the best of your ability, bearing in mind your duty under the Code and the Written Standards and the other Guidance issued by the Bar Council which has been discussed above.

7.6 Conclusion

This chapter has made it clear that professional conduct and ethical difficulties can arise throughout a case, in a variety of contexts. It has guided you through the problem areas pertinent to the key skills with a discussion of the relevant principles and other sources of guidance you will need as an intending barrister. Furthermore, several situations have been identified which are not expressly covered by the Code, but in applying its spirit with a recognition of the Code's underlying values (see **Chapter 4**), the suggested approaches should now be more easily understood.

Your alertness to these issues will ensure that they are handled appropriately paying due regard if necessary to not only the Code and the application of its spirit, but also to the 'ethical challenge' discussed in **Chapter 1**. Hence, you will continue to develop the skills set out in **Chapter 1**:

- the *identification* of potential professional conduct issues;
- the *sources* of guidance on particular issues;
- the necessity of applying the *spirit* of the Code where there is no letter;
- the need to recognise obligations towards *fair treatment*; and
- how you would deal *practically* with the matter.

Of course, in practice there will be difficult situations in which you find yourself and no matter how disciplined your approach is to handling professional conduct matters, you will struggle to know the best course of action. The point is that you are already halfway to dealing with the matter because you have recognised at the earliest opportunity that an issue has arisen. In such a situation, do not be afraid to take guidance from fellow barristers or to phone the Bar Council. Remember the need to maintain the highest standards is an ongoing obligation for all members of the Bar—the practical advice and guidance set out in this section and throughout the manual will only take you so far. You will know if you are cutting corners or deliberately ignoring professional conduct matters. However, it is hoped that you have already decided that the extra time and effort put to solving these areas of practice are the only way to ensure the solid foundation of a continuing and successful practice at the Bar.

8

The Proceeds of Crime Act 2002

8.1 The problem posed by the Proceeds of Crime Act 2002

Since it came into force, the Proceeds of Crime Act 2002 (POCA 2002) has caused considerable anxiety for lawyers. Following the decision of the Court of Appeal in *Bowman v Fels* [2005] EWCA Civ 226, the main remaining area of concern for lawyers is the reporting obligation under s 330 when working in 'the regulated sector'. However, there is also the need to advise the client when he or she is at risk of liability under s 327 and/or s 329. The Serious Organised Crime and Police Act 2005 and more recently the POCA 2002 (Business in the Regulated Sector and Supervisory Authorities) Order 2007 and the POCA 2007 (Amendment) Regulations 2007 have made amendments to the POCA 2002. There is further new legislation in the form of the Money Laundering Regulations 2007, which came into force on 15 December 2007.

To discuss the legislation, this chapter uses the specific example of ancillary relief. Ancillary relief is the process by which divorcing spouses obtain financial resolution of their affairs from the court. However, that should make it no less applicable to other situations. In ancillary relief, the client is in practice obliged to tell his or her adviser about all of his or her assets and income because of the obligation to the court of full and frank disclosure. The problem is that this process may disclose that some of those assets are the proceeds of crime.

In order for there to be proceeds of crime, somebody (usually the client or another party in the context of legal proceedings) must have engaged in 'criminal conduct' (s 340(2)). It is not necessary that he or she has actually been convicted of an offence, and your client does not necessarily need to have personally engaged in the criminal conduct, only (for example) to be in possession of criminal property (see **8.2.2**).

It may be that the client has, for example, been involved in mainstream drug dealing. More commonly, there may be issues of tax evasion, for example, the client receives money 'cash in hand'. This is not in itself 'criminal conduct'—anyone can pay their bills in cash or by cheque—but it becomes an offence if he or she fails to disclose these earnings to HM Revenue & Customs. Tax evasion is a crime, as is benefit fraud.

A number of problems face the lawyer as a result of the POCA 2002. First, there are the 'principal offences' under Part VII of the POCA 2002 (ss 327, 328, and 329) and the secondary offences under ss 333A–D (tipping off) and s 342 (prejudicing an investigation). The lawyer will need to advise the client of potential liability under these sections. There is a *small* residual risk of lawyers being liable under s 328 despite the judgment in *Bowman*. Second, since 15 December 2007, lawyers have been subject to the Money Laundering Regulations 2007, and thus may be a 'relevant person' in terms of the Regulations, while also being in the 'regulated sector' in terms of the Act (as defined by Sch 9—definitions of these terms are the same in the Act and the Regulations). Being in the regulated sector exposes lawyers to the risk of criminal liability for breach of s 330 of the POCA 2002 (i.e., failure to disclose). The risks are more acute for solicitors owing to the nature of their work (after all, they usually have first, and continuous, contact with the client and handle the client's money) but for certain types of work, the Bar is also under specific obligations and at risk of criminal liability.

The Bar Council has issued guidance to barristers in respect of the POCA 2002 and the Money Laundering Regulations 2007. This guidance is regularly updated; see **8.6** for finding the latest version.

8.2 Principal offences

8.2.1 Key differences between the principal and secondary offences

Sections 327, 328, and 329 set out the principal offences in Part VII of the POCA 2002. They differ from the secondary offences (considered below) in a number of key respects:

(a) Disclosure in respect of the principal offences is 'authorised disclosure' under s 338 (not 'protected disclosure' under s 337 which relates to the secondary offences).

(b) The disclosure defence under s 338 requires not only 'authorised disclosure' but also the 'appropriate consent' under s 335. Section 337 does not require a consent because of the fundamental difference in the duties between ss 327–329 and 330: in ss 327–329, disclosure is made in order to exonerate the discloser from criminal responsibility for what he or she would otherwise do; s 330 on the other hand is a general duty (arising from the fact of one's practice in the regulated sector) to disclose the fact that someone is involved in money laundering and in that sense is separate from any activity with which the discloser himself is involved.

8.2.2 Definitions

'Criminal conduct' is defined in s 340(2) (s 340 is in fact the definition section for Part VII of the POCA 2002). It covers conduct which would constitute an offence in any part of the UK—so, for example, tax evasion is a criminal offence in UK law. It also covers conduct which occurs abroad but would be an offence in the UK if it had occurred there, but in those circumstances defendants to offences under ss 327, 328, and 330 may be able to take advantage of the defences in those sections. These provide that if the defendant knew or believed on reasonable grounds that the relevant conduct had occurred in a particular country or territory outside of the UK, *and* that conduct was not criminal according to *local* laws at the time it occurred, *and* it was not conduct of a type prescribed by order of the Secretary of State, the defendant has not committed the offence.

'Criminal property' (s 340(3)) is that which constitutes 'a person's benefit from criminal conduct or . . . represents such a benefit (in whole or part and whether directly or indirectly)', and the alleged offender (i.e., the person accused of facilitating money laundering, etc.) knows or suspects that it constitutes or represents such a benefit.

If, for example, in an ancillary relief claim, the matrimonial home had been partially paid for by 'criminal property' in the form of unpaid tax monies—say, by paying the mortgage instalments partly with these monies—the house could 'represent' the benefit from criminal conduct. The same might be the case for other assets.

8.2.3   Sections 327, 328, and 329

Sections 327, 328, and 329 of the POCA 2002 may affect your client, and the client will need to be advised of this. Section 327 provides that:

(1) A person commits an offence if he—

    (a)   conceals criminal property;

    (b)   disguises criminal property;

    (c)   converts criminal property;

    (d)   transfers criminal property;

    (e)   removes criminal property from England and Wales or from Scotland or from Northern Ireland.

[. . .]

(3) Concealing or disguising criminal property includes concealing or disguising its nature, source, location, disposition, movement or ownership, or any rights with respect to it.

Section 328 provides that:

(1) A person commits an offence if he enters into or becomes concerned in an arrangement which he knows or suspects facilitates (by whatever means) the acquisition, retention, use or control of criminal property by or on behalf of another person.

As discussed below, 'being concerned in an arrangement' was once thought to include involvement in litigation which resulted in a settlement or an order of the court in relation to proceeds of crime. The Court of Appeal in *Bowman* made it quite clear that s 328 is not intended to affect 'the ordinary conduct of litigation by legal professionals. That includes any step taken by them in litigation from the issue of proceedings and the securing of injunctive relief or a freezing order up to its final disposal by judgment', and that such activities are not to be regarded as 'being concerned in an arrangement'. Subject to the points made at **8.7.2** *et seq*, s 328 now clearly does not apply to the involvement of a lawyer in litigation or the resolution of litigation by agreement.

However, the client may still have committed the offence in relation to an arrangement over property, *independent of the litigation process*, for example, a sham property transaction designed to conceal the proceeds of crime.

Section 329 provides:

(1) A person commits an offence if he—

    (a)   acquires criminal property;

    (b)   uses criminal property;

    (c)   has possession of criminal property.

For example, a wife in an ancillary relief claim who had not personally committed the criminal offence of tax evasion could potentially be accused of the s 329 offence— acquiring, using, or possessing criminal property—if the house that she jointly owns with her tax-evading husband was bought with money he had not declared to tax— unless she makes an authorised disclosure under s 338. The husband could conceivably be accused of both s 327 and s 329 offences, as well as tax evasion itself. In order to protect herself, the wife should make an 'authorised disclosure' under s 338.

8.2.4   Defences to the principal offences

The client (and the barrister, in the rare situation that disclosure is required of him) can obtain a complete defence by making an 'authorised disclosure' under s 338 (in the manner prescribed by s 339), *and* by getting the 'appropriate consent' (s 335).

Generally speaking, disclosure is to the Serious Organised Crime Agency (SOCA). The way that consent works is as follows:

(a) SOCA may consent within seven days of disclosure being made, in which case the client can continue with the act or transaction in question.

(b) If not, the client is required to wait for seven working days from the working day after disclosure. Once that period has passed without a notice of refusal from SOCA, the consent is deemed and the client can continue with the act or transaction.

(c) If SOCA gives notice of refusal within the seven-day period, there is then a moratorium period of 31 calendar days from the day on which refusal is received. Thereafter, the client is free to continue with the act or transaction.

Specific guidance is given by the Bar Council in 'Proceeds of Crime Act 2002' in the Guidance section of the website (see **8.6**) as to the interrelation of any obligation the barrister has to disclose (whether by reason of s 328 or s 330) and the obligations to the client—paras 8 and 9. It is very important that you consider these principles first in such a situation.

8.2.5 Does s 328 apply to the activities of lawyers?

The judgment in *Bowman* was handed down by the Court of Appeal on 8 March 2005. It is authority of considerable public importance since this was the first full examination by the Court of Appeal of the impact of the POCA 2002 on legal professional privilege between lawyer and client. It effectively overrules *P v P (Ancillary Relief; Proceeds of Crime)* [2003] EWHC Fam 2260.

8.2.5.1 Background

Prior to this decision, the word 'arrangement' was believed to cover litigation, including settlement of such litigation by agreement. Where a lawyer knew or suspected that money or assets being the subject of litigation were the proceeds of crime, then he or she could only escape criminal liability under s 328 by making an 'authorised disclosure'—in other words, by notifying the National Criminal Intelligence Service (NCIS) (note, this is now SOCA) of the suspected criminal activity and obtaining the appropriate consent to proceed with the arrangement. For lawyers, it seemed that the fundamental principle of legal professional privilege had been fatally undermined—not only would a lawyer be obliged to report suspected money laundering by the other party, but he or she would also be compelled to make disclosure to a third party of suspected money laundering by his or her own client.

8.2.5.2 The central question in *Bowman*

The Court of Appeal identified the following issues (para 24):

(a) Whether s 328 applied to the ordinary conduct of legal proceedings at all.

(b) Whether Parliament could have been taken, without using clear words to that effect, to have intended to override the very important principles of legal professional privilege.

8.2.5.3 The decision in *Bowman*

The Court of Appeal concluded as follows:

(a) (para 83) Section 328 is not intended to affect 'the ordinary conduct of litigation by legal professionals. That includes any step taken by them in litigation from the issue of proceedings and the securing of injunctive relief or a freezing order up to its final disposal by judgment'. In other words, conducting litigation does not involve 'becoming concerned in an arrangement' within the meaning of s 328, and s 328 is therefore inapplicable to such activities.

(b) (para 87) The Court of Appeal further stated that even if the above conclusion was wrong, it was quite clear that on a proper construction s 328 does not override legal professional privilege.

(c) (paras 99 and 100) The Court of Appeal also came to the view that resolution of the whole, or any aspect of, legal proceedings by agreement would equally be outside the scope of s 328.

Clearly, this guidance has brought considerable clarity to an area which caused enormous concern to lawyers involved in litigation when the POCA 2002 was first enacted. A lawyer can advise and represent a client in the vast majority of situations without fear of being obliged to breach legal professional privilege to report suspected money laundering to the authorities. However, there remain some situations where s 328 could apply to lawyers. These are discussed below at **8.7**.

8.3 Secondary offences

8.3.1 The Money Laundering Regulations 2007

A barrister acting in the course of business who is a 'relevant person' as defined in the Regulations will be subject to additional requirements and liability. Barristers most likely to fall within the ambit of the Regulations are members of the Chancery Bar involved in non-contentious advisory work, especially in relation to business or taxation or property transactions and the setting up of companies and trusts. Please refer to the Bar Council Guidance on Money Laundering Regulations issued in January 2008.

8.3.1.1 When is counsel deemed to be a 'relevant person'?

Regulation 3(1) sets out a list of relevant persons, including at (c) 'tax advisers' and at (d) 'independent legal professionals'. 'Independent legal professional' is further defined in reg 3(9) as being a firm or practitioner providing legal services in financial or real property transactions concerning: at (a) the buying and selling of real property or business entities; and at (e) the creation, operation, or management of trusts, companies or similar structures.

Most barristers will not find themselves falling within the definition of 'relevant person' under these regulations. In particular the Bar Council considers that definition will not cover employed barristers, barristers providing advice *after* a relevant transaction, barristers conducting litigation arising from a relevant transaction, or barristers advising in connection with an agreement intended to compromise a genuine dispute. See 'Money Laundering Regulations—Guidance for the Bar' (given at **8.6**) for further detail.

The Regulations are transaction based, therefore counsel has to consider for every piece of work undertaken whether he or she is a relevant person.

Barristers must be astute to determine whether any particular piece of work undertaken by them falls within the Regulations, as an error in this regard and consequential failure to implement the requisite systems will result in the commission of a criminal offence, punishable by a fine or up to two years' imprisonment.

8.3.1.2   Additional requirements under the Regulations

The additional requirements for a relevant person when conducting business include the carrying out of:

(a) due diligence procedures;

(b) record-keeping procedures;

(c) internal reporting procedures and training of employees.

The latter requirements at (c) are of less significance to the Bar than to other businesses in the regulated sector, because barristers in private practice are individuals, neither employing nor acting in association with any other person and are solely responsible for their own professional practice. Most of these latter requirements either do not apply or such individuals are exempted.

In terms of due diligence, record-keeping, and identification procedures, this will usually have been carried out by the UK solicitor or other regulated professional, and counsel's duty will often be discharged by ensuring that in the instructions a letter or certificate is included which confirms that the relevant process has been carried out. Where this is not the case, a barrister must carry out his own checks. Guidance and pro forma letters in respect of these matters can be found in the appendices to the Bar Council guidance. (See **8.6**.)

8.3.2   Liability under s 330 for barristers operating within the regulated sector

Since barristers are considered to be in the 'regulated sector', they are open to criminal liability under s 330, which is the offence of 'failure to disclose' by a person in the 'regulated sector'. However, the section includes a defence relating to legal privilege, which means that it will not catch most barristers engaged in the ordinary conduct of litigation. Section 330(1) to (5) (as amended) reads as follows:

(1) A person commits an offence if the conditions in subsections (2) to (4) are satisfied.

(2) The first condition is that he—

    (a) knows or suspects, or

    (b) has reasonable grounds for knowing or suspecting, that another person is engaged in money laundering.

(3) The second condition is that the information or other matter—

    (a) on which his knowledge or suspicion is based, or

    (b) which gives reasonable grounds for such knowledge or suspicion, came to him in the course of a business in the regulated sector.

(3A) The third condition is—

    (a) that he can identify the other person mentioned in subsection (2) or the whereabouts of any of the laundered property, or

    (b) that he believes, or it is reasonable to expect him to believe, that the information or other matter mentioned in subsection (3) will or may assist in identifying that other person or the whereabouts of any of the laundered property.

(4) The fourth condition is that he does not make the required disclosure to—

    (a) a nominated officer, or

    (b) a person authorised for the purposes of this Part by the Director General of the Serious Organised Crime Agency,

    as soon as practicable after the information or other matter mentioned in subsection (3) comes to him.

(5) The required disclosure is a disclosure of—

    (a)   the identity of the other person mentioned in subsection (2), if he knows it,

    (b)   the whereabouts of the laundered property, so far as he knows it, and

    (c)   the information or other matter mentioned in subsection (3).

Note first that, unlike in other parts of Part VII, the standard is objective, not subjective. If you have failed to 'know' or 'suspect' personally, you can be liable if there were 'reasonable grounds' on which you should have known or suspected. In other words, the 'moron' defence (that the grounds were there but you simply failed to notice them) is not available to you.

So, for any piece of work you do, you have to consider your obligations under s 330. If the conditions in ss 2 to 4 apply then, subject to the defences described below, you may have an obligation to make a 'protected' disclosure under s 337.

8.3.3 Defences

There are in fact two defences available for a failure to disclose under s 330(6):

(a) you have a reasonable excuse for not making disclosure;

(b) you are a professional legal adviser and the information (the identity of the other person in subsection (2), or the whereabouts of the laundered property, or the information or matter in subsection (3)) has come to you in privileged circumstances.

In other words, there is a legal professional privilege defence to s 330. Section 330(10) clarifies the circumstances in which it applies. However, it is to some degree limited by s 330(11), which provides that legal professional privilege will not apply where 'information . . . is communicated or given with the intention of furthering a criminal purpose'. It is not clear whose intention is relevant for the purposes of this section. Given the wide manner in which criminal behaviour prohibited by ss 327, 328, and 329 is drafted, the lawyer will have to look very closely at what the client is intending to achieve in communicating information to the lawyer. Certainly, in telling you that her husband is taking cash in hand and not declaring it for tax purposes, an ancillary relief client probably is not intending to further a criminal purpose; rather she is telling you this in order to maximise her recovery in the ancillary relief—the sole or dominant purpose of her giving you this information being the conduct of the family proceedings. For further guidance, see the Bar Council guidance 'Proceeds of Crime Act 2002' (see **8.6**).

If you do make disclosure under s 337 ('protected disclosure'), provided that you comply with the conditions of s 337, you will be protected against litigation by the client for breaching confidentiality by s 337(1). Check that you have (or should have) suspicion based on real grounds, as opposed to mere speculation, or you may be at risk that your disclosure is not in accordance with s 337 and thus leave yourself vulnerable to successful litigation by the client.

8.4 Other secondary offences

There are two other secondary offences which merit consideration. These arise particularly in the context of discussing the issue of disclosure with the client.

8.4.1 Sections 333A–D—'tipping off'

The offence of 'tipping off' has been amended and now only applies within the regulated sector. Essentially, it relates to a situation where you know or suspect that a disclosure has been made (for example, your solicitor has made a disclosure already). The offence cannot be committed in relation to a disclosure that is yet to be made (as to which, see s 342 below). Where you 'make a disclosure which is likely to prejudice any investigation which might be conducted' as a result of the primary disclosure, you may be guilty of an offence. The 'disclosure' you make could be to your client, or to the other side, the point being that by revealing what you know or intend to do, you could enable a criminal or money launderer to cover his or her tracks, conceal the evidence, etc. Defences are available—those most likely to be relevant to a barrister are set out in s 333D. Disclosure to the Bar Council or to further a proper investigation is permissible as is disclosure made without knowing or suspecting that it might prejudice an investigation under the Act. Also permitted is a disclosure made to your client and 'for the purpose of dissuading the client from engaging in conduct amounting to an offence' (s 333D(2)(b)). It is not clear how this will work in practice; it is submitted that its purpose is to enable the avoidance of an absurd, 'quasi-entrapment' scenario, where a legal adviser would be forced to stand dumbly by and watch a client commit a criminal offence that is bound to be detected, which would not be committed at all if the adviser could advise the client as to the reality of the situation.

8.4.2 Section 342—prejudicing an investigation

Unlike ss 333A–D, this offence *can* be committed in advance of a disclosure being made, and relates to conduct, including making disclosures, which could prejudice an investigation which is being made or is contemplated. (Other conduct could include, for example, concealing or falsifying or destroying relevant documents.)

A variety of defences are available, including legal professional privilege. Again, legal professional privilege is limited where there is an intention to further a criminal purpose, and again the relevant intention is that of the lawyer.

In the circumstances, it may be hard to see how a lawyer could be considered to be furthering a criminal intention of his own (in relation to 'tipping off' and the prejudicing of investigation offences) in simply advising a client of the state of the law with regard to his or her position, for example the risk of the client committing an offence under s 329.

8.5 Penalties

8.5.1 Section 334

Sections 327, 328, and 329	on summary conviction, imprisonment of up to six months or a fine or both; on indictment, a fine or imprisonment of up to 14 years.
Sections 330 and 333A–D	on summary conviction, imprisonment of up to six months or a fine or both; on indictment, a fine or imprisonment of up to five years.

8.5.2 Section 342

Section 342	on summary conviction, imprisonment of up to six months or a fine or both; on indictment, a fine or imprisonment of up to five years.

Clearly, it pays to get it right. And note that the mere fact that you advise the solicitor that he has a reporting obligation under the POCA 2002 does not discharge your own obligations. However, it is perfectly possible to make joint disclosure to SOCA on the part of the solicitor, counsel, and possibly the client. In addition, SOCA indicates in its guidance that if a solicitor has made a report in advance of instructing counsel and counsel's report would be based on the exact same facts, there is no obligation on counsel to report further.

8.6   Sources of useful information

(a) The Bar Council (<http://www.barcouncil.org.uk>)—under the section 'Guidance' you can obtain two documents which are the Bar Council's current guidance on these areas, and are referred to above. At the alphabetical list go to 'P' for POCA 2002. There you will find 'Proceeds of Crime Act 2002' and 'Money Laundering Regulations—Guidance for the Bar'; at the time of writing both of these were last amended in January 2008.

(b) *Bowman v Fels* [2005] EWCA Civ 226 can be accessed through the Court Service website (<http://www.hmcourts-service.gov.uk>)—search under the 'Legal/ Professional' section—or go directly to <http://www.bailii.org>.

(c) The Law Society (<http://www.lawsoc.org.uk>)—there is much helpful guidance on this site, under the 'Anti-Money Laundering' link on the home page, and you can download a document containing the main parts of the Act.

(d) Serious Organised Crime Agency (<http://www.soca.gov.uk>)—for information such as how to go about making a report, and for SOCA guidance.

8.7   Areas in which counsel remains at risk of liability under the POCA 2002

The decision in *Bowman v Fels* [2005] EWCA Civ 226 has provided considerable clarity on an issue of acute concern to litigators. However, lawyers still need to tread carefully in certain areas—and in others, confusion remains. References to paragraph numbers below are to paragraphs in *Bowman*.

8.7.1   Section 330 and the regulated sector

Lawyers will have to continue to keep possible liability under s 330 in mind when operating in the regulated sector (principally in relation to financial and real estate transactions). This will be of particular concern to certain sectors of the Bar, such as tax specialists and Chancery practitioners who are routinely involved in such work— although every lawyer needs to be aware of the potential application of s 330, since it is transaction based; in other words, its applicability depends on the subject matter of every individual transaction rather than the lawyer's general area of work. It may well be that specialist Bar associations issue future guidance specific to their areas in relation to s 330 obligations. Of course, availability of the legal professional privilege defence is likely to mean that you are very rarely obliged to report money laundering by the client.

As pointed out in the Bar Council guidance, it is apparent from the reasoning in *Bowman* that the ordinary conduct of litigation or its consensual resolution does not fall within the 'regulated sector' for the purposes of s 330 in any event, and so s 330 really only applies to non-contentious advisory work within the 'regulated sector'.

8.7.2   Negotiation and agreement in the absence of issued proceedings

At paras 99 to 102, the Court of Appeal considered resolution of the whole, or part, of legal proceedings by agreement. The obvious point was made that if the ordinary conduct of litigation was to be treated as outside the scope of s 328, as the court had already concluded, then it would be inconsistent and illogical to nevertheless treat any step in such proceedings taken by *agreement*, or a settlement of the litigation obtained by agreement, as subject to s 328. Given the considerable emphasis on resolution of litigation by agreement not only in domestic law (the 'Woolf reforms') but also in international law, the court concluded that consensual steps—including final resolution by agreement—were not subject to s 328.

However, the court indicated (para 101) that the situation might be different where the agreed settlement was *independent* of litigation. The court was careful to use the phrase 'in a litigious context' when discussing consensual agreement. This appears to extend to situations of *existing or contemplated legal proceedings* only. As the court pointed out (para 101), this is in line with the language of the relevant European directives, as well as relevant sections of the POCA 2002. It does, however, leave something of a grey area. Surely a lawyer with his or her client's interests foremost in his mind will attempt to negotiate a settlement without recourse to legal proceedings. At what point would a court regard him or her as negotiating in the context of 'contemplated' legal proceedings (and thus beyond the reach of s 328)? Will lawyers have to threaten legal proceedings as a first step to attempting negotiation in all cases in order to escape the confines of s 328?

There is considerable emphasis on the use and observance of pre-action protocols since the Woolf reforms. It is suggested that observance of such protocols (the purpose of which is to avoid litigation where possible by agreed settlement) could, and would, be considered by a court as negotiation in the context of contemplated legal proceedings. Clearly, legal proceedings are the likely result if negotiation under the protocol fails, and protocols additionally have as their aim the efficient preparation of the case for litigation in the event of failed negotiation. It may be that this aspect of the applicability, or not, of s 328 will serve to emphasise and increase use of the protocols.

8.7.3   Sham litigation

While not expressing a concluded view on the point, the Court of Appeal referred to the possibility that s 328 could potentially apply to lawyers in the situation in which:

one were concerned with a settlement which did not reflect the legal and practical merits of the parties' respective positions in the proceedings, and was known or suspected to be no more than a pretext for agreeing on the acquisition, retention, use or control of criminal property. (para 102)

This would be an entirely logical position on the basis of the court's interpretation of the legislation. First, s 330, used by the court to illuminate the intentions of the legislator in respect of s 328, clearly provides for a situation where legal professional privilege does not apply (s 330(11)), whereby if the client intends to further a criminal purpose (such as concealing proceeds of crime) in communicating the relevant information to his lawyer, privilege does not attach and the lawyer working in the regulated sector must report. Second, recital 17 of the 2001 Directive (Directive 2001/97/EC amending Council Directive 91/308/EEC on prevention of the use of the financial system for the purpose of money laundering), on which the court placed so much reliance in interpreting the applicability of s 328 to litigation, states:

legal advice remains subject to the obligation of professional secrecy unless the legal counsellor is taking part in money laundering activities, the legal advice is provided for money laundering purposes, or the lawyer knows that the client is seeking legal advice for money laundering purposes.

The consequences are that a lawyer conducting litigation must be astute to the possibility that the litigation is a sham in order to pursue money laundering. A good indication might be that the settlement did not substantially reflect the merits of each side's case. The Court of Appeal further made the point that this still leaves the question of at what point the s 328 offence could be said to have been committed by the lawyer. In paras 67 and 68 of the judgment, the court took the view that an offence under s 328 could not have been committed until the 'arrangement' was actually made.

8.7.4 Transactions resulting from the judgment

The Court of Appeal stated at para 59 that:

while legal advice may be given in any area, one would not often expect legal professionals assisting in the planning or execution of or acting for a client in respect of a financial or real estate transaction of a kind specified in Article 2a(5) to have received from, or obtained on, their client relevant information 'in the course of performing their task of defending or representing that client in, or concerning judicial proceedings'.

This viewpoint is doubtless entirely accurate in relation to many situations. However, the question arises, what is the position in relation to the 'fruits' of litigation? More often than not, the implementation of an order, or an agreed resolution to litigation, will involve lawyers in transactions—financial, commercial, real property. An example could be an ancillary relief case, involving the transfer of a house, or a shareholding, to one of the parties. This is clearly within the meaning of 'transaction' in Art 2a(5) of the 2001 Directive, and therefore subject to s 330. Quite often (if not always), the law firms involved in the litigation will be those dealing with the transactions required to finally resolve the dispute. To what degree could the knowledge of a client's wrongdoing gained by the litigation team be imputed to the team dealing with the transactions flowing from resolution of the litigation? Or perhaps even more acutely, what about the situation of a sole practitioner dealing with the litigation and the transactions flowing from it?

One answer to this dilemma seems to depend on how one interprets the reference to 'ordinary course of litigation' in the judgment. If it includes those transactions required to give effect to the order or agreement, then the difficulty is removed. Support for such an interpretation comes from para 62 of the judgment. Reference is made to the function of litigation—'resolving the rights and duties of two parties according to law'. Such 'resolution' would be threatened if parties were deterred from litigating due to a fear of a report of their activities at the stage of actually effecting the remedy obtained. More importantly, the court's reference to assets, being proceeds of money laundering, being 'retained *or used to satisfy any liability according to the outcome of proceedings*' seems to suggest that execution of the order or agreement would not be 'carrying out' a 'transaction' relating to money laundering.

Of course, such transactions, subject as they are to s 330, will benefit from the defence in s 330(6) and (10)—that the information has come to the lawyer in privileged circumstances and so disclosure will not be required. However, under s 330(11), privilege will afford no defence to the obligation to disclose if the client's purpose in communicating the information is a criminal purpose, and it may well be here that the problem arises.

8.7.5 Conclusion

Clearly, *Bowman* and its subsequent consideration has provided considerable clarity to lawyers in terms of their obligations under s 328 and s 330 of the POCA 2002 and the Money Laundering Regulations 2007 and to their clients in terms of legal professional privilege. However, some caution may still be required with regard to the situations suggested above. As ever, it is crucial that you are familiar with, and remain up to date with, guidance issued by the Bar Council.

Since the Act the situation has gradually become clearer and the latest guidance is the shortest and clearest yet, reflecting the increasing confidence of the profession in where this legislation does and does not apply in practice.

9

Professional conduct problems

Question 1

Objectives

    (a) To consider the meaning and importance of the cab-rank rule in all aspects of a practising barrister's work.

    (b) To consider the meaning of 'professional embarrassment'.

A solicitor seeks to instruct you to act for notoriously bad landlords in an action for possession of premises occupied by a highly regarded charitable organisation. The case is likely to draw adverse publicity. You hold yourself out to act in landlord and tenant cases, you have no connection with either party or with the premises, you have no conflicting professional commitment and the fee offered is a proper fee for you and for the case. Your clerk tells you that he wishes you to refuse the instructions because:

    (a) it is chambers' policy not to act for landlords; and

    (b) he fears that your normal professional clients will be reluctant to instruct you in future cases as their clients (tenants, consumers, etc.) would refuse to have as counsel one who had acted for these particular claimants.

What do you do?

Question 2

Objectives

    (a) To illustrate the possibility of different interpretations of the Bar Code.

    (b) To consider the relationship between the cab-rank rule and the practising barrister's duty not to discriminate nor to victimise on prohibited grounds.

You act for a white father whose former wife, who is also white, is now cohabiting with a black African boyfriend. Your client instructs you to resist her application for contact with the parties' son on grounds which you consider to be racist. Can you refuse to put forward instructions even if wrapped up as seeking to avoid 'exposing his son to a cultural environment totally alien to him . . . '?

Question 3

Objectives

    (a) To emphasise the continuing duty of confidentiality.

    (b) To illustrate its relationship with the cause(s) of professional embarrassment.

You have successfully appeared for the claimants in an action where the unsuccessful defendants now wish to seek a Part 20 indemnity or contribution from a third party who was not a party to the original action. The defendants' solicitors were impressed with your performance and want you to be able to use your knowledge of the case against the third party. Do you accept the instructions?

Question 4

Objective

To introduce the general rules governing the receipt of instructions.

A solicitor, who regularly instructs you and your chambers, telephones you and instructs you to attend at a particular police station where a lay client is about to be interviewed and to advise the client as necessary. The solicitor undertakes to pay you a proper fee. If the matter leads to a charge or charges being preferred, the brief is likely to come into chambers for someone of your experience.

   (a) Can you act?

   (b) Would it make any difference if the brief would certainly be beyond your competence?

Question 5

Objective

To show the importance of the Written Standards for the Conduct of Professional Work.

You are prosecuting a plea of guilty where the defendant is unrepresented. It is a type of case in which the Court of Criminal Appeal has given sentencing guidelines. The judge does not appear to be familiar with criminal work. You are aware from discussion with the officer in the case of a number of facts favourable to the defendant which he does not bring out when mitigating on his own behalf. What are your duties?

Question 6

Objectives

   (a) To underline that, under paras 306 and 403 of the Bar Code, the barrister is responsible for the organisation of his or her own work.

   (b) To underline that, under para 701(a) of the Bar Code, advocates must in all their activities be courteous and act promptly, conscientiously, diligently, and with reasonable competence and take all reasonable and practicable steps to avoid unnecessary expense or waste of the court's time and to ensure that professional engagements are fulfilled. Under para 610(d) of the Bar Code, if a case is to be returned it must be returned in good and sufficient time for the client and the court to be properly serviced when it is called on.

You have received and accepted instructions to appear in case 'A' (a civil case fixed to be heard on 20 April). You have done a lot of preparatory work upon it and have seen the professional and lay clients in conference on a number of occasions. You have also accepted instructions to defend in a serious criminal case (case 'B'), expected to be tried in the week beginning 1 April and to last for five days, but which may well go on longer. Before you have conferred with the client in case 'B', you learn that it will not be heard until the week beginning 15 April. Both solicitors assert priority and both clients are anxious to have your services. Which case do you do? Why?

Question 7

Objective

To illustrate some of the 'fundamental principles' applicable to all barristers.

You have represented your client successfully in court. After the hearing, the client stuffs a £20 note in your pocket and tells you to enjoy a drink on him.

   (a) Do you keep the money?

   (b) Would it make any difference if your client instead sent you a bottle of whisky?

Question 8

Objective

To consider scenarios where your client's instructions may render you professionally embarrassed, and the action you must take as a consequence.

> (a) *The defendant in a rape case instructs you that sexual intercourse took place between him and the victim with her consent. At trial, he tells you that he did not have sexual intercourse with her and gives you names of alibi witnesses.*
>
> (b) *Your client has mental health problems. His instructions differ each time you speak to him. What should you do in these circumstances?*

Question 9

Objective

To explore the relationship between the duty of disclosure and the grounds on which a practising barrister must cease to act and withdraw from a case.

You act for the claimant in civil proceedings. In the course of his evidence-in-chief, he produces several documents from his pocket which he alleges support his claim. You have never seen them before nor have they been disclosed to the defence. What do you do?

Question 10

Objective

To explore counsels' duties where conflicts of interest exist between their professional and lay clients.

You receive a set of instructions to advise and settle civil proceedings for a claimant from X and Co, a firm of solicitors who have instructed you on a number of occasions and are among your best clients. It is apparent that they have been negligent in handling the claimant's affairs. It appears to you that the claimant's chances have not been badly affected and he is likely to succeed in the litigation, but he has at least been prejudiced in the sense that, if the relevant matter 'surfaces' in the litigation, the defendants will be able to make use of it to reduce the damages or to obtain a better settlement than would otherwise have been open to them. (For example, there has been a failure to secure evidence relevant to proving the amount of the claimant's loss and damage.) What, if anything, should you do?

Question 11

Objectives

> (a) To highlight the practising barrister's overriding duty to the court.
>
> (b) To highlight the concomitant duties to the lay client.

You are defending a trial at the Crown Court. In the course of giving his evidence, the defendant makes an allegation which, although it is in your instructions, you had not put to the victim. It is apparent that it should have been, and the victim has gone on holiday and cannot be recalled. The judge is furious. What do you do?

Question 12

Objectives

> (a) To introduce the rules regarding media comment.
>
> (b) To introduce the rules regarding advertising.

You are appearing for a well-known businessman in his local magistrates' court on a charge of drink-driving. After a preliminary hearing, you are approached by a reporter from the local newspaper who asks you for information about the client and the case. What should you do?

Question 13

Objective

To illustrate the relationship between a practising barrister's duty of confidentiality to the lay client and the overriding duty to the court.

You are asked to advise, in conference, upon the acceptability of an offer of £3,000 in settlement of your clients claim for damages in a personal injury case. The medical report, which has been disclosed to the defence, is now ten months old. In the course of the conference, your client informs you that the doctor's prognosis was unduly pessimistic as his condition has improved since the report was prepared. In the circumstances, the offer is generous and more than your client is likely to receive from the court.

(a) *What advice do you give?*

(b) *Would it make any difference if the client's information was contained in a more recent, but undisclosed medical report?*

Question 14

Objective

To illustrate the relationship between the overriding duty to the court and the rules under the Civil Procedure Rules 1998 regarding witnesses at trial.

You are instructed to represent the defendant in proceedings for damages for breach of contract. Upon your arrival at court, your instructing solicitor informs you that one of your witnesses has just telephoned his office to say that she is ill and cannot attend court to give evidence. Her testimony is vital to the defendant's case. You have no option but to seek an adjournment. At that moment, your opponent approaches you and asks if he can have a word with you. He indicates that he has witness difficulties and invites you to agree to an adjournment of the hearing for two weeks. In so doing:

(a) *Do you inform your opponent and the court of your own witness difficulties?*

(b) *If not, do you make an application for the claimant to pay defendant's costs thrown away by the adjournment?*

APPENDICES

APPENDIX 1
CODE OF CONDUCT OF THE BAR OF ENGLAND AND WALES

CODE OF CONDUCT

OF

THE BAR OF ENGLAND AND WALES

AND

WRITTEN STANDARDS FOR THE CONDUCT
OF PROFESSIONAL WORK

8th Edition

Adopted by the Bar Council on 18 September 2004

Effective from 31 October 2004

The General Council of the Bar of England and Wales
289–293 High Holborn
London WC1V 7HZ

SECTION 1   THE CODE OF CONDUCT OF THE BAR OF ENGLAND AND WALES

Arrangement of Sections

Code of Conduct of the Bar of England and Wales
The Bar's Code of Conduct sets out the duties which all barristers must obey.
It is divided into the following sections:

Part I—Preliminary
The Preliminary section sets out the details about the commencement of the Code, the rules governing amendments to the Code, the general purpose of the Code, to whom it applies and the Bar Council's powers to waive its provisions.

Part II—Practising Requirements
The Practising Requirements section sets out the rules governing the circumstances in which individuals may practise as a barrister, exercise rights of audience and supply legal services to the public.

Part III—Fundamental Principles
The Fundamental Principles section includes the duty to not act dishonestly or bring the profession into disrepute, the duties to the court and to act in the best interest of the client. It also contains the duties to the Legal Services Commission, the duty to not discriminate on grounds of race, sex etc and the duty to maintain independence.

Part IV—Self-employed Barristers
This section concerns self-employed barristers only. It provides that they can only accept instructions from solicitors or other professional clients and sets out the work that they may not undertake. This section also contains further rules governing insurance, the duties of barristers and heads of chambers to administer their practice efficiently and the rules about fees.

Part V—Employed Barristers
This section sets out the rules governing Employed Barristers. It is now divided into two sections. Section 1 deals with barristers employed other than by recognised bodies. Section 2 relates to barristers employed by and/or managers of recognised bodies. Recognised bodies is the umbrella term for the new business structures permitted by the Legal Services Act 2007, namely Legal Disciplinary Practices and Alternative Business Structures.

Part VI—Acceptance and Return of Instructions
This section deals with the occasion on which barristers are required to accept instructions (the 'Cab Rank rule'), when they are required to refuse or withdraw from a case and when they may choose to refuse or withdraw from a case.

Part VII—Conduct of Work by Practising Barristers
This section contains the duties of barristers when conducting work, including the general duties to act courteously and promptly, the duty of confidentiality, duties where there is a conflict between clients, duties when drafting documents and appearing in court, the rules concerning contact with witnesses and media comment and advertising.

Part VIII—Miscellaneous
This section sets out miscellaneous provisions concerning pupillage, working at a Legal Advice Centre, dual qualification and relationships with foreign lawyers.

Part IX—Compliance
This section sets out the duty to inform the Bar Council in the event of criminal convictions, bankruptcy etc and the duties concerning the complaints procedure.

Part X—Definitions

This section contains the definition of terms used in the Code.

Part XI—Transitional Provisions

This section contains the transitional arrangements affecting people who were barristers before this edition of the Code came into force.

The Code also contains various annexes, which set out the rules for particular situations.

PART I—PRELIMINARY

101   The Eighth Edition of the Code was adopted by the Bar Council on 18 September 2004 and came into force on 31 October 2004.

102   This Code includes the Annexes.

103   Amendments and additions to this Code may be made by Resolution of the Bar Standards Board which shall be operative upon such date as the Resolution shall appoint or if no such date is appointed on the later of:

   (a) the date of the Resolution; and

   (b) the date when approval of the amendment or addition, if required, is given by the Legal Services Board under Schedule 4 of the Legal Services Act 2007.

Amendments and additions will be published from time to time in such manner as the Bar Standards Board may determine.

General purpose of the Code

104   The general purpose of this Code is to provide the requirements for practice as a barrister and the rules and standards of conduct applicable to barristers which are appropriate in the interests of justice and in particular:

   (a) in relation to self-employed barristers to provide common and enforceable rules and standards which require them:

      (i) to be completely independent in conduct and in professional standing as sole practitioners;

      (ii) to act only as consultants instructed by solicitors and other approved persons (save where instructions can properly be dispensed with);

      (iii) to acknowledge a public obligation based on the paramount need for access to justice to act for any client in cases within their field of practice;

   (b) to make appropriate provision for:

      (i) barrister managers, employees and owners of Recognised Bodies; and

      (ii) employed barristers taking into account the fact that such barristers are employed to provide legal services to or on behalf of their employer.

Application of the Code

105   A barrister must comply with this Code which (save as otherwise provided) applies to all barristers whenever called to the Bar.

105A   Part IV applies only to self-employed barristers.

105B   Section 1 of Part V applies only to employed barristers.

105C.1   Only Parts I, II, III, Section 2 of Part V, rules 606.1, 607, 701(a), 701(b)(i), 704, 705, 708, 708.1 and Parts VIII, IX, X and XI apply to barristers practising as managers or employees of Recognised Bodies regulated by another Approved Regulator when doing work of a sort that the body is permitted to do.

105C.2   In so applying, rule 606.1 is to be read as if it referred to a barrister or the Recognised Body being retained rather than receiving instructions.

106   Subject to the International Practice Rules (reproduced in Annex A) this Code applies to International work and whether a barrister is practising in England and Wales or elsewhere.

107   A registered European lawyer must comply with this Code in the manner provided for by the Registered European Lawyers Rules (reproduced in Annex B).

Waiver of the Code

108   The Bar Council shall have the power to waive the duty imposed on a barrister to comply with the provisions of this Code in such circumstances and to such extent as the Bar Council may think fit and either conditionally or unconditionally.

PART II—PRACTISING REQUIREMENTS

General

201   For the purposes of this Code a barrister practises as a barrister if:
   (a) he supplies legal services and in connection with the supply of such services:
      (i) he holds himself out or allows himself to be held out as a barrister; or
      (ii) he exercises a right which he has by reason of being a barrister; or
   (b) he acts as a manager of a Recognised Body and as such is required by the rules of that body's Approved Regulator to hold a practising certificate issued by the Bar Council:
   (c) and any reference to the supply of legal services includes an offer to supply such services.

202   Subject to the provisions of this Code a barrister may practise as a barrister provided that:
   (a) he has complied with any applicable training requirements imposed by the Bar Training Regulations which were in force at the date of his Call to the Bar;
   (b) he has complied with any applicable requirements of the Continuing Professional Development Regulations (reproduced in Annex C);
   (c) he has a current practising certificate issued by the Bar Council in accordance with the Practising certificate Regulations (reproduced in Annex D);
   (d) he has provided in writing to the Bar Council details of the current address(es) with telephone number(s) of the chambers or office from which he supplies legal services and
      (i) if he is an employed barrister, the name address telephone number and nature of the business of his employer;
      (ii) if he is a manager or employee or owner of a Recognised Body the nature of his role and the name, address, email address, telephone number and name of the Recognised Body and of its Approved Regulator

Rights of audience

203.1   A barrister may exercise any right of audience which he has by reason of being a barrister provided that:
   (a) he is entitled to practise as a barrister in accordance with paragraph 202; and
   (b) if he is of less than three years' standing his principal place of practice is either:

(i)   a chambers or annexe of chambers which is also the principal place of practice of a qualified person who is readily available to provide guidance to the barrister; or

(ii)   an office of an organisation of which an employee, partner, manager or director is a qualified person who is readily available to provide guidance to the barrister.

203.2   For the purpose of paragraph 203.1(b) and 204(c)(i) a barrister shall be treated as being of a particular number of years' standing if he:

(a)   has been entitled to practise and has practised as a barrister (other than as a pupil who has not completed pupillage in accordance with the Bar Training Regulations) or as a member of another authorised body;

(b)   has made such practice his primary occupation; and

(c)   has been entitled to exercise a right of audience before every Court in relation to all proceedings

for a period (which need not be continuous and need not have been as a member of the same authorised body) of at least that number of years.

203.3   A person shall be a qualified person for the purpose of paragraph 203.1(b) if he:

(a)   has been entitled to practise and has practised as a barrister (other than as a pupil who has not completed pupillage in accordance with the Bar Training Regulations) or as a member of another authorised body for a period (which need not have been as a member of the same authorised body) of at least six years in the previous eight years;

(b)   for the previous two years

(i)   has made such practice his primary occupation, and

(ii)   has been entitled to exercise a right of audience before every Court in relation to all proceedings;

(c)   is not acting as a qualified person in relation to more than two other people; and

(d)   has not been designated by the Bar Council as unsuitable to be a qualified person.

203.4   This paragraph 203 is subject to the transitional provisions at paragraphs 1102 to 1105.

Supply of legal services to the public

204   A practising barrister may supply legal services to the public provided that:

(a)   he complies with the requirements of paragraph 203.1;

(b)   he is covered by insurance against claims for professional negligence arising out of the supply of his services in such amount and upon such terms as are currently required by the Bar Council or alternatively (in the case of:

(i)   an employed barrister; or

(ii)   a barrister practising as a manager or employee of a Recognised Body) his employer or the body, as the case may be, is covered by such insurance in such amount and upon such terms as are required by the Approved Regulator of the employer or body (or, if none, in such amount and on such terms as are currently required by the Bar Standards Board); and

(c)   In the case of legal services supplied pursuant to paragraph 401(a)(iii):

(i)   he is more than three years' standing;

(ii) he has complied with such training requirements as may be imposed by the Bar Council or Bar Standards Board; and

(iii) he has notified the Bar Council that he holds himself out as willing to accept instructions from lay clients.

205   A practising barrister may supply legal services to the public as:

(a) a self-employed barrister:

(b) a manager or employee of a Recognised Body, subject to the rules of the Approved Regulator of that body;

(c) an employed barrister to the extent permitted by paragraph 502

206.1[1]   A barrister called before 31 July 2000 who is deemed to be practising only by virtue of paragraph 201(a)(i) in England and Wales and who does not and is not required either by the BSB or by any Approved Regulator to hold a practising certificate under this Code shall not be subject to the rules in this Code applying only to practising barristers provided that:

(a) If he supplies any legal services to any person:

(i) He provides in writing to the Bar Council details of the current address(es) with telephone number(s) of the office or premises from which he does so, and:

(1) if he is employed, the name address telephone number and nature of the business of his employer;

(2) if he is an employee or owner or manager of a Recognised Body, the name, address, email address, telephone number and the name of the Recognised Body and its Approved Regulator

(ii) Unless he is employed only to offer services to his employer, or to the Recognised Body of which he is an employee he (or, if he is supplying legal services to clients of his employer, or a Recognised Body of which he is an employee) that employer or body is currently insured by insurers authorised to conduct such business against any and all claims in respect of civil liability for professional negligence arising out of or in connection with the supply of legal services for at least the first £250,000 of each and every claim, with an excess not exceeding £500.

(b) Before supplying legal services to any person, employer or Recognised Body, and when first dealing with any third party in the course of supplying legal services, he informs them fully and comprehensibly in writing (a) of his status and the fact that he does not hold a practising certificate under this Code, (b) of the relevant limitations under this Code on the legal services he may undertake, (c) that he is not fully regulated by the Bar Standards Board , and (d) of the absence of available compensatory powers for any inadequate professional service he may render.

206.2   A barrister whenever called who is deemed to be practising only by virtue of paragraph 201(a)(i) outside England and Wales, who does not and is not required either by the BSB or by any Approved Regulator to hold a valid practising certificate under this Code and who is not subject to paragraph 4(e) of the International Practice Rules shall not be subject to the rules in this Code applying only to practising barristers provided that he complies with the provisions of paragraph 206.1.

---

[1] Paragraphs 206.1 and 206.2 are effective from 31 July 2005.

<h2 style="text-align:center">Acting in a dual capacity</h2>

207   A barrister may practice or be involved with the supply of legal services in more than one capacity in the following circumstances:
(a) in accordance with rule 806: or
(b) after:-
   (i)   having notified the BSB in writing of an intention so to do and after supplying the BSB with such information as the BSB requires in relation thereto; and
   (ii) having agreed with each employer or Recognised Body with which the barrister is involved a protocol that enables the barrister to avoid or resolve any conflict of interests or duties arising from practice and/or involvement in those capacities.

208   A barrister who practices or is involved with the supply of legal services in more than one capacity pursuant to paragraph 207(b) above must:-
(a) provide a copy of each protocol required by paragraph 207(b)(ii) to the Bar Standards Board on request; and
(b) maintain (and make available to the Bar Standards Board on request) a record of referrals by the barrister to the employer or Recognised Body and of instructions received by the barrister from the employer or Recognised Body;
(c) refuse to accept instructions in any case where so acting gives rise to a potential conflict of interest;
(d) not work in more than one capacity in relation to the same case or issue for the same client at the same time;
(e) disclose (or procure the disclosure by the Recognised Body of) the interest to the client in writing before the barrister refers a client to the employer or Recognised Body or before accepting instructions from the employer or Recognised Body.

209   If a barrister directly or indirectly has an ownership interest in a Recognised Body and is in practice other than as a manager or employee of that Recognised Body, the barrister must:-
(a) notify the Bar Standards Board in writing of the ownership interest at or as soon as reasonably practicable after, the time at which that interest is acquired or the barrister starts practising other than as a manager or employee of that Recognised Body, whichever is the later;
(b) disclose (or procure the disclosure by the Recognised Body of) the interest to:-
   (i)   any client of the Recognised Body who instructs the barrister. If the barrister has the ownership interest at the time that instructions are received by him, disclosure to the client must be made prior to the barrister accepting the instructions. If the ownership interest is acquired after instructions have already been accepted, the ownership interest is acquired after instructions have already been accepted, the ownership interest must be communicated at the time of, or as soon as reasonably practicable after, the barrister's acquisition of that interest and the client must be advised of their right to instruct another barrister.
   (ii) any person that the barrister refers to the Recognised Body. If the barrister has the ownership interest at the time that the referral is

made, disclosure to the client must be made prior to the barrister making the referral. If the ownership interest is acquired after the referral has already been made, the ownership interest must be communicated at the time of, or as soon as reasonably practicable after, the barrister's acquisition of that interest.

(c) maintain (and make available to the Bar Standards Board on request) a record of referrals by the barrister to the Recognised Body and of instructions received by the barrister from the Recognised Body.

PART III—FUNDAMENTAL PRINCIPLES

Applicable to all barristers

301   A barrister must have regard to paragraph 104 and must not:

(a) engage in conduct whether in pursuit of his profession or otherwise which is:

(i) dishonest or otherwise discreditable to a barrister;

(ii) prejudicial to the administration of justice; or

(iii) likely to diminish public confidence in the legal profession or the administration of justice or otherwise bring the legal profession into disrepute;

(b) engage directly or indirectly in any occupation if his association with that occupation may adversely affect the reputation of the Bar or in the case of a practising barrister prejudice his ability to attend properly to his practice.

Applicable to practising barristers

302   A barrister has an overriding duty to the Court to act with independence in the interests of justice: he must assist the Court in the administration of justice and must not deceive or knowingly or recklessly mislead the Court.

303   A barrister:

(a) must promote and protect fearlessly and by all proper and lawful means the lay client's best interests and do so without regard to his own interests or to any consequences to himself or to any other person (including any colleague, professional client or other intermediary or another barrister, the barrister's employer or any Recognised Body of which the barrister may be owner or manager);

(b) owes his primary duty as between the lay client and any other person to the lay client and must not permit any other person to limit his discretion as to how the interests of the lay client can best be served;

(c) when supplying legal services funded by the Legal Services Commission as part of the Community Legal Service or the Criminal Defence Service owes his primary duty to the lay client subject only to compliance with paragraph 304.

304   A barrister who supplies legal services funded by the Legal Services Commission as part of the Community Legal Service or the Criminal Defence Service must in connection with the supply of such services comply with any duty imposed on him by or under the Access to Justice Act 1999 or any regulations or code in effect under that Act and in particular with the duties set out in Annex E.

305.1 A barrister must not in relation to any other person (including a client or another barrister or a pupil or a student member of an Inn of Court) discriminate directly or indirectly because of race, colour, ethnic or national origin, nationality, citizenship, sex, sexual orientation, marital status, disability, age, religion or belief.

305.2   A barrister must not in relation to any other person, victimise that person for carrying out a protected act defined in the relevant legislation.

306   A barrister is individually and personally responsible for his own conduct and for his professional work: he must exercise his own personal judgment in all his professional activities.

307   A barrister must not:

(a)   permit his absolute independence integrity and freedom from external pressures to be compromised;

(b)   do anything (for example accept a present) in such circumstances as may lead to any inference that his independence may be compromised;

(c)   compromise his professional standards in order to please his client the Court or a third party, including any mediator;

(d)   give a commission or present (save for small promotional items) or lend any money for any professional purpose to or (save as a remuneration in accordance with the provisions of this Code) accept any money by way of loan or otherwise from any client or any person entitled to instruct him as an intermediary;

(e)   make any payment (other than a payment for advertising or publicity permitted by this Code or in the case of a self-employed barrister remuneration paid to any clerk or other employee or staff of his chambers) to any person for the purpose of procuring professional instructions;

provided that nothing in paragraph 307(d) or (e) shall prevent a barrister from paying a reasonable fee or fees required by an alternative dispute resolution body that appoints or recommends persons to provide mediation, arbitration or adjudication services, or from entering into such a reasonable fee-sharing arrangement required by such a body, if the payment or arrangement is of a kind similar to that made by other persons who provide such services through the body.

PART IV—SELF-EMPLOYED BARRISTERS

Instructions

401   A self-employed barrister whether or not he is acting for a fee:

(a)   may supply legal services only if appointed by the Court or is instructed:

(i)   by a professional client; or

(ii)   by a licensed access client, in which case he must comply with the Licensed Access Rules (reproduced in Annex F1); or

(iii)   subject to paragraph 204(c), by or on behalf of any other lay client, in which case he must comply with the Public Access Rules (reproduced in Annex F2); or

(b)   must not in the course of his practice:

(i)   undertake the management administration or general conduct of a lay client's affairs;

(ii)   conduct litigation or inter-partes work (for example the conduct of correspondence with an opposite party, instructing any expert witness or other person on behalf of his lay client or accepting personal liability for the payment of any such person);

(iii) investigate or collect evidence for use in any Court;

(iv) except as permitted by paragraph 707, or by the Public Access Rules, take any proof of evidence in any criminal case;

(v) attend at a police station without the presence of a solicitor to advise a suspect or interviewee as to the handling and conduct of police interviews;

(vi) act as a supervisor for the purposes of section 84(2) of the Immigration and Asylum Act 1999.

(c) must not supply legal services for reward otherwise than in the course of his practice except as permitted by paragraph 806.

Insurance

402.1 Every self-employed barrister (other than a pupil who is covered under his pupilmaster's insurance) and a barrister called to the Bar under Part IV(E) of the Bar Training Regulations must be entered as a member with BMIF.

402.2 Every barrister entered as a member with BMIF shall:

(a) pay immediately when due the appropriate insurance premium required by BMIF for the purpose of insurance against claims for professional negligence for such amount and upon such terms as may be Approved by the Bar Council from time to time;

(b) supply immediately upon being requested to do so such information as BMIF may from time to time require pursuant to its Rules.

Administration and conduct of self-employed practice

403.1 A self-employed barrister must not practise from the office of or in any unincorporated association (including any arrangement which involves sharing the administration of his practice) with any person other than a self-employed barrister or any of the following:

(a) a registered European lawyer;

(b) subject to compliance with the Foreign Lawyers (Chambers) Rules (reproduced in Annex H) and with the consent of the Bar Council a foreign lawyer;

(c) a non-practising barrister.

(d) a person who is:

(i) a lawyer from a jurisdiction other than England and Wales;

(ii) a retired judge; or

(iii) an employed barrister

to the extent that that person is practising as an arbitrator or mediator.

403.2 A self-employed barrister:

(a) must take all reasonable steps to ensure that:

(i) his practice is efficiently and properly administered having regard to the nature of his practice;

(ii) proper records are kept;

(iii) he complies with the Terms of Work on which Barristers Offer their Services to Solicitors and the Withdrawal of Credit Scheme 1988 as amended and in force from time to time (reproduced in Annex G1) and with any Withdrawal of Credit Direction issued by the Chairman of the Bar pursuant thereto.

(b) must have ready access to library facilities which are adequate having regard to the nature of his practice;

(c)   must have regard to any relevant guidance issued by the Bar Council including guidance as to:

(i)   the administration of chambers;

(ii)   pupillage and further training; and

(iii) good equal opportunities practice in chambers in the form of the Equality and Diversity Code for the Bar;

(d)   (i)   must deal with all complaints made to him promptly, courteously and in a manner which addresses the issues raised; and

(ii)   must have and comply with an appropriate written complaints procedure and make copies of the procedure available to a client on request; and

(iii) meet all the requirements set out in Annexe S to the Code.

Heads of chambers

404.1   The obligations in this paragraph apply to the following members of chambers:

(a)   any barrister who is head of chambers;

(b)   any barrister who is responsible in whole or in part for the administration of chambers;

(c)   if there is no one within (a) and (b) above, all the members of the chambers.

404.2   Any person referred to in paragraph 404.1 must take all reasonable steps to ensure that:

(a)   his chambers are administered competently and efficiently and are properly staffed;

(b)   the affairs of his chambers are conducted in a manner which is fair and equitable for all barristers and pupils;

(c)   proper arrangements are made in his chambers for dealing with pupils and pupillage and, in particular,

(i)   that all pupillage vacancies are advertised in the manner prescribed by the Bar Council;

(ii)   that such arrangements are made for the funding of pupils by chambers as the Bar Council may by resolution from time to time require;

(iii) that in making arrangements for pupillage, regard is had to the pupillage guidelines issued from time to time by the Bar Council and to the Equality and Diversity Code for the Bar;

(d)   proper arrangements are made in chambers for dealing with equal opportunity issues and in particular,

(i)   that Chambers appoint at least one Equal Opportunities Officer;

(ii)   that Chambers shall have a written Equal Opportunities Policy made available to all members of Chambers and Staff and to the Bar Council when required, which shall set out the policy adopted by Chambers in relation to each of the Action Areas in the Equality and Diversity Code for the Bar and shall have regard to the recommendations in the Code;

(iii) that no barrister shall take pupils until the steps set out in (i) and (ii) above have been complied with.

(e)   all barristers practising from his chambers whether they are members of the chambers or not are entered as members with BMIF and have effected insurance in accordance with paragraph 402 (other than any pupil who is covered under his pupil-master's insurance);

(f)   all barristers practising from his chambers comply with paragraph 403.2(a)(iii);

(g)   all employees and staff in his chambers (i) are competent to carry out their duties, (ii) carry out their duties in a correct and efficient manner, (iii) are made clearly aware of such provisions of this Code as may affect or be relevant to the performance of their duties and (iv) all complaints against them are dealt with in the manner set out in paragraph 403.2(d) (i)–(iii) above;

(h)   all registered European lawyers and all foreign lawyers in his chambers comply with this Code to the extent required by the Registered European Lawyers Rules (reproduced in Annex B) and the Foreign Lawyers (Chambers) Rules (reproduced in Annex H);

(i)   fee notes in respect of all work undertaken by all members of chambers and pupils and (unless expressly agreed with the individual) former members and pupils of chambers are sent expeditiously to clients and in the event of non-payment within a reasonable time, pursued efficiently;

(j)   every barrister practising from his chambers has a current practising certificate in accordance with paragraph 202(c) of the Code of Conduct and the Practising certificate Regulations (reproduced in Annex D).

404.3   In carrying out the obligations referred to in paragraph 404.2 any person referred to in paragraph 404.1 must have regard to any relevant guidance issued by the Bar Council including guidance as to:

(a)   the administration of chambers;

(b)   pupillage and further training; and

(c)   good equal opportunities practice in chambers in the form of the Equality and Diversity Code for the Bar.

Fees and remuneration

405   Subject to paragraph 307 a self-employed barrister may charge for any work undertaken by him (whether or not it involves an appearance in Court) on any basis or by any method he thinks fit provided that such basis or method:

(a)   is permitted by law;

(b)   does not involve the payment of a wage or salary.

406.1   A self-employed barrister who receives fees in respect of work done by another barrister must himself and without delegating the responsibility to anyone else pay forthwith the whole of the fee in respect of that work to that other barrister.

406.2   Subject to paragraph 805 a self-employed barrister who arranges for another barrister to undertake work for him (other than a pupil or a person who has asked to do the work in order to increase his own skill or experience) must himself and without delegating the responsibility to anyone else:

(a)   pay proper financial remuneration for the work done;

(b)   make payment within a reasonable time and in any event within three months after the work has been done unless otherwise agreed in advance with the other person.

Client money securities and other assets

407   A self employed barrister must not receive or handle client money securities or other assets other than by receiving payment of remuneration.

PART V—EMPLOYED BARRISTERS

Section 1: Barristers employed other than by recognised bodies

501   An employed barrister whilst acting in the course of his employment may supply legal services to his employer and to any of the following persons:

(a) any employee, director or company secretary of the employer in a matter arising out of or relating to that person's employment;

(b) where the employer is a public authority (including the Crown or a Government department or agency or a local authority):

(i)   another public authority on behalf of which the employer has made arrangements under statute or otherwise to supply any legal services or to perform any of that other public authority's functions as agent or otherwise;

(ii) in the case of a barrister employed by or in a Government department or agency, any Minister or officer of the Crown;

(c) where the barrister is or is performing the functions of a justices' clerk, the justices whom he serves;

(d) where the barrister is employed by a trade association, any individual member of the association.

502   An employed barrister may supply legal services only to the persons referred to in paragraph 501 and must not supply legal services to any other person save that whilst acting in the course of his employment:

(a) a barrister employed by the Legal Services Commission may supply legal services to members of the public;

(b) a barrister employed by or at a Legal Advice Centre may supply legal services to clients of the Legal Advice Centre;

(c) any employed barrister may supply legal services to members of the public free of charge (to any person).

503   A barrister employed to supply legal services under a contract for services may be treated as an employed barrister for the purpose of this Code provided that the contract is:

(a) in writing;

(b) (subject to any provision for earlier termination on notice) for a determinate period;

(c) not a contract with a Recognised Body.

504   An employed barrister shall have a right to conduct litigation in relation to every Court and all proceedings before any Court and may exercise that right provided that he complies with the Employed Barristers (Conduct of Litigation) Rules (reproduced in Annex I).

505   An employed barrister must not receive or handle client money securities or other assets other than by receiving payment of remuneration or where the money or other asset belongs to his employer

Section 2: Barristers employed by and/or managers of Recognised Bodies

506   A barrister who is a manager of or employed by a Recognised Body shall have a right to conduct litigation in relation to every Court and to all proceedings before a Court and may exercise that right provided that the barrister complies with the Employed Barristers (Conduct of Litigation) Rules (reproduced in Annex I) and with the rules of the Approved Regulator of the Recognised Body.

507   A barrister who is employed by a Recognised Body but is not a manager of that body must not receive or handle client money securities or other assets

other than by receiving payment of remuneration or where the money or other asset belongs to that body.

PART VI—ACCEPTANCE AND RETURN OF INSTRUCTIONS

Acceptance of instructions and the 'Cab-rank rule'

601   A barrister who supplies advocacy services must not withhold those services:

(a)   on the ground that the nature of the case is objectionable to him or to any section of the public;

(b)   on the ground that the conduct opinions or beliefs of the prospective client are unacceptable to him or to any section of the public;

(c)   on any ground relating to the source of any financial support which may properly be given to the prospective client for the proceedings in question (for example, on the ground that such support will be available as part of the Community Legal Service or Criminal Defence Service).

602   A self-employed barrister must comply with the 'Cab-rank rule' and accordingly except only as otherwise provided in paragraphs 603 604 605 and 606 he must in any field in which he professes to practise in relation to work appropriate to his experience and seniority and irrespective of whether his client is paying privately or is publicly funded:

(a)   accept any brief to appear before a Court in which he professes to practise;

(b)   accept any instructions;

(c)   act for any person on whose behalf he is instructed; and do so irrespective of (i) the party on whose behalf he is instructed (ii) the nature of the case and (iii) any belief or opinion which he may have formed as to the character reputation cause conduct guilt or innocence of that person.

603   A barrister must not accept any instructions if to do so would cause him to be professionally embarrassed and for this purpose a barrister will be professionally embarrassed:

(a)   if he lacks sufficient experience or competence to handle the matter;

(b)   if having regard to his other professional commitments he will be unable to do or will not have adequate time and opportunity to prepare that which he is required to do;

(c)   if the instructions seek to limit the ordinary authority or discretion of a barrister in the conduct of proceedings in Court or to require a barrister to act otherwise than in conformity with law or with the provisions of this Code;

(d)   if the matter is one in which he has reason to believe that he is likely to be a witness or in which whether by reason of any connection with the client or with the Court or a member of it or otherwise it will be difficult for him to maintain professional independence or the administration of justice might be or appear to be prejudiced;

(e)   if there is or appears to be a conflict or risk of conflict either between the interests of the barrister and some other person or between the interests of any one or more clients (unless all relevant persons consent to the barrister accepting the instructions);

(f)   if there is a significant risk that information confidential to another client or former client might be communicated to or used for the benefit of anyone other than that client or former client without their consent;

(g) if he is a self-employed barrister where the instructions are delivered by a solicitor or firm of solicitors in respect of whom a Withdrawal of Credit Direction has been issued by the Chairman of the Bar pursuant to the Terms of Work on which Barristers Offer their Services to Solicitors and the Withdrawal of Credit Scheme 1988 as amended and in force from time to time (reproduced in Annex G1) unless his fees are to be paid directly by the Legal Services Commission or the instructions are accompanied by payment of an agreed fee or the barrister agrees in advance to accept no fee for such work or has obtained the consent of the Chairman of the Bar.

(h) If the barrister is instructed by or on behalf of a lay client who has not also instructed a solicitor or other professional client, and if the barrister is satisfied that it is in the interests of the client or in the interests of justice for the lay client to instruct a solicitor or other professional client.

604   Subject to paragraph 601 a self-employed barrister is not obliged to accept instructions:

(a) requiring him to do anything other than during the course of his ordinary working year;

(b) other than at a fee which is proper having regard to:
   (i)   the complexity length and difficulty of the case;
   (ii) his ability experience and seniority; and
   (iii) the expenses which he will incur;
   and any instructions in a matter funded by the Legal Services Commission as part of the Community Legal Service or the Criminal Defence Service for which the amount or rate of the barrister's remuneration is prescribed by regulation or subject to assessment shall for this purpose unless the Bar Council or the Bar in general meeting otherwise determines (either in a particular case or in any class or classes of case or generally) be deemed to be at a proper professional fee;[1,2]

(c) to do any work under a conditional fee agreement;

(d) save in a matter funded by the Legal Services Commission as part of the Community Legal Service or the Criminal Defence Service:
   (i)   unless and until his fees are agreed;
   (ii) if having required his fees to be paid before he accepts the instructions those fees are not paid;

(e) from anyone other than a professional client who accepts liability for the barrister's fees;

(f) in a matter where the lay client is also the professional client;

(g) to do any work under the Contractual Terms on which Barristers offer their Services to Solicitors 2001 as amended and in force from time to time (reproduced in Appendix G2) or on any other contractual terms.

---

[1] On 30 April 2001 the Bar Council decided that, with effect from 1 May 2001, all cases subject to family graduated fees are no longer deemed to be at a proper professional fee for the purposes of paragraph 604(b).

[2] On 15 November 2003 the Bar Council decided that, effective immediately, all cases subject to criminal graduated fees are no longer deemed to be at a proper professional fee for the purposes of paragraph 604(b).

(h) where the potential for professional negligence in respect of the case could exceed the level of professional indemnity insurance which is reasonably available and likely to be available in the market for him to accept.

605   A self-employed Queen's Counsel is not obliged to accept instructions:

(a) to settle alone any document of a kind generally settled only by or in conjunction with a junior;

(b) to act without a junior if he considers that the interests of the lay client require that a junior should also be instructed.

606.1   A barrister (whether he is instructed on his own or with another advocate) must in the case of all instructions consider whether consistently with the proper and efficient administration of justice and having regard to:

(a) the circumstances (including in particular the gravity complexity and likely cost) of the case;

(b) the nature of his practice;

(c) his ability experience and seniority; and

(d) his relationship with the client;

the best interests of the client would be served by instructing or continuing to instruct him in that matter.

606.2   Where a barrister is instructed in any matter with another advocate or advocates the barrister must in particular consider whether it would be in the best interests of the client to instruct only one advocate or fewer advocates.

606.3   A barrister who in any matter is instructed either directly by the lay client or by an intermediary who is not a solicitor or other authorised litigator should consider whether it would be in the interests of the lay client or the interests of justice to instruct a solicitor or other authorised litigator or other appropriate intermediary either together with or in place of the barrister.

606.4   In cases involving several parties, a barrister must on receipt of instructions and further in the event of any change of circumstances consider whether, having regard to all the circumstances including any actual or potential conflict of interest, any client ought to be separately represented or advised or whether it would be in the best interests of any client to be jointly represented or advised with another party.

607   If at any time in any matter a barrister considers that it would be in the best interests of any client to have different representation, he must immediately so advise the client.

Withdrawal from a case and return of instructions

608   A barrister must cease to act and if he is a self-employed barrister must return any instructions:

(a) if continuing to act would cause him to be professionally embarrassed within the meaning of paragraph 603 provided that if he would be professionally embarrassed only because it appears to him that he is likely to be a witness on a material question of fact he may retire or withdraw only if he can do so without jeopardising the client's interests;

(b) if having accepted instructions on behalf of more than one client there is or appears to be:

(i) a conflict or risk of conflict between the interests of any one or more of such clients; or

(ii) risk of a breach of confidence;

and the clients do not all consent to him continuing to act;

(c) if in any case funded by the Legal Services Commission as part of the Community Legal Service or Criminal Defence Service it has become apparent to him that such funding has been wrongly obtained by false or inaccurate information and action to remedy the situation is not immediately taken by the client;

(d) if the client refuses to authorise him to make some disclosure to the Court which his duty to the Court requires him to make;

(e) if having become aware during the course of a case of the existence of a document which should have been but has not been disclosed on discovery the client fails forthwith to disclose it;

(f) if having come into possession of a document belonging to another party by some means other than the normal and proper channels and having read it before he realises that it ought to have been returned unread to the person entitled to possession of it he would thereby be embarrassed in the discharge of his duties by his knowledge of the contents of the document provided that he may retire or withdraw only if he can do so without jeopardising the client's interests.

609 Subject to paragraph 610 a barrister may withdraw from a case where he is satisfied that:

(a) his instructions have been withdrawn;

(b) his professional conduct is being impugned;

(c) advice which he has given in accordance with paragraph 607 or 703 has not been heeded; or

(d) there is some other substantial reason for so doing.

610 A barrister must not:

(a) cease to act or return instructions without having first explained to the client his reasons for doing so;

(b) return instructions to another barrister without the consent of the client;

(c) return a brief which he has accepted and for which a fixed date has been obtained or (except with the consent of the lay client and where appropriate the Court) break any other engagement to supply legal services in the course of his practice so as to enable him to attend or fulfil an engagement (including a social or non-professional engagement) of any other kind;

(d) except as provided in paragraph 608 return any instructions or withdraw from a case in such a way or in such circumstances that the client may be unable to find other legal assistance in time to prevent prejudice being suffered by the client.

PART VII—CONDUCT OF WORK BY PRACTISING BARRISTERS

General

701 A barrister:

(a) must in all his professional activities be courteous and act promptly conscientiously diligently and with reasonable competence and take all reasonable and practicable steps to avoid unnecessary expense or waste of the Court's time and to ensure that professional engagements are fulfilled;

(b) must not undertake any task which:

(i) he knows or ought to know he is not competent to handle;

(ii) he does not have adequate time and opportunity to prepare for or perform; or

(iii) he cannot discharge within the time requested or otherwise within a reasonable time having regard to the pressure of other work;

(c) must read all instructions delivered to him expeditiously;

(d) must have regard to any relevant Written Standards for the conduct of Professional Work issued by the Bar Council;

(e) must inform his client forthwith and subject to paragraph 610 return the instructions to the client or to another barrister acceptable to the client:

(i) if it becomes apparent to him that he will not be able to do the work within the time requested or within a reasonable time after receipt of instructions;

(ii) if there is an appreciable risk that he may not be able to undertake a brief or fulfil any other professional engagement which he has accepted.

(f) must ensure that adequate records supporting the fees charged or claimed in a case are kept at least until the last of the following: his fees have been paid, any taxation or determination or assessment of costs in the case has been completed, or the time for lodging an appeal against assessment or the determination of that appeal, has expired, and must provide his professional or licensed access client or other intermediary or lay client with such records or details of the work done as may reasonably be required.

Confidentiality

702   Whether or not the relation of counsel and client continues a barrister must preserve the confidentiality of the lay client's affairs and must not without the prior consent of the lay client or as permitted by law lend or reveal the contents of the papers in any instructions to or communicate to any third person (other than another barrister, a pupil, in the case of a Registered European Lawyer, the person with whom he is acting in conjunction for the purposes of paragraph 5(3) of the Registered European Lawyers Rules or any other person who needs to know it for the performance of their duties) information which has been entrusted to him in confidence or use such information to the lay client's detriment or to his own or another client's advantage.

Conflicts between lay clients and intermediaries

703   If a self-employed barrister forms the view that there is a conflict of interest between his lay client and a professional client or other intermediary (for example because he considers that the intermediary may have been negligent) he must consider whether it would be in the lay client's interest to instruct another professional adviser or representative and, if he considers that it would be, the barrister must so advise and take such steps as he considers necessary to ensure that his advice is communicated to the lay client (if necessary by sending a copy of his advice in writing directly to the lay client as well as to the intermediary).

Drafting documents

704   A barrister must not devise facts which will assist in advancing the lay client's case and must not draft any statement of case, witness statement, affidavit, notice of appeal or other document containing:

(a) any statement of fact or contention which is not supported by the lay client or by his instructions;

(b) any contention which he does not consider to be properly arguable;

(c) any allegation of fraud unless he has clear instructions to make such allegation and has before him reasonably credible material which as it stands establishes a prima facie case of fraud;

(d) in the case of a witness statement or affidavit any statement of fact other than the evidence which in substance according to his instructions the barrister reasonably believes the witness would give if the evidence contained in the witness statement or affidavit were being given in oral examination;

provided that nothing in this paragraph shall prevent a barrister drafting a document containing specific factual statements or contentions included by the barrister subject to confirmation of their accuracy by the lay client or witness.

Contact with witnesses

705   A barrister must not:

(a) rehearse practise or coach a witness in relation to his evidence;

(b) encourage a witness to give evidence which is untruthful or which is not the whole truth;

(c) except with the consent of the representative for the opposing side or of the Court, communicate directly or indirectly about a case with any witness, whether or not the witness is his lay client, once that witness has begun to give evidence until the evidence of that witness has been concluded.

Attendance of professional client

706   A self-employed barrister who is instructed by a professional client should not conduct a case in Court in the absence of his professional client or a representative of his professional client unless the Court rules that it is appropriate or he is satisfied that the interests of the lay client and the interests of justice will not be prejudiced.

707   A self-employed barrister who attends Court in order to conduct a case in circumstances where no professional client or representative of a professional client is present may if necessary interview witnesses and take proofs of evidence.

Conduct in Court

708   A barrister when conducting proceedings in Court:

(a) is personally responsible for the conduct and presentation of his case and must exercise personal judgement upon the substance and purpose of statements made and questions asked;

(b) must not unless invited to do so by the Court or when appearing before a tribunal where it is his duty to do so assert a personal opinion of the facts or the law;

(c) must ensure that the Court is informed of all relevant decisions and legislative provisions of which he is aware whether the effect is favourable or unfavourable towards the contention for which he argues;

(d) must bring any procedural irregularity to the attention of the Court during the hearing and not reserve such matter to be raised on appeal;

(e) must not adduce evidence obtained otherwise than from or through the client or devise facts which will assist in advancing the lay client's case;

(f) must not make a submission which he does not consider to be properly arguable;

(g) must not make statements or ask questions which are merely scandalous or intended or calculated only to vilify insult or annoy either a witness or some other person;

(h) must if possible avoid the naming in open Court of third parties whose character would thereby be impugned;

(i) must not by assertion in a speech impugn a witness whom he has had an opportunity to cross-examine unless in cross-examination he has given the witness an opportunity to answer the allegation;

(j) must not suggest that a victim, witness or other person is guilty of crime, fraud or misconduct or make any defamatory aspersion on the conduct of any other person or attribute to another person the crime or conduct of which his lay client is accused unless such allegations go to a matter in issue (including the credibility of the witness) which is material to the lay client's case and appear to him to be supported by reasonable grounds.

Conduct in mediation

708.1   A barrister instructed in a mediation must not knowingly or recklessly mislead the mediator or any party or their representative.

Media comment

709.1   A barrister must not in relation to any anticipated or current proceedings in which he is briefed or expects to appear or has appeared as an advocate express a personal opinion to the press or other media or in any other public statement upon the facts or issues arising in the proceedings.

709.2   Paragraph 709.1 shall not prevent the expression of such an opinion on an issue in an educational or academic context.

Advertising and publicity

710.1   Subject to paragraph 710.2 a barrister may engage in any advertising or promotion in connection with his practice which conforms to the British Codes of Advertising and Sales Promotion and such advertising or promotion may include:

(a) photographs or other illustrations of the barrister;

(b) statements of rates and methods of charging;

(c) statements about the nature and extent of the barrister's services;

(d) information about any case in which the barrister has appeared (including the name of any client for whom the barrister acted) where such information has already become publicly available or, where it has not already become publicly available, with the express prior written consent of the lay client.

710.2   Advertising or promotion must not:

(a) be inaccurate or likely to mislead;

(b) be likely to diminish public confidence in the legal profession or the administration of justice or otherwise bring the legal profession into disrepute;

(c) make direct comparisons in terms of quality with or criticisms of other identifiable persons (whether they be barristers or members of any other profession);

(d) include statements about the barrister's success rate;

(e) indicate or imply any willingness to accept instructions or any intention to restrict the persons from whom instructions may be accepted otherwise than in accordance with this Code;

(f) be so frequent or obtrusive as to cause annoyance to those to whom it is directed.

PART VIII—MISCELLANEOUS

Pupils

801   A barrister who is a pupil must:

(a) comply with Part V of the Bar Training Regulations;

(b) apply himself full time to his pupillage save that a pupil may with the permission of his pupil-supervisor or head of chambers take part time work which does not in their opinion materially interfere with his pupillage;

(c) to the extent that paragraph 702 applies to his pupil-supervisor or to any person whom he accompanies to court or whose papers he sees, preserve the confidentiality of the affairs of that person's client in accordance with paragraph 702.

802   A barrister who is a pupil may supply legal services as a barrister and exercise a right of audience which he has by reason of being a barrister provided that:

(a) he has completed or been exempted from the non-practising six months of pupillage; and

(b) he has the permission of his pupil-supervisor or head of chambers;

provided that such a barrister may during the non-practising six months of pupillage with the permission of his pupil-supervisor or head of chambers accept a noting brief.

803.1   So long as he is a pupil a self-employed barrister may not become or hold himself out as a member of chambers or permit his name to appear anywhere as such a member.

803.2   A barrister who is a pupil of an employed barrister or of a barrister who is a manager or employee of a Recognised Body, who pursuant to Regulation 42 of the Bar Training Regulations spends any period of external training with such a barrister or with a solicitor shall be treated for the purpose of the Code as if he were during that period employed by the barrister's employer or by the Recognised Body or by the solicitor's firm as the case may be.

Pupil-Supervisors

804   A barrister who is a pupil-supervisor must:

(a) comply with Part V of the Bar Training Regulations;

(b) take all reasonable steps to provide his pupil with adequate tuition supervision and experience;

(c) have regard to the pupillage guidelines issued from time to time by the Bar Council and to the Equality Code for the Bar.

805   Except where a pupil is in receipt of an award or remuneration which is paid on terms that it is in lieu of payment for any individual item of work,

a barrister must pay any pupil (or in the case of an employed barrister ensure that a pupil is paid) for any work done for him which because of its value to him warrants payment.

Legal Advice Centres

806   A barrister may supply legal services at a Legal Advice Centre on a voluntary or part time basis and, if he does so, shall in connection with the supply of those services be treated for the purpose of this Code as if he were employed by the Legal Advice Centre.

807   A barrister who is employed by a Legal Advice Centre:
(a)   must not in any circumstances receive either directly or indirectly any fee or reward for the supply of any legal services to any client of the Legal Advice Centre other than a salary paid by the Legal Advice Centre;
(b)   must ensure that any fees in respect of legal services supplied by him to any client of the Legal Advice Centre accrue and are paid to the Legal Advice Centre;
(c)   must not have any financial interest in the Legal Advice Centre.

Dual qualification

808.1   A barrister who is a member of another authorised body and currently entitled to practise as such shall not practise as a barrister.

808.2   A barrister who becomes entitled to practise as a member of another authorised body shall forthwith inform the Bar Council and the Inn(s) of Court of which he is a member in writing of that fact.

808.3   A barrister who:
(a)   has had his name struck off the roll of solicitors or been excluded from membership of an authorised body; or
(b)   has at any time been found guilty of any professional misconduct or is the subject of any continuing disciplinary proceedings in relation to his professional conduct as a member of an authorised body; or
(c)   has at any time been refused a practising certificate as a solicitor or had his practising certificate suspended or made subject to a condition
shall not practise as a barrister until the PCC has considered his case and, if it decides to refer the case to a Disciplinary Tribunal, until the case is finally determined.

808.4   A barrister who is a member of another authorised body and currently entitled to practise as a member of that body shall not be deemed to be practising as a barrister if he holds himself out as a barrister provided that before supplying legal services to any person or employer, and when first dealing with any third party in the course of supplying legal services, he informs them fully and comprehensibly in writing (a) of his status and the fact that he does not hold a practising certificate under this Code, (b) of the relevant limitations under this Code on the legal services he may undertake, (c) that he is not fully regulated by the Bar Council, and (d) of the absence of available compensatory powers for any inadequate professional services he may render.

Foreign lawyers

809   A barrister called to the Bar under Part IV(E) of the Bar Training Regulations (temporary membership of the Bar) may not practise as a barrister other than to conduct the case or cases specified in the certificate referred to in Regulation 39. They must either be insured with BMIF or be covered by insurance against claims for professional negligence arising out of the supply of his services in

England and Wales in such amount and upon such terms as are currently required by the Bar Council and have delivered to the Bar Council a copy of the current insurance policy or the current certificate of insurance issued by the insurer.

PART IX—COMPLIANCE

901.1   Any failure by a barrister to comply with the provisions of paragraph 202 (a) to (d), 203(1)(a), 204(b), 402, 403.2(b)(c) and (d), 404, 405, 406, 701, 709, 801(a), 804 or 905(a)(i), (d) or (e) of this Code (to the extent that the rule or rules in question apply to him, as to which see paragraphs 105A to 105C above) or with the training requirements imposed by the Bar Training Regulations in force at the date of his Call to the Bar or with the Continuing Professional Development Regulations or the Practising Certificate Regulations shall render him liable to a written warning from the Bar Standards Board and/or the imposition of a fixed financial penalty of £300 (or such other sum as may be prescribed by the Bar Standards Board from time to time) or any financial penalty prescribed by the said Regulations for non-compliance therewith. Liability under this paragraph is strict.

901.2   Any failure by a barrister to pay a financial penalty within the time prescribed by the Regulations or stipulated by the Bar Council (or any extension thereof) shall constitute professional misconduct.

901.3   In the event that a barrister is given a written warning by the Bar Council, or a financial penalty is imposed upon him for an infringement of the aforementioned provisions of the Code, the barrister shall have a right of appeal to a panel under the provisions of paragraph 23(3) and (4) of the Disciplinary Rules. The time for bringing such an appeal shall be 28 days from the date upon which the written warning or notice seeking payment of the penalty is deemed to have been received by the barrister. However, unless the Bar Council agrees or the appeal panel otherwise rules, an appeal shall not operate as a suspension of the requirement to pay the financial penalty or an extension of the time for so doing.

901.4   Any failure by a barrister to comply with the provisions of paragraph 202 of the Code shall constitute professional misconduct if the barrister concerned has failed to take the necessary action to cure any relevant non-compliance with the preconditions to practise set out therein, or has failed to pay any financial penalty imposed on him within any time limit prescribed by the relevant Regulations or specified by the Bar Council (or any extension thereof).

901.5   (1)   Any serious failure to comply with the provisions of the Code referred to in paragraph 901.1 above shall constitute professional misconduct.

(2)   A failure to comply with those provisions may be a serious failure:

a.   due to the nature of the failure;

b.   due to the extent of the failure;

c.   because the failure in question is combined with a failure to comply with any provision of the Code (whether or not that provision is mentioned in paragraph 901.1);

d.   if the barrister has previously failed to comply with the same or any other provision of the Code (whether or not that provision is mentioned in paragraph 901.1).

901.6   If a barrister is given two or more separate written warnings by the Bar Council in a period of three years for infringement of any of the provisions of the Code referred to in paragraph 901.1, or is subjected to an automatic financial penalty for any failure to comply with any such provision of the Code on two separate occasions within a period of three years, then any further failure by him to comply with the provisions of the Code within a period of two years after the later of the written warnings or financial penalties shall constitute professional misconduct even if that failure, taken by itself, would not otherwise be regarded as professional misconduct.

901.7   Any failure by a barrister to comply with any provision of this Code other than those referred to in paragraph 901.1 above shall constitute professional misconduct.

901.8   It shall be misconduct under this Code for a barrister to be convicted of misconduct under the rules of another Approved Regulator and the barrister shall be liable to disciplinary action by the Bar Standards Board accordingly.

902   If the declaration made by a barrister on Call to the Bar is found to have been false in any material respect or if the barrister is found to have engaged before Call in conduct which is dishonest or otherwise discreditable to a barrister and which was not, before Call, fairly disclosed in writing to the Benchers of the Inn calling him or if any undertaking given by a barrister on Call to the Bar is breached in any material respect that shall constitute professional misconduct.

903   A barrister is subject to:

(a)   the Complaints Rules (reproduced in Annex J);

(b)   the Disciplinary Tribunals Regulations (reproduced in Annex K);

(c)   the Summary Procedure Rules (reproduced in Annex L);

(d)   the Hearings before the Visitors Rules (reproduced in Annex M);

(e)   the Interim Suspension Rules (reproduced at Annex N);

(f)   the Fitness to Practise Rules (reproduced at Annex O);

(g)   the Adjudication Panel and Appeals Rules (reproduced at Annex P) which are concerned with inadequate professional service.

904   Pursuant to the Rules referred to in paragraph 903 a barrister may be directed to provide redress to a lay client for inadequate professional service whether or not such inadequate professional service also constitutes professional misconduct.

905   A barrister must:

(a)   if he is practising, or the Bar Standards Board has reason to believe may be practising, as a barrister:

(i)   respond promptly to any requirement from the Bar Standards Board for comments on or documents relating to the arrangements made for administering his practice and chambers or office whether or not any complaint has been received or raised arising out of those arrangements;

(ii)   permit the Bar Council or Bar Standards Board or any agent appointed by it to inspect forthwith and on request and at any time which is reasonable having regard to the circumstances and the urgency of the matter any premises from which he practises or is believed to practise as a barrister, the arrangements made for administering his practice and chambers or office, and any records relating to such practice and to the administration of his chambers or office.

(b)   report promptly to the Bar Standards Board if:

(i)   he is a manager of a Recognised Body which is the subject of an intervention by the Approved Regulator of that body;

(ii)   he is charged with an indictable offence;

       (iii) he is convicted of any relevant criminal offence;

       (iv) he is charged with a disciplinary offence by another professional body; or

       (v) he is convicted of a disciplinary offence by another professional body;

(c) report promptly to the Bar Council if;

       (i) bankruptcy proceedings are initiated in respect of or against him;

       (ii) directors disqualification proceedings are initiated against him;

       (iii) a bankruptcy order or directors disqualification order is made against him; or

       (iv) if he enters into a individual voluntary arrangement with his creditors;

(d) where a complaint about a barrister has been made to or by the Bar Council, or where the Bar Council has reasonable grounds for believing that a breach of this Code may have occurred or is about to occur, or where circumstance referred to in sub-paragraph (b) or (c) above has been reported to the Bar Council, respond promptly to any request from the Bar Council for comments or information on the matter whether it relates to him or to another barrister;

(e) respond promptly to any letter of notification sent to him or attend before any tribunal panel body or person when so required pursuant to the rules referred to in paragraph 903;

(f) comply in due time with any sentence or suspension imposed or direction made or undertaking accepted by a tribunal panel body or person pursuant to the rules referred to in paragraph 903.

provided for the avoidance of doubt that nothing in this paragraph shall require a barrister to disclose or produce any document or information protected by law or in circumstances to which paragraph 702, or the equivalent rule of another Approved Regulator to which he is subject, applies.

PART X—DEFINITIONS

1001   In this Code except where otherwise indicated:

'the Act' means the Courts and Legal Services Act 1990 and where the context permits includes any orders or regulations made pursuant to powers conferred thereby;

'the Act of 1985' means the Administration of Justice Act 1985;

'the Act of 2007' means the Legal Services Act 2007;

'Adjudication Panel' means an adjudication panel constituted under the Adjudication Panel and Appeals Rules (reproduced in Annex P);

'advocacy services' means advocacy services as defined in Section 119 of the Act;

'Appointments Board' means the Board established by the Bar Council to make appointments to the Bar Standards Board and its Regulatory committees;

'Approved Regulator' has the same meaning as defined in section 20(2) of the Act of 2007;

'authorised body' means any body other than the Bar Council authorised under the Act to grant rights of audience or rights to conduct litigation;

'authorised litigator' means an authorised litigator as defined in Section 119 of the Act;

'bankruptcy order' includes a bankruptcy order made pursuant to the Insolvency Act 1986 and any similar order made in any jurisdiction in the world;

'Bar' means the Bar of England and Wales;

'Bar Council' means The General Council of the Bar as constituted from time to time or a Committee thereof;

'barrister' means an individual who has been called to the Bar by one of the Inns of Court and who has not ceased to be a member of the Bar; and in Parts III (other than paragraph 301), VI, VII and VIII of this Code means a practising barrister;

'Bar Standards Board' means the Board established to exercise and oversee the Regulatory functions of the Bar Council;

'Bar Training Regulations' means the Consolidated Regulations in respect of anything arising before 1 September 2009 and the Bar Training Regulations in respect of anything arising on or after 1 September 2009;

'BMIF' means Bar Mutual Indemnity Fund Limited;

'brief' means instructions to a barrister to appear as an advocate before a Court;

'Call' means Call to the Bar in accordance with the Consolidated Regulations;

'chambers' means a place at or from which one or more self-employed barristers carry on their practices and also refers where the context so requires to all the barristers (excluding pupils) who for the time being carry on their practices at or from that place;

'client' means lay client or intermediary;

'Company' means a company regulated by an Approved Regulator;

'complaint' means an allegation by any person or by the Bar Council of its own motion of professional misconduct or of inadequate professional service and includes a legal aid complaint;

'Complaints Commissioner' means the person appointed as such under Regulation 17 A of the Bar Council Constitution;

'the Complaints Committee' means the Complaints Committee of the Bar Standards Board or its successor;

'conditional fee agreement' means a conditional fee agreement as defined in Section 58 of the Act;

'Consolidated Regulations' means the Consolidated Regulations of the Inns of Court;

'Court' includes any court or tribunal or any other person or body whether sitting in public or in private before whom a barrister appears or may appear as an advocate;

'Director' means a director of a company, and includes the director of a Recognised Body which is a company, and in relation to a societas Europaea includes:

(a)   in a two-tier system, a member of the management organ and a member of the supervisory organ; and

(b)   in a one-tier system, a member of the administrative organ;

'Disciplinary Tribunal' means a disciplinary tribunal constituted under the Disciplinary Tribunals Regulations (reproduced in Annex K);

'employed barrister' means a practising barrister who is employed other than by a Recognised Body either under a contract of employment or by virtue of an office under the Crown or in the institutions of the European Communities and who supplies legal services as a barrister in the course of his employment;

'employer' means a person by whom an employed barrister is employed as such and any holding subsidiary or associated company corporate body or firm of that person;

'English law' includes international law and the law of the European Communities;

'Establishment Directive' means Directive 98/5/EC of the European Parliament and of the Council of February 1998 to facilitate practice of the profession of lawyer on a permanent basis in a Member State other than that in which the qualification was obtained;

'European lawyer' means a person who is a national of a Member State and who is authorised in any Member State to pursue professional activities under any of the professional titles appearing in article 2(2) of the European Communities (Lawyer's Practice) Order 1999, but who is not any of the following:

(a) a solicitor or barrister of England and Wales or Northern Ireland; or

(b) a solicitor or advocate under the law of Scotland.

'foreign lawyer' means a person (other than a registered European lawyer or a practising barrister of the bar of England and Wales) who is authorised by a competent professional body to practise in a system of law other than English law;

'Hearings before the Visitors' means an appeal hearing constituted under the Hearings before the Visitors Rules 2005 (reproduced in Annex M);

'home professional body' means the body in a Member State which authorises a European lawyer to pursue professional activities under any of the professional titles appearing in article 2(2) of the European Communities (Lawyer's Practice) Order 1999 and, if he is authorised in more than one Member State, it shall mean any such body;

'home professional title' means, in relation to a European lawyer, the professional title or any of the professional titles specified in relation to his home State in article 2(2) of the European Communities (Lawyer's Practice) Order 1999 under which he is authorised in his home State to pursue professional activities;

'home State' means the Member State in which a European lawyer acquired the authorisation to pursue professional activities under his home professional title and, if he is authorised in more than one Member State, it shall mean any such Member State;

'inadequate professional service' means such conduct towards a lay client or performance of professional services for that client which falls significantly short of that which is to be reasonably expected of a barrister in all the circumstances;

'incorporated solicitors' practice' means a body recognised under section 9 of the Act of 1985;

'indictable offence' carries the definition set out in the Serious Organised Crime and Police Act 2005 as defined in Schedule 1 of the Interpretation Act 1978 as 'an offence which, if committed by an adult, is triable on indictment whether it is exclusively so triable or triable either way';

'Informal Hearing Panel' means an informal hearing panel constituted under paragraph 43 of the Complaints Rules (reproduced in Annex J);

'instructions' means instructions or directions in whatever form (including a brief) given to a practising barrister to supply legal services whether in a contentious or in a non-contentious matter and 'instructed' shall have a corresponding meaning;

'Interim Suspension Panel' means a panel constituted under the Interim Suspension Rules (reproduced in Annex N):

'intermediary' means any person by whom a barrister in independent practice is instructed on behalf of a lay client and includes a professional client who is not also the lay client;

'International work' shall have the meaning set out in the International Practice Rules (reproduced in Annex A);

'JRC' means the Joint Regulations Committee of the Bar Council or any successor body exercising the same responsibilities by whatever name called;

'lay client' means the person on whose behalf a practising barrister (or where appropriate in the case of an employed barrister his employer) is instructed;

'lay member' means a lay person appointed by the Appointments Board to be a member of the Bar Standards Board or one of its Regulatory committees;

'lay representative' means either

(a) a lay person appointed by the President of the Council of the Inns of Court to serve on Disciplinary Tribunals, Summary Procedure Panels, Informal Hearings Panels, Interim Suspension Panels and Appeal Panels therefrom, Adjudication Panels, Adjudication Appeal Panels and Medical Panels and Review Panels therefrom; or

(b) a lay person appointed by the Lord Chief Justice to serve on Hearings before the Visitors

save that no person may be appointed as a lay representative:

    (i) if they are a member of the Complaints Committee or of the Bar Standards Board or any of its other Committees; or

    (ii) if they were a member of the Complaints Committee at any time when the matter which the Tribunal or panel is dealing with was considered by the Complaints Committee;

'legal aid complaint' shall mean a complaint so described in section 40 of the Act of 1985 as amended by the Access to Justice Act 1999;

'Legal Advice Centre' means a centre operated by a charitable or similar non-commercial organisation at which legal services are habitually provided to members of the public without charge (or for a nominal charge) to the client and:

(a) which employs or has the services of one or more solicitors pursuant to paragraph 7(a) of the Employed Solicitors' Code 1990 or for whom the Law Society has granted a waiver, or

(b) which has been and remains designated by the Bar Council as suitable for the employment or attendance of barristers subject to such conditions as may be imposed by the Bar Council in relation to insurance or any other matter whatsoever;

'legal services' includes legal advice representation and drafting or settling any statement of case witness statement affidavit or other legal document but does not include:

(a) sitting as a judge or arbitrator or acting as a mediator;

(b) lecturing in or teaching law or writing or editing law books articles or reports;

(c) examining newspapers, periodicals, books, scripts and other publications for libel, breach of copyright, contempt of court and the like;

(d) communicating to or in the press or other media;

(e) exercising the powers of a commissioner for oaths;

(f) giving advice on legal matters free to a friend or relative or acting as unpaid or honorary legal adviser to any charitable benevolent or philanthropic institution;

(g) in relation to a barrister who is a non-executive director of a company or a trustee or governor of a charitable benevolent or philanthropic institution or a trustee of any private trust, giving to the other directors trustees or governors the benefit of his learning and experience on matters of general legal principle applicable to the affairs of the company institution or trust;

'Legal Services Commission' means a body established by or under Section 1 or Section 2 of the Access to Justice Act 1999 and includes any body established and maintained by such a body;

'Licensed Access client' means a person or organisation Approved as such by the Bar Council in accordance with the Licensed Access Recognition Regulations (reproduced in Annex F);

'litigation services' means litigation services as defined in section 119 of the Act;

'LLP' means a limited liability partnership formed by being incorporated under the Limited Liability Partnerships Act 2000;

'Manager' means a barrister who is:

(a) a partner in a partnership;

(b) a member of an LLP; or

(c) a director of a company

which is a Recognised Body;

'Mediation'[1] mediation is a process whereby the parties to a dispute appoint a neutral person (mediator) to assist them in the resolution of their dispute;

'Medical Panel' means a panel constituted under the Fitness to Practise Rules (reproduced in Annex O);

'Member State' means a state which is a member of the European Communities;

'non-practising barrister' means a barrister who is not a practising barrister;

'owner' in relation to a body means a person with any ownership interest in that body;

'partner' means a person who is or is held out as a partner in an unincorporated firm;

'partnership' means an unincorporated partnership, and includes any unincorporated firm in which persons are or are held out as partners, but does not include an LLP;

'practising barrister' means a barrister who is practising as such within the meaning of paragraph 201;

'the President' means the President of the Council of the Inns of Court;

'professional client' means a solicitor or other professional person by whom a self-employed barrister is instructed that is to say:

(a) a solicitor, solicitors' firm, LLP or company, Recognised Body regulated by the Solicitors Regulation Authority, authorised litigator, Parliamentary agent, patent agent, European Patent Attorney, trade mark agent, Notary

---

[1] Amended 23 March 2005.

or a European lawyer registered with the Law Society of England and Wales;

(b)   a licensed conveyancer in a matter in which the licensed conveyancer is providing conveyancing services;

(c)   an employed barrister or registered European lawyer;

(d)   any practising barrister or registered European lawyer acting on his own behalf;

(e)   a foreign lawyer in a matter which does not involve the barrister supplying advocacy services;

(f)   a Scottish or Northern Irish Solicitor;

(g)   the representative of any body (such as a Legal Advice Centre or Pro Bono or Free Representation Unit) which arranges for the supply of legal services to the public without a fee, and which has been and remains designated by the Bar Council (subject to such conditions as may be imposed by the Bar Council in relation to insurance or any other matter whatsoever) as suitable for the instruction of barristers, and which instructs a barrister to supply legal services without a fee;

'the public' includes any lay client of a practising barrister (or in the case of an employed barrister of the barrister's employer) other than any of the persons referred to in paragraph 501;

'public access instructions' means instructions given to a barrister by or on behalf of a lay client pursuant to paragraph 401(a)(iii);

'the Qualifications Committee' means the Qualifications Committee of the Bar Standards Board or its successor;

'the Quality Assurance Committee' means the Quality Assurance Committee of the Bar Standards Board or its successor;

'Recognised Body' means a partnership, LLP, company or sole principal authorised to provide reserved legal services by an Approved Regulator other than the Bar Standards Board other than a licensed body as defined in section 72 of the Act of 2007 but does not include a body which is deemed to be authorised by reason of section 18(3) of the Act of 2007;

'registered European lawyer' means a European lawyer registered as such by the Bar Council and by an Inn pursuant to a direction of the JRC under Regulation 30 of the Consolidated Regulations;

'relevant criminal offence' means any criminal offence committed in any part of the world except:

(a)   an offence committed in the United Kingdom which is a fixed penalty offence for the purposes of the Road Traffic Offenders Act 1988 or any statutory modification or replacement thereof for the time being in force;

(b)   an offence committed in the United Kingdom or abroad which is dealt with by a procedure substantially similar to that applicable to such a fixed penalty offence; and

(c)   an offence whose main ingredient is the unlawful parking of a motor vehicle;

'right of audience' means a right of audience as defined in Section 119 of the Act;

'right to conduct litigation' means a right to conduct litigation as defined in Section 119 of the Act;

'self-employed barrister' means a practising barrister other than

(a)   barrister who is a manager or employee of a Recognised Body; and

(b)   an employed barrister acting in the course of his employment;

'solicitor' means a solicitor of the Supreme Court of England and Wales;

'the Standards Committee' means the Standards Committee of the Bar Standards Board or its successor;

'Summary Procedure Panel' means a panel constituted under the Summary Procedure Rules (reproduced in Annex L);

'trade association' means a body of persons (whether incorporated or not) which is formed for the purpose of furthering the trade interests of its members or of persons represented by its members, and does not include any association formed primarily for the purpose of securing legal assistance for its members; any reference to the masculine shall be deemed to include the feminine and any reference to the singular shall include the plural.

PART XI—TRANSITIONAL PROVISIONS

1101   In respect of anything done or omitted to be done or otherwise arising before 31 October 2004:

(a)   this Code shall not apply;

(b)   the Code of Conduct in force at the relevant time shall notwithstanding paragraph 101 apply as if this Code had not been adopted by the Bar Council.

1102   Any barrister called to the Bar before 1 January 2002 but who has not completed or been exempted from 12 months' pupillage in accordance with the Bar Training Regulations in force at the relevant time may practise as a barrister notwithstanding paragraph 202(a) of this Code provided that such a barrister shall not be entitled to exercise a right of audience under paragraph 203.1 unless he:

(a)   has notified the Bar Council in writing of his wish to do so; and

(b)   either (i) has complied with any conditions as to further training which the Bar Council may require or (ii) has been informed by the Bar Council that he is not required to comply with any such conditions.

1103   Any barrister who on 31 July 2000 was entitled to exercise any right of audience which he had by reason of being a barrister shall notwithstanding paragraph 203 of this Code remain entitled to exercise that right of audience.

1104   Any barrister who during any period before 31 July 2000 was entitled to exercise a right of audience as an employed barrister may for the purpose of paragraph 203.2(c) of this Code count that period as if he had been entitled during that period to exercise a right of audience before every Court in relation to all proceedings provided that he:

(a)   has notified the Bar Council in writing of his wish to do so; and

(b)   either (i) has complied with any conditions (including any conditions as to further training) which the Bar Council may require or (ii) has been informed by the Bar Council that he is not required to comply with any such conditions.

1105   Any person who was entitled on 31 July 2000 or becomes entitled before 31 July 2002 to exercise a right of audience before every Court in relation to all proceedings shall be a qualified person without having satisfied paragraph 203.3(b)(ii) of this Code if he:

(a)   has satisfied the other requirements of paragraph 203.3;

      (b)   has notified the Bar Council in writing of his wish to act as a qualified person; and

      (c)   has been designated by the Bar Council as suitable so to act.

1106   Any barrister who before 31 July 2000 had delivered to the Bar Council the notification and information referred to in paragraph 212(b)(ii) of the Sixth Edition of the Code of Conduct or was exempted by waiver from that requirement shall until 31 July 2005 remain entitled to supply legal services to the public on condition that he complies with those requirements of paragraph 212(b)–(e) of the Sixth Edition of the Code of Conduct which on 31 July 2000 applied to him and provided that he shall not thereby be entitled to exercise any right of audience which he has by reason of being a barrister.

SECTION 2

Table of Annexes

Please note, annexes A, B, F1 to H, and J to Q and S are not reproduced in this manual but can be accessed via the Bar Standards Board's website, <http://www.barstandardsboard.org.uk>, under the section on 'Standards and Guidance' (go to the Code, and use the drop-down boxes to find 'Section 2, Annexes to the Code').

ANNEXE C

THE CONTINUING PROFESSIONAL DEVELOPMENT REGULATIONS

Application

1. These Rules apply;

    (a) to all barristers who have commenced practice on or after 1 October 1997;

    (b) from 1 January 2003, to all barristers who were called to the Bar in or after 1990;

    (c) from 1 January 2004, to all barristers who were called to the Bar between 1980 and 1989; and

    (d) from 1 January 2005, to all barristers who were called to the Bar before 1980.

The Mandatory Continuing Professional Development Requirements

2. For the purpose of these Regulations:

    (a) 'calendar year' means a period of one year commencing on 1 January in the year in question;

    (b) the 'mandatory requirements' are those set out in paragraphs 3 to 7 below;

    (c) a 'pupillage year' is any calendar year in which a barrister is at any time a pupil.

3. Any barrister to whom these Regulations apply and who as at 1 October 2001 had commenced but not completed the period of three years referred to in the Continuing Education Scheme Rules at Annex Q to the Sixth Edition of the Code of Conduct must complete a minimum of 42 hours of continuing professional development during that period.

4. Any barrister to whom these Regulations apply who commences practice on or after 1 October 2001 must during the first three calendar years in which the barrister holds a practising certificate after a pupillage year complete a minimum of 45 hours of continuing professional development.

5. Any barrister to whom these Regulations apply:

    (a) must, if he holds a practising certificate or certicates throughout the whole of any calendar year, complete a minimum of 12 hours of continuing professional development during that period; and

    (b) must, if he holds a practising certifcate or certificate for part only of a calendar year, complete one hour of continuing professional development during that calendar year for each month for which he holds a practising certificate.

6. Regulation 5 does not apply:

    (a) in the case of a barrister to whom regulation 3 applies, to any calendar year forming or containing part of the period of 3 years referred to in regulation 3; or

    (b) in the case of a barrister to whom regulation 4 applies, during any pupillage year or during the first three calendar years in which the barrister holds a practising certificate.

7. Any barrister to whom these Regulations apply must submit details of the continuing professional development he has undertaken to the Bar Council in the form prescribed, and at the time specified, by the Bar Council.

8. The Bar Council may, by resolution, specify the nature, content and format of courses and other activities which may be undertaken by barristers (or any category of barristers) in order to satisfy the mandatory requirements.

9. The Bar Council may, by resolution and following consultation with the Inns, Circuits and other providers as appropriate, increase the minimum number of hours of continuing professional development which must be completed in order to satisfy any of the mandatory requirements.

Waivers

10. The Bar Council shall have the power in relation to any barrister to waive any or all of the mandatory requirements in whole or in part or to extend the time within which the barrister must complete any of the mandatory requirements.

11. Any application by a barrister to the Bar Council for a waiver of any of the mandatory requirements or to extend the time within which to complete any of the mandatory requirements must be made in writing, setting out all mitigating circumstances relied on and supported by all relevant documentary evidence.

ANNEXE D

THE PRACTISING CERTIFICATE REGULATIONS

The Authority to Issue Practising Certificates

1. The Access to Justice Act 1999 (s. 46) included provision for the Bar Council to make rules prohibiting barristers from practising unless authorised by a certificate issued by the Bar Council (a 'practising certificate'). The rules may include provision for the payment of different fees by different descriptions of barristers, but the Council may not set fees with a view to raising a total amount in excess of that applied by the Council for the purposes of the regulation, education and training of barristers, and those wishing to become barristers and for any other purpose Approved by the Lord Chancellor under subsection (3)(a) of s. 46 of the Access to Justice Act 1999.

2. No provision included in the rules shall have effect unless Approved by the Lord Chancellor.

3. Section 46 of the Access to Justice Act 1999, as amended by Order by statutory instrument with effect from 31 January 2001, is at Appendix 1 to these rules.

Application

4. These rules shall apply to all barristers and registered European lawyers holding themselves out as offering legal services as barristers to the public or to their employer. They shall not apply to non-practising barristers.

The Calculation of Income from Practising Certificates

5. The income to be raised by the Bar Council from Practising Certificate Fees shall not exceed the forecast expenditure for the year ahead starting 1 January each year to be applied to the activities and purposes set out below, less any subventions for those purposes received from the Inns of Court.

6. The activities, including education and training, to which Practising Certificate Fees shall be applied shall be as follows:

    (a) The formulation and implementation of rules and regulations;

    (b) The development and dissemination to the profession of guidance, recommendations and other standards (whether binding or advisory) contributing to the control, government and direction of the profession and the way in which it practises: those activities shall include the definition, review and supervision of the standards of professional conduct and work expected of members of the profession;

    (c) Participation in the legislative process in relation to proposals relevant to the organisation or conduct of the profession;

    (d) Law reform work: that is, participation in the legislative process in relation to proposals falling outside paragraph 5(c);

    (e) Support for the administration of provision of legal services to the public *pro bono;*

    (f) the furtherance of human rights;

    (g) the development of international relations.

7.   The maximum sum to be raised from Practising Certificate Fees shall include, as agreed by the Lord Chancellor, the annual forecast full cost of work in the following areas:

    (a) Activities which are entirely regulatory:

        (i)   Professional Standards

        (ii)   Professional Conduct and Complaints

        (iii) Equal Opportunities

        (iv)   Records

    (b) Education and Training

    (c) Activities qualifying under the Statutory Instrument laid under s. 46 subsection (3)(a) of the Access to Justice Act 1999:

        (i)   Human Rights and Pro Bono administration

        (ii)   Law Reform

8.   The maximum sum to be raised from Practising Certificate Fees shall include, as agreed by the Lord Chancellor, the proportion as shown of the annual forecast full cost of work in the following areas qualifying as Regulatory activity or for purposes agreed under the Statutory Instrument laid under s. 46 sub-section (3)(a) of the Access to Justice Act 1999:

(a)	Legal Services	80%
(b)	International Relations	90%
(c)	Policy	75%
(d)	Remuneration	80%
(e)	Public Affairs	30%
(f)	Employed Bar	70%
(g)	Young Bar	60%
(h)	Information Technology	60%

9.   For the purpose of calculating the maximum sum to be raised from Practising Certificate Fees, Administration costs shall be added in proportion to the cost of activities set out in paragraphs 8 and 9, to include the following:

Chairman's office

Executive office

Council and General Management Committee work

Finance

Library/Registry

Print and Distribution

Reception and Meeting Rooms

Publications

Website

Contingency funds up to 3% of total expenditure

Provision for capital expenditure not covered by depreciation

The Issue of Practising Certificates

10.   Subject to paragraphs 14 and 15 of these Rules, the Bar Council shall issue Full Practising Certificates to all barristers and registered European lawyers notifying the Bar Council that they wish to commence or re-commence practice and annually thereafter on each renewal date.

11. A Practising Certificate shall be valid until the due date for renewal of the certificate unless:

    (a) the barrister's status changes; or

    (b) the barrister is disbarred or suspended from practice as a barrister by a Disciplinary Tribunal, Summary Procedure Panel, Fitness to Practice Panel or Interim Suspension Panel.

12. The Bar Council shall amend a Practising Certificate if a barrister changes his category from independent practice to employed practice or vice versa provided that the barrister has paid any additional amount to cover the difference in fee applicable to each category.

13. The Bar Council shall endorse a Practising Certificate to reflect any qualification restriction or condition imposed on the barrister by the Bar Council or by a Disciplinary Tribunal, Summary Procedure Panel, Informal Panel, Interim Suspension Panel or Fitness to Practise Panel.

14. The Bar Council shall not issue a Practising Certificate to any barrister who has been disbarred or is subject to an order suspending him from practice.

15. The Bar Council may refuse to issue a Practising Certificate to a barrister if it is satisfied that the barrister:

    (a) has failed to comply with the training requirements applicable to him at the date of his Call to the Bar;

    (b) has failed to comply with any applicable requirements of the Continuing Professional Development Regulations;

    (c) has not provided in writing to the Bar Council details of the current address(es) with telephone number(s) of the chambers or office from which he supplies legal services and (if he is an employed barrister) the name, address, telephone number and nature of the business of his employer;

    (d) has not paid to the Bar Council the Practising Certificate Fee currently prescribed by the Bar Council for barristers of his/her description.

    (e) has failed to pay the appropriate insurance premium so as to be insured with the Bar Mutual Indemnity Fund against claims for professional negligence, as required by the Code of Conduct;

    (f) would be practising in breach of the provisions of paragraphs 203, 204, 205, 401, 501, 502 or 503 of the Code of Conduct.

The Renewal of Practising Certificates

16. The due date for the payment of the Practising Certificate Fee for barristers in independent practice and registered European lawyers in independent practice shall be 1 January each year. The due date for the payment of the Practising Certificate fee for employed barristers and registered European lawyers in employment shall be 6 April each year.

Practising Certificate Fees

17. Each year, the Bar Council shall decide the appropriate Practising Certificate Fees for the following year so that the projected income from these fees shall not exceed the total amount calculated under paragraphs 8 to 10 of these rules.

18. The Bar Council may set different fees for different categories of barristers reflecting, for example, the barrister's seniority and whether he is in independent or employed practice.

19. The Practising Certificate Fee following Call to the Bar or registration as a Registered European Lawyer shall become due on the relevant renewal date of the year following the year of Call or registration, as appropriate to each category of barrister or Registered European Lawyer.

20. The Bar Council shall provide four weeks' notice of the date by which payment of the Practising Certificate Fee is due and shall confirm in writing the validity of the Practising Certificate following payment of the Practising Certificate Fee. notification to practising barristers of the Practising Certificate Fee shall include a statement of any separate voluntary subscription to the Bar Council, other than for a Practising Certificate.

21. On application of individual barristers, the Bar Council may reduce the Practising Certificate Fee in recognition of certified periods of continuous absence from practice exceeding three months in the previous year. The Bar Council may reduce the full Practising Certificate Fee payable by those whose certified gross fee income or salary for the previous year is less than such annual amount as the Council may decide from time to time. Applications for such reduction must be received no later than the end of the practising certificate year following the year in which the absence occurred or low fee income received.

Non-Payment of the Practising Certificate Fee

22. A practising barrister who fails to pay the Practising Certificate Fee within one month of the due date shall be liable to a penalty to cover the administrative costs of the Bar Council in dealing with the delay in payment. If the fee is paid later than one month and earlier than two months following the due date, the penalty shall amount to 15% of the full fee applicable to his seniority and status. If the fee is paid later than two months after the due date, the penalty shall be 30% of that fee. The full penalty applies even if the barrister has been granted or is eligible for any reduction of the full Fee under these rules.

23. The Bar Council shall notify any practising barrister who has not paid the Practising Certificate Fee by the due date that if the Fee is not paid within one month of the due date, he shall become liable for the surcharge under paragraph 22 and may be reported to the Professional Conduct and Complaints Committee for that Committee to investigate and consider whether there has been a breach of paragraph 202 of the Code of Conduct.

24. The Bar Council shall report all barristers who it has reason to believe are practising and who have not paid the Practising Certificate Fee and, where applicable, the penalty to the Professional Conduct and Complaints Committee unless the Fee and, where applicable, the penalty are both paid in within 3 months of the due date provided that the barrister has not incurred the penalty for more than two years out of the last five in which case his default may be reported to the Professional Conduct and Complaints Committee within such shorter time as may appear appropriate in all the circumstances.

25. The Bar Council may, with the consent of the Chairman of the Professional Conduct and Complaints Committee, withdraw any complaint made under paragraph 24 where it is satisfied that:

     (a) the Fee and surcharge have been paid within 3 months of the due date;

     (b) the barrister was not in fact practising during the relevant period; or

     (c) there is some other reason why it would be unjust to continue the complaint.

Appendix to ANNEX D

ACCESS TO JUSTICE ACT

s. 46 Bar Practising Certificates

(1) If the General Council of the Bar makes rules prohibiting barristers from practising as specified in the rules unless authorised by a certificate issued by the Council (a 'practising certificate'), the rules may include provisions requiring the payment of fees to the Council by applicants for practising certificates.

(2) Rules made by virtue of subsection (1)—

(a) may provide for the payment of different fees by different descriptions of applicants, but

(b) may not set fees with a view to raising a total amount in excess of that applied by the Council for the purposes of:

(i) the regulation, education and training of barristers and those wishing to become barristers;

(ii) the participation by the Council in law reform and the legislative process;

(iii) the provision by barristers and those wishing to become barristers of free legal services to the public;

(iv) the promotion of the protection by law of human rights and fundamental freedoms; and

(v) the promotion of relations between the Council and bodies representing the members of legal professions in jurisdictions other than England and Wales.

(3) The Lord Chancellor may by order made by statutory instrument—

(a) amend subsection (2)(b) by adding to the purposes referred to in it such other purposes as the Lord Chancellor considers appropriate, or

(b) vary or revoke an order under paragraph (a).

(4) No order shall be made under subsection (3) unless—

(a) the Lord Chancellor has consulted the Council, and

(b) a draft of the order has been laid before, and Approved by a resolution of, each House of Parliament.

(5) No provision included in rules by virtue of subsection (1), and no other provision of rules made by the Council about practising certificates, shall have effect unless Approved by the Lord Chancellor.

(6) The Council shall provide the Lord Chancellor with such information as he may reasonably require for deciding whether to approve any provision of rules made by the Council about practising certificates.

ANNEXE E

GUIDELINES ON OPINIONS UNDER THE FUNDING CODE

Status of these Guidelines

1.   These Guidelines are prepared by the Legal Services Commission. They are intended as statements of good practice to be followed when opinions are prepared on the merits of applications or certificates issued under the Funding Code. As statements of good practice these Guidelines should not be too rigidly applied. An opinion will, however, be rejected if it does not contain the information necessary for the Commission to make its decision under the Code.

2.   These Guidelines have been agreed by the Bar Council for incorporation in the Code of Conduct of the Bar of England and Wales.

Scope

3.   These Guidelines apply to legal opinions sent to the Legal Services Commission for the purpose of decisions made in individual cases under the Funding Code. The Guidelines are most relevant to decisions made under certificates or contracts covering Legal Representation or Support Funding, but also may be relevant to other levels of service.

      The Guidelines apply to counsel and to solicitors with higher rights of audience who are instructed to give an independent opinion on the merits of a case. The term 'counsel' in the Guidelines therefore includes a solicitor with higher rights of audience.

4.   The Guidelines do not apply directly to solicitors giving a report to the regional office in a case which they are conducting or proposing to conduct. Such a report may be shorter and more informal than an opinion on the merits, but these Guidelines should still be borne in mind by solicitors when such reports are prepared.

Preliminary Considerations

5.   All opinions must be prepared in accordance with the Funding Code and having regard to the Funding Code guidance prepared by the Commission. This guidance is set out in the Commission's Manual, and on the Commission's website at www. legalservices.gov.uk. Every person preparing an opinion must have access to and consult the guidance as necessary.

6.   When counsel is instructed to provide an opinion in writing, counsel should first consider whether it is necessary to have a conference, for example to enable counsel to assess the reliability of the client's evidence in a case where that evidence is likely to be contested. Where counsel considers that a conference is necessary and would be cost effective, the costs of such a conference may be covered by the certificate provided it is within any overall cost limitation on the certificate and is justified as reasonable on assessment at the end of the case. In the case of a high cost case contract, any conference must be justified within the agreed case plan for the action.

Contents of Opinions Issues to be Covered

7.   The primary purpose of an opinion is to provide the Commission with the information and legal opinion necessary to apply all relevant Funding Code criteria, rather than to provide a personal opinion on what the funding decision should be.

8.   Each opinion should state at the outset:

   (a) the level of service under which the opinion is given and if appropriate, the level of service being applied for;

   (b) the case category into which the proceedings fall, giving reasons if there is likely to be an issue as to which case category is appropriate.

9.   In every opinion counsel should identify any potentially excluded work in the case, i.e. aspects of the case which may fall within the excluded categories in paragraph 1 of Schedule 2 of the Access to Justice Act 1999. Where excluded work arises counsel should specify any of the Lord Chancellor's directions which may bring the case back into scope.

10. It is not necessary for an opinion to discuss separately every criterion relevant to the decision. For example, it is not usually necessary for counsel to refer to the standard criteria in section 4 of the Code unless, in the particular circumstances of the case, one or more of these criteria is likely to be material to the Commission's decision. Unless otherwise instructed an opinion should always cover the following:

   (a) Prospects of success (except for special Children Act proceedings or other proceedings which do not have a prospect of success criterion). The opinion should specify what constitutes a successful outcome for the client, having regard to guidance, and must specify with reasons the prospects in one of the six categories provided for in the Code. Where prospects are 'borderline', the issues of fact, law or expert evidence which give rise to that assessment must be identified. Where prospects of success are 'unclear' the necessary work to clarify prospects of success must be identified.

   (b) Cost benefit (save for those cases which do not have a cost benefit criterion). The opinion must identify the benefit to the client from the proceedings and, for quantifiable claims, provide a figure for 'likely damages' as defined in the Code. See paragraph 14 below as to estimates of 'likely costs'.

   (c) Where the application is for Investigative Help to be granted or continued, the opinion must deal with matters relevant to criteria 5.6.2 (the need for investigation) and 5.6.4 (prospects after investigation). The opinion should explain why there are reasonable grounds for believing that when the investigative work has been carried out the claim will be strong enough, in terms of prospects of success and cost benefit, to satisfy the relevant criteria for full representation.

   (d) Where the issue is whether funding should be withdrawn on the merits, the opinion should cover matters relevant to applying criteria 14.2 to 14.4, taking into account the interests of the client, the interests of the Community Legal Service Fund and relevant guidance.

11. An opinion on merits should:

   (a) where factual issues are involved (a) set out in sufficient detail, (although not necessarily at great length), the rival factual versions to enable the Commission to assess their relative strengths, and (b) express a clear opinion as to the likelihood of the applicant's version being accepted by a court and why;

(b) where legal issues or difficulties of law are involved (a) summarise those issues or difficulties in sufficient detail to enable the Commission to come to a view about them without looking outside the opinion, and (b) express a clear view as to the likelihood of the applicant's case on the law being accepted by a court and why;

(c) draw attention to (a) any lack or incompleteness of material which might bear on the reliability or otherwise of the applicant's version, and (b) any other factor which could—whether now or in the future—materially affect the assessment of the outcome of the case.

12.   Where appropriate an opinion should suggest or formulate for the Commission any limitation or condition, whether as to the scope of work that should be covered, or as to costs, which ought to be imposed on the grant of funding in order to safeguard the Fund. In complex cases, including cases proceeding on the multi-track, the opinion should specify any future point in the proceedings at which it is likely to be sensible to re-assess the merits.

Information From Other Sources

13.   There will often be information relevant to a merits decision which is not readily available to counsel. Where such information is not included in counsel's instructions, the opinion should specify the information which should be provided by the instructing solicitors, usually in the form of a covering letter to accompany counsel's opinion.

14.   The following issues should usually be dealt with by instructing solicitors:

(a) estimates of likely costs. This includes estimates of costs incurred to date, likely future costs to disposal, or future costs to trial. Assessments of likely costs may be relevant not just to any cost benefit criteria, but also to other criteria such as the thresholds for support funding, or the affordability of a high cost case. Such estimates will sometimes best be made in the light of counsel's opinion as to prospects of success and the future conduct of the case. Alternatively instructing solicitors may provide relevant estimates of costs to counsel with counsel's instructions so that such figures may be incorporated in the body of the opinion;

(b) assessments of whether a case is suitable for a Conditional Fee Agreement and whether affordable insurance is available, in cases which are being considered under the General Funding Code.

Specific Issues

15.   Where it is suggested that a case has a significant wider public interest counsel's opinion should:

(a) identify the nature of the benefits which the case might bring to persons other than the client;

(b) identify the group or section of the public who might benefit from the case, if possible giving at least a rough estimate of likely numbers;

(c) where people may benefit indirectly from a test case, explain the individual issues which other clients would need to establish in order to succeed with their claims;

(d) where the public interest of the case derives from establishing an important point of law, set out that legal issue clearly and explain the likelihood of the court resolving the issue one way or another for the benefit of other cases.

16. Where it is suggested that a judicial review or claim against a public authority raises significant human rights issues, the opinion should identify the specific articles of the Convention which may have been breached by the public body and the importance of those issues to the client and the general public.

17. Where it is suggested that a case has overwhelming importance to the client as this is defined in the Code, the nature of the importance to the client must be identified in the opinion having regard to the Commission's guidance on this issue.

18. In cases involving more than two parties, counsel should consider carefully whether separate representation for each client is justified (criterion 5.4.5). This is particularly important in many family cases and in appeals where the points at issue in the appeal may not require separate representation from every party to the proceedings at first instance. Counsel should consider whether the arguments on which his or her client relies will be put forward on behalf of another party whose interests in the proceedings are substantially the same. Counsel should report to the Commission with proposals for minimising representation by solicitors and counsel.

19. In high cost cases in which the Commission will be considering whether the action is affordable in the light of available resources (criterion 6.4) counsel's opinion should address those aspects of the case which, in accordance with the Commission's guidance, are relevant to the affordability decision. It will not be possible or appropriate for counsel to consider the question of the resources available to the Commission, or the reasonableness of funding the individual case as against other cases, as these are matters solely for the Commission.

Continuing Duties to the Fund

20. A barrister is under a specific duty to comply with the provisions of the Access to Justice Act 1999 and any regulations or code in effect under that Act (paragraph 304 of the Bar Code of Conduct). Since these duties are directed at ensuring that public funding is granted and continued only in justifiable cases, it follows that counsel acting under a funding certificate is under a duty to bring to the attention of the Commission any matter which might affect the client's entitlement to funding, or the terms of his or her certificate, at whatever stage of the proceedings that might occur.

21. Counsel and any other legal representative acting under a certificate or contract are also subject to the specific obligations set out in Rule C44 of the Code Procedures. This includes a general obligation to inform the Regional Director of new information or a change of circumstances which has come to light which may affect the terms or continuation of a certificate.

22. Where counsel is under an obligation to draw matters to the attention of the Commission, he or she may do so by drawing matters to the attention of his or her instructing solicitors and asking that they be passed on to the Commission, or counsel may contact the Commission directly if that is appropriate in the particular circumstances of the case.

ANNEXE I

THE EMPLOYED BARRISTERS (CONDUCT OF LITIGATION) RULES

1. An employed barrister may exercise any right that he has to conduct litigation provided that:

    (a) he is entitled to practise as a barrister in accordance with paragraph 202 of the Code;

    (b) he has spent a period of at least twelve weeks working under the supervision of a qualified person or has been exempted from this requirement by the Bar Council on the grounds of his relevant experience;

    (c) if he is of less than one year's standing (or three years' standing in the case of a barrister who is supplying litigation services to any person other than a person referred to in paragraph 501 of the Code) his principal place of practice is an office which is also the principal place of practice of a qualified person who is able to provide guidance to the barrister; and

    (d) if he is of less than three years' standing, he completes at least six hours of continuing professional development on an Approved litigation course during any year in which he is required to undertake continuing professional development by the Continuing Professional Development Regulations (reproduced in Annex C).

2. For the purpose of paragraph 1(c) above an employed barrister shall be treated as being of a particular number of years' standing if he:

    (a) has been entitled to practise and has practised as a barrister (other than as a pupil who has not completed pupillage in accordance with the Bar Training Regulations) or as a member of another authorised body;

    (b) has made such practice his primary occupation; and

    (c) has been entitled to exercise a right to conduct litigation in relation to every Court and all proceedings for a period (which need not be continuous and need not have been as a member of the same authorised body) of at least that number of years.

3. A person shall be a qualified person for the purpose of paragraph 1(c) above if he:

    (a) has been entitled to practise and has practised as a barrister (other than as a pupil who has not completed pupillage in accordance with the Bar Training Regulations) or as a member of another authorised body for a period (which need not have been as a member of the same authorised body) of at least six years in the previous eight years;

    (b) for the previous two years

        (i)   has made such practice his primary occupation, and

        (ii) has been entitled to exercise a right to conduct litigation in relation to every Court and all proceedings;

    (c) is not acting as a qualified person in relation to more than two other people; and

    (d) has not been designated by the Bar Council as unsuitable to be a qualified person.

4. If an employed barrister in the conduct of litigation gives an undertaking, any breach of that undertaking shall constitute professional misconduct.

ANNEXE R

THE PUPILLAGE FUNDING AND ADVERTISING REQUIREMENTS 2003

Funding

1. The members of a set of chambers must pay to each non-practising chambers pupil by the end of each month of the non-practising six months of his pupillage no less than:

   (a) £833.33; plus

   (b) such further sum as may be necessary to reimburse expenses reasonably incurred by the pupil on:

      (i) travel for the purposes of his pupillage during that month; and

      (ii) attendance during that month at courses which he is required to attend as part of his pupillage.

2. The members of a set of chambers must pay to each practising chambers pupil by the end of each month of the practising six months of his pupillage no less than:

   (a) £833.33; plus

   (b) such further sum as may be necessary to reimburse expenses reasonably incurred by the pupil on:

      (i) travel for the purposes of his pupillage during that month; and

      (ii) attendance during that month at courses which he is required to attend as part of his pupillage; less

   (c) such amount, if any, as the pupil may receive during that month from his practice as a barrister; and less

   (d) such amounts, if any, as the pupil may have received during the preceding months of his practising pupillage from his practice as a barrister, save to the extent that the amount paid to the pupil in respect of any such month was less than the total of the sums provided for in sub-paragraphs (a) and (b) above.

3. The members of a set of chambers may not seek or accept repayment from a chambers pupil of any of the sums required to be paid under paragraphs 1 and 2 above, whether before or after he ceases to be a chambers pupil, save in the case of misconduct on his part.

Advertising

4. All vacancies for pupillages must be advertised on a website designated by the Bar Council and the following information must be provided:

   (a) The name and address of chambers.

   (b) The number of tenants.

   (c) A brief statement of the work undertaken by chambers e.g. 'predominately criminal'.

   (d) The number of pupillage vacancies.

   (e) The level of award.

   (f) The procedure for application.

   (g) The minimum educational or other qualification required.

   (h) The date of closure for the receipt of applications.

   (i) The date by which the decisions on the filling of vacancies will be made.

Application

5. The requirements set out in paragraphs 1 to 4 above:

   (a) apply in the case of pupillages commencing on or after 1st January 2003;

   (b) do not apply in the case of pupils who qualified for call to the Bar pursuant to regulations 35 (solicitors), 36 (other qualified lawyers) or 55 (teachers of the law of England and Wales of experience and distinction) of the Bar Training Regulations;

   (c) do not apply in the case of pupils who are undertaking a period of pupillage in a set of chambers as part of a pupillage training programme offered by another organisation that is authorised by the Bar Council to take pupils;

   (d) do not apply in the case of pupils who have completed both the non-practising and the practising six months of pupillage;

   (e) save as provided in paragraph 3 above, do not apply in respect of any period after a pupil ceases, for whatever reason, to be a chambers pupil; and

   (f) may be waived in part or in whole by the Pupillage Funding Committee.

6. For the purposes of these requirements:

   (a) 'chambers pupil' means, in respect of any set of chambers, a pupil undertaking the non-practising or practising six months of pupillage with a pupil-master or pupil-masters who is or are a member or members of that set of chambers;

   (b) 'non-practising chambers pupil' means a chambers pupil undertaking the non-practising six months of pupillage;

   (c) 'practising chambers pupil' means a chambers pupil undertaking the practising six months of pupillage;

   (d) 'month' means calendar month commencing on the same day of the month as that on which the pupil commenced the non-practising or practising six months pupillage, as the case may be;

   (e) any payment made to a pupil by a barrister pursuant to paragraph 805 of the Code of Conduct shall constitute an amount received by the pupil from his practice as a barrister; and

   (f) the following travel by a pupil shall not constitute travel for the purposes of his pupillage:

      (i) travel between his home and chambers; and

      (ii) travel for the purposes of his practice as a barrister.

ANNEXE S

COMPLAINTS HANDLING

These new requirements relating to complaints handling in chambers have been set out in full. For complaints to the Bar Standards Board see **Chapter 6** of this manual: Professional misconduct: the complaints procedure.

Introduction

The numbered paragraphs below contain requirements which must be met by all barristers in order to comply with paragraph 403.2 (d) of the Code of Conduct.

Requirements

Provision of information to clients

1. When a barrister receives instructions from a new professional or a new lay client they must be informed in writing as soon as is reasonably practicable:-

    (a)   that there is available upon request a Chambers Complaints Procedure

    (b)   that the lay client may complain directly to Chambers without going through solicitors.

    In cases of public or licensed access using an intermediary, the intermediary must similarly be informed.

    Where the lay client is a new client but the professional client (or intermediary) is an existing client of the barrister, the barrister must ensure that the lay client is informed in writing of the information set out at 1(a) and 1(b) above.

    The notification of the information at 1(a) and 1(b) does not require a separate specific letter. It is sufficient for it to be contained in the ordinary terms of reference letter (or equivalent letter) that is sent by Chambers upon acceptance of instructions.

2. To comply with paragraph 1 it will be sufficient for the barrister (or a member of Chambers' staff), when acknowledging instructions in a new matter, to ask the solicitor (or intermediary) in writing to pass the information about the Chambers Complaints Procedure on to the client.

3. Chambers' Complaints Procedures must be provided to professional clients, lay clients and intermediaries on request.

4. Chambers' websites and literature must carry information about the Chambers' Complaints Procedure.

Response to complaints

5. All complaints must be acknowledged promptly. Together with the acknowledgment the complainant must be provided with:-

    (a)   the name of the person who will deal with the complaint together with a description of that person's role in Chambers

    (b)   a copy of the Chambers' Complaints Procedure

    (c)   the date by which the complainant will next hear from Chambers.

    The complainant must also be informed (if this is not clear from the Chambers' Complaints Procedure) of the alternative option of complaint to the Bar Standards Board and the time limits which apply

6[1]   Where a complaint is referred to Chambers by the Commissioner in accordance with Annexe J of the Code (the Complaints Rules):

(a)   The Head of Chambers shall inform the Commissioner within six weeks of the date of the referral of the progress which has been made in considering the complaint, or of the outcome.

(b)   where the investigation is not completed within six weeks of the referral, the Head of Chambers shall provide updates on progress to the Commissioner every six weeks until the investigation is concluded, and shall then inform the Commissioner of the outcome of the complaint.

Documents and Record Keeping

7.   All communications and documents relating to complaints must be kept confidential and disclosed only so far as is necessary for:

(a)   the investigation and resolution of the complaint

(b)   internal Chambers review for the purposes of improving practice

(c)   complying with requests from the Bar Standards Board in the exercise of its monitoring and or auditing functions.

The disclosure of internal Chambers' documents relating to the handling of the complaint, such as the minutes of a Chambers' meeting held to discuss a particular complaint, to the Bar Standards Board for the further resolution or investigation of the complaint is not required.

8.   A record must be kept of each complaint, all steps taken in response to it and the outcome of the complaint, together with a copy of all correspondence, including electronic mail, and all other documents generated in response to the complaint. The records and copies should be kept for 6 years.

9.   The person responsible for the administration of the procedure must report at least annually to the appropriate member/committee of Chambers on the number of complaints received, the subject areas of the complaints and the outcomes. The complaints should be reviewed for trends and possible training issues.

---

[1]   Effective from 31st March 2009

SECTION 3

WRITTEN STANDARDS FOR THE CONDUCT OF PROFESSIONAL WORK

GENERAL STANDARDS

1   Introduction

1.1   These Standards are intended as a guide to the way in which a barrister should carry out his work. They consist in part of matters which are dealt with expressly in the Code of Conduct and in part of statements of good practice. They must therefore be read in conjunction with the Code of Conduct, and are to be taken into account in determining whether or not a barrister has committed a disciplinary offence. They apply to employed barristers as well as to barristers in independent practice, except where this would be inappropriate. In addition to these General Standards, there are Standards which apply specifically to the conduct of criminal cases.

2   General

2.1   The work which is within the ordinary scope of a barrister's practice consists of advocacy, drafting pleadings and other legal documents and advising on questions of law. A barrister acts only on the instructions of a professional client, and does not carry out any work by way of the management, administration or general conduct of a lay client's affairs, nor the management, administration or general conduct of litigation nor the receipt or handling of clients' money.

2.2   It is a fundamental principle which applies to all work undertaken by a barrister that a barrister is under a duty to act for any client (whether legally aided or not) in cases within his field of practice. The rules which embody this principle and the exceptions to it are set out in paragraphs 303, 601, 602, 603, 604 and 605 of the Code of Conduct.

3   Acceptance of Work

3.1   As soon as practicable after receipt of any brief or instructions a barrister should satisfy himself that there is no reason why he ought to decline to accept it.

3.2   A barrister is not considered to have accepted a brief or instructions unless he has had an opportunity to consider it and has expressly accepted it.

3.3   A barrister should always be alert to the possibility of a conflict of interests. If the conflict is between the interests of his lay client and his professional client, the conflict must be resolved in favour of the lay client. Where there is a conflict between the lay client and the Legal Aid Fund, the conflict must be resolved in favour of the lay client, subject only to compliance with the provisions of the Legal Aid Regulations.

3.4   If after a barrister has accepted a brief or instructions on behalf of more than one lay client, there is or appears to be a conflict or a significant risk of a conflict between the interests of any one or more of such clients, he must not continue to act for any client unless all such clients give their consent to his so acting.

3.5   Even if there is no conflict of interest, when a barrister has accepted a brief or instructions for any party in any proceedings, he should not accept a brief or instructions in respect of an appeal or further stage of the proceedings for any other party without obtaining the prior consent of the original client.

3.6   A barrister must not accept any brief or instructions if the matter is one in which he has reason to believe that he is likely to be a witness. If, however, having accepted a brief or instructions, it later appears that he is likely to be a witness in the case on a material question of fact, he may retire or withdraw only if he can do so without jeopardising his client's interests.

3.7   A barrister should not appear as a barrister:

(a)   in any matter in which he is a party or has a significant pecuniary interest;

(b)   either for or against any local authority, firm or organisation of which he is a member or in which he has directly or indirectly a significant pecuniary interest;

(c)   either for or against any company of which he is a director, secretary or officer or in which he has directly or indirectly a significant pecuniary interest.

3.8   Apart from cases in which there is a conflict of interests, a barrister must not accept any brief or instructions if to do so would cause him to be otherwise professionally embarrassed: paragraph 603 of the Code of Conduct sets out the general principles applicable to such situations.

4   Withdrawal from a Case and Return of Brief or Instructions

4.1   When a barrister has accepted a brief for the defence of a person charged with a serious criminal offence, he should so far as reasonably practicable ensure that the risk of a conflicting professional engagement does not arise.

4.2   The circumstances in which a barrister must withdraw from a case or return his brief or instructions are set out in paragraph 608 of the Code of Conduct; the circumstances in which he is permitted to do so are set out in paragraph 609; the circumstances in which he must not do so are set out in paragraph 610.

5   Conduct of Work

5.1   A barrister must at all times promote and protect fearlessly and by all proper and lawful means his lay client's best interests.

5.2   A barrister must assist the Court in the administration of justice and, as part of this obligation and the obligation to use only proper and lawful means to promote and protect the interests of his client, must not deceive or knowingly or recklessly mislead the Court.

5.3   A barrister is at all times individually and personally responsible for his own conduct and for his professional work both in Court and out of Court.

5.4   A barrister must in all his professional activities act promptly, conscientiously, diligently and with reasonable competence and must take all reasonable and practicable steps to ensure that professional engagements are fulfilled. He must not undertake any task which:

(a)   he knows or ought to know he is not competent to handle;

(b)   he does not have adequate time and opportunity to prepare for or perform; or

(c)   he cannot discharge within a reasonable time having regard to the pressure of other work.

5.5   A barrister must at all times be courteous to the Court and to all those with whom he has professional dealings.

5.6   In relation to instructions to advise or draft documents, a barrister should ensure that the advice or document is provided within such time as has been agreed with the professional client, or otherwise within a reasonable time after receipt of the relevant instructions. If it becomes apparent to the barrister that he will not be able to do the work within that time, he must inform his professional client forthwith.

5.7   Generally, a barrister should ensure that advice which he gives is practical, appropriate to the needs and circumstances of the particular client, and clearly and comprehensibly expressed.

5.8   A barrister must exercise his own personal judgment upon the substance and purpose of any advice he gives or any document he drafts. He must not devise facts which will assist in advancing his lay client's case and must not draft any originating process, pleading, affidavit, witness statement or notice of appeal containing:

(a)   any statement of fact or contention (as the case may be) which is not supported by his lay client or by his brief or instructions;

(b)   any contention which he does not consider to be properly arguable;

(c)   any allegation of fraud unless he has clear instructions to make such an allegation and has before him reasonably credible material which as it stands establishes a prima facia case of fraud; or

(d)   in the case of an affidavit or witness statement, any statement of fact other than the evidence which in substance according to his instructions, the barrister reasonably believes the witness would give if the evidence contained in the affidavit or witness statement were being given viva voce.

5.9   A barrister should be available on reasonable notice for a conference prior to the day of hearing of any case in which he is briefed; and if no such conference takes place then the barrister should be available for a conference on the day of the hearing. The venue of a conference is a matter for agreement between the barrister and his professional clients.

5.10   A barrister when conducting proceedings at Court:

(a)   is personally responsible for the conduct and presentation of his case and must exercise personal judgment upon the substance and purpose of statements made and questions asked;

(b)   must not, unless asked to so by the Court or when appearing before a tribunal where it his duty to do so, assert a personal opinion of the facts or the law;

(c)   must ensure that the Court is informed of all relevant decisions and legislative provisions of which he is aware, whether the effect is favourable or unfavourable towards the contention for which he argues, and must bring any procedural irregularity to the attention of the Court during the hearing and not reserve such matter to be raised on appeal;

(d)   must not adduce evidence obtained otherwise than from or through his professional client or devise facts which will assist in advancing his lay client's case;

(e) must not make statements or ask questions which are merely scandalous or intended or calculated only to vilify, insult or annoy either a witness or some other person;

(f) must if possible avoid the naming in open Court of third parties whose character would thereby be impugned;

(g) must not by assertion in a speech impugn a witness whom he has had an opportunity to cross-examine unless in cross-examination he has given the witness an opportunity to answer the allegation;

(h) must not suggest that a victim, witness or other person is guilty of crime, fraud or misconduct or make any defamatory aspersion on the conduct of any other person or attribute to another person the crime or conduct of which his lay client is accused unless such allegations go to a matter in issue (including the credibility of the witness) which is material to his lay client's case, and which appear to him to be supported by reasonable grounds.

5.11 A barrister must take all reasonable and practicable steps to avoid unnecessary expense or waste of the Court's time. He should, when asked, inform the Court of the probable length of his case; and he should also inform the Court of any developments which affect information already provided.

5.12 In Court a barrister's personal appearance should be decorous, and his dress, when robes are worn, should be compatible with them.

6

6.1 Witnesses[1]

6.1.1 The rules which define and regulate the barrister's functions in relation to the preparation of evidence and contact with witnesses are set out in paragraphs 704, 705, 706, 707 and 708 of the Code of Conduct.

6.1.2 There is no longer any rule which prevents a barrister from having contact with any witness.

6.1.3 In particular, there is no longer any rule in any case (including contested cases in the Crown Court) which prevents a barrister from having contact with a witness whom he may expect to call and examine in chief, with a view to introducing himself to the witness, explaining the court's procedure (and in particular the procedure for giving evidence), and answering any questions on procedure which the witness may have.

6.1.4 It is a responsibility of a barrister, especially when the witness is nervous, vulnerable or apparently the victim of criminal or similar conduct, to ensure that those facing unfamiliar court procedures are put as much at ease as possible.

6.1.5 Unless otherwise directed by the Court or with the consent of the representative for the opposing side or of the Court, a barrister should not communicate directly or indirectly about the case with any witness, whether or not the witness is his lay client, once that witness has begun to give evidence until it has been concluded.

---

[1] Specific reference should be made to the Guidance on Witness Preparation issued by the General Council of the Bar, October 2005.

6.2   Discussing the Evidence with Witnesses

6.2.1   Different considerations apply in relation to contact with witnesses for the purpose of interviewing them or discussing with them (either individually or together) the substance of their evidence or the evidence of other witnesses.

6.2.2   Although there is no longer any rule which prevents a barrister from having contact with witnesses for such purposes a barrister should exercise his discretion and consider very carefully whether and to what extent such contact is appropriate, bearing in mind in particular that it is not the barrister's function (but that of his professional client) to investigate and collect evidence.

6.2.3   The guiding principle must be the obligation of counsel to promote and protect his lay client's best interests so far as that is consistent with the law and with counsel's overriding duty to the court (Code of Conduct paragraphs 302, 303).

6.2.4   A barrister should be alert to the risks that any discussion of the substance of a case with a witness may lead to suspicions of coaching, and thus tend to diminish the value of the witness's evidence in the eyes of the court, or may place the barrister in a position of professional embarrassment, for example if he thereby becomes himself a witness in the case. These dangers are most likely to occur if such discussion takes place:

(a)   before the barrister has been supplied with a proof of the witness's evidence; or

(b)   in the absence of the barrister's professional client or his representative.

A barrister should also be alert to the fact that, even in the absence of any wish or intention to do so, authority figures do subconsciously influence lay witnesses. Discussion of the substance of the case may unwittingly contaminate the witness's evidence.

6.2.5   There is particular danger where such discussions:

(a)   take place in the presence of more than one witness of fact; or

(b)   involve the disclosure to one witness of fact of the factual evidence of another witness.

These practices have been strongly deprecated by the courts as tending inevitably to encourage the rehearsal or coaching of witnesses and to increase the risk of fabrication or contamination of evidence: *R v Arif* (1993) May 26; *Smith New Court Securities Ltd v Scrimgeour Vickers (Asset Management) Ltd* [1992] BCLC 1104, [1994] 1 WLR 1271.

That is not to suggest that it is always inappropriate to disclose one witness' evidence to another. If the witness is one to be called by the other party, it is almost inevitable that a witness' attention must be drawn to discrepancies between the two statements. Discretion is, however, required, especially where the evidence of independent witnesses is involved.

6.2.6   Whilst there is no rule that any longer prevents a barrister from taking a witness statement in civil cases (for cases in the Crown Court see below), there is a distinction between the settling of a witness statement and taking a witness statement. It is not appropriate for a barrister who has taken witness statements, as opposed to settling witness statements prepared by others, to act as counsel unless he is a junior member of the team of Counsel and will not be examining the witness or there are exceptional circumstances, because it risks undermining the independence of the barrister as an advocate. Exceptional circumstances would include:

(a) the witness is a minor one;

(b) Counsel has no choice but to take a proof and this is the only practical course in the interests of justice—this would apply, for instance, where a witness appears unexpectedly at Court and there is no one else competent to take the statement.

The Cab-rank Rule does not require a barrister to agree to undertake the task of taking witness statements.

6.2.7 There is no rule which prevents a barrister from exchanging common courtesies with the other side's witnesses. However, a barrister should not discuss the substance of the case or any evidence with the other side's witnesses except in rare and exceptional circumstances and then only with the prior knowledge of his opponent.

6.3 Criminal Cases in the Crown Court

6.3.1 Contested criminal cases in the Crown Court present peculiar difficulties and may expose both barristers and witnesses to special pressures. As a general principle, therefore, with the exception of the lay client, character and expert witnesses, it is wholly inappropriate for a barrister in such a case to interview any potential witness. Interviewing includes discussing with any such witness the substance of his evidence or the evidence of other such witnesses.

6.3.2 As a general principle, prosecuting counsel should not confer with an investigator witness unless he has also discharged some supervisory responsibility in the investigation and should not confer with investigators or receive factual instructions directly from them on matters about which there is or may be a dispute.

6.3.3 There may be extraordinary circumstances in which a departure from the general principles set out in paragraphs 6.3.1 and 6.3.2 is unavoidable. An example of such circumstances is afforded by the decision in *Fergus* (1994) 98 Cr App R 313.

6.3.4 Where any barrister has interviewed any potential witness or any such witness has been interviewed by another barrister, that fact shall be disclosed to all other parties in the case before the witness is called. A written record must also be made of the substance of the interview and the reason for it.

7 Documents

7.1 A barrister should not obtain or seek to obtain a document, or knowledge of the contents of a document, belonging to another party other than by means of the normal and proper channels for obtaining such documents or such knowledge.

7.2 If a barrister comes into possession of a document belonging to another party by some means other than the normal and proper channels (for example, if the document has come into his possession in consequence of a mistake or inadvertence by another person or if the document appears to belong to another party, or to be a copy of such a document, and to be privileged from discovery or otherwise to be one which ought not to be in the possession of his professional or lay client) he should:

(a) where appropriate make enquiries of his professional client in order to ascertain the circumstances in which the document was obtained by his professional or lay client; and

(b) unless satisfied that the document has been properly obtained in the ordinary course of events at once return the document unread to the person entitled to possession of it.

7.3

7.3.1 If having come into possession of such a document the barrister reads it before he realises that he ought not to, and would be embarrassed in the discharge of his duties by his knowledge of the contents of the document, then provided he can do so without prejudice to his lay client he must return his brief or instructions and explain to his professional client why he has done so.

7.3.2 If, however, to return his brief or instructions would prejudice his lay client (for example, by reason of the proximity of the trial) he should not return his brief or instructions and should, unless the Court otherwise orders, make such use of the document as will be in his client's interests. He should inform his opponent of his knowledge of the document and of the circumstances, so far as known to him, in which the document was obtained and of his intention to use it. In the event of objection to the use of such document it is for the Court to determine what use, if any, may be made of it.

7.4 If during the course of a case a barrister becomes aware of the existence of a document which should have been but has not been disclosed on discovery he should advise his professional client to disclose it forthwith; and if it is not then disclosed, he must withdraw from the case.

8 Administration of Practice

8.1 A barrister must ensure that his practice is properly and efficiently administered in accordance with the provisions of paragraph 304 of the Code of Conduct.

8.2 A barrister should ensure that he is able to provide his professional client with full and proper details of and appropriate justification for fees which have been incurred, and a proper assessment of any work to be done, so that both the lay client and the professional client are able to determine the level of any financial commitment which has been incurred or may be incurred.

STANDARDS APPLICABLE TO CRIMINAL CASES

9 Introduction

9.1 These standards are to be read together with the General Standards and the Code of Conduct. They are intended as a guide to those matters which specifically relate to practice in the criminal Courts. They are not an alternative to the General Standards, which apply to all work carried out by a barrister. Particular reference is made to those paragraphs in the General Standards relating to the general conduct of a case (5.8), conduct in Court (5.10), discussion with witnesses (6.1, 6.2) and the use of documents belonging to other parties (7.1, 7.2, 7.3), which are not repeated in these standards.

10 Responsibilities of Prosecuting Counsel

10A The Standards and principles contained in this paragraph apply as appropriate to all practising barristers, whether in independent practice or employed and whether appearing as counsel in any given case or exercising any other professional capacity in connection with it.

10.1 Prosecuting counsel should not attempt to obtain a conviction by all means at his command. He should not regard himself as appearing for a party. He should lay before the Court fairly and impartially the whole of the facts which comprise the case for the prosecution and should assist the Court on all matters of law applicable to the case.

10.2   Prosecuting counsel should bear in mind at all times whilst he is instructed:

(i)   that he is responsible for the presentation and general conduct of the case;

(ii)   that he should use his best endeavours to ensure that all evidence or material that ought properly to be made available is either presented by the prosecution or disclosed to the defence.

10.3   Prosecuting counsel should, when instructions are delivered to him, read them expeditiously and, where instructed to do so, advise or confer on all aspects of the case well before its commencement.

10.4   In relation to cases tried in the Crown Court, prosecuting counsel:

(a)   should ensure, if he is instructed to settle an indictment, that he does so promptly and within due time, and should bear in mind the desirability of not overloading an indictment with either too many defendants or too many counts, in order to present the prosecution case as simply and as concisely as possible;

(b)   should ask, if the indictment is being settled by some other person, to see a copy of the indictment and should then check it;

(c)   should decide whether any additional evidence is required and, if it is, should advise in writing and set out precisely what additional evidence is required with a view to serving it on the defence as soon as possible;

(d)   should consider whether all witness statements in the possession of the prosecution have been properly served on the defendant in accordance with the Attorney-General's Guidelines;

(e)   should eliminate all unnecessary material in the case so as to ensure an Efficient and fair trial, and in particular should consider the need for particular witnesses and exhibits and draft appropriate admissions for service on the defence;

(f)   should in all Class 1 and Class 2 cases and in other cases of complexity draft a case summary for transmission to the Court.

10.5   Paragraphs 6 to 6.3.4 of the Written Standards for the Conduct of Professional Work refer.

10.6   Prosecuting counsel should at all times have regard to the report of Mr Justice Farquharson's Committee on the role of Prosecuting Counsel which is set out in *Archbold*. In particular, he should have regard to the following recommendations of the Farquharson Committee:

(a)   Where counsel has taken a decision on a matter of policy with which his professional client has not agreed, it would be appropriate for him to submit to the Attorney-General a written report of all the circumstances, including his reasons for disagreeing with those who instructed him;

(b)   When counsel has had an opportunity to prepare his brief and to confer with those instructing him, but at the last moment before trial unexpectedly advises that the case should not proceed or that pleas to lesser offences should be accepted, and his professional client does not accept such advice, counsel should apply for an adjournment if instructed to do so;

(c)   Subject to the above, it is for prosecuting counsel to decide whether to offer no evidence on a particular count or on the indictment as a whole and whether to accept pleas to a lesser count or counts.

10.7   It is the duty of prosecuting counsel to assist the Court at the conclusion of the summing up by drawing attention to any apparent errors or omissions of fact or law.

10.8   In relation to sentence, prosecuting counsel:

(a)   should not attempt by advocacy to influence the Court with regard to sentence: if, however, a defendant is unrepresented it is proper to inform the Court of any mitigating circumstances about which counsel is instructed;

(b)   should be in a position to assist the Court if requested as to any statutory provisions relevant to the offence or the offender and as to any relevant guidelines as to sentence laid down by the Court of Appeal;

(c)   should bring any such matters as are referred to in (b) above to the attention of the Court if in the opinion of prosecuting counsel the Court has erred;

(d)   should bring to the attention of the Court any appropriate compensation, forfeiture and restitution matters which may arise on conviction, for example pursuant to sections 35–42 of the Powers of Criminal Courts Act 1973 and the Drug Trafficking Offences Act 1986;

(e)   should draw the attention of the defence to any assertion of material fact made in mitigation which the prosecution believes to be untrue: if the defence persist in that assertion, prosecuting counsel should invite the Court to consider requiring the issue to be determined by the calling of evidence in accordance with the decision of the Court of Appeal in *R* v *Newton* (1983) *77* Cr App R 13.

11   Responsibilities of Defence Counsel

11.1   When defending a client on a criminal charge, a barrister must endeavour to protect his client from conviction except by a competent tribunal and upon legally admissible evidence sufficient to support a conviction for the offence charged.

11.2   A barrister acting for the defence:

(a)   should satisfy himself, if he is briefed to represent more than one defendant, that no conflict of interest is likely to arise;

(b)   should arrange a conference and if necessary a series of conferences with his professional and lay clients;

(c)   should consider whether any enquiries or further enquiries are necessary and, if so, should advise in writing as soon as possible;

(d)   should consider whether any witnesses for the defence are required and, if so, which;

(e)   should consider whether a Notice of Alibi is required and, if so, should draft an appropriate notice;

(f)   should consider whether it would be appropriate to call expert evidence for the defence and, if so, have regard to the rules of the Crown Court in relation to notifying the prosecution of the contents of the evidence to be given;

(g)   should ensure that he has sufficient instructions for the purpose of deciding which prosecution witnesses should be cross-examined, and should then ensure that no other witnesses remain fully bound at the request of the defendant and request his professional client to inform the Crown Prosecution Service of those who can be conditionally bound;

(h)   should consider whether any admissions can be made with a view to saving time and expense at trial, with the aim of admitting as much evidence as can properly be admitted in accordance with the barrister's duty to his client;

(i)   should consider what admissions can properly be requested from the prosecution;

(j)   should decide what exhibits, if any, which have not been or cannot be copied he wishes to examine, and should ensure that appropriate arrangements are made to examine them as promptly as possible so that there is no undue delay in the trial.

(k)   should as to anything which he is instructed to submit in mitigation which casts aspersions on the conduct or character of a victim or witness in the case, notify the prosecution in advance so as to give prosecuting Counsel sufficient opportunity to consider his position under paragraph 10.8(e).

11.3   A barrister acting for a defendant should advise his lay client generally about his plea. In doing so he may, if necessary, express his advice in strong terms. He must, however, make it clear that the client has complete freedom of choice and that the responsibility for the plea is the client's.

11.4   A barrister acting for a defendant should advise his client as to whether or not to give evidence in his own defence but the decision must be taken by the client himself.

11.5

11.5.1   Where a defendant tells his counsel that he did not commit the offence with which he is charged but nevertheless insists on pleading guilty to it for reasons of his own, counsel should:

(a)   advise the defendant that, if he is not guilty, he should plead not guilty but that the decision is one for the defendant; counsel must continue to represent him but only after he has advised what the consequences will be and that what can be submitted in mitigation can only be on the basis that the client is guilty.

(b)   explore with the defendant why he wishes to plead guilty to a charge which he says he did not commit and whether any steps could be taken which would enable him to enter a plea of not guilty in accordance with his profession of innocence.

11.5.2   If the client maintains his wish to plead guilty, he should be further advised:

(a)   what the consequences will be, in particular in gaining or adding to a criminal record and that it is unlikely that a conviction based on such a plea would be overturned on appeal;

(b)   that what can be submitted on his behalf in mitigation can only be on the basis that he is guilty and will otherwise be strictly limited so that, for instance, counsel will not be able to assert that the defendant has shown remorse through his guilty plea.

11.5.3   If, following all of the above advice, the defendant persists in his decision to plead guilty

   (a)   counsel may continue to represent him if he is satisfied that it is proper to do so;

   (b)   before a plea of guilty is entered counsel or a representative of his professional client who is present should record in writing the reasons for the plea;

   (c)   the defendant should be invited to endorse a declaration that he has given unequivocal instructions of his own free will that he intends to plead guilty even though he maintains that he did not commit the offence (s) and that he understands the advice given by counsel and in particular the restrictions placed on counsel in mitigating and the consequences to himself; the defendant should also be advised that he is under no obligation to sign; and

   (d)   if no such declaration is signed, counsel should make a contemporaneous note of his advice.

   12   Confessions of Guilt

12.1   In considering the duty of counsel retained to defend a person charged with an offence who confesses to his counsel that he did commit the offence charged, it is essential to bear the following points clearly in mind:

   (a)   that every punishable crime is a breach of common or statute law committed by a person of sound mind and understanding;

   (b)   that the issue in a criminal trial is always whether the defendant is guilty of the offence charged, never whether he is innocent;

   (c)   that the burden of proof rests on the prosecution.

12.2   It follows that the mere fact that a person charged with a crime has confessed to his counsel that he did commit the offence charged is no bar to that barrister appearing or continuing to appear in his defence, nor indeed does such a confession release the barrister from his imperative duty to do all that he honourably can for his client.

12.3   Such a confession, however, imposes very strict limitations on the conduct of the defence, a barrister must not assert as true that which he knows to be false. He must not connive at, much less attempt to substantiate, a fraud.

12.4   While, therefore, it would be right to take any objections to the competency of the Court, to the form of the indictment, to the admissibility of any evidence or to the evidence admitted, it would be wrong to suggest that some other person had committed the offence charged, or to call any evidence which the barrister must know to be false having regard to the confession, such, for instance, as evidence in support of an alibi. In other words, a barrister must not (whether by calling the defendant or otherwise) set up an affirmative case inconsistent with the confession made to him.

12.5   A more difficult question is within what limits may counsel attack the evidence for the prosecution either by cross-examination or in his speech to the tribunal charged with the decision of the facts. No clearer rule can be laid down than this, that he is entitled to test the evidence given by each individual witness and to argue that the evidence taken as a whole is insufficient to amount to proof that the defendant is guilty of the offence charged. Further than this he ought not to go.

12.6 The foregoing is based on the assumption that the defendant has made a clear confession that he did commit the offence charged, and does not profess to deal with the very difficult questions which may present themselves to a barrister when a series of inconsistent statements are made to him by the defendant before or during the proceedings; nor does it deal with the questions which may arise where statements are made by the defendant which point almost irresistibly to the conclusion that the defendant is guilty but do not amount to a clear confession. Statements of this kind may inhibit the defence, but questions arising on them can only be answered after careful consideration of the actual circumstances of the particular case.

13 General

13.1 Both prosecuting and defence counsel:

(a) should ensure that the listing officer receives in good time their best estimate of the likely length of the trial (including whether or not there is to be a plea of guilty) and should ensure that the listing officer is given early notice of any change of such estimate or possible adjournment;

(b) should take all reasonable and practicable steps to ensure that the case is properly prepared and ready for trial by the time that it is first listed;

(c) should ensure that arrangements have been made in adequate time for witnesses to attend Court as and when required and should plan, so far as possible, for sufficient witnesses to be available to occupy the full Court day;

(d) should, if a witness (for example a doctor) can only attend Court at a certain time during the trial without great inconvenience to himself, try to arrange for that witness to be accommodated by raising the matter with the trial Judge and with his opponent;

(e) should take all necessary steps to comply with the Practice Direction (Crime: Tape Recording of Police Interviews) [1989] 1 WLR 631.

13.2 If properly remunerated (paragraph 502 of the Code), the barrister originally briefed in a case should attend all plea and directions hearings. If this is not possible, he must take all reasonable steps to ensure that the barrister who does appear is conversant with the case and is prepared to make informed decisions affecting the trial.

14 Video Recordings

14.1 When a barrister instructed and acting for the prosecution or the defence of an accused has in his possession a copy of a video recording of a child witness which has been identified as having been prepared to be admitted in evidence at a criminal trial in accordance with Section 54 of the Criminal Justice Act 1991, he must have regard to the following duties and obligations:

(a) Upon receipt of the recording, a written record of the date and time and from whom the recording was received must be made and a receipt must be given.

(b) The recording and its contents must be used only for the proper preparation of the prosecution or defence case or of an appeal against conviction and/or sentence, as the case may be, and the barrister must not make or permit any disclosure of the recording or its contents to any person except when, in his opinion, it is in the interests of his proper preparation of that case.

(c) The barrister must not make or permit any other person to make a copy of the recording, nor release the recording to the accused, and must ensure that:

   (i) when not in transit or in use, the recording is always kept in a locked or secure place, and:

   (ii) when in transit, the recording is kept safe and secure at all times and is not left unattended, especially in vehicles or otherwise.

(d) Proper preparation of the case may involve viewing the recording in the presence of the accused. If this is the case, viewing should be done:

   (i) if the accused is in custody, only in the prison or other custodial institution where he is being held, in the presence of the barrister and/or his instructing solicitor.

   (ii) if the accused is on bail, at the solicitor's office or in counsel's chambers or elsewhere in the presence of the barrister and/or his instructing solicitor.

(e) The recording must be returned to the solicitor as soon as practicable after the conclusion of the barrister's role in the case. A written record of the date and time despatched and to whom the recording was delivered for despatch must be made.

15   Attendance of Counsel at Court

15.1   Prosecuting counsel should be present throughout the trial, including the summing-up and the return of the jury. He may not absent himself without leave of the Court; but, if two or more barristers appear for the prosecution, the attendance of one is sufficient.

15.2

15.2.1   Defence counsel should ensure that the defendant is never left unrepresented at any stage of his trial.

15.2.2   Where a defendant is represented by one barrister, that barrister should normally be present throughout the trial and should only absent himself in exceptional circumstances which he could not reasonably be expected to foresee and provided that:

(a) he has obtained the consent of the professional client (or his representative) and the lay client; and

(b) a competent deputy takes his place.

15.2.3   Where a defendant is represented by two barristers, neither may absent himself except for good reason and then only when the consent of the professional client (or his representative) and of the lay client has been obtained, or when the case is legally aided and the barrister thinks it necessary to do so in order to avoid unnecessary public expense.

15.2.4   These rules are subject to modification in respect of lengthy trials involving numerous defendants. In such trials, where after the conclusion of the opening speech by the prosecution defending counsel is satisfied that during a specific part of the trial there is no serious possibility that events will occur which will relate to his client, he may with the consent of the professional client (or his representative) and of the lay client absent himself for that part of the trial. He should also inform the judge. In this event it is his duty:

(a) to arrange for other defending counsel to guard the interests of his client;

(b)   to keep himself informed throughout of the progress of the trial and in particular of any development which could affect his client; and

(c)   not to accept any other commitment which would render it impracticable for him to make himself available at reasonable notice if the interests of his client so require.

15.3.1   If during the course of a criminal trial and prior to final sentence the defendant voluntarily absconds and the barrister's professional client, in accordance with the ruling of the Law Society, withdraws from the case, then the barrister too should withdraw. If the trial judge requests the barrister to remain to assist the Court, the barrister has an absolute discretion whether to do so or not. If he does remain, he should act on the basis that his instructions are withdrawn and he will not be entitled to use any material contained in his brief save for such part as has already been established in evidence before the Court. He should request the trial judge to instruct the jury that this is the basis on which he is prepared to assist the Court.

15.3.2   If for any reason the barrister's professional client does not withdraw from the case, the barrister retains an absolute discretion whether to continue to act. If he does continue, he should conduct the case as if his client were still present in Court but had decided not to give evidence and on the basis of any instruction he has received. He will be free to use any material contained in his brief and may cross-examine witnesses called for the prosecution and call witnesses for the defence.

16   Appeals

16.1

16.1.1   Attention is drawn to the Guide to Proceedings in the Court of Appeal Criminal Division ('the Guide') which is set out in full its original form at (1983) 77 Cr App R 138 and is summarised in a version amended in April 1990 Volume 1 of *Archbold* at 7–173 to 7–184.

16.1.2   In particular when advising after a client pleads guilty or is convicted, defence counsel is encouraged to follow the procedures set out at paragraphs 1.2 and 1.4 of the Guide.

16.2   If his client pleads guilty or is convicted, defence counsel should see his client after he has been sentenced in the presence of his professional client or his representative. He should then proceed as follows:

(a)   if he is satisfied that there are no reasonable grounds of appeal he should so advise orally and certify in writing. Counsel is encouraged to certify using the form set out in Appendix 1 to the Guide. No further advice is necessary unless it is reasonable for a written advice to be given because the client reasonably requires it or because it is necessary e.g. in the light of the circumstances of the conviction, any particular difficulties at trial, the length and nature of the sentence passed, the effect thereof on the defendant or the lack of impact which oral advice given immediately after the trial may have on the particular defendant's mind.

(b)   if he is satisfied that there are more reasonable grounds of appeal or if his view is a provisional one or if he requires more time to consider the prospects of a successful appeal he should so advise orally and certify in writing. Counsel is encouraged to certify using the form set out in Appendix 1 to the Guide. Counsel should then furnish written advice to the professional client as soon as he can and in any event within 14 days.

16.3   Counsel should not settle grounds of appeal unless he considers that such grounds are properly arguable, and in that event he should provide a reasoned written opinion in support of such grounds.

16.4   In certain cases counsel may not be able to perfect grounds of appeal without a transcript or other further information. In this event the grounds of appeal should be accompanied by a note to the Registrar setting out the matters on which assistance is required. Once such transcript or other information is available, counsel should ensure that the grounds of appeal are perfected by the inclusion of all necessary references.

16.5   Grounds of Appeal must be settled with sufficient particularity to enable the Registrar and subsequently the Court to identify clearly the matters relied upon.

16.6   If at any stage counsel is of the view that the appeal should be abandoned, he should at once set out his reasons in writing and send them to his professional client.

Miscellaneous Guidance

The Bar Standards Board has published Guidance notes which cover three main aspects of practice at the Bar today, namely Practicing Rules and Requirements, Administration of a Barrister's Practice, and Professional Conduct. Knowledge and understanding of these Guidance notes is an integral part of the Professional Ethics curriculum for the Bar Professional Training Course. Those published in the following pages relate to situations that arise most often during the course of a barrister's practice. Bar students should however familiarise themselves with the general content of all the guidance notes which can be found on the OUP website associated with this manual.

The section 'Written Standards for the Conduct of Professional Work' now forms section 3 of the Code of Conduct. The rest of the guidance does not form part of the Code itself, but barristers should comply with the guidance; you run the risk of committing professional misconduct if you do not.

Such useful professional and practical guidance covers a wide variety of situations in which a barrister can find him or herself and is a very useful resource. This kind of guidance can be found both on the Bar Council's and the Bar Standards Board's websites and much of it is accessible from both websites.

Further guidance and updating to existing guidance is being published more frequently than in the past and it is important to be familiar with the locations of this guidance and to check regularly and whenever you face a situation that may be covered by it.

On the Bar Council website the guidance can be found by going to the home page and following the link for 'Guidance' to an alphabetical list of titles. On the Bar Standards Board website the guidance can be found by going to the home page and following the link for 'Standards and Guidance'. This in turn offers you links to the 'Code of Conduct', the 'Equality and Diversity Code', and to 'Code Guidance'; under this latter link you will find a collection of clearly titled guides on a variety of practical and ethical issues.

Only a selection, that are most likely to be of use or interest to BPTC students, is reproduced here:

Pupillage Guidelines (Bar Council website: go to Guidance—Practice Management Guidelines—follow the link to Section 8: Pupillage Administration)

Written Standards for the Conduct of Professional Work (Bar Standards Board website: go to Standards and Guidance—Code of Conduct—Section 3)

Guidance on Witness Preparation (Bar Standards Board website: go to Standards and Guidance—Code Guidance)

Guidance on Preparation of Witness Statements (Bar Standards Board website: go to Standards and Guidance—Code Guidance)

Guidance on Preparation of Defence Case Statements (Bar Standards Board website: go to Standards and Guidance—Code Guidance)

Non-Practising Barristers supplying Legal Services—Guidance on 2006 Rules (Bar Standards Board website: go to Standards and Guidance—Code Guidance)

Guidance on Refusing Work in Criminal Cases and in respect of Plea and Case Management Hearings (Bar Standards Board website: go to Standards and Guidance—Code Guidance)

Reporting Professional Misconduct of Barristers by Members of the Bar (Bar Standards Board website: go to Standards and Guidance—Code Guidance)

The Equality and Diversity Code for the Bar (Bar Standards Board website: go to Standards and Guidance—Equality and Diversity Code)

USEFUL WEB LINKS

Bar Council: <http://www.barcouncil.org.uk>

Bar Standards Board: <http://www.barstandardsboard.org.uk>

Bar Training Regulations of the Inns of Court and the General Council of the Bar, which are the rules governing qualification as a barrister Bar Standards Board website: go to Education and Training

Crown Prosecution Service website, a useful source of guidance in relation to prosecution work and relationship between counsel and the CPS: <http://www.cps.gov.uk>

PUPILLAGE ADMINISTRATION—RECOMMENDED STANDARDS[1]

1. *Chambers should:*

    1.1 advertise all pupillage vacancies in accordance with the Pupillage Funding & Advertising Requirements (see Annex R to the Code of Conduct) and the Equality and Diversity Code for the Bar.

    1.2 consider all pupillage applications fairly

    1.3 establish and follow well-defined selection procedures

    1.4 ensure that all pupils are funded in accordance with the Pupillage Funding & Advertising Requirements

    1.5 establish and follow a written training programme based upon a written and Approved checklist

    1.6 ensure that the distribution of work is fair to all pupils

    1.7 comply with pupillage monitoring requirements.

    1.8 Chambers should ensure that they have appointed at least one Equal Opportunity Officer and have a written Equal Opportunities policy which sets out the policy adopted by chambers in relation to each of the Action Areas in the Equality and Diversity Code. These are required by the Code of Conduct and Chambers who do not have both an Equal Opportunities Officer and a policy cannot hold themselves out as offering pupillages.

PUPILLAGE ADMINISTRATION—IMPLEMENTATION ADVICE

2. *Appointment of Pupil Supervisors*

    2.1 Chambers should ensure that pupil supervisors have been Approved by their Inn, that their names appear on the current register of pupil supervisors, and that those who have been Approved on or after 1 October 1998 have attended the appropriate briefing session provided by their Inn.

    2.2 Chambers should ensure that pupils have been allocated to a named pupil supervisor at least 10 working days before the pupillage commences.

---

[1] This extract is taken from the Practice Management Guidelines which can be found on the website of the Bar Council. It is included here to give prospective pupils some idea of what they should expect from chambers.

3. **Recruitment of Pupils**

   3.1 *General*

      3.1.1 Chambers must have selection procedures for pupils in which applicants are recruited through fair and open competition and on the basis of merit.

      3.1.2 Chambers must comply with the Pupillage Funding & Advertising Requirements (see Annex R to the Code of Conduct) and the Equality and Diversity Code and other guidance issued by the Bar Council in relation to the recruitment of pupils.

      3.1.3 Issues around access to premises, facilities and services covered by the Disability Discrimination Act should be considered separate to the pupillage recruitment procedure by the Equal Opportunities Officer or others not involved in the selection process. The relevant steps to be taken by applicants should be made clear in the information provided to all applicants.

   3.2 *Advertisement of Vacancies*

      3.2.1 All pupillage vacancies must be advertised on a web-site designated by the Bar Council.

      3.2.2 Each advertisement should specify:

      (a)   The name and address of chambers.

      (b)   The number of tenants.

      (c)   A brief statement of the work undertaken by chambers e.g 'predominantly criminal'.

      (d)   The number of pupillage vacancies.

      (e)   The level of award.

      (f)   The procedure for application.

      (g)   The minimum educational or other qualification required;

      (h)   The date of closure for the receipt of applications.

      (i)   The date by which the decisions on the filling of vacancies will be made.

      (j)   Chambers willingness to consider reasonable adjustments in accordance with the Disability Discrimination Act 1995.

   3.3 *Selection Procedures*

      3.3.1 Chambers must establish and follow selection procedures which ensure that pupils are selected through fair and open competition on the basis of merit; in particular it is recommended that:

      (a)   selection criteria must be relevant and applied consistently to all applicants;

      (b)   short listing and other selection decisions must be undertaken by at least two people;

      (c)   applicants who are selected for interview must be sent a copy of chambers' pupillage policy document prior to attending for interview;

      (d)   all selectors should be familiar with the contents of the Equality and Diversity Code for the Bar.

      (e)   Selection criteria should be reviewed annually.

      3.3.2 Records of all applicants and documentation relating to selection decisions should be kept for a period of two years. They should indicate the manner in which applications are disposed of and, where known, the ethnic origin and sex of each applicant.

4. *Registration*

      4.1 Chambers should ensure that each pupil has registered their pupillage with the Bar Council in accordance with Regulation 42 and Schedule 14, part 1 of the Bar Training Regulations before the pupillage commences.

      4.2 Chambers must ensure that no more than one pupil is assigned to a pupil supervisor at a time, unless the pupil supervisor has obtained the prior approval of the Joint Regulations Committee.

5. *Funding of Pupils*

      5.1 Chambers should ensure that all pupils are funded in accordance with the Pupillage Funding & Advertising Requirements.

6. *Pupillage Policy Document*

      6.1 Chambers should prepare a document or documents setting out its policies in relation to:

- the number and type of pupillages on offer
- recruitment of pupils
- the roles and duties of pupils
- the roles and duties of pupil supervisors
- the general pattern of pupillage (e.g. whether it is served with one pupil supervisor etc)
- the checklist(s) used during pupillage
- arrangements for funding, including payment of expenses
- chambers' policy on payment of devilling and work completed for other members of chambers
- chambers' policy on the payment of clerks' fees and rent during the practising period of pupillage
- procedures for providing pupils with an objective assessment of their progress at regular intervals throughout pupillage
- complaints and grievances by pupils and pupil supervisors
- the method for fairly distributing briefs and other work amongst working pupils
- policy and procedure for the recruitment of tenants and when prospective tenants will be notified of tenancy decisions
- holiday entitlement
- pupils not taken on as tenants.

      6.2 All pupils should be given a copy of the pupillage policy document when they are shortlisted for interview and reminded of it at the start of the pupillage.

7. *Training*

      7.1 Chambers should ensure that each pupil has a copy of the Pupillage File, Good Practice in Pupillage guide and the appropriate checklist by no later than the end of the first week of pupillage.

7.2 Pupils may only exercise a right of audience as a barrister in their practising six months of pupillage provided that they have completed or been exempted from the non-practising six months of pupillage, and they have been given permission from their pupil supervisor or head of chambers.

7.3 Pupil supervisors must ensure that the pupil has the opportunity to do all such work and gain all such experience as is appropriate for a person commencing practice in the type of work done by the pupil supervisor and in any event so as to enable the pupil to complete the check list, in particular

(i)   To ensure that the pupil has an understanding and appreciation of the operation in practice of rules of conduct and etiquette at the Bar

(ii) To ensure that the pupil has gained sufficient practical experience of advocacy to be able to competently prepare and present a case

(iii) To ensure that the pupil has gained sufficient practical experience of conferences and negotiation to be able to conduct the same competently

(iv) To ensure that the pupil has gained sufficient practical experience in the undertaking of legal research and the preparation of drafts and opinions to be able to undertake the same competently.

7.4 The pupil supervisor must ensure that the pupil is provided with, and retains, the appropriate check list, and completes it conscientiously and accurately. The pupil supervisor must sign and date the check list.

7.5 The pupil supervisor must give the pupil time off to attend the compulsory advocacy training and Advice to Counsel courses and should ensure that he or she has completed the courses satisfactorily.

8.   *Distribution of Work in Chambers*

8.1 The distribution of briefs among practising pupils should be carried out in a manner fair to all pupils.

8.2 Sets of chambers in which advocacy work by practising pupils is a regular occurrence should establish a system for the purpose of regulating the distribution of briefs or instructions among pupils. The system should be made known to pupils at the commencement of pupillage. Heads of chambers should ensure that the distribution of work to working pupils is reviewed regularly. The distribution to pupils of unnamed work arriving in chambers and of work returned between members of chambers should be recorded accurately and monitored.

9.   *Certification*

9.1 Provided that the period of pupillage has been satisfactorily completed, the pupil supervisor must provide a pupil with a certificate in accordance with Consolidated Regulation 52.

9.2 If a pupil supervisor is not satisfied that the pupil has satisfactorily completed pupillage and he will not sign the certificate, he must notify the pupil of his or her options i.e. a certificate may be accepted from the pupil supervisor's Head of Chambers, the person designated by the Head of Chambers as the person in charge of pupillage, or another person acceptable to the Masters of the Bench and the Bar Council. If a pupil remains unable to obtain a relevant certificate the pupil may appeal to (a) the Masters of the Bench of the relevant Inn and then (b) the Joint Regulations Committee (Consolidated Regulation 52).

9.3 Pupil supervisors should familiarise themselves with the Equality and Diversity Code for the Bar, the Pupillage File and the guide to Good Practice in Pupillage.

9.4 If the pupil supervisor leaves chambers he or she should where possible make arrangements for the pupil.

10. *Monitoring*

   10.1 Chambers must have complaints and grievance procedures.

   10.2 Chambers must have a policy in the event of chambers dissolving in relation to current pupils and students who have been made offers of pupillage.

   10.4 At the end of each period of pupillage, a pupil supervisor's certificate of satisfactory completion of pupillage must be signed and submitted to the Bar Council.

   10.5 At the end of each year, the Head of Chambers must submit to the Bar Council an annual return in the form prescribed by the Bar Council.

   10.6 The pupillage policy document, annual pupillage return, completed checklists, the Chambers Equal Opportunity Policy and the name of the Chambers Equal Opportunity Officer must be made available to the Bar Council on request, for the purposes of monitoring of pupillage.

   10.7 Any pupil taken on as a tenant at the end of pupillage must have been issued with a full qualification certificate by the Bar Council.

GUIDANCE ON WITNESS PREPARATION

1. This guidance has been prepared by the Professional Standards Committee of the Bar Council to provide assistance to barristers on the difficult issues that arise in respect of witness coaching in the light of the recent decision of the Court of Appeal in *R v Momodou* [2005] EWCA Crim 177. This guidance applies simply to the issues surrounding witness preparation and should be read in conjunction with the relevant provisions of the Code of Conduct (notably paragraph 705) and the Written Standards for the Conduct of Professional Work (notably Section 6 on Witnesses). The guidance is not intended to affect the barrister's ability to discuss the merits of the case with his lay client.

2. Barristers play a significant role in the preparation and presentation of witness evidence. They have a duty to ensure that the evidence in support of their client's case is presented to best effect. It is also the responsibility of a barrister to ensure that those facing unfamiliar court procedures are put at ease as much as possible, especially when the witness is nervous, vulnerable or apparently the victim of criminal or similar conduct: see the Bar Council's Written Standards for the Conduct of Professional Work (para. 6.1.4). Barristers are being asked to prepare witnesses or potential witnesses for the experience of giving oral evidence in criminal and civil proceedings. The purpose of this guidance is to clarify what is and what is not permissible by way of witness preparation, in whatever form it is conducted.

3. The rules which define and regulate the barrister's functions in relation to the preparation of evidence and contact with witnesses are set out in paragraphs 704–708 of the Code of Conduct. The fundamental prohibition regarding the preparation of witness evidence is expressed in paragraph 705(a) of the Code: a barrister must not rehearse, practise or coach a witness in relation to his/her evidence. However, the line between (a) the legitimate preparation of a witness and his/her evidence for a current or forthcoming trial or hearing and (b) impermissible rehearsing or coaching of a witness, may not always be understood.

Criminal Cases

4. The Court of Appeal has recently considered this question in connection with witness training courses in the criminal case of *R v Momodou* [2005] EWCA Crim 177: see paras. 61–65 of the Judgment. The Court of Appeal emphasised that witness coaching is not permitted. However, the Court drew a distinction between witness coaching (which is prohibited) and arrangements to familiarise witnesses with the layout of the court, the likely sequence of events when the witness is giving evidence, and a balanced appraisal of the different responsibilities of the various participants ('witness familiarization'). Such arrangements prevent witnesses from being disadvantaged by ignorance of the process or taken by surprise at the way in which it works, and so assist witnesses to give of their best at the trial or hearing in question without any risk that their evidence may become anything other than the witnesses' own uncontaminated evidence. As such, witness familiarisation arrangements are not only permissible; they are to be welcomed.

5. Although the Court of Appeal did not expressly address the point in *Momodou*, it is also appropriate, as part of a witness familiarisation process, for barristers to advise witnesses as to the basic requirements for giving evidence, e.g. the need to listen

to and answer the question put, to speak clearly and slowly in order to ensure that the Court hears what the witness is saying, and to avoid irrelevant comments. This is consistent with a barrister's duty to the Court to ensure that the client's case is presented clearly and without undue waste of the Court's time.

6. The Court of Appeal in *Momodou* further stated that it is permissible to provide guidance to expert witnesses and witnesses who are to give evidence of a technical nature (e.g. crime-scene officers and officers with responsibility for the operation of observation or detection equipment) on giving comprehensive and comprehensible evidence of a specialist kind to a jury, and resisting the pressure to go further in evidence than matters covered by the witnesses' specific expertise. Again, this would not diminish the authenticity or credibility of the evidence which is given by such witnesses at trial.

7. In relation to witness familiarisation or expert training programmes offered by outside agencies, the Court of Appeal provided the following broad guidance:

   (1) General requirements:

   (a) The witness familiarisation or expert training programme should normally be supervised or conducted by a solicitor or barrister with experience of the criminal justice process, and preferably and if possible by an organisation accredited for the purpose by the Bar Standards Board and Solicitors Regulation Authority .

   (b) None of those involved should have any personal knowledge of the matters in issue in the trial or hearing in question.

   (c) Records should be maintained of all those present and the identity of those responsible for the programme, whenever it takes place.

   (d) The programme should be retained, together with all the written material (or appropriate copies) used during the sessions.

   (e) None of the material should bear any similarity whatever to the issues in the criminal proceedings to be attended by the witnesses, and nothing in it should play on or trigger the witness's recollection of events.

   (f) If discussion of the instant criminal proceedings begins, it must be stopped, and advice must be given as to precisely why it is impermissible, with a warning against the danger of evidence contamination and the risk that the course of justice may be perverted. Note should be made if and when any such warning is given.

   (2) Prosecution witnesses:

   (a) The CPS should be informed in advance of any proposal for a witness familiarisation course for prosecution witnesses.

   (b) The proposals for the intended familiarisation course should be reduced into writing, rather than left to informal conversations.

   (c) If appropriate after obtaining police input, the CPS should be invited to comment in advance on the proposals.

   (d) If relevant information comes to the police, the police should inform the CPS.

   (e) If, having examined them, the CPS suggests that the course may be breaching the permitted limits, it should be amended.

    (3) Defence witnesses:

        (a) Counsel's advice should be sought in advance, with written information about the nature and extent of the familiarisation course for defence witnesses.

        (b) The proposals for the intended familiarisation course should be reduced into writing.

        (c) Counsel has a duty to ensure that the trial Judge and the CPS are informed of any familiarisation process organised by the defence using outside agencies.

8.   Two points arise from the Court of Appeal's guidance in relation to courses offered by outside agencies:

    (1) First, the advice referred to in paragraph 7(3)(a) should be sought from defence counsel or independent counsel with no involvement in the proposed witness familiarisation course. Such advice should be provided in writing.

    (2) Second, in view of the Court of Appeal's warning that none of the course materials should bear any similarity to the issues in the relevant criminal proceedings, it would be good practice for both the party subscribing to the familiarisation course and the participants to provide signed written confirmation that the course materials do not have similarities with any current or forthcoming case in which the participants are or may be involved as witnesses.

9.   As part of a familiarisation process, barristers may be asked to take witnesses through a mock examination-in-chief, cross-examination or re-examination. The following points must be borne in mind when advising on, preparing or conducting any such exercise:

    (1) Subject to sub-paragraphs (2)–(4) below, a mock examination-in-chief, cross-examination or re-examination may be permissible if, and only if, its purpose is simply to give a witness greater familiarity with and confidence in the process of giving oral evidence.

    (2) If, however, there is any risk that it might enable a witness to add a specious quality to his or her evidence, a barrister should refuse to approve or take part in it.

    (3) A barrister who is asked to approve or participate in a mock examination-in-chief, cross-examination or re-examination should take all necessary steps to satisfy himself or herself that the exercise is not based on facts which are the same as or similar to those of any current or impending trial, hearing or proceedings at which a participant is or is likely to be a witness. If it appears that such an exercise may not satisfy these requirements, the barrister should not approve or take part in it.

    (4) In conducting any such mock exercises, barristers are reminded that they must not rehearse, practise or coach a witness in relation to his/her evidence: see para 705(a) of the Code. Where there is any reason to suspect that a mock examination-in-chief, cross-examination or re-examination would or might involve a breach of the Code, a barrister should not approve or take part in it.

Civil Cases

10.   Civil proceedings differ from criminal proceedings in the form of witness evidence and the process of its preparation. The Civil Procedure Rules provide that witness

evidence is to be adduced by way of witness statements and expert reports exchanged before trial, which are to stand as the evidence-in-chief of the witness in question unless the court orders otherwise: CPR Part 32.4(2) and 32.5.

11. The principles set out in *Momodou* apply in criminal proceedings. However, there is currently no authority on these matters in relation to civil proceedings. Until such authority emerges, it would be prudent to proceed on the basis that the general principles set out in *Momodou* also apply to civil proceedings. Thus while witness coaching is prohibited, a process of witness familiarisation is permissible in order to prevent witnesses from being disadvantaged by ignorance of the process or taken by surprise at the way it which it works.

Witness Familiarisation

12. The following guidance should be observed in relation to any witness familiarisation process for the purpose of civil proceedings:

   (1) Any witness familiarisation process should normally be supervised or conducted by a solicitor or barrister.

   (2) In any discussions with witnesses regarding the process of giving evidence, great care must be taken not to do or say anything which could be interpreted as suggesting what the witness should say, or how he or she should express himself or herself in the witness box—that would be coaching.

   (3) If a witness familiarisation course is conducted by an outside agency:

      (a) It should, if possible, be an organisation accredited for the purpose by the Bar Standards Board and Solicitors Regulation Authority

      (b) Records should be maintained of all those present and the identity of those responsible for the programme, whenever it takes place.

      (c) The programme should be retained, together with all the written material (or appropriate copies) used during the sessions.

      (d) None of the material used should bear any similarity whatever to the issues in the current or forthcoming civil proceedings in which the participants are or are likely to be witnesses.

      (e) If discussion of the civil proceedings in question begins, it should be stopped.

   (4) Barristers should only approve or take part in a mock examination-in-chief, cross-examination or re-examination of witnesses who are to give oral evidence in the proceedings in question if, and only if:

      (a) its purpose is simply to give a witness greater familiarity with and confidence in the process of giving oral evidence; and

      (b) there is no risk that it might enable a witness to add a specious quality to his or her evidence; and

      (c) the barrister who is asked to approve or participate in a mock examination-in-chief, cross-examination or re-examination has taken all necessary steps to satisfy himself or herself that the exercise is not based on facts which are the same as or similar to those of any current or impending trial, hearing or proceedings at which a participant is or is likely to be a witness; and

      (d) In conducting any such mock exercises, the barrister does not rehearse, practise or coach a witness in relation to his/her evidence: see para.

705(a) of the Code. Where there is any reason to suspect that a mock examination-in-chief, cross-examination or re-examination would or might involve a breach of the Code, a barrister should not approve or take part in it.

See paragraph 9 above.

Witness Statements

13. Barristers in civil proceedings are typically involved in settling witness statements. However, the courts have emphasised that a witness statement must, so far as possible, be in the witness's own words: see e.g. *Aquarius Financial Enterprises Inc. v Certain Underwriters at Lloyd's* [2001] 2 Ll.Rep. 542 at 547; Chancery Guide, Appendix 4, para. 1; Commercial Court Guide para. H1.1(i) and H1.2 and Technology and Construction Court Guide para. 6.10. When settling witness statements, great care must be taken to avoid any suggestion:

    (1) that the evidence in the witness statement has been manufactured by the legal representatives; or

    (2) that the witness had been influenced to alter the evidence which he or she would otherwise have given.

14. Furthermore, the evidence in a witness statement must not be partial; it must contain the truth, the whole truth and nothing but the truth in respect of the matters on which the witness proposes to give evidence: see Chancery Guide, Appendix 4, para. 6 and Queen's Bench Guide, para. 7.10.4(1). A barrister may be under an obligation to check, where practicable, the truth of facts stated in a witness statement if he or she is put on enquiry as to their truth: see Chancery Guide, Appendix 4, para. 6. Moreover, if a party discovers that a witness statement which has been served is incorrect, it must inform the other parties immediately: see Chancery Guide, Appendix 4, para. 6 and Queen's Bench Guide, para. 7.10.4(6). Barristers therefore have a duty to ensure that such notice is given if they become aware that a witness statement contains material which is incorrect.

Experts

15. It is standard practice in civil cases for barristers to be involved in discussions with experts and to consider drafts of the expert's report prior to service of the report on the other side. In this connection, barristers have a proper and important role in advising experts as to:

    (1) the issues which they should address in their report;

    (2) the form of the report and any matters which are required by the rules of court to be included in it; and

    (3) any opinions and comments which should not be included as a matter of law (e.g. because they are irrelevant or usurp the function of the court or go beyond the expert's experience and expertise).

Beyond this, however, the courts have repeatedly emphasised that expert reports should be, and should be seen to be, the independent product of the expert in question: see *The Ikarian Reefer* [1993] 2 Ll.Rep. 68 at 81; Practice Direction—Experts and Assessors, para. 1.2; Commercial Court Guide, Appendix 11, para. 1. Therefore, a barrister should not seek to draft any part of an expert's report. His or her involvement may, however, include discussing or annotating on a draft report observations and questions for the expert to consider in any revisions to the draft.

16. A barrister may, however, familiarise experts with the process of giving oral evidence, including:

(1) explaining the layout of the Court and the procedure of the trial, and

(2) providing guidance on giving comprehensive and comprehensible specialist evidence to the Court, and resisting the pressure to go further in evidence than matters covered by his or her specific expertise.

See paragraph 6 above. However, great care must be taken not to do or say anything which could be interpreted as manufacturing or in any way influencing the content of the evidence that the expert is to give in the witness box.

Professional Standards Committee

October 2005

GUIDANCE ON PREPARATION OF WITNESS STATEMENTS

PREPARING WITNESS STATEMENTS FOR USE IN CIVIL PROCEEDINGS

DEALINGS WITH WITNESSES

GUIDANCE FOR MEMBERS OF THE BAR

[Issued January 2001]

Introduction

1.   The purpose of this paper, which has the approval of the Professional Standards Committee of the General Council of the Bar, is to offer guidance to members of the Bar instructed to prepare or settle a witness statement and as to dealings with witnesses. Guidance already exists for practice in some Courts, notably Appendix 4 to the Chancery Guide, Part H1 of the Commercial Court Guide and CPR Part 32 and PD 32, paragraphs 17 to 25 to which attention is drawn. The intention is that this paper should be consistent with that guidance.

2.   This guidance is not applicable to criminal proceedings. Attention is drawn to the Guidance Note 'Written Standards for the Conduct of Professional Work' in Section 3 of the Code of Conduct.

Witness statements

3.   The cardinal principle that needs to be kept in mind when drafting or settling a witness statement is that, when the maker enters the witness box, he or she will swear or affirm that the evidence to be given will be the truth, the *whole truth* and nothing but the truth. In most civil trials almost the first question in chief (and not infrequently the last) will be to ask the witness to confirm, to the best of his belief, the accuracy of the witness statement. It is therefore critical that the statement is one that accurately reflects, to the best of Counsel's ability, the witness's evidence.

4.   Witnesses often misunderstand the function of those drafting and settling witness statements. The function of Counsel is to understand the relevant evidence that a witness can give and to assist the witness to express that evidence in the witness's own words. It is important it is made clear to the witness (by reminder to the professional client or the witness, if seen by Counsel) that the statement once Approved is *the witness's* statement. Ultimately it is the witness's responsibility to ensure that the evidence he gives is truthful. It is good practice to remind witnesses expressly of this from time to time, especially where Counsel is assisting the witness to formulate in his own words a particular aspect of the evidence or putting forward a particular piece of drafting for the witness's consideration (which is expressly permitted by the proviso to Rule 704 of the Code of Conduct).

5.   It is not Counsel's duty to vet the accuracy of a witness's evidence. We all may doubt the veracity of our clients and witnesses occasionally. Counsel is, of course, entitled and it may often be appropriate to draw to the witness's attention other evidence which appears to conflict with what the witness is saying and is entitled to indicate that a Court may find a particular piece of evidence difficult to accept. But if the witness maintains the evidence, it should be recorded in the witness statement. If it is decided to call the witness, it will be for the Court to judge the correctness of the witness's evidence.

6. It follows that the statement:

(i) Must accurately reflect the witness's evidence. Rule 704 of the Code of Conduct states:

'A barrister must not devise facts which will assist in advancing the lay client's case and must not draft any . . . witness statement [or] affidavit . . . containing:

(d) in the case of a witness statement or affidavit any statement of fact other than the evidence which in substance according to his instructions the barrister reasonably believes the witness would give if the evidence contained in the witness statement or affidavit were being given in oral examination;[1]

provided that nothing in this paragraph shall prevent a barrister drafting a document containing specific factual statements or contentions included by the barrister subject to confirmation of their accuracy by the lay client or witness.'

(ii) Must not contain any statement which Counsel knows the witness does not believe to be true. Nor should the witness be placed under any pressure to provide other than a truthful account of his evidence.

(iii) Must contain all the evidence which a witness could reasonably be expected to give in answer to those questions which would be asked of him in examination-in-chief. The witness statement should not be drafted or edited so that it no longer fairly reflects the answers which the witness would be expected to give in response to oral examination-in-chief in accordance with the witness's oath or affirmation. Although it is not the function of a witness statement to answer such questions as might be put in cross-examination, great care should be exercised when excluding any material which is thought to be unhelpful to the party calling the witness and no material should be excluded which might render the statement anything other than the truth, the whole truth and nothing but the truth. While it is permissible to confine the scope of examination-in-chief to part only of the evidence which a witness could give, that is always subject to Counsel's overriding duty to assist the Court in the administration of justice and not to deceive or knowingly or recklessly to mislead the Court (Rule 302 of the Code of Conduct). Consequently, it would be improper to exclude material whose omission would render untrue or misleading anything which remains in the statement. It would also be improper to include fact A while excluding fact B, if evidence-in-chief containing fact A but excluding fact B could not have been given consistently with the witness's promise to tell the truth, the whole truth and nothing but the truth. Whether it is wise and in the client's interest in any given case to exclude unfavourable material which can properly be excluded is a matter of judgment.

(iv) Save for formal matters and uncontroversial facts, should be expressed if practicable in the witness's own words. This is especially important when the statement is dealing with the critical factual issues in the case—e.g. the accident or the disputed conversation. Thus the statement should reflect the witness's own description of events. It should not be drafted or edited so as to massage or obscure the witness' real evidence.

---

[1] CPR Part 32.4(1).

(v) Must be confined to admissible evidence that the witness can give, including permissible hearsay.[2] Inadmissible hearsay, comment and argument should be excluded.

(vi) Should be succinct and exclude irrelevant material. Unnecessary elaboration is to be avoided. It is not the function of witness statements to serve as a commentary on the documents in the trial bundles. Nor are they intended to serve as another form of written argument.

7. Sometimes it becomes apparent, after a witness statement has been served, that the witness's recollection has altered. This may happen if the witness sees or hears how another witness puts the facts in a witness statement served by another party. Where Counsel learns that the witness has materially changed his evidence—

(i) He should consider with, and if necessary advise, his professional or BarDirect[3] client whether, in the circumstances, a correction to the original statement needs to be made in order to avoid another party being unfairly misled.

(ii) Where a correction to the original statement is appropriate, this should be done by recording the changed evidence in an additional witness statement and serving it on the other parties (and if appropriate filing it at court). If this is impracticable, e.g. because it occurs very shortly before the hearing, the other parties should be informed of the change immediately and the statement should be corrected at an early stage in court.

(iii) The underlying principle is that it is improper for a litigant to mislead the court or another party to the litigation.[4]

(iv) If a lay or BarDirect client refuses to accept Counsel's advice that disclosure of a correction should be made, Counsel's duty is to withdraw from further acting for the client.

Formalities

8. A witness statement:

(i) Should be expressed in the first person;

(ii) Should state the full name of the witness and the witness's place of residence or, if the statement is made in a professional, business or other occupational capacity, the address at which he works, the position he holds and the name of the firm or employer;

(iii) Should state the witness's occupation or if he has none his description;

(iv) Should state if the witness is a party to the proceedings or is an employee of such a party;

(v) Should usually be in chronological sequence divided into consecutively numbered paragraphs each of which should, so far as possible, be confined to a distinct portion of the evidence;

---

[2] 32PD, para. 18.2 requires the witness to indicate which of the statements are matters of information and belief and the source for any such matters.

[3] Note that under the 8th Edition of the Code, 'BarDirect' is now termed 'licensed access'.

[4] On the duty to make disclosure of material changes of evidence and new documents, see generally *Vernon v Bosley (No. 2)* [1999] QB 18.

(vi) Must indicate which of the statements in it are made from the witness's own knowledge and which are matters of information and belief, indicating the source for any matters of information and belief;

(vii) Must include a statement by the witness that he believes that the facts stated in it are true;

(viii) Must be signed by the witness or, if the witness cannot read or sign it, must contain a certificate made by an authorised person as to the witness's approval of the statement as being accurate;

(ix) Must have any alterations initialled by the witness or by the authorised person;

(x) Should give in the margin the reference to any document or documents mentioned;

(xi) Must be dated.

There are further formal requirements in 32PD, paras 17–19, relating to heading, exhibits, pagination, production and presentation, to which attention is directed.

Dealings with Witnesses

Counsel seeing witnesses[5]

9. The old rules preventing Counsel from seeing a witness, other than the client, have been progressively relaxed over recent years. The current position in civil proceedings can be summarised as follows:

(i) There is no longer any rule which prevents a barrister from having contact with any witness. Indeed, in taking witness statements and generally, it is the responsibility of a barrister, especially when the witness is nervous, vulnerable or apparently the victim of criminal or similar conduct, to ensure that those facing unfamiliar court procedures are put as much at ease as possible.

(ii) Although there is no longer any rule which prevents a barrister from having contact with witnesses, a barrister should exercise his discretion and consider very carefully whether and to what extent such contact is appropriate, bearing in mind in particular that it is not the barrister's function (but that of his professional client) to investigate and collect evidence.

(iii) The guiding principle must be the obligation of Counsel to promote and protect his lay client's best interests so far as that is consistent with the law and with Counsel's overriding duty to the Court (Code of Conduct paragraphs 302, 303). Often it will be in the client's best interests that Counsel should meet witnesses whose evidence will be of critical importance in the case, so as to be able to form a view as to the credibility of their evidence and to advise the lay client properly;

(iv) A barrister should be alert to the risks that any discussion of the substance of a case with a witness may lead to suspicions of coaching, and thus tend to diminish the value of the witness's evidence in the eyes of the court, or may place a barrister in a position of professional embarrassment, for example, if he

---

[5] This is largely taken from Guidance Note 'Written Standards for the Conduct of Professional Work' in Section 3 of the Code of Conduct Approved by the Lord Chancellor's Advisory Committee on Legal Education and Conduct and the designated judges.

thereby becomes himself a witness in the case. These dangers are most likely to occur if such discussion takes place:

(a) before the barrister has been supplied with a proof of the witness's evidence; or

(b) in the absence of the barrister's professional client or his representative.

(v)   Rule 705 of the Code of Conduct provides that a barrister must not rehearse practise or coach a witness in relation to his evidence. This does not prevent Counsel giving general advice to a witness about giving evidence e.g. speak up, speak slowly, answer the question, keep answers as short as possible, ask if a question is not understood, say if you cannot remember and do not guess or speculate. Nor is there any objection to testing a witness's recollection robustly to ascertain the quality of his evidence or to discussing the issues that may arise in cross-examination. By contrast, mock cross-examinations or rehearsals of particular lines of questioning that Counsel proposes to follow are not permitted. What should be borne in mind is that there is a distinction, when interviewing a witness, between questioning him closely in order to enable him to present his evidence fully and accurately or in order to test the reliability of his evidence (which is permissible) and questioning him with a view to encouraging the witness to alter, massage or obscure his real recollection (which is not). The distinction was neatly drawn by Judge Francis Finch in *In Re Eldridge*[6] in 1880, where he said:

> While a discreet and prudent attorney may very properly ascertain from witnesses in advance of the trial what they in fact do know and the extent and limitations of their memory, as guide for his own examinations, he has no right legal or moral, to go further. His duty is to extract the facts from the witness, not to pour them into him; to learn what the witness does know, not to teach him what he ought to know.

At the risk of stating the obvious, this is a difficult area calling for the exercise of careful judgment.

(vi)   A barrister should also be alert to the fact that, even in the absence of any wish or intention to do so, authority figures do subconsciously influence lay witnesses. Discussion of the substance of the case may unwittingly contaminate the witness's evidence,

(vii) There is particular danger where such discussions:

(a) take place in the presence of more than one witness of fact; or

(b) involve the disclosure to one witness of fact of the factual evidence of another witness.

These practices have been strongly deprecated by the courts as tending inevitably to encourage the rehearsal or coaching of witnesses and to increase the risk of fabrication or contamination of evidence: *R v Arif* (1993) 26 May; *Smith New Court Securities Ltd v Scrimgeour Vickers (Asset Management) Ltd* [1994] 1 WLR 1271.

(viii) That is not to suggest that it is always inappropriate to disclose one witness's evidence to another. If conflicting witness statements have been obtained from different witnesses or served by the other side, it may be appropriate or

---

[6] New York Court of Appeals; 37 NY 161, 171.

necessary for a witness to be further questioned about, or have his attention drawn to, discrepancies between statements. Discretion is, however, required, especially where the evidence of independent witnesses is involved.

(ix) Whilst there is no rule that any longer prevents a barrister from taking a witness statement in civil cases, there is a distinction between the settling of a witness statement and taking a witness statement. Save in exceptional circumstances, it is not appropriate for a barrister who has taken witness statements, as opposed to settling witness statements prepared by others, to act as Counsel in that case because it risks undermining the independence of the barrister as an advocate. Exceptional circumstances would include:

(a) The witness is a minor one;

(b) Counsel has no choice but to take the proof and this is the only practical course in the interests of justice—this would apply, for instance, where a witness appears unexpectedly at Court and there is no one else competent to take the statement;

(c) Counsel is a junior member of a team of Counsel and will not be examining the witness.

The Cab Rank rule does not require a barrister to agree to undertake the task of taking witness statements.

(x) A barrister should be prepared to exchange common courtesies with the other side's witnesses. However, a barrister should only discuss the substance of the case or any evidence with the other side's witnesses in rare and exceptional circumstances and then only with the prior knowledge of his opponent.

GUIDANCE ON PREPARATION OF DEFENCE CASE STATEMENTS

THE PREPARATION OF DEFENCE CASE STATEMENTS PURSUANT TO THE CRIMINAL PROCEDURE AND INVESTIGATIONS ACT 1996

GUIDANCE ON THE DUTIES OF COUNSEL

(As Approved by the PCCC on 24 September 1997)

1. It is becoming increasingly common for solicitors to instruct counsel to draft or settle Defence Case Statements, required under section 5 of the Criminal Procedure and Investigations Act 1996. Often these instructions are given to counsel with no or little previous involvement in the case shortly before the expiry of the time limit.

2. The relevant legislation is set out at §12–56 *et seq.* of the 1997 [7]edition of *Archbold*. In summary, however:

    (i) The time limit for compliance is short—14 days from service of prosecution material or a statement that there is none. The permitted grounds for an extension of time are limited;[8]

    (ii) The contents of the Defence Case Statement are obviously of great importance to the defendant. An inaccurate or inadequate statement of the defence could have serious repercussions for the defendant, if the trial judge permits 'appropriate' comment;

    (iii) Whilst it will be the natural instinct of most defence counsel to keep the Defence Case Statement short, a short and anodyne statement may be insufficient to trigger any obligation on the prosecution to give secondary disclosure of prosecution material.

3. Normally it will be more appropriate for instructing solicitors to draft the Defence Case Statement, since typically counsel will have had little involvement at this stage.

4. However, there is nothing unprofessional about counsel drafting or settling a Defence Case Statement, although it must be appreciated that there is no provision in the current regulations for graduated fees allowing for counsel to be paid a separate fee for his work. This most unsatisfactory situation (which has arisen, as a result of the 1996 Act, since the graduated fees regulations were negotiated) is being addressed urgently by the Fees and Legal Aid Committee. A barrister has no obligation to accept work for which he will not be paid. The absence of a fee will justify refusal of the instructions of counsel who are not to be retained for the trial and are simply asked to do no more than draft or settle the Defence Case Statement. Where counsel is retained for the trial, Rule 502(b) of the Code of Conduct deems instructions in a legally aided matter to be at a proper fee and counsel would not be justified in refusing to draft or settle a Defence Case Statement on the sole ground that there is no separate fee payable for this work.[9]

---

[7] Currently 2010 edition.

[8] See the Defence Disclosure Time Limit Regulations 1997 made pursuant to the Act.

[9] Editor's note: it would appear to be necessary to read this guidance in the light of the Bar Council's decision of 15 November 2003 on criminal graduated fees—see footnote 2 to para 604 of the Code. Further, the relevant rule of the Code is now 604 and not 502.

5. Many members of the Bar will nevertheless feel that, in the interests of their lay client and/or of good relations with instructing solicitors, they cannot refuse work, even where they would otherwise be entitled to do so. Those who do so need to recognise the crucial importance of:

    (i) Obtaining all prosecution statements and documentary exhibits;

    (ii) Getting instructions from the lay client, from a properly signed proof and preferably a conference. Those instructions need to explain the general nature of the defence, to indicate the matters on which issue is taken with the prosecution and to give an explanation of the reason for taking issue. They must also give details of any alibi defence, sufficient to give the information required by section 5(7) of the 1996 Act;[10]

    (iii) Getting statements from other material witnesses;

    (iv) Insuring that the client realises the importance of the Defence Case Statement and the potential adverse consequences of an inaccurate or inadequate statement;

    (v) Getting proper informed approval for the draft from the client. This is particularly important, given the risks of professional embarrassment if the client seeks to disown the statement during the course of the trial, perhaps when the trial is not going well or when under severe pressure in cross-examination. Counsel ought to insist on getting written acknowledgement from the lay client that:

        (a) he understands the importance of the accuracy and adequacy of the Defence Case Statement for his case;

        (b) he has had the opportunity of considering the contents of the statement carefully and approves it.

    This may often mean having a conference with the lay client to explain the Defence Case Statement and to get informed approval, although in straightforward cases where counsel has confidence in the instructing solicitor, this could be left to the solicitor. Where the latter course is taken, a short written advice (which can be in a standard form) as to the importance of obtaining the written acknowledgement before service of the statement should accompany the draft Defence Case Statement. A careful record should be kept of work done and advice given.

    (vi) If there is inadequate time, counsel should ask the instructing solicitor to apply for an extension of time. This needs to be considered at a very early stage, since the application must be made before the expiry of the time limit.

6. It follows that counsel ought not to accept any instructions to draft or settle a Defence Case Statement unless given the opportunity and adequate time to gain proper familiarity with the case and to comply with the fundamental requirements set out above. In short, there is no halfway house. If instructions are accepted, then the professional obligations on counsel are considerable.

---

[10] Editor's note: s. 5(7) has been repealed by the Criminal Justice Act 2003. The contents of the Defence Case Statement are now governed by s. 6A, inserted by the 2003 Act.

NON-PRACTISING BARRISTERS SUPPLYING LEGAL
SERVICES—GUIDANCE ON NEW RULES

This note seeks to inform non-practising barristers of changes to the rules affecting them, which came into effect from 31 July 2005.

The General Rule

Any barrister who does not hold a practising certificate, for whatever reason, is a non-practising barrister. The general rule is that a non-practising barrister must not hold him or herself out as a barrister in connection with the supply of legal services. Under transitional provisions, non-practising barristers who were offering legal services on 31 July 2000 have been entitled to use the title 'barrister' in connection with the supply of legal services, provided that it is qualified by the words 'not [or non-] practicing'. These provisions expire on 31 July 2005.

The Bar Council has been reviewing these rules and agreed new provisions. Copies of these provisions are attached.

Exceptions to the General Rule

The new provisions took effect from 31 July 2005 and will allow certain non-practising barristers to hold themselves out as barristers, provided that they comply with certain requirements.

The following categories of non-practising barrister may take advantage of the new provisions:

- Those who were called to the Bar before 31 July 2000;
- Those who are also qualified and practising as members of another 'authorised body';
- Those who supply legal services outside England and Wales.

The following are the requirements that need to be fulfilled in order to be in compliance with the new rules:

(i)   You must notify the Bar Council of your intention to supply legal services and provide full details of your employer and/or the premises from which you intend to supply legal services*; and

(ii)   You must be insured against claims for professional negligence up to at least £250,000*; and

(iii) You must provide a written 'health warning', explaining your status, to any potential client, employer or third party.

(*not required in the case of members of other authorised bodies)

Further Detail of The Provisions

<u>I am registered with the Bar Council as supplying legal services as a 'barrister (non-practising)'.</u> <u>Can I just continue to do so?</u>

No. The transitional provisions allowing certain barristers to supply legal services as a 'barrister (non-practising)' end on 31 July 2005. After that date, all non-practising barristers must either comply with the new provisions, or stop using any title containing the word 'barrister'.

<u>What about those called since 31 July 2000?</u>

The new provisions are an acknowledgement of the fact that barristers called before 31 July 2000 could have taken advantage of the previous provisions allowing them to supply legal services as a 'barrister (non-practising)'. Those called since that date would have been fully aware, at the time of their Call, that they would not be able to hold themselves out as barristers until they qualified for a practising certificate. For this reason, the new rules do not apply to those called since 31 July 2000 (unless they are members of other authorised bodies or supply legal services overseas), although a working group has been set up to give further consideration to the position of those in this group.

<u>What are 'authorised bodies'?</u>

'Authorised bodies' are bodies that are authorised under the Courts and Legal Services Act 1990 (as amended) to grant rights of audience or rights to conduct litigation. The following are currently authorised bodies: the Law Society, the Institute of Legal Executives, the Chartered Institute of Patent Agents and the Institute of Trade Mark Attorneys. If you are practising as a member of any of these bodies, you may hold yourself out as a barrister in addition to your other qualification, provided that you comply with the 'health warning' requirement. (NB There is no requirement for this category to notify the Bar Council or to obtain insurance.)

<u>I am qualified and practise as a lawyer in another country, but also use the title 'barrister'. Do I need to comply with the new rules?</u>

The new rules do not affect rule 4(e) of the International Practice Rules, which allow barristers qualified and practising as lawyers in jurisdictions other than England and Wales to hold themselves out as barristers, provided that:

(i)   they are undertaking international work substantially performed outside England and Wales; and

(ii)   they do not give advice on English law; and

(iii)   they do not supply legal services in connection with any proceedings or contemplated proceedings in England and Wales (other than as an expert witness on foreign law).

If you meet these requirements, you may use the title 'barrister' alongside the title under which you primarily practise, without needing to comply with the new requirements. If not (e.g. if you are only qualified as a lawyer in England and Wales or if you give advice on English law), you must comply with the new provisions in order to hold yourself out as a barrister.

<u>What notification do I need to give to the Bar Council of my intention to supply legal services under the new provisions?</u>

Please use the form enclosed with these guidelines.

<u>How do I arrange insurance?</u>

You should consult a broker specialising in professional indemnity insurance. We understand that the following insurance companies provide such insurance, but there are likely to be many others that do so also:

SBJLtd   *TLOLtd*   *Scott Taylor Associates*
www.sbj.co.uk   *Contact Vernon Taylor*   *LLP*
Contact Martyn   **v.taylor@tloinsurance.co.uk**   **www.stainsurance.co.uk**
Shorrock   *020 7839 0472*   *Contact Martin Taylor*
020 7816 2000   *01353 862268*

<u>What must be included in the 'health warning'?</u>

The warning must cover *all* of the following:

(i)   your status and the fact that you do not hold a practising certificate under the Bar's Code of Conduct; and

(ii)   the limitations on the legal services you may undertake; and

(iii) that you are not fully regulated by the Bar Council; and

(iv)   the absence of available compensatory powers for any inadequate professional service you may render.

A suggested health warning is attached to these guidelines. However, it is not compulsory to use the suggested warning, so long as you include all the compulsory elements.

<u>To whom must I supply the health warning, and when?</u>

If you are already employed to supply legal services, you must give the warning to your employer before you start holding yourself out as a barrister under the new rules. For any future employment, you should give the warning before commencement of the employment.

Whether employed or self-employed, you must give the warning to anyone to whom you propose to supply legal services, prior to any agreement to supply such services.

During the course of supplying legal services, you must give the warning to any third party, as soon as you first deal with them.

<u>What title may I use?</u>

So long as you have complied with all of the relevant requirements, you may use the title 'barrister'.

<u>Can I use the title 'barrister' on my business card?</u>

If you use it in connection with the supply of legal services, you should only provide the card to clients or third parties in connection with those services if you have given them the 'health warning'.

<u>What are the limitations on what I can do?</u>

Essentially, you must not undertake work that you could only do because you are a barrister. In essence this includes:

• exercising rights of audience as a barrister (this applies particularly in those courts where such rights are restricted—the magistrates' courts, the county courts, the Crown Court, the High Court, the Court of Appeal and the House of Lords);

• exercising a right to conduct litigation (including issuing proceedings, acting as an address for service etc);

• such conveyancing and probate services as are restricted under the Solicitors Act 1974;

- providing immigration advice or representation unless you are registered with the Office of the Immigration Services Commissioner.

Does this mean that I cannot appear as an advocate?

No. You have exactly the same rights as any other member of the public and there is nothing to prevent you appearing on behalf of a client in tribunals where rights of audience are not restricted or, with the permission of the court, in one the higher courts. You must not, however, claim to have a right of audience and, if seeking leave, should not mislead the court as to your status.

Does the work I do constitute 'legal services'?

The Code of Conduct gives the following definition of 'legal services':

'legal services' includes legal advice representation and drafting or settling any statement of case witness statement affidavit or other legal document but does not include:

(a)   sitting as a judge or arbitrator or acting as a mediator;

(b)   lecturing in or teaching law or writing or editing law books articles or reports;

(c)   examining newspapers, periodicals, books, scripts and other publications for libel, breach of copyright, contempt of court and the like;

(d)   communicating to or in the press or other media;

(e)   exercising the powers of a commissioner for oaths;

(f)   giving advice on legal matters free to a friend or relative or acting as unpaid or honorary legal adviser to any charitable benevolent or philanthropic institution;

(g)   in relation to a barrister who is a non-executive director of a company or a trustee or governor of a charitable benevolent or philanthropic institution or a trustee of any private trust, giving to the other directors trustees or governors the benefit of his learning and experience on matters of general legal principle applicable to the affairs of the company institution or trust.

If all the work that you do falls outside the definition of 'legal services', you may hold yourself out as a barrister without complying with the new provisions.

What additional rights do the new provisions give me?

None. The new provisions only allow you to use the title 'barrister'. They do not make you a practising barrister and do not entitle you to exercise any of the rights (e.g. rights of audience) that are only exercisable by practising barristers.

What rules of professional conduct apply to me?

The Code of Conduct still covers you and the Bar Standards Board can consider complaints against you. While it is true many of the rules apply only to practising barristers (notably paras. 302–307 and Parts IV–VII), you should note that you are still covered by paragraph 301 of the Code and that there are a number of circumstances (for example, acting where there is a conflict of interest, misleading a court or failing to act in good faith) which would be very likely to put you in breach of that paragraph. While the Bar Standards Board does not have the power to take action against a non-practising barrister for inadequate professional service, it is possible that seriously poor service to a client or succession of clients might justify an action for misconduct under this paragraph also.

<u>Who should I contact with queries?</u>

Please contact the Bar Standards Board, 289–293 High Holborn, London WC1V 7HZ; tel 020 7611 1444. Queries should be directed as follows:

Queries regarding the requirements of the new rules and the notification procedure:

Joanne Dixon
The Education and Qualifications Department
JDixon@BarStandardsBoard.org.uk

Queries regarding the extent to which non-practising barristers are subject to the Code of Conduct and complaints procedures:

Contact the Complaints and Investigations Department

Suggested Information Notices

1. **Information Notice to be given before supplying legal services to a client**

   The suggested form of information notice to be given by barristers without practising certificates to those to whom they intend to supply legal services is as follows:

   'I hold the degree of barrister, but I do not have a practising certificate, because [I have not completed the training required by the Bar Standards Board or I do not comply with the Bar Standard Board's rules for practising barristers]. This limits the work I am allowed to do. It also limits the rights you will have against me and against the Bar Standards Board.

   I cannot appear in court on your behalf. I cannot conduct litigation or immigration work for you.

   I am not fully regulated by the Bar Standards Board. This means that, although the Bar Standards Board can consider a complaint against me, it cannot require me to pay you compensation for inadequate professional service. The Bar Standards Board will also not pay you compensation itself for any wrongdoing on my part. Full details are available at www.barstandardsboard.org.uk.'

   This form of information notice must be given <u>in writing</u> to any person to whom a barrister without a practising certificate is intending to provide legal services <u>before</u> any such legal services are provided. The information notice must be explained in an appropriate fashion to any person who may not reasonably be expected to understand it fully for themselves.

   An information notice need be given only once to a person intending to employ a barrister without a practising certificate prior to the commencement of that employment.

2. **Information Notice to be Given to Employers**

   The following revised form of information notice may be given by barristers without practising certificates to a firm of solicitors or a legal department by whom they are about to be employed:

   'I hold the degree of barrister, but I do not have a practising certificate, because [I have not completed the training required by the Bar Standards Board or I do not comply with the Bar Standards Board's rules for practising barristers]. This limits the work I am allowed to do. It also limits the rights you will have against me and against the Bar Standards Board. I cannot appear as a barrister in court. I cannot conduct litigation or immigration work as a barrister. I am not fully regulated by the Bar Standards Board. This means that, although the Bar Council can consider a complaint against me, it cannot require me to pay compensation for inadequate professional service. The Bar Standards Board will also not pay compensation itself for any wrongdoing on my part. Full details are available at www.barstandardsboard.org.uk.'

   The Notice need only be given if the barrister intends to use the title in conjunction with his/her work for the organisation.

3. **Information Notice for those who have re-qualified as Solicitors**

   The following revised form of information notice may be given by barristers without practising certificates, who have re-qualified as solicitors, to a firm of solicitors or a legal department by whom they are about to be employed:

   'I hold the degree of barrister, but I have re-qualified as a solicitor, and I am practising as a solicitor. I do not have a practising certificate from, and am not fully regulated by, the

Bar Standards Board. This means that, although the Bar Standards Board can consider a complaint against me, it cannot require me to pay compensation for inadequate professional service or pay compensation itself for any wrongdoing on my part. The primary rules governing my conduct are those of the Law Society.'

4.   **Information Notice to be given to third parties before supplying legal services**

The suggested form of information notice to be given by barristers without practising certificates to those third parties with whom they deal in the course of supplying legal services is as follows:

'I hold the degree of barrister, but I do not have a practising certificate, because [I have not completed the training required by the Bar Standards Board or I do not comply with the Bar Standards Board's rules for practising barristers]. This limits the work I am allowed to do. I cannot appear as a barrister in court. I cannot conduct litigation or immigration work as a barrister.

I am not fully regulated by the Bar Standards Board but they can consider a complaint against me.'

The notice must be given <u>in writing</u> to any person with whom a barrister without a practising certificate is dealing in the course of supplying legal services <u>at the time of the first such dealings</u>. The information notice must be explained in an appropriate fashion to any person, who may not reasonably be expected to understand it fully for themselves.

NON-PRACTISING BARRISTERS

Notification of Intention to Supply Legal Services (Rule 206)

<u>Personal Details:</u>

Surname   ....
Previous name (if any)   ....

Other Names   ....
Title (Mr/Ms etc)   ....

Address

              ....
              ....
              ....

Telephone No   ....
Fax   ....

E-mail   ....

Inn   ....
Date of Call   ....

Please indicate how you intend to supply legal services:

Employed, supplying legal services to your employer only   ☐

Employed, supplying legal services to clients of your employer   ☐

Self-employed, supplying legal services to your own clients   ☐

Please give the following details of the place from which you will be supplying legal services (if different from details given above):

Name of employer/ organisation: (where applicable)		
Address:		
Telephone:		Fax:

1.   **Have you taken out professional indemnity insurance?**

☐ Yes   ☐ No

2.   **Please give full details of your insurer and the extent of your cover.**
        (You may wish to supply a copy of your certificate of insurance or insurance policy, but please do not send us originals)

....
....
....
....
....
....
....
....
....

3.   **I confirm that the information I have given is true.**

Signed   ....

Date   ....

Please return this form to

The Records Office
Rule 206 Notifications
General Council of the Bar
289-293 High Holborn
London
WC1V 7HZ

PROFESSIONAL STANDARDS COMMITTEE GUIDANCE TO MEMBERS OF THE CRIMINAL BAR IN RELATION TO REFUSING WORK

The PSC has been asked whether it would be a breach of the Code for barristers to refuse work in a series of particular circumstances.

In brief, the PSC has concluded after a special meeting held on Tuesday 13th September 2005 as follows:

1. Rule 604(b) of the Code provides that a barrister is not obliged to accept instructions other than at a fee which is proper having regard to

    (i)   the complexity length and difficulty of the case,

    (ii) his ability experience and seniority and

    (iii) the expenses which he will incur.

2. Until 15 November 2003, legally aided criminal defence work was deemed by the Code to be at a proper fee. On 15 November 2003, the Bar Council decided that criminal defence GFS cases should be excluded from the provision deeming them to be proper fees.

3. The Code has never contained a provision deeming criminal prosecution work to be at a proper fee. It is, therefore, governed by the same provisions as all other kinds of work.

4. In deciding in any particular case whether a fee is 'proper', a barrister must consider 2 questions:

    (1) Whether he/she in good faith regards the fee as proper having regard to the three specified factors in Rule 604(b); and

    (2) If in good faith he/she does not regard the fee as proper, whether he/she is acting reasonably and justifiably in reaching that decision.

5. Whether a fee is proper, and the questions set out above are matters of fact, which will vary from case to case. This must be kept closely in mind in considering the questions in each case.

6. Where fees are actually reduced on a particular date, barristers are unlikely to be vulnerable to an allegation that they are in breach of the Code in declining affected work after that date.

7. Where fees are not reduced, it will obviously be less easy to demonstrate that an unreduced fee is not proper. The tests set out above must be applied carefully in each case before a barrister makes a decision to refuse such work in any particular case.

<u>The position of pupils and pupil supervisors</u>

The PSC has been asked by the Pupillage Board to remind practitioners in the context of the above guidance that:

(1) A barrister who is a pupil supervisor with a pupil must not allow any decisions with regard to the acceptance of new instructions to affect or disrupt the pupillage training which the pupil supervisor is obliged to give.

(2) Whatever decisions may be taken, the pupil supervisor remains under an obligation to ensure that the pupil receives the required training so that the pupil can in turn apply him/herself diligently to the pupillage and properly complete the checklist and of course the pupillage.

(3) Similarly, it is for the Head of Chambers to ensure that, if any pupil supervisor in his/her chambers makes a decision to refuse work, arrangements are in place which allow pupils to be properly trained.

(4) Pupils have a legitimate right to proper training irrespective of any such decisions which a pupil supervisor may take, and that right should be fully recognised and respected, regardless of any steps which may be taken over the acceptance or refusal of work.

The respective duties of pupils and of pupil supervisors in this context are set out in sections 801 and 804 of the Consolidated Regulations and paragraphs 1.2 and 1.3 of the Pupillage File 2004/2005. The duties of Heads of Chambers are set out in paragraph 1.4.

Professional Standards Committee
15th September 2005

REPORTING PROFESSIONAL MISCONDUCT
GUIDANCE

Introduction

1. It is essential within a system of self-regulation, such as that operated at the Bar, that barristers recognise the important role that they play in ensuring that the profession conducts itself in the public interest and in a manner that is not discreditable, disreputable or dishonest.

2. The Bar Council is reliant on its members and members of the public to contact them if they are concerned about a barrister's conduct, ability to practise competently or if they are aware that a barrister has been convicted of a serious criminal offence. In order to highlight the importance of barristers bringing these matters to the attention of the Bar Council and to aid them when doing so, the General Management Committee of the Bar Council has decided that guidance should be issued to the Bar on the kind of conduct that should be reported and the issues that barristers should consider before reporting.

Conduct That Should Be Reported

3. The categories of conduct that we believe barristers should report can be separated into two discrete areas:

    - **What is in the public interest to be reported**

    - **What is in the best interests of the reputation of the profession to be reported**

4. In both of these categories the misconduct, incapacity or offence to be reported must be serious and of the sort which, if proved, would suggest to the public that the individual ought not to continue to be permitted to practise as a barrister offering advice to the public and might justify a sentence of disbarment or suspension from practise from a Disciplinary Tribunal. Barristers are not expected to report every minor offence or breach of the Code.

The 'Public Interest' category

5. This category can be further sub-divided into the following areas:

    - **Unfit to practise**

6. This is defined in Annex O of the Code as meaning that:

    '(a) the barrister is suffering from serious incapacity due to his mental or physical condition (including any addiction); and

    '(b) as a result the barrister's fitness to practise is seriously impaired.'

7. The Bar Council accepts that barristers are not usually medically trained, but in our view this is not necessary when deciding whether in their opinion a barrister is fit to practise. The crucial question is whether, by reason of incapacity, the ability to appear in court, advise clients or to make judgements in the client's interests is impaired. Such an assessment is something that any barrister could reasonably be expected to undertake. If the answer to the question is yes, for the protection of the public, the barrister ought to be reported to the Bar Council.

    - **Gross Incompetence**

8. We would expect a report to be made under this category only in relation to an act, or series of acts, which seriously calls into question whether a barrister is competent to practise or offer legal services to the public of the standard expected

by the profession. It is not necessary to report all acts of negligence or poor service, however the cumulative effect of a number of such acts might be sufficient to suggest that a barrister is not competent. The assessment of conduct within this category is very much subjective in nature—barristers who are unsure whether to make a report can contact the Bar Council to discuss the issues on a confidential and anonymous basis.

The 'Reputation of the Profession' category

9.   This category can be sub-divided into the following areas:

   • **Serious Criminal Offence**

10. Paragraph 905(b) of the Code of Conduct requires barristers to report to the Bar Council if they have been charged with a serious criminal offence or if they have been convicted of any relevant criminal offence.

11. We would only expect a report to be made if a member of the Bar believes on reasonable grounds that another barrister has been convicted of a serious criminal offence but had not reported it to the Bar Council. If you are uncertain whether a barrister has reported his/her conviction you should contact the Bar Council who will have a record of the convictions reported to it.

   • **Disreputable Conduct**

12. This applies to conduct in the course of a barrister's practice whether in self employed or employed practice The following are examples of the kind of conduct that we believe should be brought to the attention of the Bar Council:

Disreputable conduct within Chambers/place of work

13. Conduct which constitutes a serious arrestable offence, e.g.:

   (i)   theft from another member of Chambers or staff or pupil, or any visitor to Chambers;

   (ii) assault on another member of Chambers or staff or pupil, or any visitor to Chambers.

14. Dishonest or deceitful conduct towards other members of Chambers or staff or pupils, e.g.:

   (i)   Seeking to gain access without consent to papers or confidential information relating to a case in which a member of Chambers is instructed on the other side;

   (ii) Seeking to gain access without consent to information confidential to another member of Chambers or pupil in relation to his practice or his personal affairs (except in appropriate circumstances by a pupil supervisor in relation to a pupil).

15. In all such cases arising in self-employed practice, the person who would usually be expected to report the matter to the Bar Council is the Head of Chambers or the person or Committee within Chambers which has responsibility for the proper administration of Chambers or for investigating the matter in the first instance. However, if a barrister with knowledge of the conduct in question is aware that the Head of Chambers or other responsible person has failed to report the matter to the Bar Council, the barrister with such knowledge should bring the matter to the attention of the Bar Council.

16. For those cases arising in employed practice, barristers may wish to discuss the matter with their Head of Department or line manager before deciding who should make the report.

Disreputable conduct in relation to court proceedings

17. The Bar Council recognises that barristers cannot reasonably be expected to police the conduct of their opponents in the course of adversarial litigation. However, the profession has a duty to ensure that cases are presented fairly and honourably, so that justice can properly be done. In most cases, the Court will be able to make use of its own powers to control its procedures and to ensure that cases are properly presented. Misconduct in the face of the Court will usually be apparent to the Judge, and in such cases, it is expected that the Judge hearing the matter will bring the misconduct in question to the attention of the Bar Council. However, there are some instances in which misconduct by a barrister may not come to the attention of the Court. In addition, there are other instances in which the misconduct in question so fundamentally undermines the proper and fair administration of justice that members of the profession are expected to ensure that it is brought to the attention of the Bar Council. The following are examples of such misconduct:

    a. Dishonest or disreputable conduct, such as:

        (i) Seeking to gain access without consent to instructions or other confidential information relating to the opposing party's case;

        (ii) Encouraging a witness to give evidence with is untruthful;

        (iii) Misleading or allowing the Court or opponent to be misled.

    b. Being drunk or under the influence of drugs at Court.

Racial or Sexual Discrimination /Harassment

18. This is an extremely sensitive area and one in which victims can be reluctant to come forward themselves. We do not advocate that a report that a colleague has committed an act of racial or sexual discrimination or harassment should be made without first discussing the matter with the victim—who may have strong views that a report should not be made—however we would stress that conduct that falls within this category is wholly unacceptable and should be reported wherever possible. The Bar Council will of course offer support and assistance to the victim if a report is made.

19. It may well be the case that Chambers will be considering the matter through their own procedures and in those circumstances we would not expect a report to be made to the Bar Council unless it is deemed necessary following Chambers' investigation of the allegation.

Issues to take into consideration before making a report

20. Before making any report to the Bar Council, members of the Bar should give careful consideration to the following:

    • **Evidence**

21. What evidence or information is there of the barrister's conduct conviction or fitness to practise which causes a report to be made. A belief based on gossip or hearsay would not be sufficient. For the Bar Council to take the report forward they will need *prima facie* evidence either in the form of documents or witness statements.

22. If there is any doubt before making a report as to whether it is justified, it is open to barristers to make additional investigations and to contact the barrister concerned for an explanation.

- **Privilege/confidentiality**

23. Barristers should not breach their own duties of privilege or confidentiality in reporting misconduct without the client's consent. They must take into account the law of privilege and before reporting members of the Bar on the other side of a case for what may appear to be dishonesty or gross incompetence should ensure that they have *prima facie* evidence to support it. Consideration should also be given to the comments made by the House of Lords in the case of *Medcalf v Mardell* [2002] 3 All ER 721 about the dangers of making assumptions on apparently damning facts without first having heard the full story. Detailed guidance on this case can be found on the Bar Council's website at www.barcouncil.org.uk.

24. When deciding whether a report should be made, it may be useful to look at the provisions of the Code of Conduct to see whether the conduct causing the report seems to fall within any particular rule. This is not, of course, an exact science but it might be helpful in determining whether a report is appropriate or necessary.

25. Reports of serious misconduct, or allegations of unfitness to practise, that are made out of malice, or without supporting evidence, may be considered by the Professional Conduct and Complaints Committee actually themselves to amount to professional misconduct. Barristers should, therefore, if they are in any doubt, contact the Professional Standards or Professional Conduct Department at the Bar Council to discuss the possible report on a confidential and anonymous basis.

What action the Bar Council will take if a report is made

26. The action taken by the Bar Council will depend on the nature of the allegation and the evidence contained in the report. In all cases, the matter will be referred either to the Complaints Commissioner or to the Chairman of the Professional Conduct and Complaints Committee for instructions. As guidance, the following action is likely to be taken.

27. Where a report advises that a barrister has been convicted of a serious criminal offence the Bar Council is likely to institute proceedings under the Interim Suspension Rules (see Annex O to the Code of Conduct) and will also consider disciplinary action.

28. If the evidence suggests that the barrister is unfit to practise, the Bar Council is likely to institute proceedings under the Fitness to Practise Rules (see Annex O of the Code of Conduct). It is important to note, however, that these proceedings do not amount to disciplinary proceedings and are intended to provide support for a barrister to deal with his or her problems so that disciplinary proceedings are avoided. The main aim of the Fitness to Practise Rules is to protect the public but it is also a means of protecting the profession as it removes from individual barristers and their chambers the burden of deciding whether they are fit to practise and places it upon the Bar Council.

29. In other cases the Bar Council is likely to raise a complaint against the barrister concerned or to seek their comments prior to raising any complaint.

30. If a complaint is raised, the Bar Council may require the assistance of the barrister making the report in supplying witness statements and/or attending at any Tribunal proceedings that may follow.

Reporting the matter to the Bar Council

31. Should a barrister wish to make a report to the Bar Council they should write to the Professional Standards and Complaints Section 289–293 High Holborn, London, WC1V 7HZ, enclosing any evidence that they have in support of their report. Barristers should therefore, if they are in any doubt, contact the Professional Standards or Professional Conduct Department at the Bar Council to discuss the possible report on a confidential and anonymous basis.

Conclusion

32. The Bar functions on a system based on trust and confidence between colleagues and the Bar Council would not wish to suggest anything that might put this in jeopardy. There is however a need to ensure that the profession continues to operate at the high standard it has historically maintained. The role that self-regulation plays in achieving this is essential and, in order for the Bar Council to effectively police the profession, assistance from members of the Bar is encouraged. Our net does not extend wide enough to be able to uncover every instance of serious misconduct, incompetence or unfitness to practise. Barristers have a responsibility to uphold the reputation of the profession and we would urge them strongly therefore to bring to our attention anything that might call this into question.

The General Management Committee
The General Council of the Bar
October 2005

The Equality and Diversity Code
for the Bar

CONTENTS

FOREWORD

The Bar of England and Wales continues to lead the way among professions in its practical approach to equality and diversity within the Bar. This concern with fair treatment and respect for individual dignity is especially important in a profession whose own task is to uphold people's rights without fear or favour.

This edition of the Equality Code has been updated to take into account increasing awareness in discrimination issues and developing law, including disability legislation. Although it cannot provide comprehensive guidance to the law, it does provide practical guidance on implementation of good equal opportunities practices in areas where equality and diversity issues are most likely to arise. It places greater emphasis on:

- practice development for pupils and junior tenants
- access to good quality work
- flexible working, including maternity and paternity leave

For those accessing the document electronically, there are hyperlinks to relevant legal provisions, codes of practice, model policies and guidance.

The profession was consulted about the first draft, and the final version incorporates many of the suggestions received. The Bar Council unanimously Approved the Equality Code at its meeting on 17 July 2004.

The Bar Council's Equality and Diversity Advisers are willing to provide advice and guidance, and can provide information about planned training courses and briefings.

This Code is the result of much effort by experts in the field. We urge you to draw upon that expertise.

THE RT HON LORD
GOLDSMITH QC
ATTORNEY GENERAL

STEPHEN IRWIN QC
CHAIRMAN
GENERAL COUNCIL OF THE BAR

INTRODUCTION

The purpose of the Code

This new Equality and Diversity Code is designed to assist barristers and their employees to apply good equal opportunities practice in the development and running of Chambers. The advice is primarily for barristers in self-employed practice as employed barristers will be bound by their individual company/organisation's policies and rules for implementation. All barristers are required to comply with the broad obligations not to discriminate, as set out in paragraphs 305 and 404 of the Code of Conduct and in the anti-discrimination statutes. It is intended to be a practical guide rather than a legal handbook but seeks to reflect and give effect to the requirements of the law.

Why does equality of opportunity matter?

Equality of opportunity is **fair, commercially advantageous, necessary for compliance with non-discrimination law and constitutionally important.**

Barristers advise and represent clients from an increasingly diverse range of backgrounds. They remain the largest pool for recruitment to the judiciary. It is in the best interests of both the public and the Bar that those of the highest ability and talent are attracted to the profession. Recent statistics for entry to the Bar are encouraging but retention remains an issue of concern. Cultures and practices which may deter those of high ability from remaining within the profession or from achieving their full potential must be identified and, where possible, eliminated. Public confidence and support for the Bar can only be enhanced by systems which are seen as open and fair.

Barristers need to be able to recognise their own prejudices and to be aware of the assumptions which they make in evaluating others. They must learn how to ensure that prejudices and assumptions do not influence their treatment of others in the work context. Diversity training will assist barristers in understanding the cultures and sensitivities of others. Systems, such as fair recruitment processes, policies on flexible working and monitoring, will help to ensure that working practices really are achieving equality. Accreditation through schemes such as the Legal Services Commission's Quality Mark now require that good equal opportunities practices are applied.

The application of good equal opportunities practices will minimise the risk of breaches of discrimination law for which awards may now be substantial. But the commercial advantages go further. They entail the retention of an excellent pool of talent. Barristers in the early stages of their professional lives may be supported in their work by rent concessions and training. If they then leave Chambers because, for example, childcare commitments limit their earning capacity for a few years and a period of flexible working cannot be accommodated, their value is lost. They may be potential major contributors to Chambers whose value is lost by short-term considerations.

The Bar has a constitutional role in ensuring the independence of advocates before the Courts and in order to maintain confidence in that role, its own practices must be and be seen to be fair.

The Bar Council has now adopted a policy of 'mainstreaming' equal opportunities and Chambers are encouraged to do the same. This means that the furtherance of equal opportunity objectives and the potential for discrimination should be considered in relation to all policies, practices and decisions where equal opportunities issues may arise: for example, not just recruitment but also matters such as distribution of work, allocation of rooms, fees, the location and timing of meetings and Chambers entertaining.

Using the Code

The Code begins with a guide in Section 1 to the key areas (known as 'Action Areas') where good equal opportunities practice should be implemented. This is where practical guidance may be found, on the key areas of recruitment, maternity and fair access to work. Section 1 also includes a guide to the new statutory provisions on service provision to disabled clients.

Section 2 outlines the legal and regulatory framework which underpins the requirement not to discriminate. The duty not to discriminate is to be found not only in statute and regulations but also in the Bar's Code of Conduct. The key concepts of anti-discrimination law are summarised and some common misconceptions are clarified.

In each Section, the reader will find Links to Regulatory provisions, statutory Codes of Practice, model policies and guidance on good practice. For those reading the Code in its paper version rather than electronically, Section 3 contains Annexes with further guidance on good equal opportunities practice, such as the Bar Council Maternity, Paternity and Flexible Working Policy guidance on Monitoring and on the role of an Equal Opportunities. Officer in chambers References to 'Heads of Chambers' in the text include all management structures with overall responsibility for running chambers.

Section 1: Action Areas

The Equality and Diversity Code contains 18 action areas. Action areas A–H are reproduced here. For the full text of C and many useful links to other websites, the reader should consult the website of the Bar Standards Board, <http://www.barstandardsboard.org.uk>. Guidance on equal opportunities practices may also be find via an alphabetical index on the website of the Bar Council.

A. RECRUITMENT: PUPILS AND TENANTS

General Guidance

1.1 The same broad principles apply to the recruitment of pupils, starter tenants, established practitioners and staff. Discrimination by barristers on the ground of sex, race, disability, sexual orientation and religion or belief in recruitment is unlawful. Discrimination on the ground of age is professional misconduct.[11]

Advertisement

1.2 Vacancies should be advertised. A failure to advertise vacancies for pupils or tenants places Chambers and individual barristers at risk of allegations of indirect discrimination. It is good practice to include in advertisements:

- encouragement of applications from groups which are under-represented in Chambers;
- a statement of compliance with the Equality and Diversity Code;
- a statement indicating preparedness to make reasonable adjustments for disabled candidates.

Where Chambers use agencies or head hunters they should ensure that Chambers' equality policy is included in the instructions given to the agency.

Application Forms

1.3 An application form is generally preferable to curriculum vitae. An application form enables the assessment of candidates to be made on a clearly defined comparative basis by reference to specific qualities which are relevant to Chambers' selection criteria.

Chambers are reminded that reasonable adjustments may need to be made for disabled candidates at the application stage of the recruitment process when, for example, application forms may have to be provided in a particular format.

Selection Criteria

1.4 Candidates for pupillage or tenancy should be selected using selection criteria. Selection criteria should be objective and should relate to the work to be done.

- selection criteria enable Chambers to focus on the qualities which they require from the successful candidate.
- they reduce the opportunity for decisions to be influenced by stereotyping or unwitting prejudice.

---

[11] The Bar Standards Board website here gives a link to a number of other useful websites.

- selection criteria may be designed so that a higher score is attributed to criteria to which greater importance is attached.
- chambers should avoid criteria that are subjective, such as personality-based attributes or behavioural attributes that cannot fairly be tested at interview.
- it is good practice to provide candidates with selection criteria in advance of the interview.

They promote a consistent and objective approach to candidates by selectors.

Short Listing

1.5 Short listing should be carried out by more than one person and by reference to relevant selection criteria which should be determined in advance of the recruitment process. It is good practice to draft a job or post description and a person specification to assist in identifying the relevant criteria and enable application forms to be drafted in a way which allows candidates to address the criteria. Where shortlisters cannot agree, it may be necessary for a committee to moderate short-listing decisions.

Selection Committees

1.6 All recruitment decisions Chambers make, except for sole practices, should be made by a number of selectors, except in sole practices. Selection committees should, so far as possible, include persons of different age, gender and social, racial or cultural background. They should not include any relative or close friend of the candidates. No candidate should feel that he or she is so remote from the interviewing committee as to be denied a fair prospect of success.

1.7 Where final decisions as to recruitment are made by Chambers or designated members of Chambers rather than the selection committee, no single member of Chambers should be permitted to veto a decision and any challenge to a recommendation of the selection committee should be by reference to the selection criteria and on grounds which are substantiated.

Training

1.8 Members of selection committees should be familiar with this Code and the applicable procedures and selection criteria. It is recommended that at least one member of each selection committee should be trained in fair selection methods.

Interviews

1.9 Interviews should be planned in advance and structured so that each candidate may demonstrate his or her abilities and qualities by reference to each selection criterion. Chambers should ensure that any reasonable adjustment required for a disabled candidate has been made so that disabled candidates are not disadvantaged at interview.

1.10 Interviews should be of sufficient length to enable informed decisions to be made and to minimise the potential prejudices involved in 'gut feeling'.

1.11 It is not essential to ask each candidate identical questions, but a planned sequence of topics is recommended.

1.12 Irrelevant questions, such as personal questions in relation to family and personal background should be avoided. However, disabled candidates should be asked what, if any, adjustments may be needed to enable the candidate to practise as a barrister.

1.13 Selectors should score candidates individually on an agreed scale and should then compare scores with others on the panel so as to seek to reach a consensus. Scores should not be adjusted to reflect personal preference.

1.14 Standard exercises either in written form or by way of oral presentation may be a useful aid to arriving at objective assessments of candidates. In relation to pupils and starter tenants, such exercises should be designed in such a way that any area of law covered is one which should be equally familiar to all candidates. Alternatively, a topic may be chosen which requires no prior specialist legal knowledge but is designed to test analytical or advocacy skills.

Record-Keeping

1.15 Candidates who have been rejected may want an explanation for their rejection. If good records are kept, reasons for rejection are generally easily explained in the event of a request or even legal challenge. If explanations for rejection can be given, this should enhance confidence in the recruitment system.

Monitoring and Review

1.16 Candidates should be asked to complete monitoring forms so as to enable Chambers to review their performance by reference to reliable statistics. Monitoring enables Chambers to self-check. It may be that prejudices and attitudes of which selectors are not even conscious are influencing decisions. Monitoring enables these possibilities to be recognised and examined. Where there are significant discrepancies between proportions of applicants from a particular group and proportions of successful candidates from a particular group, recruitment practices may need to be reviewed with a view to redressing observed discrepancies and to achieving diversity in Chambers. If there are no such discrepancies, statistics may support the objectivity of a particular process in the event of a challenge.

1.17 All documents relating to exercises should be retained for two years and statistics should be prepared by reference to gender, race, disability and age of the number of persons applying, being short-listed and being recruited.

Recruitment of Pupils

1.18 This guidance is in addition to the matters set out at paragraphs 1.1 to 1.7 above.

Pupillage Policy

1.19 Chambers should have a pupillage policy which includes a pupillage selection procedure. The pupillage selection procedure should be made available to candidates for pupillage and should be reviewed regularly.

Advertising Pupillages

1.20 Pupillages must be advertised on a website designated by the Bar Council, save in the exceptional circumstances set out in paragraph 5 of the Pupillage Funding and Advertising Requirements 2003 in Annexe R to the Code of Conduct. Subject to those exceptions, all pupillages must be advertised including supplementary or late vacancies and vacancies for candidates who intend to practise outside the UK (see para 404.2 (c) of the Code of Conduct).

Private Arrangements

1.21 Private arrangements to take pupils should not be made, save where the requirement to advertise is disapplied or waived pursuant to paragraph 5 of the Pupillage Funding and Advertising Requirements 2003 (see para 1.20 above). Private arrangements are contrary to good equal opportunities practice and the Bar Council will not register pupillages by private arrangement. They breach the requirement in the Code of Conduct that pupillages must be advertised.

References

1.22 Where references are sought, a standard form should be used. Alternatively, referees should be directed as to the selection criteria being applied and the type of information which is sought from them.

Recruitment of Starter Tenants

1.23 This section is in addition to paragraphs 1.1 to 1.17 above.

1.24 Every Chambers, which recruits starter tenants, should have a policy in relation to the recruitment of starter tenants. The policy should be made available to members of Chambers and to pupils when they begin their pupillage. Pupils should be informed as to when their Chambers will identify any vacancies for starter tenants and how pupils will be assessed for any vacancies identified.

1.25 Chambers should identify, preferably at a specified time each year, how many starter tenants they wish to recruit. Chambers should, so far as possible with the assistance of the senior clerk, practice director or similar, determine the quantity and the nature of work available, or potentially available, for starter tenants.

1.26 Starter tenancies should be advertised where Chambers do not recruit from among their own pupils.

1.27 Many Chambers prefer to consider their own pupils for starter tenancies and some recruit all pupils with a view to a tenancy. This is not objectionable provided that pupillage selection procedures have been fair and non-discriminatory.

1.28 Whichever approach is taken, the following guidance is recommended:
   - all candidates for starter tenancies should be assessed according to an objective and transparent system of assessment, which may include an interview, and against the same criteria;
   - assessments in relation to the candidates' demonstrated abilities and potential should be obtained from a wide range of sources by reference to relevant criteria;
   - the sources will include records of any formal assessments of pupils conducted during their pupillage, assessments by barristers for whom the candidates have carried out work, including but not confined, to pupil supervisors, and feedback from instructing solicitors by whom candidates have been instructed;
   - all comments provided in relation to candidates should be considered solely by reference to the agreed selection criteria.

1.29 Chambers should aim to identify ability and potential with objectivity, filtering out so far as possible the subjective loyalties and favouritisms which may be felt by individual members of Chambers (in particular pupil supervisors) to particular pupils and the converse, such as subjective dislikes based on personal prejudice, whether conscious or unwitting.

1.30 Candidates for starter tenancies should be assessed by a committee of at least three members of Chambers, wherever possible excluding pupil supervisors who have supervised any of the candidates.

1.31 The decision to offer a starter tenancy should be made either by the committee as a whole or, on recommendation by the committee, by all or a substantial proportion of the members of Chambers.

Recruitment of Established Practitioners

1.32 Reference is made to the general guidance at paragraphs 1.1 to 1.17 above.

1.33 Vacancies for established practitioners should be advertised.

1.34 Exceptionally, Chambers may identify or may be approached by individuals or groups of established practitioners with particular experience or expertise in the field(s) in which the Chambers practises. In those circumstances, it may be legitimate to recruit without advertisement provided that such recruitment can be justified both in terms of Chambers' real business needs and in terms of the skills of those recruited. Chambers should be aware that recruitment of this nature may give rise to allegations of discrimination.

Mini-Pupillages

1.35 Where Chambers are unable to offer mini-pupillages to all who apply, Chambers should organise their mini-pupillages in such a way as to ensure equality of opportunity, so far as practicable, by applying objective criteria. Where mini-pupillages are assessed, the same or equivalent assessment materials should be provided to all candidates, who should be assessed by at least two assessors applying the same criteria.

B. FAIR ACCESS TO WORK

Allocation of Work in Chambers

1.36 The opportunities for barristers to develop a successful practice in their areas of interest are frequently affected by the range and quality of work on which they are instructed in the early stages of their careers and even in pupillage. Paragraph 404(2) of the Code of Conduct requires that Chambers take all reasonable steps to ensure that the affairs of Chambers are conducted in a manner which is fair and equitable for all barristers. This responsibility extends to the fair distribution of work amongst pupils and members of Chambers. Pupils and tenants are entitled to equality of opportunity in terms of being able to experience the full range of work and training undertaken by Chambers.

1.37 Pupils and junior tenants should be afforded the opportunity to develop their practices in a fair and equal manner. Discriminatory and stereotyped career assumptions may exist and procedures should be in place to ensure that patterns of instruction and briefing are transparent and open to scrutiny.

1.38 Chambers should have in place effective procedures for the monitoring of work allocation and for responding to (and rectifying where appropriate) complaints and concerns about work allocation. There should be procedures in place for ensuring the fair distribution of work, particularly un-named work and for providing support and guidance in respect of practice development and marketing.

1.39 The onus is on Chambers rather than on the individual pupil or barrister to ensure that there is fair access to work.

1.40   Chambers should ensure that its clerks use the clerks' room software to best advantage so that regular breakdowns of work are undertaken. Analysis should include the amount of work done, the type of work, fees earned and received and solicitors instructing. As a guideline, in respect of pupils and junior tenants, breakdowns should be produced at three monthly intervals. This information should be discussed with the pupil or junior tenant as part of their individual practice development, as well as being used to monitor Chambers' internal work distribution procedures and instructing solicitors' briefing practices.

1.41   One or more members of Chambers or appropriate practice manager should be responsible for overseeing the monitoring of work and should meet with the Senior Clerk on a regular basis in order to compare and review the work distribution data so as to ensure that work is distributed in a manner which is fair.

1.42   Chambers should be particularly aware of issues relating to the distribution of any un-named work coming into Chambers, and the redistribution of work between members of Chambers and pupils and junior tenants. These in particular should be systematically monitored to ensure that any disparities in allocation are identified and rectified.

1.43   Chambers should use the work distribution data to ascertain whether any instructing organisations or solicitors exhibit briefing practices which tend to favour a particular group. Any such trend should be considered by a designated member or members of Chambers to see if there is any underlying discriminatory practice.

1.44   If briefing practices are identified which disadvantage a particular group (for example allocating sex and child abuse cases predominantly to female practitioners) these should be addressed through the clerks' room. If the issue cannot be resolved through the clerks' room, it may need to be addressed by the Head of Chambers and the solicitor(s) involved.

1.45   Any unequal or unfair treatment of pupils and members of Chambers in the allocation of work should be treated as a serious matter and dealt with appropriately so that it does not recur.

1.46   Chambers should ensure that all clerks are fully briefed on the need to distribute work in a fair and non-discriminatory manner and to monitor work allocation. Clerks, and in particular those involved in the distribution and monitoring of work allocation, should be provided with equality and diversity training.

1.47   Chambers should seek to ensure, where possible, that instructions and briefs are not delivered by solicitors at such times as to preclude those with childcare and other dependent care commitments from being eligible for that work (for example, where a brief is not delivered until Friday afternoon for a trial on Monday). Late delivery of briefs may also disadvantage disabled barristers who may require the Court to make adjustments for them which cannot be made on the morning of a trial or hearing. Any solicitor who insists on a directly discriminatory allocation of work should be reported to his or her professional disciplinary body. The work should be refused.

Practice Development

1.48   Chambers should arrange regular feedback sessions for working pupils and practice development meetings for tenants. The purpose of these meetings is to enable discussion of the allocation of work, work opportunity and development of individual practices.

1.49   Chambers are encouraged to set up mentoring schemes whereby a junior tenant may be a pupil's 'mentor' and a junior tenant may be linked to a more senior member of Chambers who can offer advice and guidance regarding practice development in a mentoring role. This will be relevant also to barristers returning to practice following a career break.

Marketing of Barristers and Pupils

1.50   Marketing strategies for tenants and pupils should take into account equal opportunities considerations. For example, socialising after work in the pub may provide an effective means of 'networking' for those who do not have childcare commitments or substantial student debts or both. Socialising in the pub may exclude pupils and junior tenants whose religious beliefs preclude the drinking of alcohol. Chambers should be sensitive to these issues and should ensure that marketing and networking activities are organised so that all pupils and tenants can, so far as practicable, be equally involved.

1.51   Chambers should encourage pupils and junior tenants to take part in Chambers' seminars and lectures, attend outside seminars and lectures, write or contribute to articles in professional publications, become involved in professional organisations connected to their line of work and become involved with any legal advice or support centres or organisations.

1.52   The organisation of regular 'Practice Group Meetings' within Chambers is encouraged as a means of discussing individual and Chambers' issues and as a means of integrating pupils and members of Chambers.

C. MATERNITY, PATERNITY AND PARENTAL LEAVE

Written Policies

1.53   All Chambers of more than one tenant should have a written policy on maternity, paternity, parental leave and flexible working. This policy should contain particulars of:

- the member's right to return to Chambers after a specified period of leave;
- the extent of the periods of leave offered free of Chambers' rent and expenses;
- the manner in which the rent and expenses to be waived, deducted or reimbursed in respect of a period of leave will be calculated;
- the member's entitlement to work part-time or flexibly or to take a career break for childcare or other reasons;
- the procedure for dealing with grievances under the policy;
- Chambers' commitment regularly to review the effectiveness of the policy.

Period of Leave Free of Rent and Chambers' Expenses

1.54   The Maternity, Paternity and Flexible Working Policy Approved by the Bar Council recommends that Chambers should offer their members taking maternity leave or leave following adoption, a minimum period of six months' free of Chambers' rent and expenses. This rent-free period should apply irrespective of whether the Chambers' rent is calculated as a percentage of fees earned or is a flat rate payment. The mechanics of calculation will be a matter for individual Chambers depending upon how rent is paid. For women paying a percentage of receipts, one option is to base the calculation of the rent free period on average earnings over the preceding twelve months. The rent-free period could be applied during the six months after the woman has returned to Chambers as this would be a time of relatively low income. Policies may need to cover matters such as clerks' fees, mortgage repayments and any contributions payable in respect of one-off investments, as appropriate.

1.55 The Maternity, Paternity and Flexible Working Policy Approved by the Bar Council recommends that members of Chambers should be offered a minimum of one month's leave free of Chambers' rent and expenses following the birth or adoption of a child by their partner, where they have or share responsibility for that child and so that they can discharge that responsibility.

1.56 These recommended minimum periods of leave are not intended to discourage Chambers from adopting a more generous policy.

Right to Return to Chambers

1.57 The Bar Council recommends that a woman should have the right to return to her Chambers as a tenant following the birth or adoption of a child. The right to return should continue for a guaranteed period of at least a year. During that period, she should be able to return to Chambers without the need to re-apply for admission. Chambers are encouraged to offer a longer period of leave.

1.58 The recommendation in paragraph 1.57 should also be applied to a man who adopts and is the principal carer of the adopted child.

Assistance to Return to Chambers and to Work During Maternity Leave or Career Break

1.59 Chambers are encouraged to respond positively to members' wishes to work during their maternity leave or any career break. Chambers' written policy should set out how Chambers plan to assist their members to keep in touch with Chambers and with practice developments during any period of leave and to return to practice. Invitations to training events, social occasions and information on Chambers' business should be passed on to members on maternity leave or a career break and Chambers should endeavour to consult with them in relation to major Chambers' decisions which may affect the member's practice.

Grievance Procedures, Monitoring and Review

1.60 Chambers should adopt procedures which enable members to raise concerns about the Chambers' maternity, paternity and flexible working policy and its application. There should be one or more Chambers Equal Opportunity Officers (see para 2.14 below) who can respond to queries about the policy and provide reports on its effectiveness and value. The policy should be circulated to all members, clerks and staff of chambers so that they understand the policy and their role in relation to it.

D. FLEXIBLE AND PART-TIME WORKING AND CAREER BREAKS

Bar Council Recommendations

1.61 All Chambers of more than one tenant should have written policies permitting members of Chambers (female or male) to take career breaks, work flexible hours, part-time or partly from home to enable them to manage their family responsibilities and remain in practice. Such policies should reflect, in particular, the needs of the primary carer in relation to childcare responsibilities.

Written Policy

1.62 Chambers' arrangements for the payment of rent should not constitute disincentives to flexible working. Earnings related arrangements for the payment of rent may be preferable to fixed rates. A policy of fixed rent without any qualification is potentially indirectly discriminatory against women because it is likely to impact on a greater proportion of women than men (see para 2.18.b where indirect discrimination is explained). Rent arrangements need to reflect the economic effect on the individual and the Chambers, as do arrangements such as desk space and any capital benefit obtained from mortgage repayments on property acquired by a set of Chambers.

1.63 Members of Chambers working on flexible working arrangements should be included in Chambers' business and in Chambers' continuing professional development, marketing and social activities in the same way as full-time working members of Chambers.

Advantages of Flexible Working

1.64 Flexible working arrangements should assist in retaining some of the disproportionately high number of women who leave the Bar, including those who leave after having children. This is a loss to the Bar because the presence of women at senior levels broadens the profession's diversity, increases the number of women in the pool for judicial appointment and strengthens and enhances the profession's marketability. It is also a loss to Chambers in terms of the wasted investment in training and the gap left in seniority.

1.65 The availability of flexible working arrangements is likely to increase commitment to Chambers and the profession and improve morale.

1.66 The Bar has always accommodated flexible working: allowing barristers to combine practice at the Bar with part-time judicial appointments, writing, academic or political appointments. Flexible working for reasons associated with child care or other domestic responsibilities can and should be treated in a similar way. Barristers are already accustomed to working in teams and returning work to their colleagues when they are unavailable.

1.67 The arrangements which any particular Chambers puts in place will need to reflect the nature of the membership and the work undertaken. Systems such as telephone conferencing, and e-mail should be used to best advantage to enable members of Chambers to conduct their practices from home where desired. Different working patterns may suit different individuals: for example, working during school term times only for a parent with children of school age.

1.68 Individual practitioners should recognise that reduced working hours will have an economic effect on their Chambers and should themselves be proactive in seeking to agree fair arrangements for rent and the use of Chambers resources, including accommodation, with their Chambers. Rental arrangements should be agreed and understood before any period of flexible working commences.

E. HARASSMENT

What is Harassment?

1.69   Harassment is any form of unwanted conduct which has the aim or effect of diminishing a person's dignity or creating a humiliating or offensive environment for that person. The fact that one person may be able to ignore or deal comfortably with certain behaviour does not mean that it is acceptable if directed at another. A single incident may constitute harassment if it is sufficiently serious. The motive or intention of the perpetrator is normally irrelevant (see para 2.18 in relation to harassment which also constitutes unlawful discrimination).

1.70   There is now a criminal offence of intentional harassment. It covers harassment on any ground. The Act defines harassment as the use of 'threatening, abusive or insulting words or behaviour; or disorderly behaviour' or displays of writing, signs or other visible representation which is threatening, abusive or insulting, and includes harassment at the workplace. Harassment amounting to physical or sexual assault is also a serious criminal offence and victims should be encouraged to report it to the police.

Policy

1.71   All Chambers should have a harassment policy, which sets out a clear summary of the type of behaviour which is unacceptable in the working environment and the procedures for dealing with complaints about such behaviour. The policy should apply to all members and employees of Chambers, squatters and pupils and personal copies should be provided.

1.72   Complaints of harassment are sensitive and Chambers should adopt policies which enable them to react quickly and appropriately if a complaint is raised. It becomes much more difficult to deal with complaints effectively where there is delay.

Guidance

1.73   Harassment causes distress. It can lead to impaired work performance, sickness, and even to recipients leaving Chambers altogether. Many recipients of harassment are afraid to complain. They fear that their complaint will be trivialised or that they will be subject to ridicule or reprisals or that nothing will be done.

1.74   Examples of behaviour which may amount to harassment based on sex, race, disability, religion or sexual orientation include:

- physical assault, including sexual assault;
- demands for sexual favours in return for career advancement;
- unnecessary physical contact;
- exclusion from social networks and activities;
- isolation;
- bullying;
- compromising suggestions or invitations;
- suggestive remarks or looks;
- display of offensive materials, including on computer screen;
- tasteless jokes or verbal abuse;

- offensive remarks or ridicule;

- dealing inappropriately with complaints of harassment.

1.75 By undertaking certain specific steps, Chambers should be able to alleviate the problems of harassment in the context of work related relationships. In particular, the following is recommended:

- a policy statement which makes it clear that harassment will not be tolerated or condoned and that employees, members of Chambers, pupils and others temporarily in chambers such as mini-pupils have a right to complain if it occurs;

- effective communication of the policy to all those to whom it applies;

- active promotion of the policy by people in managerial positions;

- training for those in managerial and supervisory roles on how to keep the working environment free of harassment and how to deal with it should it occur;

- the provision of informal means of resolving harassment in the first instance;

- the designation of an adviser to assist employees and others subjected to harassment;

- a formal complaints procedure, which should be monitored and reviewed;

- an independent, objective, sensitive and fair procedure for internal investigations of complaints; and

- a principle of treating violations of the harassment policy as a disciplinary offence.

1.76 Often victims of harassment just want the harassment to stop and do not wish to see the harasser disciplined. There are various informal methods by which Chambers can deal with complaints of harassment, including:

- telling the harasser that their behaviour is unacceptable and asking them to stop immediately (if the recipient feels able to challenge the harasser directly or indirectly in this way);

- seeking the help and advice of the Inns' Student Officers where the harassment occurs in an Inn of Court or at an Inn's sponsored event;

- seeking the help and advice of the Bar Council's Equality and Diversity Advisers directly or by calling the confidential telephone number 020 7611 1310;

- seeking the help and advice of pupil supervisors or other members of Chambers.

Formal Resolution Options

1.77 Where informal methods fail to resolve the issue, or where the harassment complained of is of a more serious nature to begin with, one or more of the following formal methods of resolution may be appropriate:

- the initiation of Chambers' formal complaints or grievance procedure;

- contacting the relevant Inn to make a formal complaint where the complaint concerns a sponsor or pupil supervisor or something occurring at an Inn sponsored event;

- a complaint to the Professional Conduct Committee which has in place a special protocol for dealing with complaints of harassment;

- initiation of the Bar Council's mediation procedure in confidence through the Bar Council's EDAs. The Mediation Panel is made up of individual members of the Bar who have received training in harassment mediation. The role of the panel is to advise the complainant and, with his or her permission, to mediate between the parties, without necessarily finding fault or blame and without the imposition of sanctions;

- in extreme cases, the complainant might consider whether a complaint should be made to the police where the act complained of amounts to a criminal offence or whether a complaint of unlawful discrimination might be brought in a County Court or employment tribunal.

F. COMPLAINTS AND GRIEVANCES

Complaints Handled Internally

1.78 The Bar Council recommends that all Chambers should have a written grievance procedure and that this should include procedures for handling complaints of discrimination and harassment. The procedure should be brought to the attention of every pupil, tenant and Chambers' employee.

1.79 It is important for a person who has a complaint about discrimination, particularly where harassment is alleged, to have access to someone who can give them sympathetic advice and, if necessary, counselling. This should take place in an atmosphere of total confidentiality.

1.80 Complaints and grievances should be dealt with promptly, objectively and fairly.

1.81 In order to assist in the effective resolution of grievances within Chambers it is recommended that, in addition to the formal procedure, Chambers should nominate one or two members of Chambers to act as informal advisers to potential complainants, and to assist, when asked, in the informal resolution of grievances.

1.82 Barristers who have paid their voluntary subscriptions and their clerks may also approach the Bar Council Arbitration and Conciliation Service to resolve disputes between barristers themselves and between barristers and their clerks.

1.83 Chambers' employees are able to raise complaints through the new statutory grievance procedures which, together with statutory dismissal and disciplinary procedures, are an implied term of all contracts of employment in all Chambers regardless of size or number of employees.

1.84 When a complaint is made, in the interests of all concerned, confidentiality should be maintained throughout any investigatory process as far as possible and as appropriate in the circumstances. Names of complainants must not be released (save to those conducting the investigation and to the person complained against) without their consent.

Formal Procedures

1.85 Formal grievance procedures should include:

- the allocation of responsibility for investigating complaints to at least two members of Chambers, including one senior member, each of whom should be familiar with the Code of Conduct and the Equality and Diversity Code for the Bar. In the event of a conflict of interest, provision should be made for the involvement of additional members of Chambers, or other nominated persons;

- names of Chambers' informal advisers;
- an undertaking that complainants will not be victimised or suffer detriment because of a complaint made in good faith;
- an undertaking that all procedures will, as far as practicable, be confidential;
- a requirement for the complaint to be made in writing;
- a time limit within which a written response should be delivered;
- the range of remedial actions where complaints are substantiated;
- identification of the relevant Bar Council Committees and external bodies to which complaints may be addressed;
- an indication of opportunities for support and counselling provided by the associations and groups for women lawyers, members of minority ethnic groups, disabled people, lesbians or gay men, the Pupil Barristers' Group or the Mature Entrants' Group. Confidential assistance may also be sought from the Equal Opportunities Officers at the Bar Council.

Complaints of Unfair Work Allocation

1.86 By establishing regular monitoring and reviews of allocation of work, Chambers should reduce the need for formal complaints by providing a regular opportunity to identify and remedy problems. Where there is a complaint about the distribution of work from a pupil or tenant, the complaints procedure set out above should apply. A set period during which more detailed monitoring of the distribution of work will take place, may be included as a step in the investigation of the complaint.

Complaints of Harassment

1.87 See paragraphs 1.73 to 1.77 above.

Remedies

1.88 Where, following investigation of a complaint, actual or potential discrimination has been identified, remedial action should be taken immediately. This may include all or some of the following:

- a re-evaluation of the applications and/or another interview with another panel (eg for a complaint from an unsuccessful applicant for pupillage, tenancy or a job);
- a change of practice (eg in relation to unfair work allocation);
- implementation of a reasonable adjustment (in relation to a complaint from a disabled person);
- further advice, briefing or training for the members of selection panels, Chambers clerks and staff;
- advice and support to ensure that the complainant is not victimised as a consequence of making a complaint in good faith;
- disciplinary action.

1.89 A report on all complaints, and on the findings of the investigations, should be made to the Head of Chambers. Chambers should maintain confidential records of all complaints and records of meetings. These should be reviewed annually to ensure that the procedures are working effectively.

1.90 Chambers may be required to explain how they investigated any complaint that is taken to the Bar Council or other external body. An analysis of any complaints received will also be useful in identifying problem areas, training needs or scope for further action when Chambers review their procedures.

Complaints Made to External Bodies

1.91 Any individual (member of Chambers, pupil, employee or client) may complain about the conduct of an individual barrister to the Professional Conduct and Complaints Committee of the Bar Council, or to the Inn about a pupil supervisor.

1.92 Where an individual has a statutory complaint of unlawful discrimination, the complaint may be pursued through the employment tribunals or County Court as appropriate.

G. SERVICE PROVISION

Service provision to disabled clients

Introduction

1.93 This section will focus on the practical issues connected with service delivery, as it relates to disability, within the context of the legislative framework. It is designed to assist Chambers and individual barristers to comply with the disability legislation and generally to improve the services offered to disabled people by the Bar.

1.94 Disability is not always visible and many disabled people choose not to disclose their disability. Disability encompasses, for example, certain musculo-skeletal problems, circulatory conditions and mental illness.

1.95 Barristers are likely to come into professional contact with many disabled people including lay and professional clients, colleagues, pupils, members of the judiciary, witnesses and staff within the judicial system.

Obligations Under the Disability Discrimination Act 1995 ('DDA')

Who are the Clients to Whom Duties are Owed?

1.96 Obligations are owed to 'disabled' persons. The term 'disabled' receives a statutory definition in section 1 of the DDA. The disabled person may be the lay client or any person from the instructing solicitors. The duties under this code will also apply to other persons to whom the barrister or set of Chambers provide services or come into contact (such as witnesses in a case).

Who Owes the Duties?

1.97 A set of Chambers will be a 'service provider' for the purposes of the provisions of the DDA dealing with discrimination in the provision of services. A set of Chambers will therefore owe duties under section 19 of the DDA both to the lay client and to the professional client. An individual barrister will also be a service provider and will therefore owe duties as such under the DDA.

What are the Duties?

1.98 The DDA makes it is unlawful for a barrister or set of Chambers to discriminate against a disabled person:

- by refusing to provide (or deliberately not providing) any service which it provides (or is prepared to provide) to members of the public; or

- in the standard of service which it provides to the disabled person or the manner in which it provides that service; or

- in the terms on which it provides a service to the disabled person (section 19 DDA).

1.99 Pro bono cases remain part of service provision and are subject to exactly the same duties as paid cases. Providing conference facilities at Chambers is also deemed to be the provision of a service.

1.100 It is also unlawful for service providers such as a set of Chambers or an individual barrister to discriminate in failing to comply with a duty to make reasonable adjustments (section 21 DDA).

1.101 The following are the duties owed by a service provider to a disabled person:

- not to discriminate against the disabled person by treating the disabled person less favourably for a reason related to the disabled person's disability (section 20(1));

- not to discriminate against the disabled person by failing to comply with a duty to make a reasonable adjustment causing the disabled person to find it either impossible or unreasonably difficult to use the service provider's services for example by failing to remove, alter or avoid physical features which make it impossible or unreasonably difficult for the disabled person to use the service;

- not to victimise any person (whether disabled or not) by treating them less favourably because they brought proceedings, gave evidence or information or made allegations relating to the DDA.

1.102 It is possible to justify discrimination against a disabled person but only in certain limited circumstances, defined in the DDA.

Less Favourable Treatment

1.103 A service provider discriminates against a disabled person if, for a reason which relates to the disabled person's disability, it treats the disabled person less favourably than it treats (or would treat) others to whom the reason does not (or would not) apply and it cannot show that the treatment in question is justified (section 20(1) DDA).

It is not necessary that the barrister knows that the person is a disabled person for less favourable treatment to occur.

1.104 It is unlawful to refuse to serve a disabled person or deliberately not serve the disabled person for a reason relating to the disabled person's disability (section 19(1)(a) DDA).

1.105 It is unlawful to provide service of a lower standard or in a worse manner to a person for a reason relating to the disabled person's disability (section 19(1)(c) DDA).

1.106 It is unlawful to provide a disabled person with a service on worse terms (for example by charging more) for a reason relating to that person's disability (section 19(1)(d) DDA).

1.107 Chambers should note that the DDA does not prohibit positive action in favour of disabled people (see para 2.2 for distinction between positive action and positive discrimination). The protection of the DDA confers positive advantages on disabled people in certain respects.

The Duty to Make Reasonable Adjustments

1.108 As a service provider, a set of Chambers is required to make reasonable adjustments in several areas unless it can show that the failure to make a reasonable adjustment is justified.

1.109 The duty to make reasonable adjustments is owed to disabled people at large and not just individual disabled people. Barristers and Chambers therefore should not wait until a disabled person wants to use their services before investigating the need to make reasonable adjustments. It is recommended that barristers and Chambers should look at adjustments that they can make on an ongoing basis (whether or not they currently provide services to disabled people). The idea is to anticipate the requirements of disabled people and in order to do this effectively consultation should take place with existing disabled clients or disabled potential clients. Whilst this may not be possible to do on an individual basis, barristers and Chambers should consider consulting organisations of disabled persons to obtain their views.

1.110 The law requires reasonable adjustments to be made in the following areas:

- changing practices, policies and procedures;
- providing auxiliary aids and services;
- adjusting a physical feature by either removing the feature or altering it or ensuring that it can be avoided, or providing services by alternative means.

1.111 The service provider has a duty to take reasonable steps to change the policy, practice or procedure which makes it impossible or unreasonably difficult for disabled people to make use of its services.

1.112 When considering whether the services of a barrister or Chambers are unreasonably difficult for disabled people to use, account should be taken of whether the time, inconvenience, effort, discomfort or loss of dignity entailed in using the service would be considered unreasonable by other people if they had to endure similar difficulties. There may be unreasonable difficulty, for example, where a client in a wheelchair has to be carried up three steps to a conference room.

1.113 It is sensible to try to anticipate the needs of disabled clients rather than acting in a wholly reactive way. Consultation with organisations of disabled people about the needs of a group which may use the services of Chambers will help to give Chambers an idea of the kind of adjustments that it may need to make. Similarly an individual barrister should consider consulting such organisations if he or she anticipates working with a disabled person on a particular case. Chambers and individual barristers should therefore indicate that reasonable adjustments will be made on request if this will assist disabled people to use their services.

1.114 Chambers or a barrister may discriminate unlawfully even if they do not know that a client is disabled. It is worthwhile remembering that not all disabilities are visible. What is important is not to act on assumptions, but to be prepared to ask in advance what reasonable adjustments can be made to ensure that the service of Chambers or the barrister can be used without the disabled person being put to unreasonable difficulty. If it is not reasonable to anticipate a particular requirement the barrister will not act unlawfully if he or she does not anticipate it.

1.115 The duty to make reasonable adjustments is a continuing duty, and it may be necessary to make more than one adjustment. The best approach is to consider what changes can be made in practical terms to ensure that the disabled person can use the barrister's or Chambers' services without unreasonable difficulty. The disabled person should be consulted about what he or she believes is the best solution. That view is not going to be conclusive and the barrister will have to consider what is a reasonable step to have to take in order to achieve this end.

1.116 In deciding whether it is reasonable to take any particular step, consideration could be given to whether it would be effective in overcoming the difficulty that disabled people face in accessing the services of Chambers or the barrister. Consider whether it would be practicable to take the step, and the financial and other costs of making the adjustment. Some steps which are suggested would cause disruption. A certain amount of disruption can be required but not a disproportionate amount. Chambers and barristers are entitled to take account of financial and other resources as well as the amount of resources already spent on making adjustments.

1.117 What needs to be borne in mind is the ultimate aim of rendering services accessible without unreasonable difficulty. Making adjustments for one group of disabled people will not absolve the Chambers from making different adjustments for different disabled people.

1.118 Providing access to Chambers for any purpose is also covered. Both the set of Chambers and also the Inns of Court may owe duties to members of the public attending Chambers. If the Inns of Court do not provide a reasonable means of access to Chambers through the common parts so that access through them remains impossible or unreasonably difficult for disabled people (which may result from difficulties in obtaining planning permission), the Chambers may have duties to provide a reasonable means of avoiding the physical feature which is causing the difficulty. In those circumstances, Chambers will also have a duty to provide a reasonable alternative method of making its services available to disabled persons. For example a Chambers which does not have wheelchair access may have to consider holding conferences with a wheelchair user away from Chambers.

1.119 If Chambers decides to make adjustments to its premises these should be drawn to the attention of disabled people (for example by a sign). Similarly if it is the intention of Chambers to make its services accessible by providing auxiliary aids, this should be made known.

1.120 It will be exceptionally rare for a Chambers or a barrister not to have to make any adjustments that would render services accessible to disabled persons. It is strongly recommended that a periodic audit be conducted by a nominated person in Chambers who should be mandated to discuss matters with individual barristers.

1.121   There is no obligation on Chambers or a barrister to take any steps which would fundamentally alter the nature of its service.

1.122   When a barrister or Chambers complies with the duty to make reasonable adjustments they are not entitled to pass on any additional costs of compliance solely to disabled clients.

1.123   The duty to make adjustments may affect the Chambers' policies (what it intends to do), its policies (how it plans to go about providing its services) and its practices (what it actually does when providing services).

1.124   The barrister or set of Chambers must take reasonable steps to provide auxiliary aids including equipment or services if these would facilitate disabled people using its services. An auxiliary aid may be the provision of a special piece of equipment but it is more likely, in the case of barrister services, simply to be the provision of some extra assistance to disabled people.

1.125   The obligation is to take such steps as it is reasonable for the barrister or Chambers to take in all the circumstances of the case to make it services accessible to disabled people. Therefore consideration needs to be given to the size and resources of the Chambers (or the resources of the individual barrister) as well as the cost of providing the auxiliary service.

1.126   The Disability Rights Commission (DRC) Code of Practice gives examples of the kind of auxiliary services or aids that may be appropriate for people with hearing disability (para 5.23 and following) and visual impairments (para 5.26 and following).

Adjustments to Physical Features

1.127   In terms of physical features it is advisable that an access audit should be carried out on a Chambers' premises. During this the views of people with different disabilities or those representing them should be sought, as this may help in identifying barriers and developing solutions. The best approach to removing the effect of physical features on accessibility is to alter the physical feature itself so as to create an inclusive environment. Removal of physical barriers will be preferable to alternative arrangements. There is an inherent loss of dignity for the disabled person in having to use some alternative route for example. It is only if it is not reasonable to remove the physical feature, or to alter it, that such alternative route adjustments should be made.

1.128   The DRC Code contains specific guidance on how the building regulations and leases affect reasonable adjustment duties. What needs to be borne in mind is that the duty to make adjustments will still arise in respect of any access issues and regardless of whether no physical adjustments are required or permitted.

1.129   Adjustments to physical features may require the consent of the landlord. Regulations provide that it is reasonable for the service provider to have to request consent but that it is not automatically reasonable for the service provider to have to make an alteration just because consent has been given. In essence the landlord may not unreasonably refuse consent to a reasonable alteration which is necessary to comply with the duty to make adjustments. The landlord is entitled to attach reasonable conditions to the consent. Detailed guidance is given in the DRC's Code concerning these regulations and the obtaining of consent (see para 1.126 above).

Justification

1.130 Both less favourable treatment and a failure to make reasonable adjustments may be justified on specific grounds which are set out in section 20(4) of the DDA provided that the discrimination is not direct discrimination. The Chambers or the barrister must reasonably believe that one or more of the following conditions are satisfied:

- the service provider is not obliged to do anything which would endanger the health or safety of any person;

- the disabled person is incapable of entering into an enforceable agreement, or of giving an informed consent, and for that reason the treatment is reasonable in that case;

- (in relation to refusing to provide, or deliberately not providing, any service) the treatment is necessary because the Chambers or barrister would otherwise be unable to provide the service to members of the public;

- (in relation to the standard of service or the terms on which it is provided) the treatment is necessary in order for the Chambers or barrister to be able to provide the service to the disabled person or to other members of the public.

- (In relation to the terms on which the service is provided) the difference in the terms on which the service is provided to the disabled person and those on which it is provided to other members of the public reflects the greater cost to the provider of services in providing the service to the disabled person. However any increase in the cost of providing a service to the disabled person resulting from compliance with the duty to make reasonable adjustments is disregarded for this purpose.

Other Areas of Potentially Discriminatory Service Provision

1.131 Discrimination by barristers as service providers on the ground of race or sex is unlawful. Discrimination on any other ground covered in paragraph 305 of the Code of Conduct is prohibited.

1.132 Examples of discriminatory service provision include the following:

- the racial or sexual harassment of a professional or lay client;

- a refusal to accept instructions to act on behalf of individuals or groups defined by their race, sex, sexuality, religion or belief;

- providing a service that is inappropriate (eg timing of conferences with clients with childcare responsibilities);

- failing to take account of the religious needs of clients in relation to dress, food and drink or religious observance;

- asking irrelevant questions based upon assumptions about client's sexuality.

1.133 Chambers should ensure that their members are equipped to provide an appropriate level of service for their clients by arranging diversity training for members of chambers and chambers staff. Clients whose first language is not English may have particular needs for interpreters and the Bar Council has produced a guidance document on this subject.

H. STAFF IN CHAMBERS

1.134 Practice Management for the Bar sets out standards and guidelines covering the main areas of practice management. This includes recruitment and a section on personnel management which states the recommended standards for managing staff together with detailed guidance on their implementation. The comprehensive guidance in Practice Management is not replicated in this document. The recommendations for good practice set out here in earlier chapters are equally applicable to chambers staff and many of them explicitly include chambers staff.

1.135 Recruitment of chambers' staff should follow the recommendations relating to pupillage and tenancy recruitment wherever appropriate, for example open advertisements, clear and objective selection criteria and panel interviews.

1.136 It is important to ensure that all equal opportunity policy initiatives developed in Chambers cover staff as well as members of Chambers whenever appropriate. The Equal Opportunities Commission, Commission for Racial Equality and Disability Rights Commission have all developed Codes of Practice in recruitment.

Maternity, Paternity, Parental Leave

1.137 A policy for staff will differ markedly from a policy for members. Chambers should set out their policy for staff on maternity, paternity and parental leave and flexible working. This should, at least, meet the minimum legislative requirements. These provide for:

- time off for ante-natal care;
- periods of paid and unpaid maternity leave for women following childbirth;
- paternity leave and pay for fathers;
- adoption leave and pay for individuals who adopt or one partner of a couple who jointly adopt;
- paternity leave and pay for the other member of the couple;
- parental leave for up to 13 weeks for parents with children (including adopted) under the age of six. This is extended to eighteen if the child is disabled.
- a reasonable amount of unpaid time off to deal with an emergency situation.

Complaints and Grievances

1.138 Chambers should have a written complaints and grievance procedure for staff which includes procedures covering complaints of discrimination and harassment. These should provide for both formal and informal routes for making complaints. Chambers should nominate an 'approachable' person in chambers to act as an informal adviser to staff. For further information see Action Area F.

SECTION 2: LEGAL & REGULATORY FRAMEWORK

Statutory Regulation

2.1 Barristers owe a legal duty not to discriminate on grounds of race, sex, disability, sexual orientation or religion or belief and a duty not to discriminate indirectly or to victimise in:

- the recruitment of staff and the selection of pupils and tenants;
- the terms, opportunities for training or gaining experience, benefits and services for prospective or current members of staff, pupils and tenants;

- the termination of service of staff or the termination of pupillage or tenancy, including pressure to leave;
- subjecting staff, pupils or tenants to detrimental treatment.

2.2   Discrimination following termination of the relationship between barristers and staff, pupils or tenants may be unlawful where there is sufficient connection between the relationship and the discriminatory act complained of, for example in the provision of references or post-employment benefits.

2.3   It is unlawful for barristers to discriminate against lay or professional clients in the provision of services on grounds of sex or race or for reasons relating to disability.

2.4   Discrimination 'on racial grounds' encompasses nationality, race, colour and ethnic origins.

2.5   Sex discrimination encompasses not only gender but also marital status, pregnancy and gender reassignment. Discrimination on grounds of pregnancy is a particular type of sex discrimination where no comparator is required, so that it is no defence to a claim based on pregnancy that a man absent by reason of sickness would have been treated in a similar fashion.

2.6   Many of the duties apply to barristers' clerks as they apply to barristers.

2.7   Disability is a legal concept defined in the DDA. It includes not only obvious visible disability but may include conditions such as manic depression or other mental impairment. Particular rules are made in respect of progressive conditions such as cancer. There is a positive duty to make reasonable adjustments to accommodate a disabled person, such as providing communications equipment or alterations to premises.

2.8   Age discrimination will be outlawed as from 2006.[12]

2.9   The relevant statutory provisions are to be found in the Sex Discrimination Act 1975, Race Relations Act 1976, Disability Discrimination Act 1995, Employment Equality (Sexual Orientation) Regulations 2003, Employment Equality (Religion and Belief) Regulations 2003, Disability Discrimination Act 1995 (Amendment) Regulations 2003; EU Equal Treatment, Race Discrimination and Framework Employment Directives.

Bar Code of Conduct

2.10 Paragraph 305 of the Code of Conduct prohibits discrimination directly or indirectly by a practising barrister in relation to:

- any other person including a lay or professional client, another barrister, a pupil or student member of an Inn of Court

on the following grounds:

- race, colour, ethnic or national origin, nationality, citizenship, sex, sexual orientation, marital status, disability, religion or political persuasion.

2.11 To the extent that discrimination *in the provision of services* is not unlawful (for example, where discrimination is on grounds of sexual orientation or religious belief), the Code of Conduct makes such discrimination a matter of professional misconduct.

---

[12] See Age Discrimination (Employment) Regulations SI 2006/1031.

2.12 Discrimination on grounds of age in relation to pupillage and tenancy selection is prohibited unless it can be shown to be objectively and reasonably justifiable (para 305 (ii)).

2.13 The Code of Conduct, paragraph 403 requires a barrister to have regard to this code, which is likely to be taken into account by Courts, tribunals and disciplinary panels in deciding whether discrimination has occurred.

2.14 Paragraph 404.2(d) of the Code of Conduct[1] requires that Chambers

a. appoint at least one Equal Opportunity Officer; and

b. have a written equal opportunities policy made available to all members of Chambers and staff and to the Bar Council when requested, which shall set out the policy adopted by the Chambers in relation to each of the Action Areas in the Equality and Diversity Code and shall have regard to the recommendations in the Equality and Diversity Code;

c. shall not hold itself out as offering pupillages until the steps set out in a. and b. above have been complied with.

2.15 The Pupillage and Funding Requirements 2003, set out in Annexe R of the Code of Conduct, require that

2.16 all vacancies for pupillage are advertised on a website designated by the Bar Council, subject to limited exceptions.

Bar Council Equal Opportunity Policy Statement

2.17 The Bar Council, in pursuit of its constitutional function to represent the interests of the Bar and its statutory functions under the Courts and Legal Services Act 1990, will promote equality of opportunity irrespective of race, colour, ethnic or national origin, nationality, citizenship, sex, marital status, sexual orientation, disability, age, religion or political persuasion.

In accordance with the Code of Conduct of the Bar of England and Wales, discrimination by a barrister is professional misconduct and the Bar Council will take disciplinary action against any barrister or employee of the Bar Council found to have discriminated.

The Bar Council will monitor the effectiveness of its policy and the achievement of its objectives.

Key Concepts

2.18 Unlawful discrimination generally falls into one of three categories:

a. Direct discrimination: where one person is treated less favourably than another was or would be treated in the same or similar circumstances because of a particular characteristic identified in the anti-discrimination legislation (gender, race, disability, sexual orientation or religion or belief);

b. Indirect discrimination: where an apparently neutral provision, criterion or practice has a disadvantageous impact upon a particular group and where the provision, criterion or practice is not a proportionate means of achieving a

---

[1] This amendment to paragraph 404 is awaiting the Department for Constitutional Affairs' approval.

legitimate aim (for example, holding an internal Chambers training seminar at a time when a particular group of members will find it difficult to attend and when the meeting could reasonably be held at some other time which would not exclude any particular group);

c. Victimisation: where a person is treated less favourably because he or she has brought proceedings under the anti-discrimination legislation, given evidence or information relating to proceedings or has alleged that unlawful discrimination has occurred (or is suspected of intending to do any of the above).

2.19 It is not a defence to claims for direct discrimination and victimisation that there was no intention to discriminate or that the discrimination was justified, save that discrimination for a reason related to disability can be justified if the reason for the treatment is substantial and material. This defence of justification has been applied very narrowly by the courts. In relation to indirect discrimination, treatment may be justified if it can be shown that it is a proportionate means of achieving a legitimate aim but the lack of an intention to discriminate is not a defence.

2.20 Discriminatory treatment may amount to harassment. Harassment is any form of unwanted conduct which is intended to, or which creates the effect of, violating a person's dignity or which creates an intimidating, hostile, degrading, humiliating or offensive environment for that person. The fact that one person may be able to ignore or deal comfortably with certain behaviour does not mean that it is acceptable if directed at another. A single incident may constitute harassment if it is sufficiently serious. The motive or intention of the perpetrator may be (but is not invariably) relevant. Where harassment is on a ground identified in the anti-discrimination legislation, it will be unlawful. There is a new free-standing definition of harassment contained in various regulations; the relevant provisions are the Race Relations Act 1976 (Amendment) Regulations 2003; the Employment Equality (Sexual Orientation) Regulations 2003; the Employment Equality (Religion or Belief) Regulations 2003; and the Disability Discrimination Act 1995 (Amendment) Regulations 2003.

2.21 Any 'detriment' on a prohibited ground and in a protected area (e.g. employment and provision of services) will amount to unlawful discrimination. Detrimental treatment includes any treatment which the complainant reasonably perceives as disadvantageous.

2.22 The concepts applicable under the Disability Discrimination Act 1995 ('the DDA') are in some respects different from other discrimination legislation. The DDA covers claims for direct discrimination which cannot be justified. Barristers and their clerks have a further duty under the DDA to make reasonable adjustments to ensure that a disabled person is not placed at a disadvantage.

Clarifying Some Common Misconceptions

2.23 Proof of discrimination does not depend on showing motive or bad faith. It is possible to discriminate without intending to discriminate. Even treatment which is well-intentioned may amount to discrimination.

2.24 There is no defence of 'joke' or 'banter'. Jokes and banter which cause offence may be discriminatory even though there was no intention to cause offence.

2.25 Discrimination which involves the more favourable treatment of a member of a disadvantaged group ('positive discrimination') is unlawful in relation to persons encompassed within the anti-discrimination legislation, save that a form of positive discrimination may be exercised in relation to disabled persons who may require particular adjustments to be made. Applications may be encouraged from groups which are under-represented in an organisation (this is known as 'positive action') but applicants from such groups cannot be positively advantaged in any selection process.

2.26 Individuals from the same protected group may commit acts of unlawful discrimination against each other: a woman may unlawfully discriminate against another woman, for example, or a barrister in one racial group against another member of that group.

2.27 Some common misconceptions can be dispelled by appropriate diversity training or by access to information such as that provided to judges by the Judicial Studies Board's Bench Book (see para 1.133).

How Does an Individual Prove Discrimination?

2.28 If there is a difference in treatment and a difference in the relevant identifying characteristic (eg gender) of two persons in the same or similar circumstances, an inference of unlawful discrimination may be drawn. It is rare for discriminatory attitudes to be expressed overtly and unlawful discrimination may take place without the perpetrator being conscious that he or she is discriminating. The inference drawing process is the method by which Courts and tribunals test whether there has been unlawful discrimination.

2.29 In looking at whether inferences should be drawn, Courts and tribunals look at factors such as whether there have been assumptions or stereotyping which have influenced the complainant's treatment.

Sometimes, an organisation may demonstrate a preference for individuals in their own image: 'people like us' or someone 'whose face fits' or who will 'fit in'. Ignorance of cultural difference may lead to the application of inappropriate evaluations of behaviour or attitude.

2.30 An explanation for the difference in treatment which is objectively adequate will usually prevent any inference arising. Good practice gives a large measure of protection. For example, if objective criteria have been applied to all candidates in a recruitment exercise by a panel of interviewers and a reasoned decision has been made and recorded, a Court or Tribunal is more likely to be persuaded that a decision has not been influenced by excessively subjective and discriminatory judgments.

2.31 Whilst the civil standard of proof applies in discrimination cases in the employment tribunal and County Court, the criminal standard of proof applies in disciplinary proceedings for breach of the Code of Conduct. In the employment tribunal and the Courts in race, sex, religion or belief and sexual orientation discrimination cases, the burden of proof shifts to the employer/respondent/defendant where an employee/applicant/claimant establishes facts from which unlawful discrimination could be inferred in the absence of an adequate explanation.

APPENDIX 2
FURTHER PROBLEMS

2.1 Specific issues in criminal defence

2.1.1 The defendant absconds

You appear in the Crown Court defending in a robbery case. There is a co-defendant. After a number of preliminary hearings, your client has absconded. The main evidence against him is the fact that, on arrest, stolen items were found in the jacket that he was wearing. He has provided an unsigned proof of evidence suggesting that the jacket in fact belonged to the co-defendant, who had asked to swap jackets prior to arrest. There is some material in the prosecution evidence to support these claims (items belonging to the defendant were found in the co-defendant's jacket; and CCTV footage). A defence statement was signed by your client prior to absconding, but confirmation of his proof of evidence, and comments on the prosecution evidence were not provided before he disappeared. The judge decides to hear the case in your client's absence, and asks you to represent him. Your solicitor takes the view that, as he has no clear instructions, he must withdraw.

(a) Should you agree to the judge's request?

(b) If so, what part can you play in the trial?

(c) Are you allowed to use the material contained in the unsigned proof of evidence and the defence statement?

(d) Would it make a difference if your solicitor considered that he had sufficient instructions to continue to represent the client?

Tip—you may wish to consider the judgment of the Court of Appeal in *O'Hare* [2006] EWCA Crim 471, *R v K* [2007] EWCA Crim 1339, and the Written Standards for the Conduct of Professional Work and the Guidance note 'Client Absconds without Instructions' which you can find on the Bar Council's website, under 'Guidance' – Section D.

2.1.2 Defence statements

(a) You are asked to draft a defence case statement, but it is not clear that the case you are being asked to state is actually the defendant's own account, as opposed to what his solicitor anticipates will be his client's account (based on some discussions and the police interview). You will not be paid for this work, which will take many hours. The matter is urgent, and you are reluctant to antagonise the solicitor. What should you do?

Tip—consider 'The Preparation of Defence Case Statements' issued by the Bar Council in September 1997 (but still current); it is available on the Bar Standard's Board website under Standards and Guidance—Code Guidance—do not forget to scroll down or you will miss the section on 'Guidance on the Professional Conduct of Barristers', which contains the relevant material. You can also look at 'Failure to Draft Defence Statements and Skeleton Arguments' and 'Preparation for PCMH Hearings' on the Bar Council's website under Guidance—Letter 'D'/ Defence Case Statements.

(b) You see the defendant in conference on the morning of the first day of the trial. He insists that his solicitors (who continue to act for him, and who drafted the statement) have misunderstood his instructions. As a result, you realise that his defence case statement does not accurately reflect the case that he wishes to put forward. You hadn't appreciated the problem until this conference. What action should you take?

(c) The defendant is cross-examined by the prosecution on differences between his defence case statement and his evidence. These differences only arise because of your misunderstanding of his proof of evidence (it is a complex case and you were obliged to prepare the defence case statement in a hurry, and without payment). What are your obligations in this situation?

2.1.3 The defendant is suicidal

Your client has smuggled a razor blade into the cells, which he shows to you. He tells you that he will commit suicide if he gets a sentence of imprisonment. He specifically instructs you not to tell the prison authorities. What should you do?

2.1.4 The defendant makes threats against another person

You are seeing a client in conference in prison. He repeatedly, and apparently seriously, threatens to kill a prosecution witness once he is released from prison. You believe him capable of it. What should you do?

2.2 Specific issues in family practice

You act for the mother of a two-year-old boy in care proceedings. The local authority have placed the child in temporary foster care, and are seeking to persuade the court to grant a care order on the basis of a plan to have the child adopted. Your client naturally seeks the return of her son. During a conference on the second day of the hearing, she tells you that she has recently been tested for HIV, and was found to test positive. You are aware that the court might find this information relevant to decisions on the child's welfare. Should you disclose this information to the court and the other parties?

Tip—see the guidance from the Bar Council Professional Practice Committee, 'Disclosure of Unhelpful Material Disclosed to Counsel in Family Proceedings' (available on the Bar Council's website, under Guidance—Alphabetical 'D').

2.3 The rule in *R v Cox and Railton* [1884] QBD 153

You are advising partners in a firm whose main activity is importing antiquities from Iran. During a conference with the clients, it becomes apparent to you that the real purpose for which they are seeking your advice is to identify a way of disguising the import of antiquities in breach of both Iranian and English law. Are the contents of your conference subject to legal professional privilege?

INDEX